Hollywood Bohemians

ALSO BY BRETT L. ABRAMS

*Capital Sporting Grounds: A History of Stadium
and Ballpark Construction in Washington, D.C.*
(McFarland 2008)

Hollywood Bohemians

*Transgressive Sexuality
and the Selling of the
Movieland Dream*

BRETT L. ABRAMS

McFarland & Company, Inc., Publishers
Jefferson, North Carolina, and London

LIBRARY OF CONGRESS CATALOGUING-IN-PUBLICATION DATA

Abrams, Brett L., 1960–
   Hollywood bohemians : transgressive sexuality and the selling of the movieland dream / Brett L. Abrams.
       p.   cm.
   Includes bibliographical references and index.

   ISBN 978-0-7864-3929-4
   softcover : 50# alkaline paper ∞

   1. Gay motion picture actors and actresses—United States—Anecdotes.   2. Bohemianism — California — Los Angeles — History — 20th century.   3. Hollywood (Los Angeles, Calif.) — Social life and customs.   I. Title.
PN2286.5.A27   2008
791.43086'64 — dc22   2008030114

British Library cataloguing data are available

©2008 Brett L. Abrams. All rights reserved

No part of this book may be reproduced or transmitted in any form or by any means, electronic or mechanical, including photocopying or recording, or by any information storage and retrieval system, without permission in writing from the publisher.

On the cover: Nazimova as the title character in the 1923 film *Salome* (United Artists/Photofest)

Manufactured in the United States of America

McFarland & Company, Inc., Publishers
   Box 611, Jefferson, North Carolina 28640
       www.mcfarlandpub.com

Acknowledgments

There is always a long list of people who deserve acknowledgment. I want to thank my parents, Al Abrams and Betty May Abrams, my stepmother Linda Gagliardi Abrams, and my brother Mark for the solid foundation they provided for me. I had excellent instructors at Rutgers, Northeastern and American universities, particularly Richard Heffner and Clay McShane. Professors Vanessa Schwartz, Douglas Gomery, and Rodger Streitmatter aided me immensely in completing my dissertation. I also appreciate the views of contemporaries and scholars whom I have read or spoken with at various conferences.

A number of the people working in archives and libraries around the country have been extremely helpful in locating documents and photographs. The staffs at the Academy of Motion Picture Arts and Sciences' Margaret Herrick Library, the USC Moving Image and Warner Brothers archives, the One Institute, and UCLA's Film and Television Archives have proved extremely knowledgeable about their collections. I also received great assistance from the people at the Los Angeles City Archive, the Lesbian Herstory Archive in Brooklyn, the Library of Congress's research centers and reproduction division, and the Billy Rose Theatre Collection at the New York Public Library. Staff at the Lilly Library of Indiana University at Bloomington and the Los Angeles Public Library helped me obtain important photographs. Dr. Karen Schoenewaldt of the Rosenbach Museum and Library, Nancy Kauffman at the George Eastman House, and Mary Ilario of NARA's Still Pictures Branch served as surrogate photo researchers.

I appreciated attending American University with a dedicated group of thoughtful and intelligent history graduate students, particularly Debbie Doyle, Heidi Hackford, Jeffrey Harris, Uday Mohan, and Elizabeth Stewart. Other friends heard many stories and offered suggestions over the years, especially the following, who appear in alphabetical order: Thomas Drymon, Daniel Emberley, Deborah Garcia, Peter Hoefer, Willard (Bill) Hillegiest, Michael Hussey, Jon Carl Lewis, William Megevick, Jim O'Laughlin, Michael Seto, and Tim Tate.

There is one person with whom I share daily trials, stories, passions and interests. He has been there through all my struggles, dramas, and accomplishments. With all my love I dedicate this book to Ira Tattelman.

Table of Contents

Acknowledgments	v
Preface	1
Introduction: Bohemians in the Depictions of Hollywood	3

ONE. Hollywood Nightlife
    Female Impersonators and Cross-Dressing Females   13

TWO. The Public Hollywood Party
    Star Arrivals and Emotions   50

THREE. The Private Hollywood Party
    Secret Love at the Wild Party   78

FOUR. The Hollywood Star Home
    Chic Bachelor and Odd Bedfellow Digs   113

FIVE. Hollywood Behind the Scenes
    Glamour and Mystery in the Workplace   159

Conclusion: Hollywood Bohemians Today	193
Chapter Notes	199
Bibliography	221
Index	237

Preface

As a child growing up in suburban New Jersey during the 1970s, I had a great interest in Hollywood's Golden Age. I enjoyed watching the *Million Dollar Movie* on one of the syndicated stations. Afterwards, I often consulted reference books for information about the lives of the stars and directors. My parents both grew up during that era and would sometimes watch the movies with me and tell me about their favorites. The movies fueled two of my enduring passions: seeing other worlds and learning about other people's lives.

When I was pursuing graduate work in history at Northeastern University, my interests returned to Hollywood. This time I focused on the business of the movies. I wrote a thesis about the labor strife between the artisan unions and the motion picture studios during the 1940s.

I decided to get my Ph.D. in history at American University. For my dissertation I wanted to continue my research on Hollywood before World War II. One seminal work in gay, lesbian, and queer studies, George Chauncey's *Gay New York*, appeared to offer a possible avenue for investigating the world of homosexuality and sexual identity in Hollywood. After trips to archives in Los Angeles and New York, it became apparent that written materials, the core of what historians use to delve into an era, were very limited. Many of the sources that others in this area of study had successfully used, such as court records, proved almost nonexistent in Hollywood. Another pathway became blocked when only a few of the persons from the era who were still living expressed interest in discussing the topic with me.

As part of my research, I began detailed reading of the major Los Angeles newspapers from the era. While some of the articles about the industry had interesting information, the gossip columns proved enlightening; they contained highly suggestive material. I recognized code phrases and humorous items that appeared to indicate adulterous behavior and homosexual interests.

Initially surprised at these thinly coded topics, I began to wonder why these items appeared somewhat regularly. I decided to examine other descriptions of Hollywood. I found more characters that defied the culture's sexual and gender norms. The focus of my possible topic shifted from a social history to a cultural history about the appearance of sexual others in descriptions of Hollywood and the movie world.

Fortunately, I received a junior fellowship at the Library of Congress in their Motion Picture, Broadcasting and Recorded Sound Division. I had the opportunity to view most of the movies the studios created that featured Hollywood as the primary location. I found several movies with sexual bohemians. I also read nearly 70 Hollywood novels written between 1917 and 1950 and found even more adulterers, cross-dressers, and homosexuals. I continued to research gossip columns and news stories in a number of the metropolitan newspapers in the U.S., which provided allusions to these figures in the Hollywood milieu.

Many scholars have examined images of non-conformist sexuality in mass media. The images have been far from pretty or positive. In general, movies depicted homosexuals and adulterers as unfortunate and suicidal figures, or forced them to renounce their lives and redeem themselves before the final credits rolled. Novels faced censorship for using such depictions or made the characters into outcasts, suicide victims, or self-loathers because they failed to follow cultural norms. The rare instances in newspapers showed homosexuals and adulterers as criminals. I realized that I had a unique group of images and descriptions about Hollywood, the place that stood apart from those described in other scholarship in both gay and lesbian history and the history of the mass media in the United States.

The images needed to be organized. I sought to relate them back to the social environment of Hollywood and Los Angeles. It proved best to relate them to the major landmarks of Hollywood. These locales included nightclubs, parties and houses; the completed dissertation included five places in all.

In the years since the dissertation's completion, a few popular books on Hollywood have focused on homosexual stars and homosexuals in the industry. They have effectively detailed a star's life or some activities and contributions of gays and lesbians to Hollywood. These writers observed that the people running Hollywood generally suppressed information about homosexuals. My book differs significantly. The images of adulterers, homosexuals and cross-dressers appeared in a much more positive light in fictional movies and novels about Hollywood. They also appeared in the publicity materials that the Hollywood studios and news media released. My book provides explanations of Hollywood's relationship to and sometimes promotion of non-conformity that the other popular books have been unable to explain.

Introduction
Bohemians in the Depictions of Hollywood

Thelma Todd was pleasure-loving and temperamental, not the domestic type at all. Miss Todd and Roland West frequently participated in the gay parties at Miss Catherine Hunter's Hollywood bungalow. Miss Todd often remained overnight with Miss Hunter at her home. West, who had testified on business matters twice, refused to answer questions about Miss Todd's love life. "I am determined at all costs to protect her memory."[1]

Movie star Thelma Todd's sex life took center stage during the grand jury investigation into her death. The movie industry, newspapers, magazines, and book publishers produced endless publicity. Their articles fed and stoked audience members' desire to connect with the stars and other people in the movie industry. Most of this publicity showed virile men and virtuous women, dating males and females, and faithful husbands and wives in Hollywood. However, the newspaper articles on Thelma Todd hinted that the actress was not content as a wife and had a romantic life that her friends wanted to keep secret.

The image of Thelma Todd was not unique. Newspaper and magazine articles, Hollywood novels, and Hollywood movies featuring Hollywood between the late 1910s and early 1940s showed audiences a whole lot more. Actress Greta Garbo defined herself as a bachelor. Screenwriter Mercedes De Acosta wore mannish attire. A trio of male heartthrobs attended a party and showed no romantic interest in women. Homosexual designers picked up men in nightclubs. The industry and the media covering Hollywood developed and disseminated these real and fictional characters, whom I call Hollywood's bohemians. In an era when many thought there was a connection between a person's sexual interests and their gender behavior, why did homosexuals, adulterers, effeminate males, and butch females appear in all these depictions of Hollywood?

The Hollywood bohemians appeared because they contributed significantly to the construction of the movie capital's image. They helped forge the perspective of Hollywood as the most racy, risqué and unconventional place in the country. Hollywood was the dream factory, a place to project our fantasies and reflect our desires, no matter how outlandish. The usual Hollywood publicity enabled audience members to develop a sense of intimacy with the celebrity so that readers could imagine themselves as having a greater understanding of the star.

Hollywood bohemian images increased the appeal to audiences' prurient interests in sexual naughtiness. As homosexuals, adulterers, effeminate males, and butch females, the bohemians embodied the pleasures of the forbidden and the taboo. Hollywood bohemians linked the industry to exposure of (previously) guarded secrets. They played an important role in developing Hollywood's image as a place of sexual abandon, further enhancing the Hollywood "mystique." The brilliance of these images was that they set the bohemians at familiar Hollywood locations. The presence of the sexual "other" makes the location more exciting, and the familiar location makes the "other" less threatening.[2]

Most publicity images and descriptions of Hollywood in novels and movies used Hollywood as their setting. In the 1920s and 1930s, Hollywood was known for its nightclubs and restaurants, movie premieres and the Academy Awards, private parties, star homes, and the giant studio lots. A movie about Hollywood from the era, Warner Brothers' *Hollywood Hotel* (1937), offered audiences a tour of Hollywood and revealed each of the important locales.

As a newcomer landed at the airport in Hollywood and drove toward the studio, the audience saw what they envisioned as the movie capital of the world; a building shaped like a derby hat and another with engravings and pillars at the entry passed by. The Brown Derby and the Cafe Trocadero were two of the top restaurants and clubs that formed the Hollywood nightlife. Along Hollywood Boulevard, the car passed Grauman's Chinese Theater, one of the places where the staged events and semi-public affairs that composed the public Hollywood parties happened. A sign selling personal guides to movie star homes flashed past. The panorama of Hollywood ended with an image of the studio gates, and inside them were the stage sets, dressing rooms, and studios of Hollywood — behind the scenes.

Unlike all the other images of Hollywood, the bohemians linked these famous movie industry places with unusual people and behaviors. By binding these places to things that the culture viewed as taboo, the Hollywood bohemians made those locations appear wild and spectacular. Bohemians made Hollywood, the town and its industry, stand apart and appear to be something that people thought they had to see and experience — more intriguing than any other place in the country.

Each chapter will examine one of these important Hollywood locations and show how the Hollywood bohemians made the place stand out. Beginning with the most public locations, the restaurants and nightclubs that formed Hollywood nightlife, each chapter will center on a three-part examination of media images: A presentation of the media images of the location in other cities and towns will provide a standard for how the location usually appeared in the media; a focus on the way the location appeared in most Hollywood publicity and many novels and movies that described the movie industry and its town is the second part of this examination.

This focus will show how Hollywood publicity worked, with its elaborate description of a location and the revelation of information about a star's personality. The focus will display the publicity's emphasis on showing how both the location and star conformed to society's expectations. The publicity and images that form Hollywood novels and movies with Hollywood bohemians will demonstrate how the bohemians made each location appear fun and crazy.

The first chapter covers female impersonators and women in men's clothing who lit up Hollywood's neon night scene. The second describes how Hollywood stars emoted at the Hollywood public parties of the Oscars and movie premieres. The middle chapter discusses the beautiful people making all kinds of love at Hollywood private parties. Chapter four shows how chic bachelor women and odd bedfellows made happy homes. Finally, the fifth chapter reveals temperamental artists plying their trades behind the scenes at the studio lots.

The Hollywood bohemians worked within almost every profession in the industry. They included actors and actresses, screenwriters and publicists, directors and producers, and costume designers and makeup artists. Actors and actresses formed the most publicized group in Hollywood and they appeared in the majority of the images.

The performers and other professionals who composed the Hollywood bohemians appeared in three types of media material. The novels featured Hollywood as the primary setting for the story and a major character who worked in the movie industry. Known as Hollywood novels, these books spanned across genres, including drama, romance, farce, and musical comedy.

Hollywood novelists ran the gamut of the writing profession. They included literary lights such as F. Scott Fitzgerald (*The Last Tycoon*, 1941) and the currently respected authors, like James M. Cain (*Serenade*, 1937). The group also featured popular writers of the era like Vicki Baum (*Falling Star*, 1934) and virtual unknowns such as John Preston Buschlen (*Screen Star*, 1932).

Movies that centered on Hollywood and its workers, "Hollywood on Hollywood" motion pictures, also slipped Hollywood bohemians into scenes. Like the Hollywood novels, these movies crossed genres and types and included money-making pictures such as *Going Hollywood* (MGM, 1933) and box-office failures such as *Hollywood Party* (MGM, 1934). Some achieved critical acclaim, such as Preston Sturges's *Sullivan's Travels* (Paramount, 1941), while others like *Stunt Pilot* (Republic, 1939) were B-movies intended to be minor time fillers.

Newspapers and magazines, including metropolitan dailies and tabloids, depicted Hollywood bohemians in feature articles and gossip columns. The magazines that carried these images ranged from trade types such as the *Hollywood Reporter* and fan magazines such as *Photoplay* to general interest types, including *Life* and *Time*.[3]

The novels, movies, newspapers and magazines used different words and degrees of detail to describe the Hollywood bohemians and their activities. Generally, only the novels used the word "homosexual." The movies and newspaper and magazine articles opted for code words or phrases, such as "pansy" or "the happy couple." Rarely did any of the media use the word "adulterer," and all three tended to show effeminate males and masculine females through the clothing that they wore. The three types of media rarely depicted the "illicit" activities of the adulterers and homosexuals. Instead, they usually hinted at the action.

The vast majority of the images of Hollywood bohemians showed people who appeared to enjoy rich and happy professional and social lives. The stars and character actors and behind the scenes artisans all earned high salaries. They also worked on some of the best Hollywood productions. They owned homes, cars, and beautiful clothes. The bohemians received respect from their fellow movie people and formed friendships and loving relationships inside and outside the industry. Hollywood bohemians lived like few others.

Readers and viewers occasionally encountered images of adulterers and homosexuals in the mass media during the first half of the twentieth century. Depictions of these figures in books, such as in Upton Sinclair's *Oil!* (a girl seducer) and William Faulkner's *Sanctuary* (rape and voyeurism) and Radclyffe Hall's *The Well of Loneliness* (masculine women, lesbianism), sparked censorship efforts to keep them from being printed and distributed. The supporters of censorship saw these images as vulgar and disgusting. They believed that the people who saw these images, particularly the young and the simpleminded, would have their morals corrupted. This corruption of morals would destroy the civilized world, so they saw it as their job to stop the images before the world as they knew it was lost.[4]

The legal efforts failed to stop the presentation of adulterers and others in the media. Still, books were not awash in these images. The images that did appear, including those in the books previously mentioned, showed that these characters' activities made them feel miserable. No character escaped experiencing emotional turmoil because of their sexual behavior. The figures appeared occasionally in the newspapers and magazines of the era usually because they engaged in criminal activity.

Otherwise, their appearance in articles carried a pejorative tone. When the newspapers ran stories about a Hollywood celebrity whose scandalous behavior sparked a public outrage, the industry responded by firing or demoting their nonconformist stars and other employees. Writers, including David Ehrenstein in *Open Secret* and William Mann within *Behind the Screen*, noted the studios' negative responses, but did not discuss the industry's promotion of their bohemian employees.[5]

Characters who did not conform to the culture's norms for sexuality also appeared in movies that did not feature Hollywood as the main setting. As in the non–Hollywood books and newspapers, the adulterers and homosexuals encountered a hostile world and negative experiences. Adulterers, gold diggers, and other "fallen woman" either met unfortunate ends or redeemed themselves at the end of the movie.

Even before the increased reviewing of movies that occurred under the Production Code Administration, scripts eliminated the racy woman. The movies either tried to marry the racy woman off to a good man at the end of the movie or sought to show that she learned a life lesson. Male and female homosexual images in general Hollywood productions from the early 1910s to the mid–1970s led lonely lives. These figures experienced derision and sometimes became victims of murder or suicide. During the Great Depression of the 1930s, effeminate males appeared in a range of movies where they faced derisive comments and were linked to members of other groups viewed unfavorably in the culture. Books, including Vito Russo's *Celluloid Closet* and Richard Barrios's *Screened Out* and Janet Staiger's *Bad Women,* documented these findings while missing the Hollywood bohemians.[6]

These negative presentations in literature, news, and general Hollywood movies of adulterers, homosexuals and others strengthened the status quo. The images provided entertainment for audiences. They laughed at the characters in comedies and rooted against them in dramas. The images gave audience members the opportunity to feel personally superior and feel the satisfaction of knowing that they did not occupy the bottom rung of society.

Indeed, scholars who studied these negative images argued that they appeared in the media to maintain the dominant gender and sexual norms in U.S. society. The images presented stereotypes of homosexuals and adulterers so audience members would supposedly know about them. The stereotypes experienced horrible lives to establish sharp boundary definitions for whom and what the culture considered unacceptable. The depictions indicated that rewards came only from following behaviors the culture considered acceptable. This system of reward and punishment aimed to keep audience members from wanting to or believing that they could cross the lines.[7]

Hollywood bohemians composed a distinctly different set of images. While many portrayed similar gay and lesbian stereotypes, others did not. Most uniquely, this book shows us that Hollywood presented figures who successfully suggested to audience members that crossing the lines was not fatal or harmful. The Hollywood bohemians illustrated that those who did not follow these norms could lead successful lives. At least in Hollywood, they could obtain material goods, be a part of a community, and have friends, lovers, and spouses.

The Hollywood bohemians had a complexity that made them more than simplistic stereotypes of homosexuals and cross-dressers. The Hollywood bohemian images appeared similarly to the main character in a novel, a fully realized person who changes over time. They were figures who created successful lives beyond the culturally mandated boundaries of acceptable behavior. This suggested to audience members that crossing the lines was fun and exciting. The bohemians undercut the system of reward and punishment and made the boundary lines appear less firm.

The need to solidify gender and sexual boundaries was particularly important during the late nineteenth and early twentieth centuries. A variety of cultural and economic forces resulted in an era of impressive change. The woman's movement promoted more educational, work, and political opportunities for women and led to more females engaging in experiences outside the home. Industrialization and technological developments sparked the expansion of bureaucratic work environments, resulting in men having less control over their work lives.

The waves of new immigrants brought their different cultural traditions into American society. Together with the women's movement, they created a muddle of the appropriate behaviors for men and women. These developments spurred the need to create new definitions for appropriate male and female behaviors. Factors including rising divorce rates and the expansion of commercial leisure activities promoted greater discussion of sexuality and changes in the behavior and expectations regarding sex. Men and women discovered that older avenues for demonstrating masculinity and femininity and proving sexuality had closed and entirely different venues had emerged. The medical and psychological professions informed everyone in society that sexuality had great importance in human lives. This made the desire to demonstrate masculinity and femininity and prove sexuality become even more important to individuals in this era.

The mass media blossomed amid this time of transition. New innovations in communications led to new and different mass media forms. These products ranged from phonographs to movies to radio. The emergence of a consumer culture offered plentiful goods and services.

This new mass entertainment media became the prime location for the presentation of both male and female behavior and sexuality. The media began to establish appropriate behaviors for men and women of all classes. It also presented a greater amount of sexual discussion and titillation.

The working and middling classes gained larger incomes and leisure time during the early twentieth century. They spent a good portion of these resources on their enjoyment of the movies and related publications. Hollywood provided this audience with fantasy lives and celebrity images. Many people desired human images and identified with stars to escape the stresses and anxieties of daily life and the limitations and restrictions of the culture.[8]

This growing mass media presented more images in general and racier ones in particular immediately after World War I because of changes in the country. The United States witnessed the breakdown of genteel culture and its restrictions on topics of discussions in the aftermath of the war. The new "modern" culture invited greater presentation of sexual innuendo and sexuality in the mass media. Indeed, as the first era to revise notions of sexuality around desire and fulfillment, the culture interpreted sex as central to personal identities. The entertainment for this culture would logically focus on presenting such an important topic to its audiences.

Around this same time, changes in the movie industry resulted in the production of both more celebrity and more risqué imagery. The studios changed their publicity approach. The divorces and other off-screen activities of several major stars forced the industry to shift away from promoting stars as picture personalities. Picture personality publicity used the star's on-screen character as a mirror image of their off-screen lives. The studio publicity featured the star's supposed everyday life and developed stories about their personalities. The beginnings of the cult of personality necessitated the discussion of the star's sexual behavior since that was considered central to personal identities.[9]

The number and variety of media that featured Hollywood people expanded significantly during the era. Newspaper coverage included regular articles about the industry's personalities and featured daily gossip columns from the six major syndicated writers on the beat. General interest magazines, such as *Time* and *Life*, and the fanzines, like *Photoplay* and *Silver Screen*, reached millions of readers with their weekly photographs, features, and gossip items on Hollywood. The Hollywood novel changed its focus during the late 1910s away from the technology of movie making to presenting readers with stories about characters within the industry. Hollywood movies about the industry increased as movie production solidified itself in the southern California cultural climate.[10]

Hollywood was not alone among places to present themselves in the mass media. Other cities perceived the advantage of reaching a wide variety of audiences through the mass media. Cities like Paris, France, and Atlantic City, New Jersey, used the press, wax museums and postcards to depict their spectacular realities and sensual pleasures. This enabled individual businesses to promote themselves and also the entire area to become known as a destination point.[11]

Like the media that featured Hollywood, these mass media depictions offered their audiences stories. They contained narrative suspense, novelties, and a faithful depiction of the city and industry. Each city's presentation of this sensationalized reality contained a familiarity that promoted audience members' sense of participation and belonging in that reality. The depictions also contained enough celebrities and fantastic events to prompt audience members to wish that they were there and desire to find out what more there was to know. While Paris sensationalized crime coverage and Atlantic City presented bathing beauties, only Hollywood depicted itself as populated with "bohemians."

None of the other mass media businesses in the era associated themselves with adulterers or homosexuals. Vaudeville presented female impersonators and male impersonators on stage. However, the publicity for these performers described the first as tough and virile and the second as sensitive and demure. The Broadway stage might have had homosexuals in its ranks. Yet neither plays about the theater nor the publicity about theatrical people ever mentioned their presence, nor the presence of other breakers of the culture's sexual norms. When producers such as the Charles Froham Company and Mae West put plays featuring lesbians and drag queens on stage, the city government closed down one production and no theater owner would offer a Broadway location to the other. Immediately afterwards, the New York state legislature passed the Wales Padlock Law in early 1927, granting municipal authorities the power to lock up any theater if its owner put a play with homosexuals in it on its stage.[12]

Hollywood successfully accomplished something that other cities and mass media industries could not. Hollywood was a wild place. As one contemporary noted, "I lived in Hollywood because as a kid I got used to carnivals."[13] Hollywood studios, insiders and newspapers and magazines focused on selling characters to attract audiences. One of its most marketable assets was the presence of different people and outsiders in its midst.

However, Hollywood's marketing of these characters differed from carnivals and sideshows in key ways. Sideshows featured people with physical and cultural differences within bizarre environs to showcase their inability to adapt to the prevailing cultural norms. Audiences experienced reactions of superiority to the "freaks of nature" or, at best, pity. Hollywood bohemians appeared as understandable figures in recognizable yet fantastic environments with whom audience members could forge and build an identification. Indeed, Hollywood bohemians offered audience members the opportunity and motivation to identify with the "other."

This book will motivate us to reconsider what we think about Hollywood during the studio era. Hollywood was the dream factory of the masses because of its great climate, wealth, and glamorous romances between a man and a woman. But the Hollywood bohemians revealed another part of the equation that has been omitted from the Hollywood story. The dream included people pursuing wild, outlandish, and "illegal" sexual activities and interests. Audiences enjoyed being exposed to the culture's marginalia, and the bohemians illustrate that the movie industry humanized these outsider images. *Hollywood Bohemians* will show that one of the primary image-makers in the world used the images of "bohemians" not only for purposes of entertainment and derision but as an integral part of its self-definition.

Hollywood Bohemians will offer us the opportunity to understand how entertainment industries work and what audiences enjoy. The discovery of Hollywood's intentional use of risqué and racy images provides an explanation for why so many religious and other groups opposed the movie industry then and today. The images helped the movie industry sell both its product and Hollywood in general.

The Hollywood bohemians influence our current media. They are the forerunners of today's highly sexualized images. They show us how we arrived at two controversial features of the way our media operates: The bohemians highlighted celebrity and public figure's personal lives, which has become the focus of extensive coverage now. They represented the media presenting culturally controversial behavior images on display, pushing the envelope of what the media showed. This "cutting edge" then built and maintained audience size and interest. The Hollywood bohemians appalled some groups of audiences, but they appealed to many more, and they kept everyone watching and talking. *Hollywood Bohemians* shows us the background for how the U.S. culture arrived at contemporary attitudes about the media and sexuality.

ONE

Hollywood Nightlife
Female Impersonators and Cross-Dressing Females

La Boheme Cafe owner Karyl Norman delighted patrons by dressing up in yards and yards of lace and feathers whenever he performed his incredible female impersonations. His impersonation of Joan Crawford doing a scene as Sadie Thompson brought down the house nightly, occasionally with Crawford enjoying the laughs.[1]

Hollywood publicity frequently showed celebrities inside the fancy and fantastic environments of nightclubs and restaurants. The stars ate and drank lavishly, fought and danced wildly, and dated and romanced extravagantly. However, some Hollywood nightlife images also depicted celebrities hanging out with exotic and decadent figures or engaging in exotic and decadent behavior themselves.

Hollywood bohemian imagery, such as Norman's impersonation of Crawford, played a significant role in forming the mystique of Hollywood's nightlife. The image informed readers about Crawford's nighttime activities and her interaction with others. These two pieces of personal information offered readers the chance to believe that they knew the star more intimately. Presenting a female impersonator provided readers with a glimpse of something they rarely saw and the thrill of experiencing behavior and persons the culture labeled taboo.

The association with the unusual and taboo enabled Hollywood nightlife to stand apart from depictions of the nightlife in other cities. It enhanced the usual movie industry publicity that made Hollywood nightlife seem fun and adventurous by linking the nightlife to decadence, making it appear wild. Hollywood was not the only place in the United States whose restaurants and nightclubs received coverage in the newspapers and magazines, nor was it even the first city to receive such coverage.

The coverage of nightclubs was a relatively recent phenomenon in the early twentieth century. It centered on clubs and restaurants in New York City. Few public entertainment places in the middle to late nineteenth-century United States received significant coverage in the press. Saloons limited their clientele to males and rarely became the subject of newspaper reporting except when a disturbance appeared in police reports. Brothels, dance halls, and other nightlife locations existed within city vice and tourist districts and had reputations as such debased places that they rarely appeared in the mass media.

Many of the media readers, including members of the Women's Christian Temperance Union, viewed places of public nightlife as disreputable and worked to close them down. In addition, these nightlife locations did not attract the people whose activities newspaper readers wanted to follow. Most middle- and upper-class men and women spent their leisure time in private homes and locations where admission came through membership in either a formal or informal social circle. The dominant social life for most people functioned around the private party.[2]

By the end of the nineteenth century, a new nightlife emerged as locations moved to more respectable areas within United States cities. Commercial locations increasingly emerged to replace the family, neighborhood, and private clubs as places to meet people and receive a variety of stimulation. Restaurants in hotels opened in more respectable neighborhoods and attracted both men and women from the upper classes. With the movement to different neighborhoods and the drawing of upscale crowds, leisure locations attracted more print media coverage.

The sensationalist newspapers of the major cities discovered increased readership interest in the activities of the upper classes. They began expanding the coverage of their parties and their dining out in restaurants in the society columns. General interest magazines also depicted the activities of the wealthy in these urban locations. During the first decades of the twentieth century, dailies in the largest U.S. markets regularly ran weekday columns and Sunday sections that chronicled "Society's" affairs. Many newspapers began running columns containing notes on the lives of those in the theatrical world that included their activities in restaurants and nightclubs.[3]

Images of Socialite Nightlife

The newspaper and magazine images of socialite nightlife reflected the genteel culture of the early twentieth century. To ensure that their customers behaved according to the generally accepted strict standards, management of the hotels and restaurants maintained a bevy of restrictions regarding entrance and behavior in their establishments. Lobster palaces—large restaurants that featured numerous courses of very expensive food and drink—were not open to the "fast" crowd of show business people or to the newly wealthy from the professional ranks. The places insisted on respecting social and economic hierarchies, dressing their staffs in uniforms, and providing guidelines to enforce gentility among their workers.

Even those Broadway restaurants that opened their doors to the "nouveau riche" and theatrical crowd, a group of people with less "decorum," maintained a variety of rules governing behavior within their establishments. Like the lobster palaces, these Broadway restaurants featured a lavish decor that mimicked aspects of earlier great civilizations and offered enormous amounts of food and the opportunity to watch other patrons. Most of the patrons in both types of restaurants helped maintain the environment. They supported the door policy, inside, they respected social class distinctions. Customers generally stayed seated at their tables and accepted that no entertainment or dance floor existed. Both sets of restaurants stayed within the bounds of propriety and insisted on a formal, hierarchical, and restrained nightlife world, leading to bland images in print.[4]

The lobster palaces and voluminous Broadway restaurants lost a significant amount of their appeal by the early 1910s. Customers wanted nightspots that departed from viewing nightlife as an extension of the private home. They wanted more than eating a large meal as the only entertainment.[5] Cabaret businesses began with the establishment (and immediate failure) of the *Folies Bergere Theater* in the heart of New York City's theater district in 1911. Other ritzy locations opened in the Broadway hotels, and their dances, contests, and stress on drinking produced an atmosphere of greater interaction among the customers.

Some patrons enjoyed the excitement of acting on their private impulses within a cabaret or other nightspot. Much more frequently, patrons feared that acting on those impulses would compromise their morals, so they restricted how they behaved inside the nightclubs and restaurants. The high entrance fee and cost of meals meant that attendance at cabarets was limited to a small section of the population. Cabaret management further hampered the interaction among audience members through policies that restricted drinking to tables and discouraged patrons from cutting in on dances and making new contacts. The images that appeared in the newspapers and magazines portrayed this highly structured nightlife.

Despite these limitations, the cabaret of the 1910s expanded the level of interaction among patrons and between audience members and performers and led to the development of the nightclub in the post–World War I.[6] These lobster palaces, volume restaurants, and cabarets sprang up in the country's largest cities; rural America and small towns like Hollywood, California rarely participated in this leisure world.

Nightlife in the Sleepy Hollywood

Hollywood entered the twentieth century as a small town with several Protestant churches that supported the local ban on the public sale and consumption of alcoholic beverages. The town voted to join the larger city of Los Angeles in 1910 to receive water and sewer lines. As movie-making companies began settling in the area in the early 1910s, Hollywood incorporated bordering towns on each of its sides and organized a YMCA. Despite these changes, the population numbered only 7,500 and Hollywood retained its village quality. The C.C. Hall grocery store was considered the main gathering place in town. Much of Hollywood's citizenry desired to maintain the town as the religious hamlet. They disliked the reputation of entertainers and imposed restrictions on their activities and access, using signs above entryways that read, "No dogs or actors allowed."[7]

The small number of nightspots in Hollywood and greater Los Angeles limited the places where industry celebrities could escape for evening amusements. The Hollywood Hotel on tree-lined Hollywood Boulevard was the center of the community's social activities, offering chaperoned dances. Los Angeles's largest cluster of eateries were the small cafes and lunchrooms located in and around Spring Street. In the evenings, people went out to eat at the Pig 'n' Whistle and the few Italian restaurants downtown. Movie people characterized the city as dull and unsophisticated. As screenwriter Ralph Block noted "...[the] only relation between Hollywood of 1920 and Hollywood later is that the latter grew somehow out of the former."

The small number of restaurants and nightclubs offered only occasional opportunities for the newspapers to present Hollywood nightlife. Gossip columns mentioned the industry's celebrities engaging in communal celebrations, such as the Thursday dances at the Hollywood Hotel. An article noted the presence of chaperones at the event, which hinted to readers that the events in these environments fell well within the boundaries of genteel culture.

The newspapers and industry magazines began linking the industry nightlife with lavish dining and the forging of romance between movie celebrities. An item in the *Los Angeles Times* movie industry society column informed readers that "[Actress Miriam Cooper and director Raoul Walsh] went to Nat Goodwin's restaurant down on the beach which over-looked the ocean in Venice, Calif. Everything was glass and [you could] hear the waves breaking on the pier." A letter from the actress to Walsh confirmed the impression of romance, as Cooper called the scene romantic and noted after their goodnight kiss that she loved him.[8] With such limited options among public evening establishments, newspapers covered the evening activities of Hollywood's movie community members at social clubs and private parties. Occasionally, the representations in area newspapers centered on the activities of motion picture actor and female impersonator Julian Eltinge.

Female Impersonators in Early Hollywood Nightlife

At a swank party, a man approached the head of a movie studio and his wife. He told the wife where she purchased her dress. The owner of the Matzene Feature Film Company, Mr. Matzene, said, "You must be mistaken, sir, only ladies' clothes are made at the place." "Yes, of course," Eltinge said.[9] Julian Eltinge, the top female impersonator in the country, showed off his unique position as a man who knew about things female at a Hollywood nightlife event and shocked some of the attendees.

Born in Newtonville, Massachusetts, in 1883, William Julian Dalton made his professional debut at the tender age of ten years old. He wore feminine apparel, and you could say it stuck with him ever after. He worked in the world of Boston revues, gaining raves and eventually the attention of Broadway producers. He made his Broadway start as Julian Eltinge in the musical comedy *Mr. Wix of Wickham* in late 1904. He became one of the most notable female impersonators in vaudeville and Europe.

Eltinge posed an interesting problem as a legitimate theater star. The theatrical star system centered on promoting the star's stage image as the star's personality. In Eltinge's case that would have required building his star image around a man behaving like a woman. A person acting like a member of their opposite biological sex flipped the cultural expectation that people behave according to their biological sex. The medical experts called behaving in a manner opposite one's biological sex "gender inversion."

During the late nineteenth and early twentieth centuries, doctors and sexologists thought homosexuality occurred because of gender inversion. The homosexual man or woman had the traits of the opposite sex within themselves and thus acted out the gender desires "appropriate" to that opposite sex. This prompted female impersonation to acquire a link with homosexuality. Eltinge and the theater owners worried about this connection, so the star and industry created publicity that promoted distance between his stage image and his outside life. In the *Julian Eltinge Magazine of 1911*, articles discussed the star's masculine activities and interests in his private life, or "revealed" his manhood by showing him fighting those who made untoward comments about him.[10]

Eltinge succeeded beyond the others in his profession. He appeared in vaudeville and embarked on a tour of Europe. Eltinge had the honor of performing in front of King Edward VII in a "command performance." Theater producers took advantage of the popularity and began creating plays that centered on Eltinge's unique abilities. He appeared on stage in *The Fascinating Widow* in 1911. The show was much more of a success around the country than in New York City, but he received another opportunity to perform in *The Crinoline Girl* and, in 1915, *Cousin Lucy*.[11]

Regardless of the connection, female impersonation drew large crowds to vaudeville. Hollywood studios have always needed new stars. In 1916, two of the top motion picture studios in Hollywood, Paramount and Mack Sennett, reached into the ranks of vaudeville's female impersonators and gave contracts to its biggest sensations, Julian Eltinge and Bothwell Browne. Although Browne starred in only one motion picture, Eltinge played in several motion pictures in the middle and late 1910s that Paramount designed to showcase his image and talent. With the hiring of Browne and Eltinge, female impersonators became one of the first groups of proven performers from another entertainment field to receive contracts and star in motion pictures.[12]

The publicity and gossip that emerged during the early years of Eltinge's stay in Hollywood featured his being a man playing at being a woman. The stories about Hollywood nightlife put Eltinge's Hollywood bohemian behavior in the forefront. Besides giving readers the sense that they knew the Hollywood nightlife scene and Eltinge more intimately, putting his untypical gender behavior in the publicity made the Hollywood nightlife a spectacular show. Hints about Eltinge's sexuality emerged from the images in a manner that granted a playful decadence and exoticism to the Hollywood nightlife.

Gossip column images placed Eltinge amid Hollywood evening circles. In one item, Eltinge threw a party with fellow actor Carlyle Blackwell at Al Levy's Cafe for members of the Photoplayers' Club. This gossip placed readers inside one of Hollywood's important nightspots and exclusive industry organizations while revealing that bohemians like Eltinge belonged in these crowds.[13] The item gave readers the opportunity to wonder if Eltinge created a scene by wearing one of his famous gowns at this gathering or other club affairs.

At other Hollywood nightlife events, like the party that opened this section, Eltinge acted on his Hollywood bohemian interests. The party scene showed Eltinge making comments that demonstrated a sly humor that centered in playing with a man's knowledge of things woman, thus hinting at gender inversion. The suggestion of the taboo in this story made Hollywood nightlife appear as a place where people discussed private, racy topics.

One elaborate publicity piece tied the expression of a star's deep secret and the sexually taboo to Hollywood nightlife.

> Eltinge has lots of fun working on location since he is frequently taken for a woman when he appears in his beautiful feminine togs. Eltinge having a few moments to spare strolled down the beach. He looked unusually beautiful, that day, he says, due to having on a sport suit of pale blue with a saucy little hat to match. Down on the beach he met a youth, obviously country bred but not the least bit backward. The youth pursued and while Eltinge pretended to run away he let the young man catch up with him.... The two strolled, Eltinge using his "other" voice. The youth asked Eltinge out to an ice cream festival and Eltinge consented.... Later he met at the spot dressed in male attire. "Howdy," he said to the country swain. "Why, I had a date with a lady!" stammered the youth. "Well, you aren't going to meet her 'cause I got a date with her myself." The boy wanted to fight and Eltinge was about to accommodate him just to keep in trim

when director Fred Bailshofer appeared and convinced them to call it off. Then the youth took another look at Eltinge and became the most sheepish-looking swain in the world.[14]

This passage presumably appeared as part of Eltinge's publicity campaign to retain industry and audience interest in his motion picture career. In

Eltinge before bringing female impersonation to Hollywood (courtesy Lilly Library, Indiana University, Bloomington, IN).

Hollywood, however, after three successful productions, including *The Countess Charming*, Paramount did not renew the performer's contract. Eltinge weighed over 170 pounds and the camera magnified his figure so he had to be cast with ever-larger women in order to appear demure in his female role. This story suggested that Eltinge still retained a figure and the mystique to be a successful female impersonator and movie star.

Maintaining his career might have been Eltinge and his studio's motivation behind the story. The gossip provided readers with an intimate look at the star's personal life by showing his "dating" habits. The image linked Hollywood nightlife to one man presenting himself to another man as a date. Eltinge knew that he was really a male, yet he offered himself as a date to a "not backward swain." The swain's, or boyfriend's status as "not backward" indicated that he was not easy to fool regarding Eltinge's biological sex. If he was not easy to fool then was he not fooled? Perhaps Eltinge believed him not to have been fooled? Did either believe that they would go out on a date as two men? We will not know, but the image presented that possibility. The image stretched the component of romantic adventure in Hollywood nightlife into the realm of potential same-sex romantic interest. This offered readers the thrill of experiencing the cultural taboo and the decadent and bound both of these outlandish things to Hollywood nightlife.

The images of Eltinge aided the industry in making the Hollywood nightlife as something special and apart from the depictions of the nightlife in other urban locations. They also revealed that Hollywood bohemians lived good lives in the movie industry. Unlike the images of effeminate men and homosexuals in other media and places, Eltinge lived well in Hollywood. The female impersonator attended important industry affairs and also sponsored events. He belonged to social and industry clubs and had friends in the industry. Eltinge built Villa Capistrano, one of the most lavish estates in the Hollywood area, where he lived with his mother and entertained for their numerous friends.

A fan magazine featured a group of eastern society people viewing Eltinge's new California home. The place caused one visitor to comment on the female impersonator's romantic life. "It's too beautiful for a bachelor — it's a shame." Eltinge offered no apology for his bachelorhood and took ownership of the house's design. "[I] had been planning and dreaming this for ten years and at least I'm going to get it finished according to my own ideas."[15] Since home decoration was considered women's work, the female impersonator showed that off stage he would put his Hollywood bohemian status on display. In vaudeville Eltinge played up masculine traits. In Hollywood, Eltinge displayed his feminine traits and toyed with a potential interest in taboo sexuality. He also admitted to living in the home with his mother. This publicity would anticipate the type of coverage that some bachelors received in Hollywood materials during the 1930s. This will be examined in the chapter on houses.

By the early 1920s, Eltinge returned to the stage and again promoted himself in more masculine terms. The outrageous performances of female impersonators Francis Renault and Bert Savoy and the drag balls and gay speakeasies of the '20s "pansy craze" in New York made Eltinge's style appear old-fashioned. He began to drink heavily and in 1923 was caught smuggling liquor from Canada. Despite a sensational trial and bad press, he managed to get an acquittal. But it was the beginning of his decline.[16]

Nightlife After World War I: From Prohibition to World War II

The nightlife in U.S. cities changed dramatically during the period of Prohibition from 1920 to 1933. Reformers fought against the presence and operation of nightclubs prior to World War I. The Anti-Saloon League won the passage of legislation banning the sale of alcohol in many states. However, the reformers' activities culminated in the passage of the Volstead Act, which banned alcohol sales throughout the country after 1919.

The Act drove many saloon and bars out of business but also hurt other establishments as well. Many lobster houses and older respectable cabarets throughout the country disappeared, losing the profits that came from alcohol sales, while facing competition from speakeasies that offered customers illegal drinks. Organized crime moved into this business world and cut the emphasis on food, services, and other extras. These factors significantly reduced the upper- and middle-class nature of nightclubs and their emphasis on respectability. Yet the top echelon of society and entertainment celebrities flocked to the new nightclubs, helping the public increasingly perceive these spaces as exciting places full of romance and adventure.[17]

The new nightclubs served as the setting for newspaper columnists who wrote about the doings of the country's wealthy and famous. These writers wrote syndicated columns that appeared in newspapers throughout the country. This national distribution led to the increasing concentration upon those people known by readers of newspapers across the country. The emergence of illustrated tabloid newspapers, such as the *New York Daily News*, prompted the need for more photographs of celebrities and also led to the increased focus on nationally known personalities.

The coverage of society figures, local politicians, and business people declined as the space devoted to entertainers rose. By 1930, celebrities from the entertainment world replaced cafe society as the main attraction for newspaper coverage. The press and public sought more information about people whose fame arose from attracting and maintaining the mass media's focus than those individuals known because of their family or their productive activities.[18]

Nightclubs existed in more disreputable parts of cities and they began to draw sizable crowds. The clubs in the other areas, such as Greenwich Village, offered white middle class people the chance to see "exotic" people as performers, an activity termed "slumming." Since the late 1800s, slummers visited ethnic neighborhoods to see different people and gawk at their "different" ways.

Beginning in the 1920s, they attended theatrical shows that featured "new" performers. The performers included the "New Negroes," "pansies," and working-class performers and offered very specific and sometimes highly stereotyped acts for the audiences' entertainment pleasure.[19] Historians described slummers as people who enjoyed the titillating experience of seeing something different from themselves from a distance, before returning home to their daily routine without having their lives and perspectives disrupted. Slummers enjoyed the appearance of being knowledgeable, daring, sophisticated, jaded urbanites in front of their friends and neighbors. Their familiarity with "decadence" served in some way as a sign of status. However, these adventurers cared little for the "different" people themselves and held patronizing attitudes toward the cultures these performers represented.[20]

The most extensive coverage of nightlife occurred in New York and Los Angeles/Hollywood. These cities had the greatest concentration of all the necessary elements: entertainers and society figures, nightclubs and bars, and newspapers and gossip columnists. The majority of this coverage focused on the established nightlife areas of Times Square and the Sunset Strip. The contrast between the nightlife of these two cities during the late 1920s through the early 1930s showed that while New York City opposed attempts to link its nightlife with effeminate males and homosexuality, Hollywood promoted such images in the media.

Scenes from Times Square

The success of the clubs that attracted slummers prompted New York City nightclub owners to bring exotic entertainers to the bright lights of middle-brow Times Square. Several people involved in the theater business and the nightclub business realized that they could make a profit and/or inform people about the city using effeminate males and homosexuality. The first efforts occurred on the legitimate stage during the late 1920s; two Broadway plays, *Sex* and *The Captive* respectively, brought an unapologetically wanton woman and a lesbian to the stage. However, the city's newspaper reviewers and reporters covering these plays generally avoided direct mention of lesbianism and referred to both plays' themes as revolting.

In early February 1927, city officials raided *Sex* and *The Captive* as part of a larger clean up of sexuality on stage. That same month Broadway theater owners denied producers of *The Drag*, a play that included effeminate, homosexual males among its characters, a location to stage their show. These plays demonstrated that both New York City local government officials and the city's theater owners objected to bringing the perceived disreputable nightlife world of degenerate prostitutes and homosexuals into plain view on stage.[21]

A few nightclub owners along Broadway observed the success of a small number of Greenwich Village clubs that featured effeminate males as performers and waiters. They decided that they could cash in on the appeal of this novelty and brought female impersonator entertainment to their Times Square nightclubs. Manhattan's nightclub columnists covered the clubs, labeling their entertainment as the "pansy craze scene." They revealed to their readership that these performers acted effeminately and were "pansies playing pansies."

The majority of the newspaper coverage attacked the scene as degenerate, and their campaign against the nightclubs prompted the city government to take repressive action within the year. Police raided several clubs in early 1931 and frequently placed themselves at the club doors, making access to gay nightlife and illegal liquor nearly impossible. The actions finished the pansy acts and their presentation in the New York media. The New York City politicians, newspapers, and citizens would not allow for the open display of effeminate males and homosexuals in their nightlife and did not want their city associated with these subcultures in any way.

After the repeal of Prohibition in early 1933, the New York State Liquor Authority instituted a policy that provided a license to serve alcohol only to places they deemed "orderly." The agency interpreted the presence of lesbians and gay men as "disorderly" and threatened bars that served gay and lesbian clientele with the loss of their licenses and livelihood. Historian George Chauncey interpreted this repression as part of a powerful backlash against the visibility of homosexuals in the public sphere, where they were perceived as a threat to the gender and sexual arrangements already in crisis because of the Great Depression.

This perceived threat proved so powerful that even the *representation* of homosexuals disappeared from many media forms. New York, the city with the largest nightlife in the country, stopped the media presentation of images of homosexuals, effeminate men, and female impersonators in the early 1930s.[22] Drag did not disappear from New York City, as gay males continued to don women's apparel and enter city automats and cafes. However, newspaper and magazine readers would rarely read about female impersonators and drag performers.

What was true for the Big Apple was true for other cities across the nation. Several cities experienced pansy crazes in their nightclubs during the 1930s. Many of the clubs faced legal action and other pressures to stop using female impersonators as their entertainment. Few images of these female impersonators appeared in the mass media of these cities, which ranged from Chicago to New Orleans. Instead, the newspapers featured accounts of successful attempts to drive shows out of town or ban female impersonation from their city. City officials and the gatekeepers of the media did not want these "deviants" in the highly visible spaces of their nightclubs and daily and evening newspapers.[23]

By the mid–1930s the proprietors of nightclubs in the urban United States reduced nightlife's association with deviance and decadence. Media images reflected this change. New restaurants sprang up on Broadway. These nightclubs contained large enough spaces to offered lower cover charges and alcohol prices, allowing more of the middle class to enter. Known in the day as volume restaurants, these nightclubs teased their customers with acts and environments that provided excitement without scaring them. This gave their clientele the opportunity for a "dangerous love": they could have a heterosexual romance yet also receive hints of fatal attractions and sex across forbidden boundaries.

These volume restaurants, which were an important part of the Times Square New York nightlife, provided middlebrow theatrical entertainment to club visitors. They also shared that middlebrow taste with readers who learned about the evening events in gossip columns. Even a magazine depiction of a Harlem after-hours club provided little raciness. The piece stated, "On a typical evening four bands played in the Lenox Avenue ballroom and while some people danced many sat half-asleep at the tables." The article did not mention heterosexual romance, the central element to most Hollywood nightlife images.[24]

As Los Angeles grew during the 1920s and into the 1930s, nightlife locations blossomed around the city. When movie stars and celebrities frequented these new restaurants and nightclubs in Hollywood, particularly along Sunset Strip, the movie industry and the media took the opportunity to show everyone these people enjoying the new Hollywood nightlife. The depictions of Hollywood nightlife, unlike the images coming out of other cities in the country, continued the association of nightlife with decadence.

Hollywood Nights

Nightclubs and restaurants blossomed as Los Angeles's population, industry, and cultural importance grew spectacularly after World War I. By 1930, Hollywood had "more Neon lights than Broadway.... It is gayer, newer, brighter, and younger than anything in the history of man." During the 1920s Hollywood's population quadrupled as the area expanded west through Beverly Hills and north into the San Fernando Valley. Los Angeles developed a manufacturing base in automobiles and aircraft, expanded its oil refinery industry, and emerged as one of the top tourist locations in the country. The city developed a notable research institute in the Huntington Library and a major institution of higher learning with the University of Southern California. Los Angeles also developed the Mediterranean and Spanish Revival architectural styles and Southland literature.

The Hollywood motion picture industry played the greatest part in Los

Angeles's cultural growth. Moviemaking became the eleventh-largest industry in the nation. The large studios transformed the "barn" structures of the early 1910s into the series of buildings and sets behind tall gates, giving the studios the look of fiefdoms. The production wings of the big eight studios functioned like factories. Each studio employed nearly 3,000 people and a single department, such as MGM's makeup, could handle 1,200 actors in an hour through its production techniques.

As the movie industry grew, related industries including costume and prop stores expanded. Between 1917 and the early 1930s, the number of restaurants and lunchrooms quadrupled. They spread, as did nightclubs, from the Spring Street area to Sunset and Hollywood Boulevards and Melrose Avenue. The blocks around the intersection of Hollywood and Vine contained luxurious hotels, elaborate beauty parlors, shops, and widely publicized restaurants such as the Brown Derby. The old town of Sherman, later to become West Hollywood, clustered its stores, nightclubs, and restaurants in groups along Santa Monica and Sunset Boulevards.

Despite this growth, Los Angeles retained numerous orange groves and undeveloped areas, providing its inhabitants with the freedom available in open spaces. This freedom was literal, the spaces offering people places where they could sneak away and not be observed. This freedom was also cultural, in the perception of California, and the West in general, as an open place where a person was not known and could reinvent himself or herself.[25]

The city's old and new wealth participated in the development of the area's nightspots. The Ambassador Hotel started as a heroic civic enterprise to bring more civilization to the area. Its opening drew Los Angeles's society, but shortly thereafter the hotel opened the Coconut Grove nightclub and developed an industry clientele. Stars continued to go to clubs run by Frank Sebastian, such as The Cotton Club, and to towns like Vernon and Culver City to go slumming in cabarets and speakeasies.[26]

Hollywood nightclubs grew during the decade and the majority of the "in" places congregated along the "Sunset Strip," a three-square-mile area that bordered Hollywood and Beverly Hills. The area remained outside the city of Los Angeles and was policed by the Los Angeles County Sheriff's Office. Many a famous star greeted the boys in the patrol cars by name in this unincorporated area of West Hollywood. Such familiar relationships led to a more relaxed attitude toward the enforcement of laws.[27]

Hollywood boasted several of the most famous nightclubs in the country. Two of the more renowned, the Trocadero and Earl Carroll's Theatre Restaurant, offered their patrons high-quality food, elaborate decor, and late-night ambiance that often included impromptu events and performances. The Sunset Strip gained notoriety as one of the most famous hot spots in the country. Of the nightclubs in the area, The Barn, La Boheme, the Club New Yorker, and the Back Yard Café all featured cross-dressing performers and clientele.

The Strip, along with Hollywood Boulevard, sported many well-known eateries, including the Montmartre Cafe, the Oasis, the Bullpen, Hula Hut, Burp Hollow, and the Toad in the Hole. Despite the protests of religious figures and other citizens that the bars and nightclubs, gambling houses, and houses of ill repute invaded the best residential districts, the Strip drew the stars, the society and the politicians.[28]

The nightclubs and restaurants offered industry clientele and the readers of newspaper and magazine items fantasy environments. The Montmartre Cafe seated 350 people and served them on 2,400 pounds of solid silver service. Chandeliers from Czechoslovakia hung above their heads. La Boheme created a version of the Normandy seaside, and the Ambassador provided a Moroccan motif with gold leaf and etched palm tree doors leading into a grand expanse. The Coconut Grove decorated its expanse to create exotic environs such as a Venetian carnival. The Embassy Club's French ballroom and roof garden offered the best to the stars. Earl Carroll's Theatre Restaurant, housed in an ultramodern building, had two revolving stages 80 feet in diameter and a neon lighting system used in extravaganzas. The six tiers accommodated 1,000 people, and inner-circle club members paid $1,000 to sit in the first tier.[29]

The publicity featured the attire and activities of stars in the beautiful environs and made Hollywood nightlife into a fantasy for the audience members. Columnists and reporters described stars' clothing and jewelry, creating a sense of style and wealth beyond the readers' dreams. They described the special celebrations in the nightclubs, including birthdays, wedding anniversaries, welcome-back soirees, and affairs to honor visiting guests, turning the nightlife scene into an ongoing party. In one example, a group of stars feted actress Thelma Todd at George Olsen's club; they honored her with a horse-shoe-shaped table banked with roses and surrounded by miniature palms and papier-mâché Deauville dolls.

Newspaper items also promoted Hollywood nightlife as a fantasy by tying a star's appearance at a club or restaurant to romance, such as "Magnificent Gloria Swanson was seen the past week lunching with the new boy friend, Michael Farmer." Even the top gossip columnist in the country, Walter Winchell, joined the chorus that adored Los Angeles's nightclubs and noted Hollywood's sexually free ways. "Nowhere in the East is there so enchanting a rendezvous as the Coconut Grove ... where the celebrated of the screen and even the lesser prominent sip and sup and stay up until almost 12:30 in the morning.... And swap loves almost daily."[30]

The nightlife publicity added stars' feelings to these glamorous environs and enhanced Hollywood nightlife's reputation. Items captured real and imagined professional feuds between certain stars, like a jousting scene between Garbo and Dietrich at the Trocadero. Items carrying the suggestion of extramarital affairs that provoked fights in nightclubs and hotels provided flair. As the owner of Ciro's noted, "I guess we have about the highest-priced pugilistic talent west of Madison Square Garden." Occasionally, a gossip piece hinted that the romance of Hollywood figures might cross sexual boundaries. A piece noted that "The Billie Dove-Howard Hughes affair is still 'on' but rumor has it that there are certain legal matters of a marital nature which must be ironed out before the romance can be officially culminated." These items suggested the presence of Hollywood bohemians in the industry's nightlife.[31]

Throughout the 1930s, local government officials and citizen groups attempted to forcefully sever this link between Hollywood nightlife and the taboo, but the nightlife locations and their appearance in the depictions of Hollywood lasted. That they could not sever the link revealed that the bohemians and their favorite locations were deeply ingrained in the definition of Hollywood nightlife, as we can see in the forthcoming images.

Doing Lunch: Proper Attire in Hollywood Restaurants

With the development of the new Hollywood nightlife in the early 1930s, the first significant appearance of Hollywood bohemians in Hollywood nightlife involved women wearing men's clothing to Hollywood's restaurants. Women have worn suits, hats and other clothing associated with men in a variety of world cultures, often in order to spend their lives disguised as men. However, in Hollywood, the women did not deny their biological sex. The women wore the men's clothes as a feminist statement, as an indication of gender inversion, or both.

Media portrayals of these women echoed the general pattern of Hollywood nightlife images by emphasizing the trendy environs and presenting information about the activities and personalities of Hollywood celebrities. The images used the depiction of women defying the culture's standards for clothing as a way of showing the sophistication of Hollywood and making its nightlife appear taboo and more spectacular than the nightlife in New York City or anywhere else.

The creative team behind the motion picture *What Price Hollywood?* (RKO, 1932) attempted to "tell the truth about Hollywood." Producer David O. Selznick thought the "trouble with most films about Hollywood was that they gave a false picture, that they burlesqued it, or they oversentimentalized [sic] it.... And my notion ... dialogue was actually straight out of life and was straight 'reportage.'"[32] The Brown Derby restaurant in Hollywood attracted actors, directors, producers, and screenwriters of the industry from noon until the early morning hours. The Vine Street location reserved its booths and the north wall front tables for stars and executives while others sat in the center. All hoped to get noticed.[33] One of the earliest scenes in *What Price Hollywood?* occurred inside this restaurant:

Drunken motion picture director Max Carey walks in throwing gardenias he bought from an old woman outside. Smiling, he greets the people he knows. He briefly exits the screen. [The viewer sees a section of the restaurant as the shot switches from a medium to a long shot.] Carey continues walking around the restaurant and bumps into the mannishly attired woman as she rises from her table. His mouth drops as he steps back and says, "I beg your pardon, old man." As she straightens her suit jacket, Max slowly looks down then up her torso and rolls his eyes back in his head. Reaches out his hand and taps her elbow. "Pardon me, who's your tailor?" She turns her back and strides out as he smirks then carries on giving out the flowers.[34]

The movie placed its audience inside this famous Hollywood night spot. The scene put a variety of Hollywood types on display, including a lecherous agent, an egotistical actor, and a producer with his sycophant dining in a booth. The presence of the mannishly dressed woman indicated that these women were part of Hollywood nightlife. Her introduction differed from the presentation of other Hollywood types. Carey briefly exited before he returned into view and immediately bumped into the woman in a man's suit. Of all the Hollywood types presented in this scene, the movie tried to surprise its viewers only when it introduced the Hollywood bohemian.

The separation of this woman's image from the other industry types illustrated the significance of the role of Hollywood bohemians in Hollywood nightlife. The image made the restaurant seem like a wild and fantastic place. The woman's mannish dress hinted that she held lesbian interests. The difference in her introduction indicated that the image represented a unique type of person and spurred the belief that Hollywood nightlife was wild because it contained special places where people who acted on taboo interests dined. The image provided audiences with the perception of Hollywood nightlife as fantastic through giving them the experience of seeing a person who pushed the culture's sexual boundaries beyond their everyday experiences.

The scene at the Brown Derby and the image of the mannishly-dressed woman enhanced the reputation of the motion picture for RKO. The scene corroborated how many people around the world perceived Hollywood. As the critic for the trade magazine *Motion Picture Herald* informed theater owners, *What Price Hollywood?* was a serio-burlesque load of inside dope on what folks everywhere thought Hollywood was. The box office returns from most U.S. cities validated the trade reviewers' perceptions that the motion picture would fulfill audience expectations.[35]

The image sacrificed truth for entertainment value. The mannish female character's tailored suit was too large and ill-fitting, which prompted Carey's quip about wanting to know about her tailor. Among the Hollywood women wearing masculine tailored suits during the era, actress Marlene Dietrich, director Dorothy Arzner, and screenwriter Mercedes de Acosta wore suits with impeccably sharp lines and style. Certainly, producer David Selznick, director

George Cukor, and the four screenwriters knew about women who dressed in the sharp style of men's clothing. But the production team wanted to add humor to the scene and chose to make her the object of the joke. Still, the "mannish woman" in the movie had more "positive" attributes than depictions of mannish women in the literature of the era: she had an attractive face, a torso that was neither overly boyish nor overweight; she treated herself well, dining at a hot spot, and had a place within the motion picture industry community.

Hollywood women in masculine attire appeared occasionally in newspaper and magazine gossip columns. The items ran, "Director Dorothy Arzner, who favored 'man-tailored suits,' dined with actress friends at La Maze"; "...[Arzner] lunched with a variety of women friends, including actress Claudette Colbert, at the exclusive Vendomes," and placed women in men's clothing at a variety of Hollywood's eateries and watering holes. Like the character in *What Price Hollywood?* the gossip items associated Hollywood nightlife with the fantasy of seeing people who defied the typical clothing style for women. In the late 1920s and early 1930s, their choices to wear male clothing signaled gender inversion, an understanding of the holding of homosexual interests, thus tying Hollywood nightlife to people who pursued taboo sexual behaviors.[36]

The gossip column items discussed the activities of living people. The pieces indicated that these Hollywood bohemians enjoyed fine lives in Hollywood. The women in men's clothing were important industry figures. They worked for the major movie studios on big-budget pictures. They earned large salaries that enabled them to dine at exclusive nightspots. The women forged friendships, attended and hosted parties, and built a community of like-minded women in Hollywood.

Many of these women appeared on the Hollywood scene around the same time. The image of a woman wearing mannish slacks and suits created an impression of same-sex interest and titillated Hollywood fans by associating the nightlife with this risqué behavior. Actress Katharine Hepburn came to Hollywood in 1932 after Broadway success. The daughter of a successful doctor and a suffragette, who was a tomboy in her early life, wore slacks out of personal preference. Her studio, RKO, one of the smaller in size and influence in the industry, generated less of the publicity using this image for the actress that other studios did for their stars. A few images showed Hepburn attending clubs wearing slacks.

The images worked, as they caught the attention of the public reading the Hollywood materials. They made the nightlife more interesting and sparked the readers enough to offer comments. "The trousers worn outside of work by Dietrich and Hepburn are as comfortable, not to say as charming and logical, as the drapes with which they are gowned for the public eye...." This woman from Los Angeles obviously enjoyed the style and supported Hepburn and Dietrich without qualms. Another reader wrote in a more tongue-in-cheek manner to the editor of *Photoplay*. She observed that the actresses might

> be sued for disrupting home life, parading in masculine attire! ... I won't be able to tell the boyfriend from my old maid aunt, whom insists upon "Marlegging" in her latest "Dashabout Dandy," which comes, mind you, with an extra pair of trousers![37]

Hepburn herself observed years later that people thought of her as a lesbian because she always wore mannish clothes and was constantly seen in the company of Laura Harding. Clothing designer Howard Greer noted that Hepburn always came to his shop with the beautiful and unassuming Miss Harding, who lived with Hepburn. While the actress claimed that Miss Harding returned to New York during 1933, Greer noted that Harding was still coming to the shop with Hepburn while the later was doing the film *Bringing Up Baby*, which would be in 1937–1938.[38]

The contradiction between what the actress said and what a contemporary saw raised questions if not eyebrows. Certainly, Hepburn's Hollywood bohemian image resulted from the actress's unconventionality. Perhaps the contradiction and Hepburn's comment on Hollywood's perception of her sexuality revealed a degree of truth. One scholar referred to the actress as a bisexual, noting Hepburn's affair with Laura Harding. Of course, Katharine Hepburn was well-known for her decades-long love affair with Spencer Tracy. The unconventionality continued as Tracy remained married to another woman and the pair did not live together.[39]

Another one of the first actresses to incorporate the image of mannish dress as a part of publicity was Tallulah Bankhead. Born in 1902 as Tallulah Brockman Bankhead, the Alabama native lost her mother three weeks after being born. Her father, William Bankhead, the son and brother of prominent Alabama politicians, worked as an attorney before obtaining a seat in Congress in the early 1910s.

Tallulah soon realized that behaving theatrically garnered for her the type of responses that she sought. She craved more and more attention and found other sources for that attention as she attended several boarding schools. While her older sister planned to get married at age sixteen, Tallulah had other interests. Still wedded to theater and movies, she read the movie and fan magazines religiously. A contest for readers to enter guaranteed a small group the chance to win a bit part in a movie. Each reader submitted a photograph and the *Picture Play* staff chose who won based on their photographs. The blossoming southern belle won and went to New York.[40]

Miss Bankhead was not a stranger to the city despite her young years. She had attended school in the city briefly and one of her aunts resided in New York. The success in this "beauty contest" fueled her desire to perform and provided the means to attempt to become an actress. Both the New York movie studios and the stages of Broadway proved difficult to woo.

While she worked to convince both her father and grandfather to allow her to act in the stage production of *The Squab Farm*, her father wrote to the Shuberts to convince them to cast his daughter. The play received a critical lambasting. While admitting that it contained clever lines and garish characters, the critics considered it a crude drama and the play lasted only 45 performances. Tallulah played Gladys Sinclair and received no mention in her walk-on child role. The actress summed up her experience with the quip, "A mute child in a flop."

Tallulah had forsaken attempting a career in the movies. She broke through with the help of playwright Zoe Akins, attaining her first substantial role in a play entitled *Footloose*. Later she received positive reviews for a few other small roles in stage plays, but she could not make any significant headway. Over four years after arriving in New York, she left for London, England and a start at a different stage.[41]

The change of scenery proved fantastic for the actress's career. She became part of a crowd-pleasing play called, *The Dancers*, in 1923 and would perform regularly until opting to leave for Hollywood in 1930. She became vogue in England's capital, meeting with both theatrical and gentry societies. What she did and what she said became the talk of the country. People followed stories on her clothes, cars, home, jewels, and personal assignations. She gained the admiration of matinee girls and beaus in boxes and the studios had to have her. Paramount won out.[42]

The Hollywood publicity machine began creating material for the new star. Since some if not many movie fans might not know much about the actress, Hollywood studios and the press provided information. The publicity claimed that Hollywood waited nervously, slightly apprehensively for Tallulah Bankhead's arrival. What reportedly concerned the studios the most was that the actress "thinks like a lawyer and acts as she jolly well pleases."

The actress lived up to

Tallulah Bankhead, 1931 (Library of Congress).

her reputation. The publicity department of Paramount and the newspaper gossip columns worked at presenting the image through Bankhead's clothing. Ironically one of the first mentions of Bankhead's clothes included her old friend from New York City and the director of the movie that contained a mannishly-dressed woman character, *What Price Hollywood?* "Director George Cukor and screenwriter Zoe Akins held a party for their friend actress Tallulah Bankhead [who frequently donned mannish attire] at a downtown French café." Even at the close of her Hollywood career the image continued. Readers learned that Tallulah created a furor at the Assistance League. The actress made an appearance as the guest of honor in heavy white silk slacks and a long white wool coat. She took the restaurant by storm and signed everything the tourists put in front of her.

While Miss Bankhead created excitement in Hollywood's restaurants and nightclubs the gossip columnists also described her exploits in other areas of Hollywood. One gossip informed that after spending several hours sunning herself Tallulah acquired a tan so notable that she just had to show it to someone.

> Slipped on a bathing suit, covered herself with a coat and dashed over to Paramount. Rushed out to the Mae West set and with a "Look at me!—" cast aside the cloak and pranced about like a bronze peacock. Mae thought it looked fine. So did the electricians.[43]

This last gossip item informed the public that a star wore little or no clothing on one studio set. This made the behind-the-scenes area in Hollywood appear that much more wild and crazy than even the nightclubs and restaurants.

Despite the publicity efforts Tallulah Bankhead did not make it as a Hollywood studio star. The actress blamed the studio in her autobiography, asserting that the Paramount movies were mediocre at best. She returned to New York City and the Broadway stage in late 1933. She appeared in at least a play per year, winning the New York Drama Critics Award for her performance in *The Skin of Our Teeth* in 1942. The success led to a return to Hollywood for character roles in two movies.

In Hollywood certain actresses might wear mannish clothes in nightclubs and restaurants. Their style created a stir and carried the suggestion of the taboo, whether accurate to Bankhead's personality or not. Contemporaries such as the actor Laurence Olivier did not mention this behavior specifically, although he described Tallulah as "great fun to be with ... and unusually attractive with overtones of sensuality...."

However, other contemporaries did. Comedian Robert Benchley joked about going out on the town with two gay men and Tallulah.

> All my high-class girls seem to be in Europe this summer, and Harlow is tied up with Powell and Lombard with Gable. I can't turn my back for a minute without their running out on me. However, Tallulah is here and Bill Haines, and I understand that Jerry Zerbe is coming out, so we can just kid around in drag if there are no girls.

Benchley joke centered on his view of the gay men as possible substitutes for women. In addition, the comment carried the humor of not considering Tallulah a "real girl."[44]

Biographers seem split on the issue, noting that the lesbian affairs occurred in Tallulah's youth. Writers on the actress have addressed her sexuality differently. The issue rarely appeared in one of the biographies. Others suggest that Tallulah was a favorite but maybe not the lover of certain lesbians, such as producer Cheryl Crawford. During her later years she lived with Patsy Kelly, a former movie comedienne who was lesbian and is examined in chapter four. Most of the sources believe her to have had a large sexual appetite that included both males and females that she found attractive. The actress herself made several jokes regarding sexual behavior, both heterosexual and homosexual.[45]

The mannishly dressed woman in Hollywood nightlife reached a cultural apex with a different Paramount Studio star. The publicity featured actress Marlene Dietrich. Born two days after Christmas in 1901 in Berlin, Germany, Marie Marlene Dietrich studied music before embarking on a career as a chorus girl and actress. She appeared in the plays of noted theater actor and director Max Reinhardt. Although she appeared in minor roles in the German movie industry, Dietrich's career did not blossom throughout the 1920s.

The UFA (Universum Film AG) production *The Blue Angel*, released in 1930, provided her the role of Lola-Lola. Dietrich made this cabaret singer whose seduction brings about the downfall of a respected schoolmaster her breakthrough. With the help of director Josef von Sternberg, Paramount Studio contracted with Dietrich, bringing her to Hollywood for her first movie in 1930. Ironically, this movie, *Morocco*, would be the only one for which Dietrich earned an Academy Award nomination.[46]

The star wore tuxedos in two of her early Hollywood movies and gossip columnist Louella Parsons noted Dietrich's preference for pants in her daily life as early as the fall of 1930. However, Paramount avoided discussing the star's clothing preferences. With the box office failure of her movie *Blonde Venus* in late 1932 and Paramount signing Dietrich to an expensive five-year contract, the studio's publicity department launched a huge publicity campaign for Dietrich's new movie, *Song of Songs* (1933).[47]

In January 1933, a few articles and several industry columnists chronicled Dietrich's attire. A tabloid piece provided abundant detail about Dietrich's apparel. "Marlene Dietrich gave the photo snappers and autograph hounds a real thrill yesterday by appearing at the Brown Derby with long gray flannel trousers, blue sweater, cap to match, dark gray mannish coat and her attorney, Ralph Blum." An item in the *Los Angeles Times* offered more context for the images. "Lunching with Mamoulian [Dietrich was] still wearing trousers and coats and evidently having them made to order. It is said she has just ordered two or three Tuxedo suits to wear in the evening. It is also said that she ate considerable humble pie in coming back to Paramount."

Marlene Dietrich in one of the suits that created such a stir, 1932 (Rosenbach Museum & Library, Philadelphia).

Another tabloid item suggested a reaction to readers as it informed them that Dietrich's Hollywood nightlife style caused heads to turn. "Marlene Dietrich created a mild sensation when she arrived at the El Mirador hotel in Palm Springs.... She wore masculine attire for all occasions at the desert resort...." These items accomplished the studio's goal of significant media coverage for their star. Promoting the star actress wearing men's clothing at Hollywood restaurants made Hollywood nightlife appear wild.[48]

The studio offered readers an interpretation of these images that did not promote the connection between Hollywood nightlife and the star's romantic life. Paramount's publicity department framed this "new" Dietrich image as the start of a fashion trend. This linked her image with a cultural understanding of woman as display object of consumer culture products. Some contemporaries writing on the Dietrich masculine attire interpreted the image similarly. "'Will it be overalls next?' an industry columnist wondered. 'Depends probably on how much publicity Katharine Hepburn gets out of her favorite garb. Anyway, they seem to be organizing a publicity campaign on them. It's probably rivalry for Dietrich's troussers [sic].'"[49]

Others perceived that the "new" Dietrich image offered hints about Dietrich's interest in women. The images spurred readers to connect the star's romantic life with Hollywood nightlife. An alluring woman wearing men's clothing enabled different people to fantasize. Dietrich's occasional beau and confidant Maurice Chevalier expressed the star's attractiveness to heterosexual males. "I told Marlene myself that if she would wear men's clothes and women's garments even to the extent of fifty-fifty, I would find it the most attractive and charming idea.... She looks wonderful in men's attire."

Director Josef von Sternberg noted that Dietrich's adoption of masculine dress also appealed to another group's romantic interest. Von Sternberg described his intention of outfitting Dietrich in male tuxedos in two motion pictures. "The formal male finery fitted her with much charm, and I not only wished to touch lightly on a Lesbian accent ... but also to demonstrate that her sensual appeal was not entirely due to the classic formation of her legs."

The Dietrich images revealed that Paramount's publicity department devised a campaign around presenting one of the industry's biggest stars as a Hollywood bohemian. The decision to promote their star wearing tailored suits and slacks in restaurants and other locations illustrated both the studio's intentional use of Hollywood bohemian imagery and the promotional value of the imagery. The Dietrich campaign worked. People remembered the images.

Other creators also connected the Dietrich Hollywood bohemian image to Hollywood nightlife. The great songwriting team of Richard Rogers and Lorenz Hart wrote "I'm One of the Boys" for the motion picture *Hollywood Party* in mid-1933. The song chronicled the activities of a woman who, they joked, was one of the boys.

The Rogers and Hart character acted like a male, having habits that the culture usually associated with a man, such as hard drinking and gambling. The woman in the song carried her association with mannishness so far that she wore men's suits in order to look more like a male. The tie-in to the world of Hollywood in the song was that this character supposedly went to a tailor to get her man's suits fitted. The tailor happened to be the same one that Dietrich supposedly went to get her own suits fitted properly. The possibility that the song might appear in the movie caused the Studio Relations Committee's head to write to MGM executive Eddie Mannix. As the chief of the censorship organization for the industry, he advised Mannix that caution be used against playing "I'm One of the Boys" in any way that might be suggestive of lesbianism.[50]

Did the image and its suggestion of the taboo contain more of a description of Dietrich's personality than her choice of clothes? The biographies of contemporaries and analysis from writers on the era agree that the star had same-sex interest. Screenwriter Mercedes de Acosta, who will be examined in chapter four, described Dietrich charming her with gifts, food, her soft personality and radiantly lovely looks. De Acosta called the period spent at Dietrich's rental beach house happy times.

Years later another contemporary also mentioned Dietrich's bisexual interests. Actress Barbara Stanwyck, herself featured in an interview book entitled *Hollywood Lesbians*, observed, "I know the women from Europe swung both ways."

The writers on the studio system and Dietrich assert that the star had bisexual interests. Axel Madsen detailed her relationships, including love affairs that Dietrich and other actresses and screenwriters had amongst each other during the 1930s and 1940s.[51]

Dietrich's daughter, Maria Riva, noted her affairs, how the homosexual boys sent her mother violets as a tease about her lesbianism. She spitefully attacked Mercedes De Acosta, observing that De Acosta loved her mother and that her mother let her flounder. Two other writers note Dietrich's presence among groups of women with sexual interests in other women, described as a "sewing circle," or "the girls."[52]

The Dietrich campaign proved successful because audience members remembered it years later. When readers visited Hollywood a few years later they regularly asked whether Miss Dietrich really wore trousers. Guides told visitors that the Brown Derby would be a good place to see the star for themselves. The guides' advice confirmed the accuracy of the Dietrich publicity campaign. They also gave the visitors the chance to experience the Hollywood nightlife fantasy themselves.[53]

Women in men's clothing formed an unmistakable addition to the mystique of Hollywood restaurants. These Hollywood bohemians grabbed peoples' attention and remained in their minds. Their presence helped the restaurants appear wild and fantastic, places where alluring and out-of-the ordinary figures met and participated in an atmosphere of decadence that their taboo behavior created. The women in men's clothing made Hollywood nightlife different from all other depictions of city nightlife in the media.

The style and image of the mannishly dressed woman began as a portion of the lesbian subculture. Women in the community and others signaling a specific sexual preference adopted the clothes as a method of standing apart to be identified in the subculture. Particular actresses in Hollywood and other females in the industry followed suit. Within a decade the slacks and trousers for women, if not the tailored suit, had become co-opted and part of women's apparel.

Swinging Clubs to International Cafes: Merriment in the Great Depression

While images of certain female Hollywood figures provided hi-jinks in the restaurants, female impersonators performed in Hollywood's nightclubs in the early 1930s. The metropolitan dailies, tabloids, and trade newspapers featured the nightclub establishments in their industry columns because they drew Hollywood celebrities. The presence of the nightclubs in Hollywood novels and newspaper articles over the remainder of the decade illustrated that the "pansy craze" in Hollywood lasted longer than scholars have thought and demonstrated the importance of these bohemians to Hollywood nightlife.

Two figures in Hollywood's version of the "pansy craze" received the majority of press coverage in the early 1930s. Long-time vaudevillian Karyl Norman, who billed himself as "the Creole Fashion Plate," established himself at a nightclub called La Boheme. Jean Malin, a key figure in Manhattan's short-lived pansy craze, served as master of ceremonies of the Club New Yorker.

Norman, born George Paduzzi, joined a minstrel show at 16 years of age in 1913 and began his vaudeville career in 1918. Norman's act frequently required him to sing in soprano and in baritone. The switch from a tone associated with female singers to one associated with males amazed audiences not only for its versatility but also for the alternating between the genders. Some in vaudeville provided him with an alternative sobriquet, "The Queer Old Fashion Plate." This disparaging comment showed the degree of vaudeville's coarse homophobia and clever wordplay.

The other significant person among the new wave of female impersonators was Brooklyn-born Victor Eugene James Malin. Malin competed for prizes at Manhattan's drag balls while in his mid-teens during the early 1920s. After losing several chorus-boy jobs because Broadway directors perceived him as too effeminate, he became a professional female impersonator. He worked at Paul and Joe's, a personality club in Greenwich Village, the Rubaiyat in Greenwich Village, and then as master of ceremonies at Broadway's Club Abbey during the 1920s. The six-foot, 200-pound man with a lisp, attitude, and sharp tongue left for Los Angeles after the shutdown of the female impersonator nightclubs in Times Square in early 1931.[54]

Occasionally publicity items appeared in newspapers and trade magazines about the sexuality of these performers prior to their arrival in Hollywood. As with Eltinge, the publicity for these men attempted to give these performers

Karyl Norman prior to becoming the host at La Boheme (courtesy Lilly Library, Indiana University, Bloomington, IN).

the image of sexual conformity. One set of items in the early 1920s featured Karyl Norman's engagement to male impersonator Ruth Budd. When Norman called off the engagement, Budd claimed that the affair was actually a publicity stunt, stating, "I'm glad I found out in time."[55] Budd's comment highlighted that in vaudeville Norman strove to receive publicity that focused on a conventional sexual path. In order to get that publicity, the female impersonator would even create a false marriage, known in the era as a marriage of convenience.

The female impersonator nightclubs made Hollywood nightlife seem exciting and wild because the top Hollywood stars came for the shows. "[There was a] large film turnout for the revue headed by Karyl Norman.... This was for the opening of La Boheme cafe. The spot just outside city limits can feature dancing until wee hours," and "A flock of celebs turned out for Jean (swish!) Malin's return to the Club New Yorker last eve." Stars willingly lent their names to help the female impersonators. "[Karyl] Norman is preparing a Club La Boheme menu, autographed by Claudette Colbert, Wallace Beery, George Raft, Jean Harlow, and others to serve as souvenirs for guests."[56] These items informed readers that the female impersonator nightclubs were the places to be. The big names thought that those nightclubs offered the most exciting Hollywood nightlife.

The movie magazines also carried images that showed the connection between the female impersonators, industry stars, and nightlife in Hollywood. Two photographs depicted several celebrities out on the town at the Club New Yorker. Malin sat in the middle of the crowd in both images. The captions highlighted the presence of stars such as Colleen Moore and popular leading ladies such as Sally Eilers. The magazine also made a game out of the captions. The photographs included some people who had not been around in the industry recently, with captions like, "Remember Stanley Smith?" (He was a leading man of the era.) The magazine asked the readers if they remembered who the person was, making a game out of the reader's knowledge of the movie industry.[57]

The gossip items expanded upon the connotation of sexual taboos by showing that both of the top female impersonators defied the culture's norms offstage as well. An item mentioned, "Norman sat in the dressing room sewing buttons on LaVerdie's dress." The piece depicted Norman as a mother hen. One of the aforementioned items regarding celebrities in the audience for Malin's performance used the word swish. The use of the word to describe a male's movement implied that Malin behaved very effeminately.

Another item more blatantly suggested that Malin transgressed gender and sexual boundaries offstage as well. "There's an artist chappie (in New York) who wears brown VELVET suits with WHITE polka dots, and he wants Jean Malin to return that bathrobe he borrowed ... his name is Samson, if you're interested ... so there!"[58] Readers were left to wonder what situation Malin had been in that required him to borrow a bathrobe from another man. Given the labeling of that other man as an "artist chappie" and the flamboyant clothes that he wore, the most obvious conclusion centered on the men being homosexuals.

A few publicity items in the tabloid and mainstream press made the connection between the nightclubs and homosexuality very obvious. One issue of *Broadway Brevities* stated that Hollywood had "two new eateries given over to exploiting nances." Nance was a slang term for homosexual man, emerging from the phrase "nancy boy." In a 1933 issue, *Hollywood Magazine* linked female impersonators with places for homosexuals in Hollywood. "There's B.B.B.'s Cellar where the boys dress up like girls; there's Jimmy's Back Yard, where the girls dress up like boys ... there's the Bohemian Club where Karyl Norman ... puts on a revue."[59]

One newly signed actress, British star Benita Hume, arrived in Los Angeles fresh from the British film industry in late 1932. Signed with MGM, Hume made over fifteen movies during the period from 1933 to 1938, frequently as the second female lead. When she arrived in Hollywood the publicity described her as preparing for marriage. Hume reportedly went to the beach, bought Christmas presents to ship back to England, and acquainted herself with such newer bright spots as Karyl Norman's La Boheme and Jean Malin's New Yorker.[60]

However, the publicity also made Hollywood nightlife appear to undercut the reader's slumming experience. The images humanized the female impersonators and showed that famous and respected people formed personal relationships with them. Readers learned that female impersonators had relationships with each other, such as Norman looking after the needs of one of his charges (sewing buttons for La Verdie). They discovered that Hollywood stars maintained personal relationships with the impersonators. Some stars lent their names and aid to female impersonators.

Others like MGM's star William Haines and Hal Roach studio comedian Patsy Kelly maintained friendships with Malin. Performers such as actress Fifi D'Orsay invited Malin and Norman to her industry parties. As fans of Hollywood stars, readers of these images identified with the star. If one of their favorite stars was friendly with female impersonators, the reader would continue to identify with the star, thus assuming the star's position of friend of the female impersonator.[61]

Some among the female impersonators joined the industry workforce as well. Jean Malin received two roles in movies. First, he worked on the Fox lot in a movie entitled *Arizona to Broadway* in 1933. Malin appeared in an uncredited role as "Ray Best," a Broadway performer. Best is a female impersonator, and in the scene, the gangster is trying to coerce all the best performers of the day to take part in a show he is producing. Malin impersonates the actress Mae West.

Later that year Malin appeared in a small role in an RKO studio movie. The story centered on the attempt of Joan Colby (Ann Harding) to get playboy millionaire John Fletcher (William Powell) to marry her. The female impersonator appeared in the opening scenes as the owner of a dress shop. However, unlike at Fox, the executives at RKO deemed Malin "too flamboyant a presence." The studio replaced him with another character actor and re-shot the scenes. This cost RKO a not-insignificant sum of near $1,700. Studio president B.B. Kahane wrote in an intra-studio memo that "I do not think we ought to have this man on the lot on any picture — shorts or features."[62]

The image that began this chapter dramatically shows how female impersonators made readers feel connected to a taboo person. Norman's imitation of Crawford enabled Crawford and other audience members from the movie industry to see themselves or someone they knew embodied by the female impersonator. This demonstrated the thinness of what theater scholars term "the fourth wall," the artificial distance between the person on stage and the audience.[63] The elimination of the distance between the performer and the celebrity audience made the female impersonator and the stars in the audience feel closer to one another. Since fans identify with celebrities, the readers also shared in the closer connection between the female impersonators and the celebrities.[64]

The female impersonators dramatically shaped perceptions of Hollywood nightlife. The images of female impersonators in Hollywood nightclubs were extraordinary. Hollywood insiders promoted these "drag queens" at a time when no other media wanted to show them and no officials wanted them to perform in their city. These bohemians made a living in Hollywood, established connections amongst themselves and friendships with people in the movie industry. They made Hollywood nightlife a wild and fantastic adventure that offered audience members a personal connection with decadence and the kind of culturally forbidden experiences that other cities attempted to eliminate from their own nightlife locations.

The information on the sexual preferences of these men is not voluminous. Comedian Milton Berle, who saw these figures in vaudeville and Hollywood, stated, "I did shows with some of the greatest female impersonators, Karyl Norman, Bert Savoy and Julian Eltinge. Of course, I worked with straight men too." Berle, along with two male dancers, performed in his mother's act. Norman gave Berle notes to pass on to one of the male dancers in the act. His mother caught on and admonished Berle to stay away from the homosexual.[65]

Female impersonators developed such a prominent role in Hollywood nightlife that they appeared in a book about Hollywood during the mid–1930s. Irish novelist Liam O'Flaherty arrived in the late 1920s to work on the script for the motion picture *The Informer*. He used these experiences to pen *Hollywood Cemetery* (1935).[66] In this novel, a producer's assistant used his humor and player nature in Hollywood's nightlife to climb the ladder in the movie industry.

The plot of *Hollywood Cemetery* featured a small studio's attempt to make a movie. Mortimer faced pressure from his talented director to make a prestigious motion picture of Brian Carey's novel *The Emigrant*. The producer wanted to keep the director happy so he decided to make the movie, but also conduct a search to find a new sexy female star so that it would be a box office hit. Mortimer traveled overseas and found an Irish lass having sex in the woods.

The producer brought the surprised girl to his hotel room. As he opened the door, Mortimer and the lass found his assistant, Larry Dafoe, draped in a white sheet. Preening in front of a full-length mirror, Dafoe declared, "I am Queen Victoria."[67] Mortimer laughed; the producer hired this female impersonator as his assistant after deciding that Dafoe's humor and style were a necessity on any trip to Hollywood's nightclubs. The Hollywood bohemian enhanced Hollywood's nightlife not only for gossip column readers but for the motion picture insiders.

The assistant's female impersonator skills played a larger role in Hollywood star making and nightlife glamour. Mortimer named the woman he found Angela Devlin. He placed Dafoe in charge of teaching Devlin how to become a female movie star. Dafoe's bohemian nature, particularly his ability to act like a woman, made him valuable to the studio. Dafoe played a key role in helping the studio create a star actress. Dafoe taught Devlin women's styles, behaviors, and attitudes, ranging from putting on perfume to the proper carriage she needed as she walked. The actress used these womanly behaviors both on screen and in the Hollywood restaurants and nightclubs. Dafoe and other female impersonators played an important behind-the-scenes role, shaping the look and behavior of the people who brought glamour and style to Hollywood and its nightlife.[68]

Tumultuous relationships existed between the main characters. Screenwriter Carey and actress Devlin fought while slowly falling in love. Devlin alienated herself from the producer. Mortimer and Dafoe fought often. As the publicity campaign for the movie increasingly focused on the as yet unseen Devlin, she proved unsatisfactory as an actress and sex object. Devlin and Carey fled the floundering movie production. They settled in Mexico where they married and sent press releases damning Mortimer. The producer had no star and no movie. The studio executives put pressure on him to show them something immediately.

Dafoe proposed that they replace Devlin with his male friend Jesse Starr, whose extremely effeminate manners and appearance made it impossible for him to appear in movies as anything but a chorus boy. Amid the chorus boys Starr met many who donned female clothes for performance and personal reasons.[69] They may have helped him fine-tune his own abilities. Increasingly desperate from the bad publicity, Mortimer agreed to Dafoe's plan. Dafoe and Mortimer hired Dr. Karl Zog to remake Starr physically. Dafoe used his bohemian talents to help perfect Starr's actions as a woman. The introduction of this female impersonator as Angela Devlin left the studio staff enthralled.

Mortimer and Dafoe then watched as the new Devlin met the public. The crowd let out a thunderous cry and chanted, "She is. She is. She is. She is."[70]

O'Flaherty used the images of female impersonation to critique the industry as a "cemetery" of the values that the author treasured, truth and nature. The author attacked Hollywood because its products dealt in surfaces and false images. He thought Hollywood studios were so corrupt that they believed they could make anything appear better than the item did in nature. O'Flaherty believed that only the motion picture industry would sabotage the nature of a woman's beauty and would promote a female impersonator as a "better" woman.[71]

The critique extended to the major characters. Mortimer cared most about making money, so he would perpetrate any hoax on the public as long as it proved profitable. Dafoe thought about advancing in the industry and maintained relationships to make others serve his ends. Starr looked ridiculous as a man so he willingly made himself available to become a woman.

Despite this stinging critique, *Hollywood Cemetery* granted its Hollywood bohemians positive attributes and a positive influence on Hollywood nightlife. Dafoe and Starr achieved success in the industry. Dafoe had friends in the industry and helped his friend Starr become a big success. Dafoe showed his intelligence by concocting the idea that put a major talent on the screen. His skills shaped Starr/Devlin into a star and a figure on the Hollywood nightlife scene. Starr/Devlin placed his talents on the screen for the world to enjoy, and his ability enabled him to bring glamour and fantasy to the Hollywood nightlife. In his attempt to debunk the mythologies surrounding Hollywood, O'Flaherty's novel presented other myths about Hollywood, including filling the city and movie industry with zany characters, unusual events and people engaged in double-crossings.[72]

Hollywood Cemetery continued the presentation of female impersonators as key bohemians in Hollywood nightlife. O'Flaherty's novel depicted that nightlife as a fantasy place tied to taboo people and decadent behavior. *Hollywood Cemetery* represented a first in the United States' literary tradition. Since the movie was successful, Dafoe became influential in the industry, and Starr became a star as Angela Devlin. *Hollywood Cemetery* marked the first time that a book made a female impersonator and a transsexual an antihero.

Some powerful figures on the city's political scene shared O'Flaherty's distaste for the Hollywood nightlife. One newspaper carried the report of a politician's lament. "They are openly soliciting patrons of lewdness and degeneracy with signs on their windows.... One place is so well-known people come from all over the city to see it." In late 1935, Councilman John Baumgartner launched an attack against the "hell holes and dives" operating in his district.

Two years prior to the publication of *Hollywood Cemetery*, the Los Angeles City Council tried to limit female impersonators and cross-dressing females in Hollywood nightlife. The officials complained that these establishments attracted homosexually inclined performers and audiences and argued that these nightclubs were dangerous. The Council passed a law that prohibited the appearance of people in drag within a cafe, unless employed by the cafe. Contemporary observers and current scholars observed the numerous raids on female and male cross-dressing nightclubs in late 1933 and thought the law would close nightclubs featuring female and male impersonation. This did not work. As Councilman Edward Thrasher declared, "While we sit here debating, these men of degenerate tendencies continue to dance in Councilman Baumgartner's district."[73]

Baumgartner's district represented an unusual urban location for homosexual nightlife during the early twentieth century. The Twelfth District was neither the poor, vice-ridden area of the city nor the tourist area of Los Angeles.[74] The district lay northwest of downtown and included portions of the Colegrove, Edendale, and Wilshire–Pico sections of the city. The area contained mostly middle- and working-class housing (single-family detached houses with garages and small courtyard apartments), a few hospitals and motion picture studios, and large undeveloped tracts. Stores appeared in patches along South Western Avenue and on a few of the numbered streets in the Wilshire–Pico portion of Baumgartner's district. Small clusters of stores and restaurants appeared in the eastern Hollywood area where Santa Monica Boulevard and North Vermont Avenue met and across from the Sunset Studio on Sunset Boulevard. This was an important place where the nightclubs operated.[75]

The female impersonators in Hollywood nightlife publicity provided the politicians with more ammunition. As we have seen, even with the vaudeville theater owners' efforts to create a decorous place of entertainment, female impersonators still carried a link to homosexuality. Hollywood publicity traded upon that link. In addition, the publicity located the female impersonators in nightclubs. Bars, according to respectable middle and upper-class Americans, had questionable moral orders in terms of who patronized them (deviants) and what was thought to go on in them (lewd, lascivious, bawdy, drunken, and illegal behavior among strangers). While Prohibition had been repealed, many Americans and psychology professionals continued to believe in the evils of alcohol. A psychologist even linked alcohol consumption to male homosexual activity when he stated that "when drinking, men fall on each other's necks and kiss one another."[76]

These factors helped the City Council enact new legislation. In 1935, the City Council's Welfare Committee introduced a resolution to control nightclubs with female impersonator entertainment. The resolution noted that these nightclubs had "entertainment which is detrimental to morals and a disturbance of the peace because it led to the congregating and loitering of undesirable and vicious people...." The full Council then passed an ordinance that required any place serving liquor to apply for a permit from the Police Commission if they wanted to hold shows. The Los Angeles Police tried to control the activities of the nightclubs in Hollywood. Police Chief James E. Davis, beginning his second term in 1933, made an effort although the majority of their attention focused on attacks on Communists and their offices.[77]

The policing efforts achieved mixed results in Hollywood. The city's black community had female impersonator Karyl Norman drawing crowds in his nightclub but also had others performers and activities that received publicity in newspaper gossip columns. The queer folk were a part of the regular nightlife activities in the Hollywood milieu. As a columnist discussed the latest stars and their "book-law" marriages he noted the other activities on the street at night. "Whassat! Nothing! Just the little bunch of open-air 'Reefer' boys at the corner of Reefer Alley taking bold whiff.... Queer folk hiding out since Chief Davis ordered 'Pick 'em up....'"

The nightlife continued, as a column from months later noted. Chauncey Highland made thousands of dollars holding drag balls in Hollywood during the recent past. Despite the police presence, gossip noted that plans for another "pansy ball" called "drags" were afoot. However, objections to the "...bizarre spectacle of 'queer' guys parading in skirts, high heeled slippers, rouge and lip-stick while queer 'women' in manless parties throng the ringside [arose.]"

The columnist supported the plan to put the kibosh on the drags, such as the efforts of recent California laws. Regardless of the harsher attitude displayed toward the female impersonators, these images showed that they appeared in all of Hollywood's communities. Furthermore, the men in female attire and the "manless" women made black Hollywood nightlife more exciting and offered the readers of these newspapers knowledge of their existence and the titillation of learning about these bohemians.[78]

Despite the politicians' pronouncements and the City Council's new ordinance, female impersonation remained a part of the Hollywood nightlife. The nightclubs remained open and drew crowds as Hollywood figures continued to attend female impersonation clubs. B.B.B.'s Cellar drew the Hollywood stars to its female impersonator in the early 1930s.

Industry fan magazines in the late 1930s described his Swing Club as the spot for industry stars in the wee hours of the morning. "The lines could be ten deep, and an occasional raid was taken in stride, for the patrons are never molested." The gossip piece informed readers that this type of club remained a part of the night lives of Hollywood's stars. The addition of raids made the Hollywood nightclub a wilder scene.

Others understood that audiences enjoyed images of Hollywood nightlife and some even desired to participate in it. The book *How to Sin in Hollywood* appeared in 1940 and provided descriptions of Hollywood restaurants, cafes, and nightclubs. The author divided the book into sections based on the type of nightlife experience the reader wanted. Each section contained a page of details including the nightclub's location, entertainment, and food and drink offerings to help tourists find and experience Hollywood nightlife. One item described a nightspot on the west side of town.

> "When Your Urge's Mauve," [go to] the Cafe International on Sunset Boulevard. The location offered supper, drinks, and the ability to watch boy-girls who necked and sulked and little girl customers who ... look like boys.[79]

The book included a visual presentation of this Hollywood bohemian world. Opposite the descriptive information, a cartoonist drew two women in tuxedos

... the little girl customers ...

Typical customers at Café International, 1940 (Jack Lord and Lloyd Huff, *How to Sin in Hollywood*).

above the caption, "the little girl customers." One is smoking a cigar and the other wore prominent lipstick, an image reminiscent of the women in men's clothing who appeared in the Hollywood eateries discussed earlier in the chapter.[80]

The description and cartoon extended the connection between Hollywood's bohemians and nightlife into something readers could experience directly. As part of a tour book, the image provided readers with the address of this place so they could easily visit the club and take part in Hollywood's nightlife. The presence of Cafe International in this tour book suggested the strong connection between Hollywood nightlife and its bohemians and the high level of interest that Hollywood visitors had in participating in this experience. Audiences wanted to try out the clubs where homosexuals, women in male attire, and female impersonators went as couples or hung around with their friends within their communities. Audiences wanted to experience the unusual and sexually forbidden. *How to Sin in Hollywood* and Hollywood nightlife in general provided them with that rare opportunity.

The connection between Hollywood nightlife and its bohemians promoted anxiety among some Hollywood insiders. When a studio purchased the movie rights to his novel *Miss Lonelyhearts*, Nathanael West went to Hollywood. He worked as a screenwriter on westerns and gangster pictures. Concerned with the emptiness of twentieth century life, West captured his experience of Hollywood in *The Day of the Locust* (1939). The novel indicted the motion picture industry and the culture it forged, including the loss of masculinity among American men. West featured a female impersonator in the Hollywood nightlife to make this particular point.[81]

A movie set designer took two "losers" who wanted to go out on the town to a nightspot in Hollywood. They approached a building shaped like a lady's slipper. The Cinderella Bar's design created a public presence that was hard to miss and advertised the presence in the bar of people who pursued taboo sexual behavior. West located the bar on Western Avenue which bordered Councilor Baumgartner's district. The author described how the central characters in the novel, Homer Simpson, Faye Greener, and Tod Loomis, watched a young man in a tight evening gown of red silk sing a lullaby.

> He had a soft, throbbing voice and his gestures were matronly, tender and aborted a series of unconscious caresses. What he was doing was in no sense parody; it was too simple and too restrained. It wasn't even theatrical. This dark young man with his thin, hairless arms and soft, rounded shoulders, who rocked an imaginary cradle as he crooned, was really a woman.
> When he had finished, there was a great deal of applause. The young man shook himself and became an actor again. He tripped on his train, as though he weren't used to it, lifted his skirts to show he was wearing Paris garters, then strode off swinging his shoulders. His imitation of a man was awkward and obscene.
> Homer and Tod applauded him.
> "I hate fairies," Faye said ... "They're dirty," she said.[82]

West's view challenged the previous depictions of the Hollywood bohemians and the nightlife they helped create. His female impersonator was "obscene," not fun and glorious. The nightclub where he worked was not the voluminous, decorous place that generated thoughts of wild, romantic adventure in audiences, but rather a seedy dive. Instead of linking nonconformity with celebrities, this imagery bound the female impersonators with the fringe of both the movie industry and the city's population. West's depiction stripped Hollywood's bohemians of their accomplishments, humor, and celebrity connections. The image also removed the spectacle they created from Hollywood nightlife, making the link between decadence and that nightlife appear depraved and deleterious to the culture.

West illustrated the danger he saw in Hollywood nightlife through his depiction of the audience. Most of the audience enjoyed the performance. They greeted its conclusion with a great round of applause and appreciated the female impersonator's role in their Hollywood nightlife. West contended that everything about Hollywood led citizens to suffer the dual loss of their spirituality and critical minds. Thus, they could applaud an emasculated performer and be oblivious to their own emasculation and how this led to the crisis of the American male. Reviewers of the novel agreed with West's analysis of female impersonators and the unfortunate Hollywood nightlife. They argued that "perverts" added to Hollywood's strange people and denied the humor and entertainment value these performers brought to Hollywood nightlife.[83]

City authorities renewed their efforts against the bohemians in Hollywood nightlife. Los Angeles City Attorney Raymond Chesboro told the media he would draft a new ordinance that empowered the Police Commission to deny or revoke permits for shows it deemed threatening to the "public welfare." Although no mention of this action appeared in the city records, the Council did pass a law in an effort to control public homosexual activity. Following New York City's lead, the Los Angeles City Council adopted a stricter disorderly conduct ordinance in early 1940. The law declared that any man who frequented or loitered about any public place soliciting men for the purpose of committing a crime against nature or other lewdness would be arrested for disorderly conduct.[84]

That year, the Police Commission began fulfilling its mandate to monitor shows in nightclubs. The first Police Commission action toward female impersonator shows involved Julian Eltinge. Eltinge applied to the Commission to receive a permit to present his famous act at the Rendezvous Cafe in January 1940. During the hearing several vice squad officers testified that "many people of questionable character frequent the place." The president of the Commission, Henry G. Bodkin, announced that while Eltinge's entertainment was "clean and wholesome," the nightclub had a notorious reputation. The Commission denied the nightclub the permit to allow Eltinge to perform. Female impersonators and other Hollywood bohemians formerly linked with

Hollywood's humorously spectacular and decadent nightlife now found themselves associated with a morally deleterious nightlife.[85]

These limitations on female impersonators received mixed reactions from Hollywood. David Butler, a former silent film actor who became a director and producer in the 1930s, gave Eltinge a walk-on role as himself in the motion picture *If I Had My Way* (Universal, 1940). Eltinge appeared in drag during a brief floor show scene with two other former vaudevillians. Reviewers panned the picture, and Eltinge received no other movie roles.

The general industry response became evident during Eltinge's opening show at *The White Horse* on Cahuenga Boulevard later in 1940. Eltinge received a permit for the show only after agreeing to display his female costumes on a clothes rack rather than wear them. He stood beside each outfit as he performed the appropriate impersonation. The critic for *Script* magazine, a small publication popular with movie people, noted that only a dozen people attended on opening night, and Eltinge closed the act after a few dates.[86] The female impersonator craze that had richly contributed to the depictions of Hollywood nightlife reached its end.

Two

The Public Hollywood Party
Star Arrival and Emotions

The crowd awaiting entrances of the stars at the premiere for *The Gold Rush* watched a movie of Rudolph Valentino swimming in the Pacific, unaware that thieves were stealing his clothes. Valentino realizes he is late for the premiere and rushes away in the movie to appear seconds later at the premiere clad only in his bathing suit.[1]

Both the movie screen set up outside a movie premiere and the surprise arrival of a big movie star illustrated the pageantry associated with Hollywood's public parties. Whether the Academy Awards banquet or the parties before and after the premiere of a new motion picture, Hollywood marketing let the public into the scene. The words and images spurred the public to imagine that they had never experienced as many splendors as could be found at a Hollywood party.

Hollywood public party imagery distinguished the industry's formal events through the arrival of and revelations about movie stars. The stars turned the arrival into its own event within the larger event of the party or movie premiere. Some of the images showed celebrity emotions felt so deeply that they revealed the star's sexual interests. The Hollywood bohemian images made the arrival and responses of the movie stars more exciting. They associated the Hollywood public party with titillating and taboo behavior that made it stand apart from any other type of formal public or semi-public party that appeared in newspapers and magazines or on the stage and the screen.

The Hollywood bohemian image from *The Gold Rush* premiere focused on the arrival of the celebrity. Valentino's highly sensual and erotic presentation of his body as an object to be seen bent the rules for the male gender in this era. Men of the era in the United States observed female bodies. While men were thought of as "sex symbols," they did not put their bodies on display.[2] The inclusion of "unmanly" behavior, the exposure of the male body, enhanced the excitement surrounding the star's arrival. This turned the staged party at this movie premiere into a circus atmosphere that distinguished it from the panoply of other premieres. The image was so effective that it appeared in a book as an example of a Hollywood premiere party over a half century later.

Three types of parties appeared within the pages of Hollywood books and newspaper articles. Public events were highly formalized and structured functions intended for public consumption; these events provided specific times and locations for attendees to interact with the press. Semi-public occasions were composed of a public party and a private affair of invited people and press that occurred in public locations. These events were often leaked to the press so that the reading public could informally experience the event. Private parties consisted of personally invited people and excluded the formal media; these parties usually occurred inside individuals' homes. This chapter will examine the first two types of parties. The next chapter will analyze the latter.

The public party utilized a location where attendees enjoyed an extravagant atmosphere and dining experience. The participants were members of a community that attended the event in order to recognize the achievement of one of their peers. Public parties occurred in gorgeously decorated ballrooms or mansions. Individuals or small groups were feted during the course of the afternoon or evening for their work achievements, or for their attainment of group membership or social position. During the affair, the individuals appeared before their peers and received their honor. The honorees became members of the larger group, like Elks or Rotarians, or a circle of winners, such as in professional associations.

The mass media offered audiences peeks at these affairs for decades. Society parties appeared as a regular feature in the *New York Herald* during the 1830s. By the 1860s, newspapers including the *New York Times* devoted front-page coverage to the inaugural balls of the presidents. However, coverage of all parties expanded significantly in the last decades of the nineteenth century.[3] Newspapers, magazines, and novels carried depictions of the parties held by the elite Four Hundred, Cafe society and its theatrical friends, and various local groups, including the Elks, college and professional clubs. These ceremonies and galas monopolized the media coverage through the first decade of the twentieth century, helping to establish the standard for the coverage of the public party.

Public Parties: Structured Affairs

The galas of the wealthy and the politically notable were among the first public parties to garner media coverage. The images of these public parties revealed that they functioned like public ceremonies. These staged affairs, such as presidential inaugural balls, the opening of a new municipal or civic building, or opening night for a new opera, represented a ritual at which to publicly congratulate an elected official or a member of the city elite with food and drink. More importantly, they were rites of passage and represented the acknowledgement of an individual for the assumption of a new job or the attainment of work-related excellence.[4]

Tacit and written rules governed how the affair functioned. These rules structured all the guests' activities, dress, and interactions. Everyone wore highly formal attire and expensive jewelry. They arrived and departed at particular times. Guests sat at assigned tables and ate, or danced with their spouses. The prearranged seating restricted movement and limited interactions among the individuals and groups in attendance. The most prominent guests faced the greatest limitations, as their interactions with others often centered on exchanging greetings at specific times and within a particular location within the ballroom or hall. Similar to the early years of nightlife at the lobster palaces and cabarets, the rules of genteel culture added a heavy layer of decorum to the behavior of the elite participants at these public parties.

The elite within cities across the country in the late nineteenth and early twentieth centuries held annual balls. The descriptions of the Assembly Balls in Philadelphia and the Veiled Prophets Balls of St. Louis captured their formal nature. The newspaper items describing these affairs listed who among the city elite and government officials attended and wrote about the clothes they wore for the occasion. When the party merited coverage in the newspaper's society column, the image contained information detailing the type of food and drink available in the main hall along with description of the environment, such as bunting hanging from facades and the flowers on the large tables.

While the images might carry the official statements of civic leaders, these pronouncements rarely mentioned their emotions. Few of the general society figures provided quotes for attribution in the columns and consideration of how the party made them feel occurred even more rarely. Dance cards and chaperons remained pervasive through the 1910s, restricting activities within the public party and providing little risqué activity to include in the coverage of the party.[5] Thus, the images of these public parties contained the most mild and inoffensive descriptions and mundane official comment. They contained little information that might offer insight into these figures. This restricted most readers' experience of the party to the decorations and food and clothes, limiting their ability to identify with these partygoers and gain vicarious enjoyment from the public party.

Public Parties: Washington Style

Although many of these city parties were large and occurred annually, the country had an enormous regularly scheduled public party that seized the public's attention every four years. The importance of the president and the rarity of the inaugural balls provided this public party with an air of greater significance than the annual city political and society balls. And the less frequent occurrence of this Washington, D.C., party made it appear that much more special.

The inaugural ball for the President of the United States, the nation's largest public party, has a long and rich tradition. The coverage of this event in the media has varied significantly over one hundred years. Inaugural balls began after the second inauguration of James Madison in 1813. They served as the centerpiece of James and Dolley Madison's attitude toward socializing. During James Madison's second administration as president, he and his wife Dolley extended the official social season from six to ten weeks. The balls and dinners that they hosted sparkled with gaiety.[6]

One of the first descriptions of the Presidential Ball was highly negative. Newspapers lambasted the celebration of Andrew Jackson's first election because the party resulted in the ransacking of the White House. While most readers accepted the media's perspective on the event, some enjoyed the drunken rowdiness of the celebration. The public party presented a display of emotional exuberance that entertained and provided these readers with the opportunity to understand and identify to a greater degree with the attendees.

In light of the critical coverage, future images of inaugural balls featured the stateliness of the public party. Martin Van Buren and his four sons hosted the event with excellent food and wine. But the dignity of the affairs from President William Henry Harrison to James Buchanan often arose from both the dryness of the affair and a press more interested in covering the procession to the swearing-in than the party at night.

The atmosphere of tension in official Washington did not add to the images of the parties as glamorous affairs. The political partisanship and positions on the issues facing the nation drove a wedge between Northerners and Southerners within Washington's official society. The division was significant enough to cause snubs by people on both sides of the slavery question. This division reached its apex with Abraham Lincoln's inaugural ball in March 1861. The *Washington Evening Star* noted that a Northern crowd danced quadrilles to the music of the Marine Band inside a temporary structure of wooden frames covered with cloth. This "white muslin palace of Aladdin" sat behind City Hall.[7]

By the end of the nineteenth century, the newspaper articles about inaugural balls filled several columns on the first few pages. Most of the images focused on the details of the outfits and jewelry for each of the most significant female figures in attendance. Occasionally, the articles mentioned particular male clothing as well. Other features of these pieces described the decorations in the hall and the food and drink that filled the serving tables.[8]

In the early twentieth century, the coverage of the presidential balls declined. Newspapers devoted less space. The articles described the clothing of the attendees, and the decoration and food, much more succinctly. The articles that appeared in tabloid newspapers beginning in 1920 with Harding's ball followed the trend of the other newspapers. They provided small accounts that described the decorations and attendees. However, the tabloids tried to increase the connection between readers and the figures at the ball by including photographs of the dignitaries. The series of photographs depicting the ball often filled a single page.[9]

By the late 1920s, Washington politicians had developed personal relationships with Hollywood executives and stars. The Hollywood studio heads enjoyed the association with power and the politicians enjoyed basking in the greater limelight associated with the movie industry. Many of the tabloid photographs of the inaugural balls featured the motion picture stars and executives at the affair as often as the politicians.[10]

Similarly, a small group of these images included the official statements from a few of the attendees. This enabled readers to gain a little insight into how the person felt about the public party. Overall, the descriptions of the ball's setting and of the attendees presented to readers an air of dignity and being in control and provided very little of the excitement and emotional content of the public party.[11] The motion picture industry gave their public party the glamorous surroundings and clothing that were key to the inaugural ball. But, being smart businessmen, they added excitement and celebrity emotions to their affair.

Public Parties: Hollywood Style

Similar to the inaugural balls, the public Hollywood parties featured a highly ceremonial environment. Hollywood public party imagery included descriptions of lavish decorations, splendid food and drink, and the presence of important people clothed in fine gowns and jewelry. The Hollywood public party images differed from the inaugural balls because they contained more information about the attitudes of the celebrities in attendance, which the industry realized its audiences wanted to see.

The Academy of Motion Picture Arts and Sciences began as the brainchild of MGM studio chief Louis B. Mayer. Mayer wanted to lend the movie industry prestige and control its labor force through a professional organization. The Academy started as a non-profit corporation in May, 1927, with 36 members. This original membership included 13 production executives, two lawyers, and six from the ranks of the industry's best known actors, directors, and screenwriters. Three members worked in the technical arenas.

The Academy of Motion Picture Arts and Sciences sought to advance the arts and sciences of motion pictures through fostering cooperation among creative leaders for cultural, educational and technological progress, recognizing outstanding achievements, cooperating on technical research, improving methods and equipment, and providing a common forum and meeting ground for various branches and crafts.¹² The industry leaders wanted to give their motion pictures greater credibility as an art form, as opposed to "just" entertainment, and they saw the Academy as playing a significant role.

The Academy assisted the moguls in this regard less through educational and technological progress than through the manner in which they recognized outstanding achievements. The Academy established the Academy Awards ceremony to bestow the recognition on people within the movie industry. The ceremony, better known as the Oscars, became the premier Hollywood public party.

The industry believed that the giving out of glitzy competitive prizes would grab audiences' attention. Once this public party had the audiences' attention, the Academy Awards conveyed a sense of professional achievement upon the industry. The ceremony showed the many professions and workers involved in making a movie. The reception of the Oscar singled out an individual as the best in his or her category. Winning conveyed that the person achieved artistic excellence. The positive reception the winners received both at the party and afterward confirmed their artistic achievements.¹³

The first annual award dinner occurred in the Blossom Room of the Hollywood Roosevelt Hotel on May 16, 1929. The crowd topped 250 people and tickets cost $10. Over the next 15 years, the Academy Awards banquet affairs took place at the Ambassador or the Biltmore hotels. One of the first grand hotels in the city of Los Angeles, the Ambassador grew famous as the hotel that housed the well-known nightclub Coconut Grove.¹⁴ The ballroom seated over 400 people, with a large dance floor in the center. A huge panorama of a tropical island shone from the rear wall as tall cocoa palms with fake monkeys hanging from their branches surrounded the tables.

The Biltmore Hotel in downtown Los Angeles housed an enormous ballroom with long, elaborate brocade drapes. The guests added to the elegance with their specially made gowns and fine jewels. Many industry figures worried about the lavishness surrounding the Academy Awards. As Cary Grant acknowledged years later, "There is something embarrassing about all these wealthy people publicly congratulating each other...."¹⁵

The Oscar ceremony did as the industry expected—it appealed to the interests of people. The awards offered the excitement of winners and losers. They involved the audiences to a greater extent than a typical contest because the contestants were people in whom audiences were greatly involved and invested. The industry used its publicity departments to make media outlets aware of the Oscar ceremony, and the news reports and articles promoted the magic of the event and of winning the golden statue.

The studio publicity departments aided the effort of selling the public on the importance of the Academy Awards. Studio press releases proclaimed that various movie people were Academy award winners. Industry articles informed the public that the Academy awards were interesting because "it is always interesting to find out what Hollywood thinks of itself."

Eventually, advertisements would proclaim the number of Oscar nominations that particular movies and individual stars obtained and describe how excited everybody felt over the possibility of winning. After the awards ceremony, advertisements trumpeted the wins of the movie and stars, using phrases such as "the new movie queen" that likened the triumphant actress to a reigning monarch.[16]

Other media quickly began covering the party. In 1930, a Los Angeles radio station presented the Oscar party live for one hour. Producers perceived that their stars or their pictures would probably win awards and quickly had the stars and others giving radio interviews to take advantage of the publicity gained by a national radio hook-up. Throughout the 1930s, the Academy Awards party generated increasing media and audience attention. People wanted to know about the attire and activities of their favorite celebrities at this important Hollywood public party. Media mogul William Randolph Hearst wanted the Academy Awards to have prestige, so Hearst syndicated columnist Louella Parsons covered them extensively.

Other publications, both in the trade and general interest magazines, covered the event and featured the reactions of the stars. The awards received expanded coverage from the broadcast media during the decade. By 1940, the ceremony appeared as a short subject in theaters. In the late 1940s, the entire ceremony appeared on television for the first time. The publicity worked as fans in Hollywood flocked to the ceremony to try to witness the arrival of the stars and gain insight into their personalities. "Streets outside the Biltmore and the lobbies of the hotel were congested with thousands of people, trying to get a glimpse of their favorite actor or actress...."[17]

The Academy Awards eventually held more interest for the media and its audiences than the other public parties in the United States. By the early 1930s, the newspaper coverage illuminated that the Academy Awards attracted a larger and more prominent crowd than the inaugural balls. One article observed that at the recent Academy Awards, "The brilliant crowd outnumbered those who attended President Herbert Hoover's ball two years earlier."

The Hollywood public party outdistanced Hoover's affair in population of prominent people, including Vice President Charles Curtis, California Governor Rolph, the members of the American Newspaper Publishers Association, and every major actor and actress in Hollywood." Prestigious speakers came from within the industry, including the renowned director D. W. Griffith. Notable speakers also came from other arenas, including President Franklin Roosevelt, who addressed the 1941 banquet and recognized the industry's importance in cementing continental solidarity.

The public interest in the Academy Awards and the prominent people who attended the public party resulted in increasing media overage of the affair.

These images of the Award ceremony featured descriptions of the splendid environment. Newspaper readers learned about the decorations of the hotel's ballroom. Occasionally items mentioned the food and drink that the guests consumed.[18] However, these articles devoted less attention to the descriptions of the decorations and the feast than the depictions of the late nineteenth-century inaugural balls had.

The depictions of Hollywood's most important public party strove to accentuate the glamour and style of the public party. Academy attendees wore clothing more elegant and stylish than the attire at the inaugural balls. Will Rogers, the master of ceremonies for the 1934 Academy affair, quipped that the brilliant gathering was "...the last roundup of the ermine." In 1936, a tabloid reporter observed that the Academy's ceremony contained "...the beautiful and immaculately groomed who sported millions of dollars worth of jewels that flashed as they dined, and sipped, and danced till the wee hours."[19] The photographs in both the metropolitan dailies and the tabloids vividly illustrated the style and glamour of the Hollywood public party. The pictures of a variety of stars showed the particular styles adopted by each celebrity at the Academy Awards ceremony.

As one might expect, a staged public party like the Academy Awards would not serve as a location for the presentation of Hollywood's bohemians. However, the Oscar Hollywood public party added elements to the images of the public party that made it appear more exciting than inaugural balls and society parties in other cities. The images from the Academy Awards moved away from presenting information about the attendees' personalities that highlighted their dignity and control to placing the emotional expressions of Hollywood figures and visiting dignitaries on display. The increased emotional information in images from the Oscar ceremonies enabled readers to believe that they had secret information about these celebrities' feelings and thus knew them more intimately.

One of the earliest Academy Awards images presented testimony from a distinguished visitor that the Hollywood staged party was a spectacular experience. Vice President Charles Curtis's speech suggested that he established an emotional bond with Hollywood. "This is my first venture into your *new and strange* [italics added] world. I am pleased and interested with that which I see and hear...." This feeling sparked Curtis to make the bold statement linking awards won for great courage during wars and for world-changing activities with those bestowed at Hollywood's staged party. "[I note the] other great awards of distinction and honor, such as Napoleon's Legion of Honor, the Nobel Prize, and America's Distinguished Service Medal, and observe that the Academy Award is significant of much the same spirit that accompanies these famous badges."[20]

Other images informed readers that the Academy Awards moved many other people who attended the party. Readers learned that the stars in attendance applauded so loudly that they almost raised the raised the roof when the aging and ill Marie Dressler won a Best Actress Oscar in 1931. The stars cried, applauded voraciously, and laughed during the presentation of a special Oscar to director D. W. Griffith a few years later. As they read and later watched the Academy Awards ceremonies, audiences encountered imagery that revealed their favorite Hollywood figures lavishly expressing love and adoration.

Most often, the images from Hollywood's premier public party focused on the reactions of individuals. Stars entering the event offered gushing praise about attending the party and seeing everyone else there. The most powerful emotions occurred as the honorees received their awards. Actor Spencer Tracy provided effusive praise of Father Flanagan while accepting the Best Actor award for *Boys Town* (1938). Ginger Rogers fought the tears welling up in her eyes as she accepted the Best Actress award for her performance in *Kitty Foyle: The Natural History of a Woman* in 1940. Most remarkably for the era, audiences for this Hollywood public party heard and read of an African-American being honored. After winning the Best Supporting Actress award, Hattie McDaniel attempted to thank the important people in her life. Audiences heard and saw that the pleasure of the moment became so great for McDaniel that she cried.[21]

These representations of intense emotions distinguished the Hollywood public party from other public parties. Indeed, the Hollywood stars expressing their "private" emotions bound excitement to the public party. Even more, the expression of the stars' emotions provided "knowledge" about the celebrities. This gave audience members the sense that they knew the star better. The inclusion of emotional expression enabled the Hollywood public party to distinguish itself from images of other public parties.

The depictions of the Academy Awards admirably conveyed the splendor of the Hollywood public party. However, the Academy Awards presented little information about the attendees' romantic and sexual lives.[22] The Hollywood premiere parties, though, occasionally demonstrated that Hollywood's stars expressed intense emotions about romance. Including this intense romantic component made Hollywood semi-public parties distinct from the variety of semi-public parties that received media coverage during the 1920s and 1930s.

Semi-Public Parties: Staged Segues into the Private

Newspapers and magazines covered semi-public parties in daily and weekly gossip columns and occasionally in feature articles. These semi-public parties included a staged public affair followed by one large or several smaller parties. Like the public staged parties, semi-public affairs occurred in public locations. However, the staged component of the semi-public party rarely attained the degree of formality and regimentation that characterized the staged party.

The semi-public parties of city socialites, which included debutante balls, dances, and cotillions, tended to be smaller affairs. These parties contained a smaller number of public figures among the guests than the public parties like the inaugural balls. While debutante balls and cotillions shared an induction component with the public parties, this attribute did not have the same prominence for them.

The semi-public party's after-parties were conducted with greater regimentation than the private parties to be discussed in the following chapter. Additional distinctions between these two affairs center on the location of the party and the presence of certain figures. The semi-public party's after-party usually occurred at a public place, such as a restaurant, ballroom, or nightclub. This offered a degree of public scrutiny and exposure that was not present at a private party within a home. This after-party, since it followed after the staged component of the semi-public party, usually included executives and other figures from the working world and media figures among the guests. The presence of these people was likely to have lessened the amount of acting out and frivolity present at the semi-public party's after-affair compared to a private party, in which guests were specifically invited to enter one person's home.

Every section of society in cities around the country held semi-public parties. The parties of the older society, the group Mark Twain called the "Antiques," received a great deal of coverage. This group attracted newspapers and magazines because of their long-standing family names and the traditions behind the events that they held.

The new aristocracy, nouveaux riche, or the "Parvenus," according to Twain, held parties that attracted their share of media attentions. Their events carried a brash and opulent style that came from the mixture of great wealth and inexperience in the elite class. In Washington, D.C., and a few of the state capitals, a group of the powerful people in government forged an official society whose events received a degree of press coverage because they carried the allure of power and political position and the cache of attendees, such as foreign notables and dignitaries.

Semi-public parties constituted the majority of the representations of parties that appeared in newspaper society pages and magazine articles. Newspaper editors and writers filled the columns of their pages with simple descriptions of cotillions, coming-out parties and wedding notices. The majority of these gatekeepers and the readers of the society pages in the late nineteenth century tended to love the bland sameness of the section. At the beginning of the twentieth century, metropolitan dailies expanded the daily column and added several pages of society news on Sundays. The weekend sections devoted the additional space to the descriptions of the decorations and floral designs in the churches and ballrooms and the glittering clothing and jewelry on the prominent persons in attendance at each semi-public party.[23]

The newspaper coverage of society's semi-public parties sparked attacks. Many society members criticized this new style of reporting as an invasion of their lives. However, society reporters, such as Frank Carpenter and Emily Edson Briggs, saw their work as giving the readers information about parties held in public spaces, spaces that they felt belonged to the public. Some society members saw how they could benefit from coverage of their semi-public parties. Months before his run for president in 1824, John Quincy Adams and his wife, Louisa Catherine Adams, held a ball in honor of his political rival Andrew Jackson. Adams hoped that newspaper coverage of this celebration of the anniversary of Jackson's victory in the Battle of New Orleans would display Adams's patriotic and personal virtues and enhance his chances to win the presidency.

Several years later another presidential administration would try to use publicity to increase its popularity and standing. Mrs. Julia Dent Grant and the majordomo at the Grant White House, Valentino Melah, each gave interviews and information to society reporters to create a fashionable image. Others in the president's cabinet and even his family saw the value of coverage in the newspaper society columns. During the 1860s, Kate Chase, daughter of Treasury Secretary and later Chief Justice of the Supreme Court Salmon P. Chase, enjoyed the balls of Washington's official society. Married to Senator William Sprague of Rhode Island in late 1863, she enjoyed her public position as part of the most fashionable couple in the capital.

Society figures could benefit from media attention but could also be stung by the press. Mrs. Sprague experienced marital unhappiness. She began being seen regularly at official parties with the married senator from New York, Roscoe Conkling, and this led to her declining visibility on the social scene and in the society columns. As soon as her husband's last Senate term ended in 1875, reporters linked Kate Sprague's name with Conkling's in print. The exposure of the adulterers was rare, and although the press made the suggestion of impropriety indirectly, the tone of the articles was condemning. Several newspapers, such as the *Providence Press*, editorialized that the scandal should be laid to rest. The Spragues successfully deflected the accusation, but the exposure proved fatal for Mrs. Sprague in society and her continuing appearance in the press.[24]

The newspaper society coverage altered slightly after World War I. Metropolitan dailies divided Sunday pages into sections with headlines such as "Affairs of the Week" and "In the Realm of Society." The stories about the parties that ran in these sections occasionally included additional details about the persons who attended the parties, such as "...the bride was a direct descendent of an officer under the first Napoleon." These details provided audiences with additional information about some society figures. This enabled readers to believe that they knew more about the personalities of these people and gave them a greater sense of intimacy with these figures.

Tabloid society pages regularly featured photographs of the notable and beautiful. These articles offered descriptions of the decorations and attendees at weddings and college fraternity and sorority suppers. However, both sets of newspapers offered little detail regarding the activities of the individuals at these semi-public parties or provided little suggestion that anyone had adulterous or homosexual interests.[25]

Magazines in the late nineteenth century depicted society semi-public parties, but printed nearly as many articles that examined how newspapers covered society. Magazine articles on debutante balls mentioned the music at the affair and the lighting, such as the footlight arcs framing the debs' figures. These articles noted that the young people were well bred as were their parents. No attendee at these society semi-public parties was an inferior or eccentric person.[26]

The height of magazine coverage of society's semi-public parties occurred during the early twentieth century and declined quickly thereafter, numbering less than ten articles during each of the four years between 1915 and 1918 and 1925 through 1928.[27] The representations of debutante balls reflected that the events maintained strict decorum; thus the images of these parties showed nothing that deviated from society's conventions.[28] The semi-public political affairs, such as a dinner for diplomats, included descriptions of the choice blooms and plants and graceful palms that added stately grandeur both to the affair and audiences' perceptions of the events. The images briefly described the backgrounds of the attendees.

Very infrequently, readers learned about those excluded from the guest list. One article noted that selecting guests had many pitfalls and the party host needed to make sure that she/he maintained propriety. "The visitor glanced [at the list of guests' names] then exclaimed in shocked surprise. 'Oh, my dear, you surely aren't going to ask her! ... She has no right whatever to be asked to an embassy ... Why, before she was married — — ....'"[29] While it did not state what the woman did, the piece acknowledged that people who might have committed adultery or engaged in sexual activity before marriage were often excluded from attending semi-public parties.

A few depictions of semi-public parties revealed that on rare occasions society people in attendance acted highly indiscreetly. However, the people redeemed themselves before the end of the party. A magazine story about the ball at Delmonicos in 1863 centered on a widow named Mrs. DeLancey, who attended the affair on the arm of Mr. Delano, a married man. A dowager explained the man's situation to her and the woman promptly sought and found redemption while the married man returned to his wife and left New York society for Europe.

The image presented the principals as unaware of their adulterous activity and used negative terms to describe them until they learned their lesson and responded appropriately. After they renounced their bohemian natures, Mrs. DeLancey married a good man and Mr. Delano reunited with his wife, and this enabled both to find happiness.[30] This choice between renouncing bohemian activities and facing a horrible life became a staple in mass culture's depictions of people who crossed sexual boundaries for nearly a century after this magazine article's appearance.

By the end of the period of this study, a few images of semi-public parties made the affairs appear somewhat racy. Individuals with less than "proper" decorum generally attended not as invited guests but as the entertainment for the amusement of the partygoers. Performers such as striptease artist Gypsy Rose Lee entertained at parties like the Beaux Arts Ball during the mid–1930s.

By the early 1940s, descriptions of balls suggested that guests might have enjoyed greater latitude with player behavior. An article on the 1940 Architects Ball in Chicago noted that colored lights played briefly on bare limbs as people danced. A photograph from the Rhode Island Fisherman's Ball in the fall of 1941 revealed that a man donned a caveman costume that left him barechested.[31] These images did not necessarily suggest that adulterers and homosexuals did not attend these affairs, nor did they imply that this behavior occurred at these parties. Still, these presentations made these semi-public parties of the late 1930s and early 1940s appear more risqué and fun than parties from earlier in the century. Yet even these images could not match the raciness of Hollywood semi-public party images, particularly when Hollywood bohemians attended the affair.

The Semi-Public in Hollywood

The calendar of Hollywood semi-public parties featured two major staged events that occurred throughout the season. During the 1920s, the heads of the major Hollywood studios began the Mayfair Ball at the Mayfair Club as an event for Hollywood society. These Hollywood executives envisioned the Mayfair Club as the place where the "Hollywood Four Hundred" met. Attendees to the nine annual parties included Hollywood's elite producers, directors, actors and actresses. The balls occurred during several seasons of each year and became the event that many in Hollywood and in the reading public awaited anxiously.

Depictions of the Mayfair balls enhanced the perception that Hollywood parties contained the best of everything. Descriptions noted the parties occurred within the city's most magnificent colonnaded ballrooms. The elaborate decorations and motifs created glamorous environments. "Blue of smiling skies, flecked with daisy white, was even in the tablecloths last night when members of the Mayfair Club gathered.... The ballroom had been changed into a bower of flowers.

"The fabulous decorations given by the Mayfair Club at the best hotels in Hollywood were but part of the brilliant party...." Fan magazine articles and gossip column stories emphasized that stars wore spectacular clothes and expensive accessories to this semi-public party. Stars and industry executives donned white tie and tails and other formal finery and "...strove to better a 'high-class' society affair as they danced until the wee hours of the morning." The stars and studio elite often brought royal persons to the affair. During the height of the Great Depression, the Jean Hersholts brought Prince and Princess Sigvard Bernadotte to the Mayfair spring affair at the Beverly Wilshire Hotel.[32]

The decorations and the Hollywood and international royalty created elegance and brought sophistication to the semi-private party. The depictions also included star emotions. The winter party at the Victor Hugo Café received the vote of many as one of the most brilliant events in the movie colony history. "Hollywood in its gayest and giddiest mood 'went to town' socially, romantically, vocally and historinically [sic]."

Like the other Mayfair Club events, this party had its beautiful environment and the attendance of every important star, major executive and directors. In addition, the party showcased histrionics as the entrances of the stars were announced by the footman in silken breeches over loudspeakers to the guests in the two rooms and the autograph seekers congregated outside. Romantically, the Mayfair disclosed new twosomes, with rumors of mutual interest between Clark Gable and Carole Lombard. The columnist noted this almost gleefully, despite later in the column mentioning that Ria Gable (Clark's wife) was present at a different party.[33] This coverage of the adulterers carried on for the next four years and is examined later in this chapter.

The movie industry also created a second semi-public party that occurred on a regular basis. The world premieres of major movies created a more exciting and spectacular party environment than the Mayfair Ball. Premiere parties at Los Angeles's movie palaces along Hollywood Boulevard brought music, humor, and excitement into one location. Theaters with names from the most important world civilizations of the past, such as the Riviera and the Granada, offered the industry opulence and enormous scale for its world premieres.

Two of the most famous, Grauman's Egyptian Theatre and Grauman's Chinese Theatre, were grandiose parodies of ancient building styles. Holding events at these places fueled the perception that the Hollywood semi-public parties were exceptional and emblems of "high civilization." The studios situated searchlights, grandstands, orchestras, and walkways made of everything from wood to red carpet in front of these theaters to create a vibrant atmosphere for their unveilings. In front of the entrance, radio announcers greeted the stars and character actors with microphones to carry their words to eager audiences nationwide. Premieres frequently featured promotional gimmicks, such as fashion shows, that added excitement to their "best of everything" environment.

The premieres generated significant audience interest. Spectators lined up the day before to get views of the stars attending the premiere. Some shows, such as Cecil B. DeMille's *The King of Kings*, drew over 100,000 "people-spectators." Even Hollywood insiders otherwise unimpressed with the city, such as cinematographer Harold Sintzenich, immensely enjoyed a premiere that included a marvelous harmonica band in front of the Gaucho Theater, which, Sintzenich wrote, "is impressive in its riot of colouring [sic] and oriental atmosphere."[34]

Similar to other images of semi-public parties, articles featured descriptions of the environment, including the beams of forty arc-lights fencing in the sky and lean limousines purring at the head of the procession of stars. They focused on stars' arrivals, including what the stars wore and their dates, using cute phrases to indicate a romantic coupling. In Hollywood, information about the star's sexual life was expected, and performers who did not bring a person of the opposite sex to a premiere party had their sexual interests questioned.

Like the Academy Awards staged party images, the imagery of the premiere semi-public party featured stars' emotions. Descriptions noted that stars approached the announcer and uttered verbal bouquets, such as being thrilled to be there and finding the premiere quite astounding. These images offered readers a fantasy environment that they could "experience" and the anticipation of "seeing" the stars. When the stars arrived and provided a comment about the semi-public party, the images provided readers with the thrill of "receiving" supposed insight into these figures' feelings.[35] Semi-public party images with Hollywood bohemians made the stars' emotions more exciting because they titillated readers with very highly personal information about the stars.

Hollywood's Bohemians Arrive at the Theater

A few images of premieres added an exotic sexual behavior to the publicity depiction of the star arrival at the Hollywood semi-public party. The Hollywood bohemian made the usual star's arrival more exciting for two reasons. First, the information about the star's "sexuality" provided audience members with the belief that they had received more insight into the star's personality. Second, the image indicated that a person engaged in a sexuality that was culturally taboo, providing the thrill of encountering the forbidden to audience members and making that premiere semi-public party more of a standout event.

> Greetings ladies and gentlemen, is this a party? You should see them pouring in with boofy looks and their big blue eyes. Gorgeous girls! Brunettes who once were blondes. Blondes who were once brunettes. Hello. [He nods to a couple walking past.] And here comes a little platinum. Hello, Pansy. [He says as he steps away from the microphone to greet a female walking past. He rushed back to the microphone.] That was a girl, not a man.[36]

In MGM's *Hollywood Party* (1934), actor Robert Young, playing himself, offered these comments to the radio audience after the station's announcer grabbed him before he got inside a Hollywood party. The large industry party, thrown by Jimmy Durante as a ploy to get what he needed to make his next movie, created a stir among the stars and the media. Everybody in town came to his house for the celebration. The presence of a radio announcer at the entrance to Schnarzan's mansion made the party appear more like a premiere than a typical private party. As the announcer provided the radio audience with details about the stars arriving at the party, he grabbed Young. The actor took the microphone and described the scene.

The actor's comments captured the procession of Hollywood stars entering the party as if they had arrived at a movie premiere. The punch line of Young's comments suggested that the attendees of Hollywood semi-public party included homosexuals, or men who acted effeminately. The kicker in the joke, the word "pansy," was a slang term for a male homosexual. Young's denial that the person he spoke to was a man implied that homosexuals existed in the industry. In his attempt to be accurate, he informed the audience that the person who walked into the party was not a homosexual or highly effeminate man.

The joke carried an additional suggestion. The denial of the homosexuals' presence to the radio audience suggested that this fictitious radio audience already knew that homosexuals attended private parties in Hollywood. The need to deny the homosexual's presence to the fictional audience suggested that the real radio audience would also have this same knowledge. In addition, the use of the word pansy, and denial of its association with effeminate and homosexual males, provided titillation to the real movie audience for *Hollywood Party*.

The fictitious radio audience and the movie's real audience learned that attendees of this party and those of other important motion picture celebrities might "be" pansies.[37] They entered the Hollywood semi-public party like any other movie figure and pursued their Hollywood bohemian sexual interests. The scene linked the star arrival at the "premiere" with the taboo sub-cultural group, male homosexuals. The mention of Hollywood bohemians in this movie scene added sexual titillation and the excitement of being associated with a forbidden sexual behavior to the splendid environment of the Hollywood semi-public party imagery.[38]

The party scene exposed the movie audience to a star's emotions. Young bubbled with joy and enthusiasm as the movie people entered the party. After issuing his last greeting, the star rushed back to the microphone somewhat flustered. He snidely made his correction. The scene's mention of a Hollywood bohemian with its association with the taboo and its exposure of more emotions from movie star Robert Young made the Hollywood semi-public party appear distinct from any other semi-public party. Many critics found the comedy a little disappointing. The audiences appeared more charitable, as *Hollywood Party* achieved moderate success at the box office.[39]

The arrival of an actual Hollywood bohemian star to movie premieres generated emotional reactions from attendees. Before Paramount's publicity campaign for Dietrich discussed in the last chapter, the star wore her masculine attire and created a scene at a premiere. A gossip column noted that Marlene Dietrich caused no end of chatter by appearing in formal male evening attire at the premiere of *The Sign of the Cross*. Readers learned that Dietrich brought her defiance of feminine clothing standards with its hint of lesbianism to her studio's premiere.[40]

As she did with nightclubs, Dietrich's Hollywood bohemian behavior gave the star's arrival to the premiere party additional excitement while it offered hints regarding the star's emotions. The assurance that everyone in attendance at this Hollywood semi-public party did not stop talking about the star's appearance provided readers the sense that this was a fantastic event. The information titillated many readers while inducing them to become aware of Dietrich's Hollywood bohemian clothing and the bending of appropriate female behavior. Their interest in the star grew.

Another international star raised questions about her romantic life with her arrival at a movie premiere. British-born actress Lilian Harvey arrived in Hollywood in 1933 after becoming a star in Europe. Like Pola Negri, Greta Garbo, and Marlene Dietrich before her, Harvey carved a niche for herself in Europe, becoming known as the most popular star of her day in the screen operetta genre. Her biggest box office and critical successes came when Harvey was paired with actor Willy Fritsch. The two made German, French and English-language versions of several movies during the early 1930s. Hollywood studios quickly interpreted her as another successful European who might make it in the United States. She made several movies, but none made her a star. After returning to Europe, she left during World War II, became a nurse in Los Angeles, and eventually retired on the French Riviera.[41]

Fox Studios sought to create their version of Paramount's Dietrich and MGM's Garbo. To create this box office star from the new European actress, the studio needed to publicize her beauty and her nature as a femme fatale. They chose to introduce her to the Hollywood world by having her attend a premiere for one of their movies. A newspaper gossip column mentioned Harvey's arrival. "Lilian Harvey referred to the men, fashion designer Joseph Strassner and director Paul Martin, as 'the harmless ones.'"

The humorous component in Harvey's comment suggested two potential interpretations, both of which illustrated Harvey's image as a Hollywood bohemian. One option involved the actress knowing that Strassner and Martin's harmlessness emanated from each man's adoration of her. Both would abide her whims, including illustrating in public their shared status as Harvey's beaus. In this case, the star would be violating the era's standard of seriously dating only one person at a time. Since a physical relationship ensued between dating partners, the star's dating two men simultaneously made her appear quite the Hollywood bohemian.

A second interpretation of the image centered on the men's sexual interests. The humorous part of the story created the suggestion that Harvey understood these men posed no threat to her romantically. The actress knew that their harmlessness emanated from their lack of sexual interest in her. This lack of interest occurred possibly because the men had their sexual interest in men, not in women. This offered a possible reason for the two men arriving to the semi-public party together. The image, by forging either one of these possibilities, bound Harvey's arrival to violation of the culture's sexual boundaries. This behavior made the actress a Hollywood bohemian, making Harvey stand out, a significant asset for a person the studio hoped to turn into a star. Her Hollywood bohemian attitude brought her romantic emotions and a forbidden sexual behavior to the image of the Hollywood semi-public party. The star's entry created a scene and made a spectacle of the movie premiere.[42]

The expectations that premiere parties served as locations to engage in romance resulted in the exposure of a Hollywood bohemian through his lack of dates to the premieres of his movies. Born in Durango, Mexico, in 1899, as José Ramón Gil Samaniego, he came from a wealthy and prominent family. However, the Mexican Revolution during the early 1910s forced the family to move to Los Angeles. The man who would become Ramon Novarro worked odd jobs, including as a signing waiter and on the vaudeville stage during the mid–1910s. He started getting parts through Central Casting as an extra in a few movies before getting a series of bit parts.

Ramon's talents caught the interest of Marian Morgan, who offered him a job in her dance company. He then met Louis Samuel at a dance studio and hired him as his manager. He began getting more pronounced roles. Through the help of friend and screenwriter Mary O'Hara, he saw director Rex Ingram. The charismatic and eccentric Ingram had recently had a falling-out with Rudolph Valentino. Samaniego convinced him to cast him in a period romance named *The Prisoner of Zenda*. With a success on their hands, MGM sought out a new vehicle for their new star. When the New York business office saw Ramon's surname they demanded it be changed. The company changed his last name to Novarro and launched him in 1922 as a "Latin Lover" in the mode of the wildly popular Valentino. Two years later, he achieved enormous success in the original making of the movie *Ben-Hur*. Despite its enormous production problems and costs, the movie achieved great success and launched Novarro to great heights.

He seemed to make a box office hit every year during the 1920s and early 1930s. These movies included *The Pagan, The Student Prince in Old Heidelberg, The Flying Fleet* and *Mata Hari*. Novarro played the important male lead to most of the biggest stars and the most glamorous of all the Hollywood studios. He appeared with Greta Garbo, Joan Crawford, Myrna Loy, Helen Hayes, Norma Shearer and Jeannette MacDonald.[43]

As was the studio way, once a performer had a niche, the studio continued to cast the star in similar roles. Novarro continued playing romantic leads until 1934. However, the star did not date regularly and would not consider marriage. Consequently, images of Novarro's arrival at premiere parties did not include his romantic interests. An article about the premiere of his movie *Devil May Care* noted that Novarro was "host de luxe [sic]" to a distinguished group of guests. The article made it apparent that the star's mother and sister attended the party. The piece also noted that Novarro engaged in an animated conversation with Dolores Del Rio, for whom Novarro's lovely sisters are often mistaken. The item did not link the star to a date, raising questions about Novarro's love life. While implying that Novarro might have had a Hollywood bohemian status, the piece created a spectacle of his premiere. In addition, the piece offered a positive depiction of Novarro, his relationships with his friends and family, and the premiere party for his movie.

Earlier in his career Novarro also attended premieres without a date. He went to the premiere of *Ben-Hur* in New York City at the George M. Cohan Theater the day prior to New Year's Eve, 1925. At that event, Novarro appeared with the cast. Later, there was no mention of any appearance at the premiere's semi-public party.

The gossip columns described the studio's major effort for another Novarro premiere. The premiere featured one novelty: "There will be the selection of a special block of seats for the feminine feature players, dialogue, scenario and title writers of the M.-G.-M. organizations [sic]. Ramon Novarro, it was announced yesterday, will be present in person at the premiere." The huge number of women attending this premiere provided beauty, glamour and probably a strong "swooning" section for the movie. It also highlighted Ramon's movies as appealing to women primarily. The image placed Ramon at an event with a large number of women yet linked him romantically with none of them.[44]

The lack of a date at these events presumably did not spook regular readers of Hollywood gossip columns and fan magazines. They learned that Ramon traveled extensively yet never with a woman. In Rome, during the filming of the movie *Ben-Hur*, the star paid no attention to all the Italian women swooning over him. Fans reading *Photoplay* learned, "The Italian girls went wild over Ramon Novarro, but he came back as fancy free as ever. The romantic young actor never gave them a tumble, having other matters on hand. He was too busy trying to make a success of his role of Ben-Hur."

The comment provided in the gossip item might have had some validity. However, the caption below one photograph noted that the actor and the magazine article writer Herbert Howe "have been looking into a lot of those places on the continent we have read so much about." Underneath another photograph, the caption said, "We see them at Cafe de Paris of Monte Carlo." Perhaps Novarro was busy, but apparently not so busy that he could not see the sights and sit at the cafes with Herbert Howe. Obviously, the correspondent from *Photoplay* was chronicling Novarro's experience in Rome from close proximity.

Howe continued his description of Novarro's trip as seemingly a mutual excursion. The purchase described at the end of the paragraph sent a signal to the aware reader, as the statue of David carried meaning to the homosexual community of the era.

> Whenever Novarro had a day free he would set off to inspect some museum or historical spot of interest.... A connoisseur with a keen eye and lightning wit, [Novarro] is an unfailing source for the writer.... In Florence he was especially attentive to Michelangelo's David and bought countless reproductions of the sculpture, declaring he was going into training until he [matched] it physically.[45]

Other stories about Ramon Novarro's public appearances during his travels to other countries also provided interesting bits of gossip. He traveled to France with his brother Eduardo and to South America with his sister Carmen Samaniegos. Intriguingly, the article on the star in Rio de Janeiro began with the assertion that the story focused on romance. Readers learned that the romance was not about Ramon Novarro but about his sister, who was engaged to marry.[46]

Hollywood articles continued to try to label Novarro's personality: A mystery, too handsome, "arty," and "the highly romantic type," common code words of the era for effeminate and homosexual men. As an article on romance in Hollywood noted,

Ramon Novarro and his sister Carmon, 1935 (National Archives and Records Administration).

Novarro is still a bachelor, even though many have been stirred by him. But I recall being swiftly restored to neutrality, as it were, by the fact that Ramon used to look spiritual and muse about going into a monastery some day.... Ramon himself seems to have wandered from it somewhat ... but the girls would naturally remind themselves that this enchantful [sic] male is really a monk at heart. That, gentlemen, is Ramon's line.[47]

Near the end of his career as a top-flight movie star, readers received very specific information regarding Novarro's love life. During a personal appearance in New York for the premiere of his movie *The Cat and the Fiddle* (1934), Novarro appeared without a date. Reporters caught up with him amid a throng of female admirers and asked him about his upcoming concert tour and his personal life. During this interview, which appeared in newspapers around the country, Novarro offered audiences insight into his attitude regarding dating and marriage. Novarro declared that an actor who married was a fool. This deeply felt comment confirmed suspicions about why Novarro did not bring dates to his premieres.

Newspapers and fan magazines articles offered reasons for Novarro's romantic emotions, including making the suggestion that he lacked a sexual interest in women. As one piece in the *Philadelphia Ledger* stated, "Romance still stays far away from the handsome Ramon.... [His] name is never linked with that of a woman." Indeed, even to the opening of movies that Novarro directed, he did not bring a woman companion, despite looking "quite dashing in a mess jacket."[48]

Novarro left the movie industry in the mid–1930s. He performed concert tours. He wrote a play and went to London to star in a play. This was a disaster, and a theatrical event in Budapest resulted in Ramon becoming the sixteenth foreign star that this manager refused to pay after he performed. He returned to Hollywood, and his new studio felt so confident about the success of their movie that they sent Novarro to New York City for its premiere. The gossip piece noted that although pursued by feminine armies, he [Novarro] remained unmarried and romantic.[49]

The disinterest in the women fans and lack of traveling and appearance partners appeared to signal that Novarro acted upon a same-sex sexuality. His contemporaries knew this. Actress Myrna Loy derided the studio-manufactured romances of the era, noting that the stories of a love affair between Ramon Novarro and herself had no basis in fact. "Ramon wasn't even interested in the ladies...." Silent film actress Lina Baskette observed to a film historian years later, "He was always a kind and nice gentleman. Women were crazy about him, but of course Ramon preferred another personal lifestyle which in those days was kept very much in a secret closet." MGM publicist Hal Elias stated, "We had our Bill Hainses and Ramon Novarros.... Those are the people who were discussed. Not negatively exactly.... They weren't condemned for it, let me put it that way."

Current scholars have arrived at the same conclusion. In an examination of homosexuals in the industry, William J. Mann observed that Navarro was known to be gay throughout the industry. Not only did the MGM publicity agents know but some members of the media covering the star knew as well. Certainly Herbert Howe knew, and he may have engaged in a love affair with the star as well.

Biographer Allan Ellenberger did not support the claim of a carnal rela-

Ramon Novarro's House from 1929 to 1938 (courtesy Department of Cultural Affairs, City of Los Angeles; John Bolton, photographer).

tionship between Novarro and Howe. He observed that the pair developed a close friendship but found no tangible evidence of more. However, Ellenberger clearly understood Novarro to be homosexual. He described Novarro's several relationships with men and noted that his house in the wealthy district of West Adams in Los Angeles had seventeen rooms for his mother and other family members. His wing in the back had a secret passageway to a private side entrance and exit.

The actor's sexual interest did not play a large role in his career decline. He tried his hand at foreign-language movies and directing but became bored. He came back as an actor with Republic Films but asked for his release after two movies. He continued to perform concerts during the early 1940s and returned to the screen as a character actor later in the decade. However, his drinking grew more excessive over the years, which led to cirrhosis of the liver in the early 1960s. During the decade he began using a Hollywood escort service. In the six months prior to his death in October 1968, Novarro had written nearly 140 checks to male prostitutes. He hired two men he found to provide him with services. Brothers Tom and Paul Ferguson would be convicted of murdering Novarro.[50]

The images of Ramon Novarro at the public portion of the semi-public parties spurred a significant amount of interest in these premiere parties. As they showed the romantic star without a female companion, these images spurred questions about the star's sexual interests. These premiere parties became seen as places to discover information about the star's private life and "see" a star who belonged within a culturally taboo group of people.

Hollywood bohemians appeared at the private party portion of the Hollywood semi-public party. The images revealed that the Hollywood bohemians held emotions that were so intense, those emotions made them cross the boundaries of sexual propriety. The Hollywood bohemians' presentation of this taboo sexual behavior turned Hollywood's semi-public party into a scene more wild than the usual party.

Another actor and an actress who crossed society's marital boundaries appeared in a gossip item about an after-premiere party. Clark Gable appeared in the piece at this Hollywood semi-public party as the date of actress Carole Lombard despite being married. Born in 1901 in Cadiz, Ohio, William Clark Gable lost his mother before turning one. After quitting school at sixteen, Clark worked in a tire factory before deciding he wanted to become an actor while watching the play *The Bird of Paradise*.

After a few years of bouncing around odd jobs and working in various theater companies, Gable met Josephine Dillon. The acting coach, seventeen years his senior, became his first wife and manager when they moved to Hollywood. A few years as an extra and in bit parts led Gable to return to the stage. A triumph in a local show prompted MGM to sign him to a contract in 1930. The actor and Dillon had divorced and he married Texas belle Ria Langham, then in her late 40s.[51]

In 1931, Gable played a supporting role in *The Easiest Way* and made a favorable impression to the studio and fans. MGM began casting him in a variety of roles until a formula became clear: Gable would be an aggressive romantic hero. Studio publicity focused on convincing audiences that he was rugged off-screen as well. His on-screen characters, a series of charming, handsome rogues, made him incredibly popular. Even a female fan's court case that claimed Gable fathered her child hardly damaged his image. Gable was rough but a swell guy, and women liked that. The image solidified with his rough-shaven look as Jean Harlow's love interest in *Red Dust* in 1932.[52]

Gossip columns during the mid–1930s exploited this fan adoration as Gable attended Hollywood semi-public parties. At one such event, Gable's image is linked with overly emotional and histrionic behavior. At the preview of the movie *China Seas*, Gable emerged from the theater and police and publicity men formed a flying wedge to run him through a throng packed at the long entranceway. "...souvenir hunters ripped at Gable's clothes, pulled off buttons and fought for his handkerchief." This image indicated that even when the star behaved, he sparked the fans to become overwhelmed with emotion.

At others of these premieres and other semi-public parties, columnists indicated that actor Clark Gable attended with his wife Ria. Sometimes only Mr. Gable's name appeared among the attendees and actress Carole Lombard's name also appeared, next to his. By 1935, images of Gable at the parties noted that he and his wife were "estranged," or attended the same party but did not arrive at the same time.[53]

Over the next year, as Gable separated from his wife, gossip items noted that Gable and Lombard attended public affairs and places together. After the aforementioned Mayfair Party, gossip indicated that mystery surrounded their activities. Soon, the romance reached the "sizzling stage," drawing quips from Hollywood figures like producer Hal Roach, who noted during a party, "If they could only act as well in front of the camera." Other articles informed readers that the stars were "palsy-walsy" and having a barrel of fun together although they are not sure about marriage.[54]

The couple attended events together. They even traveled to other cities as a couple. One newspaper based out of Paris captured an image of the pair watching a boxing match. The French and others on the continent had a great interest in Hollywood stars. Here they learned that Gable enjoyed boxing, but the charming Lombard appeared to have little interest in the match. The photograph also enabled them to see that the two were a couple despite the marriage status.

MGM invited their star Gable to the movie premiere and post-show party for the movie *Marie Antoinette* (1938). The party occurred at one of the best-known nightclubs along the Sunset Strip. Lombard accompanied Gable despite the star's position as a married man. A huge photograph in *Life* magazine showed the pair smiling as they sat at a table. The caption noted, "Carole

Lombard and Clark Gable had the best time at the Trocadero. Always full of fun and careless of dignity, they are one of Hollywood's delightful couples. They cannot marry because Gable's wife has refused to divorce him."[55]

The photograph and caption depicted the stars in a remarkable manner. The image presented the two stars as adulterers who were respected, enjoyed, and liked in the movie world. Unlike the two New York Society people attending the ball at Delmonicos, this pair at the Hollywood semi-public party received acceptance in the community and the mainstream media. The stars continued their relationship, earned very good salaries and made big-budget movies.

A photograph taken inside a studio party by a major media entity would only have happened with studio cooperation. Usually studios encouraged publicity when they believed that the image benefited the stars and the industry and also could not hurt either star's fan base. As noted earlier, the studios strove to link publicity images to either a real or imagined personality trait of the star. They also hoped to make the image something that fans could identify with so that they would feel closer to the star and continue coming to their movies. Adultery, in this case, was an accepted behavior in Hollywood. Stars fall out of love and Gable had fallen out of love with his wife a few years before. He was in love with Carole Lombard. The studio in earlier images promoted Gable and Lombard as the perfect couple; with this image from the party they took Gable's character a step further. After all, the actor was no gentleman and his fans liked him that way.

Carole Lombard developed her popular screen persona based on several screwball comedies during the 1930s. After her short marriage to the actor William Powell, Lombard forged an off-screen personality as a single woman, quirky, feminine, and independent. The actress was so well known for her big parties that many Hollywood insiders missed them when she threw the galas less often. Her party across the entire Venice Pier Amusement Park late in 1937 was a big hit with industry people; it generated some racy publicity images, including photographs of Dietrich, Claudette Colbert and Lombard showing their legs.

Hollywood insiders noticed a difference. A fan magazine reporter summed up the attitude of some in Hollywood with an article entitled, "What ever happened to Carole Lombard?" This reporter and other Hollywood media and friends of the actress missed the Lombard parties and wildness. Like Hollywood insiders who enjoyed her personality, many of her fans enjoyed Lombard's antics and lifestyle and presumably thought her appropriate for the rogue Gable.[56]

Could the image of the pair committing adultery at the semi-public party be consistent with their established images? Apparently, yes.

Another image in a fan magazine sought to cement the bond between these Hollywood bohemians and their public. The article offered a reason for why the two stars pursued their extraordinary relationship. The reporter's answer centered on the pair experiencing deeply-felt emotion, claiming the romance was about something uncontrollable: love. The story informed readers that the stars experienced intense emotion for one another, offering the readers insight into the stars' feelings while enabling readers to imagine experiencing this emotion themselves. Indeed, the readers' imaginations were enhanced by another statement in the article that described the relationship as something the reader could experience: "It's just two people in love, faced by a problem that might be yours."[57]

The publicity about Gable and Lombard did not condemn the stars for their behavior. This attitude established for the readers of these materials that they also could adopt a non-condemnatory position. The article expanded the identification audience members felt with either or both of the stars by

Clark Gable and Carole Lombard at a boxing match, 1937 (National Archives and Records Administration).

declaring the similarity between the stars' dilemma and what the reader could have experienced. The article made it clear that the pair would marry one another as soon as possible.

Regardless, the Gable and Lombard publicity promoted by a studio and presented in a magazine aimed at a large, general audience linked the emotional expression of two popular stars to Hollywood bohemian behavior at the Hollywood semi-public party. The photograph and article combined to create the impression that the Hollywood semi-public parties were wild and whoopee-filled places that topped the best private party the audience member might experience either in person or through a media depiction. The flouting of adultery laws and moral conventions made the Hollywood semi-public party appear like the place of dreams where one could pursue one's desires outside the restrictions imposed by the culture.

Writers on Gable and the era observed that the actor regularly had affairs outside his marriages. One noted that his affair with actress Loretta Young resulted in the birth of a daughter. Another biographer revealed that Lombard and Gable saw his wife Ria sitting at a table with her lawyer and the attorney's wife when they left the Mayfair Ball in January 1936. Lombard asked Gable, "Doesn't that old bag belong to you?" He replied, "Yeah, and from the look in those eyes, I figure her asking price for a divorce just went up by about a hundred grand."[58]

One image of the Hollywood semi-public party took a rare condemnatory attitude toward the Hollywood figures who pursued an intense emotional affair. Disgruntled with his experience as a screenwriter, novelist John Dos Passos expressed his satirical perspective on the motion picture industry in *The Big Money* (1936). The author criticized the idolization and imitation of the industry's romantic stars while he also critiqued the carnival of greed and corruption in the pleasure worlds of New York, Detroit, Hollywood, and Miami.[59]

The Big Money, which received rave reviews and sold well, featured both portions of the Hollywood semi-public party. In this novel, up-and-coming actress Margo Dowling, despite being married, attended the premiere of her movie on the arm of her fiancé, director Sam Margolies. Under the beating glare of lights outside Grauman's Chinese Theater, Margo and co-star Rodney Cathcart met the media. Similar to other depictions of the premiere portion of the Hollywood semi-public party, the stars spoke glowingly about their new picture and association with Sam Margolies.

After dining at a restaurant, Margolies brought his stars home to dine at his apartment for the private party. The director walked out of the room, leaving Cathcart and Margo seated on the couch. Cathcart took off his coat and vest, then reached over and lifted Margo onto his knee. The actor kissed Dowling and his hands explored under her dress. After protesting, Dowling declared, "Oh, hell, I don't give a damn." Both drank more champagne; then Cathcart jumped on her. She fell on the couch with his arms crushing her.

This image expanded upon the association of the Hollywood semi-public party with stars expressing emotions effusively. The movie director, the actress's fiancé, set up the date at the premiere to promote Dowling's career. Outside the theater the performers gave the media glowing tributes about their product. Margolies brought the pair to his apartment for a private party, knowing that the private portion of the Hollywood semi-public party represented a place where stars who built up sexual tension while filming a motion picture together could release that passion. He disappeared at the party for a while so that the male star could release his brutish energy through sex with the actress.

In Hollywood semi-public parties all behavior could happen. A female star could engage in sex while technically married to one man and days away from marrying another. Despite the novelist's belief that the presence of this type of emotional behavior corrupted relationships in the motion picture industry, none of the Hollywood bohemians experienced problems in the movie industry because of their sexual activities. Cathcart did not lose his popularity within or outside of Hollywood. Dowling married her successful director and continued her career.

Some readers of the novel did not advance negative opinions regarding the bohemians at the semi-public party. Two reviewers did not deem Cathcart worthy of mention. Each expressed qualified support for Dowling without comment upon Dowling's sexual activity with her co-star. Her marriage to the director prompted one reviewer to express pleasure that Dowling at least escaped from her first husband. Another reviewer critiqued Dowling for her career-climbing ways but also noted her virtues and her core of softness.[60] In the eyes of the critic, Margo Dowling might have been adulterous, but the Hollywood bohemian was still a good and virtuous woman. The Hollywood bohemian could act without propriety about sexual behavior and retain the affection and support of audience members.

The public and semi-public parties depicted in this chapter generally occurred within hotel ballrooms and theaters. Hollywood's private parties happened within the bungalows and houses of Hollywood figures, particularly those of its executives and biggest stars. While Hollywood's audience members could wait outside the theater and listen by the radio for a glimpse or news of a star entering a premiere party, Hollywood private parties did not offer this degree of access.

However, Hollywood insiders and the media understood the value of presenting images of private parties to promote leisure time enjoyment and pleasure among audience members. The images of the public and semi-public parties in this chapter revealed that Hollywood insiders enjoyed many pleasures at these affairs, and sometimes the insiders suggested that those joys included sexual interests which diverged from what was culturally accepted. This pleasure, the opportunity to engage in all kinds of sexual behavior, helped forged the reputation of the Hollywood private party.

Three

The Private Hollywood Party
Secret Love at the Wild Party

Bonnie's friend Anita met a writer who will take them to a party. It was at a beach house where this director holds bathing and other parties. All kinds of pawing occurred after enormous amounts of great food and drink.... [When] Bonnie ran away as Tom Muro himself put a hand on her shoulder [publicity director] Strickland tells Bonnie to come across and she'll get into pictures.[1]

Publicity materials and other Hollywood imagery depicted the industry's private parties as locations where wild events occurred. Many independent observers of the Hollywood scene, such as author Nina Putnam in her novel *Laughter Limited*, suggested that more than the nightlife locales and Hollywood premieres, Hollywood private parties offered movie stars and their guests a location where they could express their most intense emotions. In the midst of these pleasurable and exciting environments, some movie people seized the opportunity to pursue their romantic interests regardless of the marital status or biological sex of the person they pawed.

This perception of the Hollywood private party as a highly sexual place was widely held. A journalist of the era noted, "[The Hollywood party was] the last word in American social relaxation, rich with the super costly meats and drinks, alive with the unrestrained wit, whoopee and love-making of the Republic's most romantic characters."[2] These private parties occurred in the Santa Monica bungalows, the famous places along Malibu Beach, and in Hollywood star homes.[3]

As Bonnie and readers of the novel learned, these locations offered the privacy necessary for Hollywood stars and other figures to act upon their appetites. Images of Hollywood's bohemains expanded upon the Hollywood private party reputation for the last word in lovemaking. The usual imagery of Hollywood private parties brought audiences to the bedroom door without a key to enter or a glass to hear. The Hollywood bohemians let the audiences inside and offered them the voyeuristic thrill of "watching" sexual activity. The sexual outlaws offered audiences the joy of discovering secret, forbidden love and the intimate details about favorite movie stars. The images also provided audiences the excitement of vicariously witnessing other people experience wish fulfillment.

The Hollywood bohemians images distinguished the Hollywood private party from the images of private parties in other cities. However, the positive attributes associated with this behavior in images from the early 1930s declined over the decade because of the increasing acceptance of the U.S. culture's emergent romantic standards. By the beginning of the 1940s the appearance of bohemians within the private parties in Hollywood fiction declined. Among Hollywood celebrities the pressure increased on them to follow the culture's attitudes toward sexual behavior. However, during the 1920s and 1930s, the presentation of sexual activities and interests made the Hollywood private party images significantly different and more enjoyable than images of parties from any place else in the U.S.

Glimpses of Private Parties Across the Nation

The greatest number of private party images around the country appeared in the society pages of newspapers. The images described the tea and card-game gatherings and dinners among the social elite of the local area. During the late nineteenth century, these items featured discussions of the people present and the decoration of the houses. Readers generally received a lot of details about the courses of food offered.

Famous columnists, such as Emily Edson Briggs and Frank Carpenter, used pen names for their society pieces. Their columns featured the names in attendance and the food served at formal dinners, such as a White House state dinning room affair. They also described these elements at the sedate but elegant annual birthday parties of society figures, such as those of Senator Justin Morrill of Vermont. Occasionally, the representations of society parties were particularly memorable. They appeared to be spectacular, such as Mrs. Stuyvesant Fish's 100-person dinner on solid gold dinner service, or were intentionally odd, like Mrs. Fish's dinner party for dogs.[4]

Society party stories in the early twentieth-century metropolitan dailies noted the pretty decorations of flowers and greens and catalogued the guests of honor and other attendees. Sometimes, the newspaper items also noted the musical performance or the playlet that entertained the invitees after they had partaken of the food. The representation of a society All Fools' Party described the decorations at the affair, and then noted that jokes and tricks awaited partiers. However, the image did not provide details about these jokes or tricks, let alone mention the reactions of the party attendees.

Sensationalist newspapers generally offered similar coverage to the metropolitan dailies. However, the occasional suggestions of homosexuality and effeminate males appeared. For example, one Sunday society column contained the following item. "There's a sad story going the rounds about a certain manly man with a lady-like nickname not the lady-like man with the manly name who has the same surname."

This piece represented the raciest description of a party in a society gossip column. Although the remainder of the story concentrated upon the "manly man," the piece acknowledged the existence of a person who showed some gender inversion amid the society private parties. The story provided hints for readers to guess at each man's identity, but did not provide the person's name or information about the partygoers' attitudes, activities, behaviors, or character.[5] The lack of this information significantly limited all but the most informed of readers' chances to guess the person's identity. The lack of specifics also limited the readers' ability to understand the situation or build a sense of identification with any of the figures at the party.

The coverage of society people in every type of newspaper after World War I increased. Despite the growth, depictions of private parties did not spur racier or more risqué imagery. Descriptions of home weddings, card parties, and other events continued the same focus on decorations and the names of the people who attended these parties. Descriptions included the same type of phrases as were used before World War I, such as "handsomely-appointed," "delightful party," and "gorgeous flowers." Even one of the most sensationalist newspapers, the Hearst tabloid and its "Thru Eyes Gadabout" column, generally contained announcements of weddings, births, and the sightings of societal figures while offering few details about the sexual behaviors of the private party attendees.

While newspapers carried the bulk of the private party images, magazines featured these images as well. The majority of magazine articles about private parties featured suggestions for readers to make their own parties more successful. One example from the first decade of the twentieth century offered advice about the best food and drinks to serve. Later in the piece, the reader received suggestions about possible decorations, such as placing Japanese lanterns on the verandah to create a successful garden party.

By the early 1920s, the magazine advice article changed slightly. While the type of décor and food at one's party remained important, the main focus of these advice articles switched to the preparation of successful invitations and party events. These events included masquerade parties, dancing, and a tennis tournament. Other party advice articles focused on different methods to make a private party a success. These articles suggested theme events, such as acting out a movie or acting as if guests were foreign dignitaries.[6]

According to their depictions in magazines, early twentieth-century private parties featured enormous amounts of food and bland dinner conversation.

Conversations excluded political and religious controversy, money, servants, gossip, and sex as permissible subjects to maintain decorum. Caustic wit was also frowned upon as impolite.

This changed somewhat after World War I. At one private party the attendees engaged in profanity as a style and "degeneracy" as a topic. The image revealed that many diners showed disgust with the topic, suggesting that people who engaged in "degenerate" behaviors did not attend these parties. If they were invited, they needed to repress their interests and behaviors at the party or face direct condemnation. The images that filled magazines after World War I, such as the annual affair hosted by Mrs. Beale of Decatur House in Washington, D.C., were white-tie affairs that put elegance and formality on display. These articles and photographs depicted the parties as restricted affairs that occurred within a person's sanctuary, a place where conversations excluded much of what occurred in the outside, public world.[7]

High society private parties also appeared in the literature of the era. Many novelists whose books included elite society characters also depicted private parties in their works. These writers contrasted the beautiful surroundings of the party against the constraints that society placed upon the actions and thoughts of party attendees. Statesman and novelist John Hay recalled parties in provincial cities during the 1880s as three sets of people clustered into three separate areas of the party.

While women drew a little entertainment from gossip as they sat in the living rooms, men recounted their everyday affairs to one another in dens, and the young clustered together in little knots. Novelist Henry James emphasized the perfection of the settings and service at an early turn-of-the-century dinner party in his works. Transgressions, such as adultery, occasionally occurred in the thoughts of his characters, but would be considered in poor taste to mention at the party. Certainly, no character acted upon such interests at these events.[8]

A few novelists presented figures who defied norms at private parties. However, this activity cost each character dearly. In Edith Wharton's *The House of Mirth*, parties served as places where women appeared on display in order to attract husbands with wealth and standing. Parties served as places where one must conform to the culture's standards for women in order to establish one's position in society. These expectations about the woman's role in society forced women to display clothes and jewelry at parties that cost them a great deal financially. This cost exacted an emotional toll, pushing many women into unhappy marriages.

Wharton's character Lily Barth made choices at these parties that brought about her demise. Barth's selectiveness about a marriage partner created difficulties. However, her unladylike display of her bodice while performing a tableaux at a party created the appearance that she had lost her sexual propriety. Her unmarried status and the perception of her impropriety led to Barth's increased difficulty in fulfilling her role as a society woman. Barth had to earn her keep, slid out of society, and died shortly thereafter. The mere appearance of sexual impropriety had the ultimate disastrous effect for this female character in popular literature during the early twentieth century.[9]

After World War I, private parties in novels featured cafe society and theatrical figures along with the older, elite society. Though these books described the theatrical world, most of the characters at the private parties in these novels did not transgress sexual boundaries. At most, these characters appeared without grace or value or as heavy drinkers who exhibited little compassion or concern.

One of the best known writers of the twentieth century included a few adulterous characters in his signature novel of the jazz age. In F. Scott Fitzgerald's *The Great Gatsby* (1925), most of the characters paid for their adultery. The host of the big private party, Jay Gatsby, stepped outside the culture's sexual boundaries by coveting a married woman. He did not fulfill his interest in her physically, and his emotional involvement resulted in Gatsby dying in order to protect her. Mabel, a woman who committed adultery, appeared as a vicious, horrible person. She eventually met a grisly death. Society figure Tom Buchanan did survive his adultery. However, Fitzgerald also depicted him as a reprehensible character, not a person whom readers would have liked or identified with in any way.

Another noted author of the period featured sexually adventurous people at a big private party. Thomas Wolfe's *The Party at Jack's* (1940) roundly condemned the theatrical and Wall Street figures who attended a party within an elegant New York City apartment on Fifth Avenue. Wolfe viewed his characters' actions and attitudes as the degradation of society that capitalist culture promoted. Several characters crossed sexual boundaries as a result of their decadence and boredom with all the elements of life. A sculptor who made crude and aggressive sexual advances to all the women and a scandalous socialite who could not speak a complete sentence appeared as shallow, tasteless, and talentless people. Both characters lacked any redeeming qualities.

Wolfe also included negative depictions of one male and one female homosexual character at the party. However, the editors of the magazine that serialized the story and the editor of *You Can't Take It with You* (the novel in which the story appeared) removed them. This removal of these homosexual characters signaled that readers interested in Wall Street and Broadway parties could or would not accept the characters' presence and/or that the editors themselves could not accept them. Thus, in one of the rare instances in which an author of a non–Hollywood novel included homosexual characters at a private party, the characters disappeared before publication.[10] The censoring of materials that featured Hollywood private parties did not appear to occur very often.

Hollywood Private Party Publicity

The studios knew that private parties played a major role in the promotion of Hollywood as a glamorous location. The parties occurred within the mansions and beach houses of the industry elite. They happened under canopies and tents on their sprawling estates. They took place inside an entire roller rink or amusement park.

William Randolph Hearst with Bette Davis, Louella Parsons and Mary Brian at his 74th birthday party (Herald Examiner Collection, Los Angeles Public Library).

Most images of Hollywood private parties promoted their amazing and exciting atmospheres. These images featured the presence of white-jacketed boys carrying trays around spacious rooms, or enormous orchestras whose great playing motivated everyone to fill the dance floor. Other images described estate grounds that contained a wooden dance floor and hanging lanterns that created paths around the yards. Still more featured once-in-a-lifetime locations, such as the circus, complete with a carousel, at William Randolph Hearst's 74th birthday party and the Carole Lombard party across the entire Venice Pier.[11]

Another approach to party images heightened the glamour quotient through presenting the unrestrained wit and sophistication of Hollywood. Images revealed that the guests at producer Arthur Hornblow Jr.'s soirees including the worldly and witty Charles Laughton and Elsa Lanchester, both of whom displayed sophistication and verbal dexterity. Edgar Allan Woolf, one of the wits of the screen colony, staged novel dinner parties where he performed his vaunted mimicry of notables.

Gossip columns fueled this perception with descriptions of parties that featured important artists and writers or showed them engaged in banter, such as the battle of wisecracks at Zoe Akins's party between the host and guest William Haines. Insiders saw the wit and whoopee present at Hollywood private parties. Screenwriter Anita Loos realized how far Hollywood advanced from its naive beginnings after a party at Tallulah Bankhead's because of the actress's enormous vitality, kindness, generosity, wit, and Bankhead's genuine naughtiness. "She adored perversity for its own sake and only required that ... it had to be mixed with fantasy and wit."[12]

While glamour and wit were important, the sexuality and interests of stars served as the centerpiece of the Hollywood private party's reputation. Descriptions of the Lombard party mentioned stars reveling in joy as their sports clothing revealed sensuous legs and shapely bodices. At actress Dagmar Godowsky's baby party, star Alla Nazimova appeared in a diaper pinned with a cluster of cherries. Director Tay Garnett held parties at his aptly named Hangover House. Character actor Frank Morgan christened one area of his house the Whoopee Room during a garden party. These place names suggested reckless abandon in the pursuit of the pleasures of superior drink, verbal jousting, and the flesh. Gossip items fueled the suggestion of an ever-present sexuality at Hollywood parties. One piece described the attendees at makeup department head Ernst Westmore's swimming party as scantily clad.

The Hollywood insiders, news media, and other industry observers had to carefully construct their images of stars' sexuality at private parties. These images were designed to sell Hollywood but not start a scandal that would hurt the industry. The famous movie comedian Fatty Arbuckle attended a large, exciting party in a San Francisco hotel during which former actress Virginia Rappe died under mysterious circumstances. His trials during the early 1920s made the Hollywood private party a site of sexual escapades and death.[13]

The coverage of the Arbuckle incident illustrated the important difference from the private party images discussed later in this chapter. Like the feature on Thelma Todd's death which opened this book, Rappe's death and Arbuckle's subsequent trials posed a great threat to the industry. They held a significantly greater potential for danger to the Hollywood motion picture industry than the usual Hollywood bohemian images. In the Arbuckle case, the studios and gossip columnists could not simply set the terms for how the player and scene would appear in the media. Unlike the Hollywood bohemian images, Hollywood insiders and semi-independent observers were not the sole generators of the images. Other groups advanced perspectives that the Arbuckle affair was indicative of social problems that required collective and legal action against the motion picture industry.

It appeared that Arbuckle might be a murderer, or at least a menace to other people. This possible threat motivated the Hollywood industry to work to remove the Arbuckle party images from media and public attention as soon as possible. The industry quickly worked to placate their opponents.[14] They did this by exiling Arbuckle and expanding their self-censorship mechanisms. The sexual outlaws in Hollywood private parties did not start sparks that led to significant threats to either the movie industry or to the conception of Hollywood. Instead, the images promoted the Hollywood private party as an exciting place where audience members might catch glimpses of movie stars making love in their real lives.

Bohemian Parties: Whoopee Without Restraint

As noted in the previous chapter, one of the few movies about Hollywood private parties, *Hollywood Party* (MGM, 1934), linked these gatherings with Hollywood bohemians through a joke and a song. Through a visual montage and the Richard Rodgers–Lorenz Hart song "Hollywood Party," the movie offered insight into the secret world of Hollywood private parties. Telephone switchboard operators handled the barrage of calls being made throughout the industry about the evening's event. The operators rose from their switchboards and assured the spectators in the movie theaters that they were getting the inside news on the happenings within this secret world when they exclaimed: "This is our dish."

The song and montage depicted the Hollywood private party as an exciting, glamorous, romantic, and sexy event. After telling viewers that nobody would sleep tonight, the second stanza of the song focused on the Hollywood partiers' activities. The movie audience learned about the type of behavior that went on at a Hollywood party. A man might bring one female date but did not have to leave with that date. Instead, if he were so inclined, a man attending a Hollywood party could leave with another man's date. He could even leave with another woman's date.

After a Busby Berkeley–like dance scene with the operators whirling on a dais, the montage showed people bathing, dressing elegantly, then dancing and romancing at a party. The song lyrics reinforced these impressions. The best people of Hollywood attended the party. Not only were the producers and directors there, but all the biggest-name stars attended the party as well, such as Garbo and Gable. Everyone wore the best clothing. The women were particularly glamorous. They donned beautiful dresses and wore the most expensive animal pelts as wraps, including mink and sable.

The movie audience learned that the elite of Hollywood attended Hollywood private parties because they were raucous events. The music blared. Everybody drank the best wines. Laughter rippled across the rooms from all the groups of people. The noises and great cheer were so great that they prompted the presence of the preeminent diabolical figure at the party. The Devil came and enjoyed it so much that he joined his voice to the chorus of celebration. Satan affirmed that he liked the party environment and invited others to join in the fun.[15]

This scene from the movie offered viewers "secret" insight into the world of the Hollywood private party. More intriguingly, the song's lyrics assured viewers that the partygoers engaged in activities that Satan supported, including "sins" of the flesh. At the party, a man could leave with a different woman than he brought to the affair and the date could leave with another man. The movie depicted the Hollywood private party as a place with the probability of sexual behavior outside of wedlock. The song and montage added the promise of "debauched" secret love and cultural taboos to audience members' perception of the Hollywood's private party. This made the party appear wilder than any other groups' parties because it was a place where people could pursue their desire to "swing."

Novelists were some of the first observers of the Hollywood scene who regularly described industry private parties. Syndicated reporters noted who attended the parties in the movie gossip columns within the country's newspapers. Gossip columns linked industry figures together in actual and purported romantic couplings on the basis of how they supposedly arrived at Hollywood private parties.

Scholars of Hollywood have argued that this reporting helped construct the understanding of the Hollywood private party as a place for heterosexual lovemaking. People read the gossip columns to discover the romantic behaviors between male and female movie personalities. Yet people also read these columns for different information as well. Gay activist Harry Hay observed that he and his friends met at a coffee shop to read the gossip columns to identify stars who attended the private parties but held same-sex sexual interests.[16]

One of the earliest images of a Hollywood bohemian couple came after a death at one of their private parties. William Randolph Hearst and his film company's top actress, Marion Davies, had appeared in photographs and articles in newspapers at the Hollywood premiere parties as producer and star. In this image from a private party on Hearst's yacht, the Oneida, they appeared to have a more personal relationship. At the party, film producer Thomas H. Ince died. The articles that described his sudden death observed that Marion Davies was one of the few guests.

By the time of the Ince incident in late 1924, the newspaper publisher and movie producer Hearst and his protégée Davies had been a couple for eight years. Born in April 1863 in San Francisco, the heir of a mining fortune attended Harvard but was expelled for a crude prank. William Randolph Hearst began his newspaper empire with the San Francisco Examiner and by the 1890s forged a national syndicate, with newspapers in New York, Chicago, Los Angeles and Boston. Most famous for their coverage of the Spanish-American War and scandals that drew the derisive term "yellow journalism," the newspapers and later his magazines had innovative aspects to them as well.[17]

While expanding his publishing empire, Hearst began seeing a 16-year-old girl named Millicent Veronica Willson. From a struggling working-class family on the Lower East Side of New York, Millicent and her older sister Anita met Hearst after he befriended their vaudevillian father. Hearst escorted both sisters around the city, even living with Millicent in a house with separate quarters for Anita. He married Millicent in 1903, and the coupled eventually had five sons between the years 1904 and 1915.

Ever ambitious, Hearst cleaned his personal life up in a move to make himself appear respectable for politics. Simultaneously, his newspapers began one of the many moral campaigns to clean up popular entertainment that they would run over the next half-century. Hearst established himself as a leader in the Democratic Party, then ran for the U.S. House of Representatives and won twice. The most distinguishing feature of his service during the terms in Washington was his high rate of absence. He returned to New York City and failed in his attempts to become mayor in 1905 by a reported 3,000 votes. Hearst then lost his 1906 run for governor of New York State and for mayor in 1909.

Despite these losses, Hearst retained political ambitions. He convinced the Tammany machine to back his candidacy for governor in 1922. He and Tammany needed Governor Al Smith to run for the U.S. Senate on the ticket. Smith refused because three years earlier Hearst's papers ran cartoons accusing Smith of withholding good milk from babies on the Lower East Side. Hearst withdrew his candidacy and Smith won the election.[18]

Perhaps the magnates' business and personal activities made a political life difficult. After experimenting with the film medium, Hearst established a news reel company in the early 1910s and began making serials and feature movies. He had also met and developed an attraction to Marion Davies. By 1918, the Hearst newspaper Broadway gossip columnist noted that "Hearst entertained the Davies girl in Palm Beach...."

The youngest of five children of a mildly successful lawyer and a hardened matriarch, Marion Cecilia Douras had not turned ten when the family split. Marion left their father in Brooklyn and joined her mother and sisters in a place on the Lower East Side of Manhattan. While her mother washed clothes, her older sisters made careers in vaudeville and looked to use the stage to find a successful man to marry. Marion's mother schooled her daughters in the ways to please a man and in the perils of romantic love. Young Marion had little interest in schooling and soon obtained her mother's permission to perform on stage. Marion went from a "pony girl" on the dance lines in small-time revues to a chorine with musicals. She made her Broadway debut in *Chin Chin* in 1914.

Marion's sisters led the way on and off the stage. Reine, perhaps the most talented of the singing and dancing Douras daughters, made a stunning impression physically as well. She married the leading vaudeville producer of the time, George Lederer. Ethel and Rose also performed well on stage but did not have the same fortune in their personal lives. Rose annulled her first marriage and found little solace afterwards. Ethel became involved with a wealthy Chicago manufacturer who died of a heart attack after failing to convince his wife to grant him a divorce.

Marion's biographer quipped that Hearst had a stronger heart than Ethel's suitor. He had other decided advantages as well. Hearst usually spent his evenings alone except at political functions and charity events, when Millicent accompanied him. Davies offered competing versions of how she met Hearst, and Hearst never disclosed the information. Davies attracted male attention with her sexy and friendly qualities. Hearst reportedly followed Marion's burgeoning career, and during the 1915 run of the revue *Stop! Look! Listen!* the pair began their affair, when Marion was fifteen years old and Hearst fifty-one.[19]

Mrs. Douras did not appreciate "her baby" seeing Hearst. The publisher was a married man and the newspapers regularly covered his family. Marion's mother took her to Florida over Easter in 1916 with the hope of separating her child from the publisher. When she returned to New York, Marion earned a part in the chorus and sketch in *The Ziegfeld Follies of 1916*. Hearst sat in the front row often and within a year had won Marion's love.

The pair began a business partnership as well. Hearst now starred Marion in his movies, with the first, *Runaway, Romany*, being directed by her brother-in-law George Lederer and released for Christmas 1917. In the spring of 1918, they released their first movie made for the company that the pair made famous, Cosmopolitan Pictures. In 1920, the studio moved to California and Hearst built his mansion, San Simeon. Davies would soon own a bungalow along Santa Monica Beach, closer to the movie industry and Hollywood.[20]

A few years after the Ince death, another private party aboard the yacht provided the opportunity to present Hearst and Davies. While the marital problems of another passenger, Charlie Chaplin, served as the focus of the article, the image mentioned that he was a guest of Hearst. "The party, which in addition to the film comedian and Mr. Hearst includes Marion Davies, motion picture actress...." The image placed the Hollywood private party in a new milieu, a rich person's yacht. The presence of the unmarried couple added titillation to this private scene.

Near the end of the 1920s the private parties which the pair attended also occurred on land and in the midst of Hollywood. In the late summer of 1929, the couple began appearances at a string of weddings. First, they went to the wedding of Mary Eaton and Millard Webb, continuing on to the reception at the Beverly-Wilshire Hotel. The private wedding party contained all the beautiful environs that movie money could buy and the glamour from the celebrity attendees. The non-married Hearst-Davies presence made the party a little risqué.

In two other Hollywood private party weddings Hearst and Davies were amusing the few intimate friends who witnessed the ceremony. At the first party, actress Constance Bennett attended the event with the Marquis Henri de la Falaise. The description of the wedding included one paragraph noting who appeared in the wedding party and concluded with the short guest list: "...Gene Markey, Mr. and Mrs. Fitzmaurice, Marion Davies and W.R. Hearst also were present." When Joan Bennett, film actress, and screenwriter Gene Markey married several months later both the article and the headlines included W.R. Hearst and Marion Davies. In both of these occasions, the party seemed more exciting because so few people had the opportunity to see the affairs. The readers were among these few intimates to be included in the experience of these parties and they "attended" along with an adulterous couple.[21]

Hearst and Davies appeared at other types of Hollywood private parties as well. They appeared several times in the "Society of Cinemaland" column that ran in the *Los Angeles Times*. The fifty invitees to actress and studio owner Mary Pickford's party for Lady Louise Mountbatten, a cousin by marriage to the Prince of Wales, followed a description of the gathering. The married couples appeared in the list as Mr. and Mrs., single women as Miss, single males by name only, and near the end of the list appeared Marion Davies and William Randolph Hearst. No Miss appeared before Marion's name and they were the only non-married male and female couple listed together.

On other occasions, the pair hosted visiting dignitaries as well. Marion Davies performed the functions of hostess when the MGM studio restaurant hosted playwright George Bernard Shaw. William Randolph Hearst sat at the table along with the film celebrities—Charles Chaplin, studio head Louis B. Mayer, and actors Clark Gable and John Barrymore. Davies and Hearst managed an electrical pageant that Governor Roosevelt attended at the Olympic Stadium before the presidential election, in September 1932. The pair were two of Hollywood's chief champions of the Democratic candidate.[22]

Thus, in Hollywood even royal and dignitary parties were more fun. Readers of these gossip items experienced the royal affairs and saw that an adulterous couple attended like a husband and a wife. The "mistress" even served as the hostess of one of the parties and became a favorite of the noted playwright and the President of the United States.

Their parties were so well known that letters to the editor mentioned them. One person noted that he won a bet that President Roosevelt would comes to Los Angeles and "he will dine, lunch, or have tea or what have you with Marion Davies via the William Randolph route." Another two mentioned the parties within their larger comments about Hearst and his public opinions. The first writer complained about Mr. Hearst's support of the "Bonus Army" that marched on Washington in 1932. The approximately 31,000 veterans of World War I were suffering under financial hardship due to the Great Depression. They came to the capital seeking immediate cash payment of Service Certificates granted eight years earlier. These Service Certificate offered the soldier the soldier's promised payment plus interest. The writer claimed that if Hearst was so concerned about the men "...why doesn't he turn his immense ranch over to them instead of entertaining his friends there in sybatrical luxury? Or let Marion Davies get along with a mansion or two less?"

The third letter writer commented on the parties as part of another of Hearst's activities during the early 1930s. Hearst's newspapers and newsreels began another campaign to "clean up" the movies. The Hearst newspaper's timing fit nicely with the efforts of religious leaders in the U.S. to boycott the industry until it "cleaned up" its product. With tongue in cheek, letter writer "Simon Pure" observed that if Hearst wanted to clean up the movies he needed to make a movie "portraying the true story of his upright life as an example to the movies. It would make a wonderful theme in which to star Marion Davies." The publicity and the lifestyle of the glamorous parties in the privacy of the mansions and estates made one open to charges of hypocrisy depending upon one's public opinions. They did grasp public attention and a hold on their imaginations.[23]

Contemporaries in Hollywood certainly knew of the pair and their adulterous relationship. Few appeared bothered by the relationship. The community's elite held the 1931 Mayfair Ball in Marion Davies's honor. Hearst and Davies were well known for their private parties in Hollywood circles and many people attended. San Simeon, Hearst's castle and estate, once was intended for his wife and children to enjoy with him. It became the Hollywood party place, even drawing the likes of sitting New York City Mayor James J. Walker when he visited California.

Those among the upper echelons in Hollywood were not the only ones who knew about the pair's relationship. Davies made San Simeon available to other groups within Hollywood for fun affairs. Actor Douglass Dumbrille, known for his character in the *Blondie* movies, stated that Marion invited the cast and crew on her various productions to spend a weekend at San Simeon. He noted that "the cast and crew had great respect for her."

Fellow producers and actors maintained close friendships with them.

Screenwriter Anita Loos traveled with Hearst and Davies on their grand tour of Europe. Despite their shared personal self-absorption and theatrics MGM Studio boss Louis B. Mayer considered himself Hearst's "son." He visited Hearst several times before the newspaper titan died. Actor Rudolph Valentino maintained a beloved sister relationship with Marion. He understood her disappointment at being unmarried and in the "bird in a gilded cage" situation. Actors Clark Gable and Tyronne Power, and others visited before and after Hearst's death in the summer of 1951.[24]

Friends also knew where to find them when necessary. Actress Alma Rubens, a former star in Hearst's studio and co-worker and friend of Marion's, needed help following her arrest for possession of forty tubes of morphine. Born one month after Davies, Alma Smith began as a chorus girl on the stage. She played several minor movie roles before starring as Douglas Fairbanks's romantic interest in *The Half Breed*. The stunningly beautiful brunette made a series of successful movies through the early 1920s. Thrice married, she developed a narcotic habit that she could not lose.

The San Diego Police arrested her after finding morphine sewn into her dress. After the booking and spending time in a cell, Alma made calls to a Hollywood movie executive that went unanswered. The news article stated, "She then telephoned Miss Marion Davies at the ranch of W. R. Hearst. According to Sergeant Alvin Lyle, Miss Rubens declared that Miss Davies assured her she would 'take care of the attorney's expenses.'" Rubens died less than three weeks later.[25]

William Randolph Hearst wearing hat; Anita Loos and Marion Davies in a beer hall in Germany, 1931 (National Archives and Records Administration).

One significant group of Los Angeles citizens maintained a highly negative perspective on the pair, particularly because of Hearst's political perspectives and activities. Area leftists created two issues of a mock Hearst newspaper that they called the Anti-Hearst Examiner. The coverage usually concerned Hearst's political activities, such as a visit to talk with Adolph Hitler. However, the newspaper included a cartoon with images of Louella Parsons and Marion Davies nestled in the lap of an image of Hearst as an ogre. Also during the mid–1930s, some theater productions included characters roughly based on Hearst. One that starred actor, director and overall auteur Orson Welles lampooned the media titan and presented him as holding pro-fascist views.[26]

One perspective of the couple and their relationship remains available to viewers in the present day. The same Orson Welles from the stage production now directed, starred, and produced *Citizen Kane*. The masterpiece presented Welles's cinematic vision of Hearst and, of course, Marion Davies, in 1940. The titanic struggle of RKO to release the movie in 1941 included intimidation, extortion, and Federal Bureau of Investigation casework. This story is detailed in Thomas Lennon and Michael Epstein's 1996 documentary *The Battle Over Citizen Kane*. The movie has a tremendous reputation for its technical and storytelling innovations as it depicted a spiritually failed man. The lead character, Charles Foster Kane, shared many similarities with William Randolph Hearst, including being a media tycoon, holding very specific political ambitions, owning a palatial home and having an affair, though not an extramarital one, because of the Hays Code's restrictions against presenting extramarital affairs in movies.

Welles's version of the Hearst-Davies life had several differences from their real life. While Marion Davies succeeded in the motion picture business, Susan Alexander, the character in the movie similar to her, experienced humiliation while attempting to be an opera singer. Alexander attempted suicide and eventually split apart from Kane. Davies and Hearst did not experience either of these circumstances. Hearst also maintained two families in real life, maintaining his wife Millicent and children in New York while living with Marion Davies in California. As significantly, both Charles Foster Kane and Susan Alexander fall in love not with the real person but with an illusion. The movie indicted her as the reason Kane loses his political and social stature.[27]

Scholars have recognized that Hearst and Davies had a love relationship. Some observe that Hearst lived according to a version of Victorian morality, with the ability to lead two distinct lives. They note his ability to live on one coast as a devoted family man and on the second as a bon vivant. These writers observed his great love for Marion. Similarly, they maintain that Marion Davies had great ambition but deeply loved Hearst. Some argue that Marion compromised with the "backstairs" life, while others emphasize her unhappiness with the arrangement and her being "chained" to his reputation.

After Hearst's death in 1951, he left Marion 300,000 preferred shares of stock in Hearst Corporation. Apparently, he thought her years of support in the decisions of the business enabled her to continue making valuable decisions despite her problem with alcohol. His sons and corporation decision makers did not. They arranged a deal with Davies for her to receive the monetary benefit from the shares without holding voting rights. They also granted Davies the ability to advertise her charities in the Hearst publications.

The public that had followed this couple in Hollywood for twenty-five years did not learn about the agreement. The court settlement of William Randolph Hearst's will became public knowledge and the articles contained the praise he lavished on Marion for her support. In addition, they contained his statement that Marion received his present home in total. However, the final portion of this paragraph contained the statement "revoked this bequest without explanation." The post–World War II Hollywood played under different rules. Only the eldest son, George, maintained contact with Marion over the remaining decade of her life. She died after a lengthy illness in Hollywood in September 1961.[28]

The largest private parties in the palatial locations such as San Simeon and Davies's beach house drew the film colony elite. They were not the only parties where Hollywood bohemians swung. Author Jim Tully, who worked as a publicist for Charlie Chaplin in the early 1920s, presented two smaller parties where guests played with great abandon in his novel *Jarnegan* (1926).

Publishers Albert and Charles Boni had the reputation for publishing controversial and influential writers. As major figures in the establishment of the mass-market paperback book, their company promoted *Jarnegan* as the first honestly written novel about Hollywood. Tully's book sold well in its first printing but did not warrant a second. Over the remaining two decades of his life, Tully continued to write about the movie industry. His articles on Hollywood appeared in periodicals ranging from *Vanity Fair* to *The New Movie Magazine*.[29]

Tully presented Hollywood private parties as places where all kinds of sexual activity occurred without negative repercussions. The small party began when Jarnegan invited his friend and assistant director Jimmy, Jimmy's girlfriend, an actress named Velma, and Velma's friend Miss Dale to his home for a dinner party. As soon as they passed out the drinks, Jarnegan and Miss Dale realized that they liked each other. The movie director broke up the party before the group had eaten so he could go for a ride with Miss Dale and engage in a little sexual activity.[30]

The image indicated that the Hollywood private party served as a method for people to meet others for sex and romance. The party offered a space where Hollywood bohemians, such as Jarnegan and Miss Dale, could engage in a secret tryst. Since the culture believed that only married couples should have sex, the Hollywood private party facilitated crossing into sexual impropriety. The image gave the impression that the Hollywood insiders, like Jimmy and Velma, knew the Hollywood private party was the place to bring a friend to meet a friend and engage in fun and games. The novelist, an insider himself, passed along this perception of the Hollywood private party as the place to meet someone interested in sex, regardless of cultural prohibitions.

Later in the novel, Jarnegan, Jimmy, and two female friends drove into the exclusive residential area high in the Hollywood Hills. Angry over a fellow director's misbehavior with a female extra he cared about, Jarnegan crashed this large Hollywood private party to find the man. He walked into the petting party of a movie producer. He and his friends looked around and saw "...women at the party were semi-nude — not in happy abandon, but in middle-class vulgarity. The producer Leedman thought himself Napoleon reincarnated and Bernard looked grotesque in his Roman costume."[31]

Jarnegan's readers recognized the petting party from similar occasions in their lives. Many high school boys and girls had been to these parties, where they engaged in kissing and light petting. Peers generated the social pressure that placed limits on how "far" the sexual activities would go, even with the person they intended to marry.[32] Leedman's Hollywood private party carried the petting party further than the realities readers experienced. As a movie producer, he lived in a mansion with very expensive decorations and more style than the vast majority of homes in the country. As a Hollywood party, Leedman's affair outdid any party in the amount of food and drink, and in the number of gorgeous partiers. Leedman's arrogance, Bernard's costume, and the partially nude women each formed an element unique to the Hollywood private party and created a distinct image of the wild Hollywood party scene.

The director's Hollywood private party offered attendees splendid costly food and drinks and the most beautiful people in the movie colony. Despite Jarnegan's jaundiced view of the affair, Hollywood people could use the Hollywood private party as a place to engage in a variety of sexual activities with any other attendees regardless of any person's marital status or sexual interests. This party image confirmed to the novel's readers that everything was better at the Hollywood private party.

The novel did not punish any of the bohemians at the Hollywood private parties. All the bohemians at the private parties in *Jarnegan* had a place within the movie colony. Most had the wealth and status of a lucrative career as a producer, director, or performer. The bohemians maintained friendships and other associations with people in the business. They freely engaged in the expression of their sexually taboo activities and interests without facing ramifications.

Critics enjoyed *Jarnegan*, describing it as a vivid picture of life out of the commonplace and written directly from material observed at first hand. As a story about a rough customer, they perceived the novel as part of the expansion of the scope and intensity that changed the formerly polite American novel. Reviewers viewed the Hollywood private parties as part of the depiction of a feverish populace's pursuit of wine, women, and song. However, the populace did not care very much if they missed the singing. While not addressing the question of the truth to the party presentations, the reviewers noted that Tully's experience meant that he should know of what he wrote. However, one reviewer believed that a small audience would encounter the party images, stating that the story remained a novel for the literary rather than the general reader.[33]

Hollywood producers like Hearst and directors like Jarnegan were not the only males engaged in complex marriages and affairs of the heart. As noted in the examination of Katharine Hepburn's imagery in the nightlife chapter, she and Spencer Tracy enjoyed a twenty-year coupling while Tracy remained married to his wife. Tracy played in summer stock during the mid to late 1920s, and in Cincinnati he met a woman in the company that he found to be a "knockout." He explained that she was a darn good actress but had other ideas on his mind. They got married soon after, Tracy at 28 and his wife a little younger. His critically acclaimed performance in *The Last Mile* as the character of Killer Means drew him the attention that resulted in a Hollywood contract. The family moved to Hollywood in 1931.

While the actor made a series of mediocre movies for Fox over three years, the publicity agents kept busy. During 1932, the actor's public image appeared somewhat traditional. His fans read that he rushed back from location shooting to be with Mrs. Tracy as she had their daughter. The couple happily attended Hollywood parties, including the English lawn party hosted by Joan Bennett and husband Gene Markey.[34]

In 1933, Tracy made the movie *Man's Castle* with actress Loretta Young. Loretta had acted in movies since she was three; Loretta's parents divorced and her mother moved them from Salt Lake City to Los Angeles during the mid–1910s. After education in parochial schools, she helped her mother run the family boarding house but remained interested in having a career in the movies. Her sisters, Sally Blane and Polly Ann Young, had already broken in, and Loretta trailed closely behind. At seventeen she starred with Grant Withers in the romantic comedy *The Second Floor Mystery*, hit it off with him and chose to get married. He had many of the qualities of her father, including a charming but unpredictable personality. Her mother sought to have the marriage annulled; at any rate, the marriage did not withstand their next movie together, *Too Young to Marry* in 1931.[35]

Tracy and Young began to spend time with one another at Hollywood parties and other events. In the summer of 1933, the pair lunched with longtime director Frank Borzage, his wife, and a few others in the Columbia studio commissary. In the fall they went out with a few other couples to the Loyola Speedway motorcycle races and dined at the Biltmore Supper Room, Beverly Wilshire Gold Room, and other locations throughout Hollywood. The actors even doubled up on parties over a weekend. They attended producer David Selznick's affair, then were among a group of many other actors who packed Fox producer Winfield Sheehan's place later that evening. The couple even enjoyed an evening at the movies, attending a performance of *Ah Wilderness* at the El Capitan Theater. Their evenings together became so common that one gossip observed "Spencer Tracy alone at the Hat because Loretta Young had to rehearse."[36]

The discussion of Mr. Tracy's marital status and situation rarely appeared. He may have separated from her, but he was still a married man dating a beautiful single woman. Hollywood party throwers and friends did not seem to mind the situation as the pair received invitations and went out with other friends. When the pair ended their relationship, party hosts would invite Mr. and Mrs. Tracy to attend their affairs. On occasions like Twentieth-Century-Fox producer Harry and Tai Lachman's fete honoring the Marquis Polignac, Miss Young and Mr. and Mrs. Tracy appeared. Both increased their fan base over the next years, becoming challengers to the ranks of the top ten most popular movie stars.[37]

The image appeared based in reality to contemporaries. The Tracy-Young attraction had such intensity the others in the cast felt like intruders while they worked on the set. Tracy issued a denial of the relationship to reporters, stating, "Aw, it was all platonic, anyway." Star Helen Twelvetrees remarked, "When was Spence sober enough to say a thing like that?" MGM actor Clark Gable knew about this affair as well. Gable would work at the studio for many years with Tracy and would have his own affair with Miss Young during 1935–1936. This relationship resulted in Miss Young giving birth to a daughter.

A few writers on the movie industry of the era gave the Tracy-Young affair brief consideration. According to Katharine Hepburn's most recent biographer, the Tracy-Young affair had to be non-sexual. He cited Young's Catholicism and Tracy's situation and believed the denials of the actors. Meanwhile, a recent book on actress Joan Crawford noted that she had an interest in Spencer Tracy. Crawford felt that an affair could be possible because "Neither was it a closely guarded secret that, like Clark Gable, the supposedly happily married Tracy had also 'been through' Loretta Young."[38]

The biographers of Tracy and Young accorded the pair's relationship very different emphasis and coverage. Tracy's biographer saw the movie the pair made as "a rather insipid romance." The consideration of the affair lasted only two paragraphs and a good portion of the space went to the three of the denials that the actors issued to the press.

Young's biographers noted that the actress supposedly held an attraction for the actor out of humanitarian reasons, having noticed his heavy drinking and his separation from his wife. However, Tracy embraced the Hollywood lifestyle he so despised over the year that the pair were together, attending parties and movie premieres with Loretta. Loretta Young did bristle over being portrayed as "the other woman," insisting that Tracy had separated from his wife before Young and Tracy had even met. The writers offer a few theories centered on Young's not wanting to wait for Tracy to get divorced or to continue the relationship as it was. They mention that Tracy reconciled with his wife after having a talk with his mentor, theater luminary George M. Cohan, in the fall of 1934.[39]

Hollywood novelists read these gossip items and noted the activities of the industry's biggest stars as they included the "wild abandon" vision of the Hollywood private party. Nina Putnam's *Laughter Limited*, the story of a star's orbit through the Hollywood galaxy, included a producer's private party. As the scene at the beginning of this chapter showed, Hollywood private parties offered industry people and their guests a location where they could meet the upper echelon of the movie industry.

From the author's perspective all the people attending the parties acted as Hollywood bohemians. Indeed, after sating their eating and drinking desires, Tom Muro and the other partiers began acting to satisfy their libidos. They used the private party as a place where they pursued any sexual activity that their hearts desired. Most of the partiers reveled at the party. Others, like the lead character in the novel, potentially perceived the experience as a form of extortion. While this image suggested that Hollywood sexual outlaw activities might be seen as coercive to some, it also suggested that other women enjoyed the revelry. In addition, none of the revelers at the party hurt their professional or social lives through participation in the party activities.

One of the few reviewers of the novel mentioned the party. Although she thought the book entertaining, she believed that the "age-old story" of the "job party" was beneath Mrs. Putnam's capabilities. This reviewer likened the women at the party to the Forty Niners going west to stake their claim at striking it rich and having as likely a chance at success. She saw no reason to doubt the party's realism but suggested that a focus upon the producers and directors who received the women's favors would prove as truthful and more interesting.[40]

Another novelist did provide readers with a Hollywood private party scene that focused on a person different from the neophyte starlet.

> Chatting together in a group in the corner were Raymond Cauldwell, William Pearson and Rudolph Norman, famous throughout the world as romantic heartbreakers, but the fair sex seemed to hold no attraction for them off the screen — they appeared always far more interested in one another. It was probably fortunate that their female film admirers could not listen in on their conversation.[41]

A movie reviewer and author of several nonfiction books on the film colony invited readers into the inner sanctum of a Hollywood party. In this 1932 novel *Hey Diddle Diddle*, Tamar Lane noted the presence of Hollywood bohemians romantic stars at industry private parties. A movie critic and non-fiction writer, Lane's 1924 book *What's Wrong with the Movies?* helped Lane to forge a reputation as a person who "...discusses with utter frankness their [producers, directors, author and public] faults, shortcomings, and misconceptions."[42]

Lane used a tactic that enhanced the audience's belief in the truth of his Hollywood private party image. He mixed the names of living stars with his fictional characters only in the private party scene. Combined with the previous perception of Lane through his nonfiction writing, the addition of real names helped readers believe they were receiving truthful information about Hollywood and might have led them to place real identities onto the fictional characters. Lane's private party scene informed them that bohemians who talked about their secret love interests fit within the Hollywood private party milieu.

The scene contained all the elements that made the Hollywood private party a ballyhooed experience. Similar to images that appeared in newspaper gossip columns, this party scene included a description of the costly foods and the beautiful environs. However, it offered the excitement of providing the real names of stars at the private party. The length of the private party scene gave readers the chance to feel as if they were at the affair and receive the titillation of feeling like a Hollywood insider. They saw the trio of heartthrobs standing in the corner with their interest in and emotions for one another. The closed nature of actors' conversation suggested that they talked about highly personal feelings and interests that were to be kept amongst themselves. This allowed the reader to feel the excitement of receiving knowledge about stars' feelings.

The trio's lack of interest in the "fair" sex suggested that they did not pursue heterosexuality, the culture's normative sexual interest for males. The statement hinted that they held another interest, homosexuality. The scene provided readers with the pleasure of learning about the secret of Hollywood romantic stars. The secret carried the additional kick of exposing a forbidden love. The trio of Hollywood bohemians' pursuit of culturally taboo sexuality gave this Hollywood private party a compelling twist that made it very memorable to the readers and thus helped shape the perception of the Hollywood private party while selling Hollywood.

Like Tully and Putnam, Lane noted that Hollywood sexual outlaws fit within the movie community. These romantic stars enjoyed success in the motion picture industry professional and leisure circles. The image informed readers that the trio had many fans, suggesting that they were all top actors who earned large salaries and owned the finest in clothing, housing, and automobiles. Their attendance at this important affair and the use of the word "always" in assessing their party behavior indicated that these heartthrobs regularly appeared at all of Hollywood's party scenes. At Hollywood's private parties, the trio could discuss their secret love in this industry location and form a small community amongst themselves and remain on the invitation lists of future party holders.

The gossip columns and magazine articles throughout the 1930s included many items about actor and singer Nelson Eddy. The male portion of "America's Sweethearts," he attempted to live in Hollywood similarly to the male romantic figures in the novel *Hey Diddle Diddle*. Born in Rhode Island in 1901,

Nelson Ackerman Eddy was the sole child of a machinist father and homemaker mother. The family moved frequently because of his father's need to find work.

Both of his parents had musical abilities. While father William Darius Eddy sang in the church choir, he also performed in local stage productions in New England. Nelson Eddy's mother, Isabel Kendrick Eddy, was the daughter of a singer and a church soloist in her own right. When their son reached his early teens, the parents divorced. Eddy accompanied his mother to Philadelphia.

According to Hollywood publicity, Eddy worked in Philadelphia as a switchboard operator and reporter with a few newspapers. His big break came when he won a competition to join the Civic Opera in 1922. The musical director of the Opera became Eddy's coach. Eddy would study with a few other voice teachers, and by the end of the 1920s, he appeared with the Philadelphia Civic Opera Company frequently.

After success in concerts and on radio, MGM signed him to a motion picture contract in 1933. While Eddy engaged in old-fashioned courtship with Jeannette MacDonald in movies between 1935 and 1942, he refused to date women off-screen at Hollywood parties during the first half of his career.[43]

Eddy created an image of himself as a Hollywood bohemian through depictions of private parties. The cinema society pages of newspapers and fan magazines reported Eddy's attendance at Hollywood private parties. Unlike other stars at the private parties whose names often came paired with another to make it look as if this was a date, mentions of Eddy's name within these columns did not link his name with that of a starlet or actress. These columns linked the actor with the woman with whom he frequently attended Hollywood parties, his mother Isabella Eddy. Readers learned that at Jeannette MacDonald's first party as a married woman, attendees were actor Basil Rathbone and his wife, Ginger Rogers, and Nelson Eddy and his mother. At this and other Hollywood private parties, Eddy and his mother made a memorable pair. The pairing also enabled Eddy to depict himself as a good, thoughtful son. This image enhanced Eddy's standing with the fans of his and MacDonald's "old-fashioned" operettas.

The romantic star also hosted his own private parties with his mother's help. Eddy's Hollywood parties were known as very democratic assemblies of musicians, writers, photographers, stars, and publicity men. A broad guest list was unusual among most stars, who tended to befriend members of their own ranks and figures in the studio's higher echelons. The attendees at Eddy's parties represented people working in a variety of studio occupations, including positions with the reputation of having a predominantly homosexual male composition.[44] The Hollywood private parties appeared to offer Nelson Eddy the opportunity to be with his mother and, like the trio of heartthrobs, spend time with his friends. The unique style of his Hollywood bohemian position prompted many media outlets to investigate Eddy's attitudes and choices.

These private party images depicted Eddy's lack of dating and created the impression that this handsome man had little interest in women. Fan magazine articles confirmed this disinterest as they observed that the actor entranced secretaries and typists when he entered the studio offices. The reporters noted that women regularly expressed the desire to get to know him, but Eddy paid no attention to them. The star's attitudes and his regular attendance at private parties with his mother created a mystery audience members wanted resolved.

The entertainment-reporting organizations published articles that claimed to present the secret of Nelson Eddy's attitudes toward romance to their readers. The star furthered his image as a Hollywood sexual outlaw through depictions showing Eddy sincerely and almost belligerently pronouncing that would never marry. The romantic star used this declaration to justify his lack of dating.[45] His answer raised the question of whether Eddy had a secret love that might provide the answer to why the actor did not want to marry. One answer returned to the star's lack of interest in women. Since these images of Eddy appeared after the publication of *Hey Diddle Diddle*, where the trio of heartthrobs exhibiting a similar lack of interest in the fair sex, readers could envision heartthrob Nelson Eddy behaving similarly at Hollywood private parties for reason of "secret love."

The Hollywood media continued to seek an answer to the Eddy mystery. A fan magazine article attempted to explain the actor's behavior regarding dating and romance. "Too many have typed their message to the world that Nelson Eddy's abiding loyalty to a mother who has done everything in the world for him amounts to that suggestive word: fixation...." The reporter observed the effusive emotional attachment between mother and son but explained this connection as the result of a long, hard life together and interpreted it as beautiful and sweet. He viewed their attendance at the exciting and glamorous Hollywood parties together as the sharing of the positive portions of their lives as the mother and son had shared her divorce and the subsequent difficult times.[46] This analysis offered an explanation for Eddy's party attendance while denying one possibility for Eddy's sexual outlaw attitudes. However, the question of what Eddy did for love remained.

An article on the relationships between mothers and single motion picture performers offered what became the typical answer for Nelson Eddy's behavior. The reporter observed:

> Isabel Eddy, mother of girl-shy Nelson, is another of these Hollywood mothers said to be behind the bachelorhood of her 36-year-old son. She runs his house, protects him from unwelcomed [sic] feminine visitors, giving Nelson all of the comforts and none of the drawbacks of a wife-run domicile.[47]

This piece must have had a studio publicist involved in its creation. It seemed to answer the mystery, yet the piece also allowed for conflicting readings so as to continue the mystery. Certainly, actor and mother shared powerful emotions toward one another. Phrases including "his mother protects him" and "girl-shy," depicted the baritone as a mama's boy. Yet the phrase, "unwelcomed feminine visitors," suggested that women did come to Eddy's home and perhaps the actor entertained the welcome ones. The last sentence provided the image of Nelson receiving all the comforts without any drawbacks to home, hinting that the star had his cake and ate it too. What that exactly meant in this situation remained for the interpretation of the reader.

Eddy's image was not the rogue who enjoyed the company of women. His continued appearances with his mother at Hollywood private parties ensured that he would not be viewed that way. The remaining strong image was that Eddy was a mama's boy. This positioned Eddy as a classic case of the homosexual, according to the theories of psychoanalyst Sigmund Freud. Freud's thinking had become popularized in the United States during the 1920s and 1930s. Being labeled a homosexual lacked the subtlety and the humor inherent in the vast majority of Hollywood bohemian imagery.

As I noted in the nightlife chapter, Hollywood faced increasing pressure against the presence of its Hollywood bohemians during the late 1930s. MGM, Eddy's studio, placed more pressure on the star to marry. Eddy offered a few stipulations, then allowed the studio to arrange a marriage between himself and Ann Demitz Franklin, the ex-wife of director and producer Sidney Franklin, in early 1939. The couple remained married for twenty-seven years, until Eddy's death in March 1967.

Comment on the image from contemporaries is extremely limited. Louella Parsons wrote an innuendo in one of her columns during 1936 implying that Eddy was gay. She stated "the big laugh in Hollywood these days is Nelson Eddy's feminine pursuers.... Come on, Mr. Eddy, even the hinterlands are wise to you." Screenwriter Anita Loos commented on the lack of forcefulness to Eddy's personality and mentioned that "[he and Jeannette] never liked each other very much. The animus was mostly on Jeanette's side. Nelson was too mild ever to dislike anybody. He used to take any amount of up-staging on the part of Jeannette. Anita liked her because she acted the star."

One scholar included the Parsons comment in his brief discussion of Nelson Eddy. After noting simply that the actor's sexuality appeared unclear to him, he observed that perhaps the gossip item from Louella Parson came from one of her gay assistants. Scholar Sharon Rich had unprecedented access to a range of materials and concluded that Jeannette MacDonald and Nelson Eddy were very much in love and prevented from marrying by MGM.[48]

Eddy's marriage might have been arranged, perhaps in more ways than one. They were not unusual for celebrities in other industries. The presence of people who held homosexual interests in the theater led to the development of methods for them to present heterosexual interests to the public. The motion picture industry borrowed these two types of disguises from the theater world.

A "beard" appeared as a romantic interest in public for a person of the opposite biological sex. The beard disguised his public partner's secret homosexual romance.

The second form of marriage received the name of "twilight tandem." This pairing occurred when a man and a woman who each held same-sex romantic interests married one another. Afterwards, both husband and wife could pursue a romance with a person of their own biological sex.[49] Several private party images revealed that the Hollywood private party served as a place where romantic stars emerged from behind these marriage arrangements and fulfilled their sexually taboo interests.

Newspapers and magazines regularly covered the weddings of notable motion picture industry figures. Revelations about their private parties after the ceremony appeared in this coverage and sometimes in the articles that detailed the couple's subsequent demise. The quintessential male romantic figure of the 1920s, Rudolph Valentino, had private wedding parties that suggested the presence of Hollywood sexual outlaws.

Rodolfo Alfonso Piero Filiberto Guglielmi, the son of an Italian army veterinarian, enrolled in a variety of schools during his early years because he frequently did not attend classes or pay attention when he did. At seventeen, he left for a life in Paris and struggled there for one year. His middle-class family paid for his return trip to Italy in 1913 where he failed to build a career, including qualifying as an officer in a military academy.

The family sent him to the United States, and he landed in New York City. The funds the family provided him with went quickly, so the pampered soul had to wait tables and tend gardens to earn a living. Shortly thereafter, he took work as a taxi dancer with the connotations of being a "gigolo." The dancer appeared to engage in bisexual behavior during this period because of his financial straits. His skill enabled him to move into the lucrative world of show dancing. He met socialite Blanca de Saulles, whose unhappy marriage to her husband businessman John de Saulles led to a sensational divorce trial. Rodolfo testified in that trial and later became implicated in the murder trial after Blanca killed her ex-husband. After these trials, Rodolfo Guglielmi changed his name to various variations of "Rudolph Valentino" to avoid the previous scandal and partly because his new countrymen struggled to correctly say his born surname.

The dancer began earning small roles in the New York movie industry. From background extra, he moved to small parts as typecast villains. He enjoyed the work and began improving his acting skills. He was ambitious and perceived that the place to make his way in this industry lay in Hollywood. He had not settled on his name but opted to move west. He began getting extra and bit parts in Hollywood in 1917.

The big break came when screenwriter June Mathis saw him playing the role of a "cabaret parasite" in the movie *The Eyes of Youth*, starring Clara Kimball Young and Edmund Lowe. A recently formed motion picture production company, Harry Garson Productions, and Clara Kimball Young Films reportedly spent nearly $300,000 on the movie, a significant amount of money for the era. The plot focused on the story of a woman trying to decide if she should marry or not. Young received excellent reviews while the *New York Times* reviewer commented that the supporting cast did not have the opportunity or did not shine.[50]

In late 1919 Valentino met a Metro contract player named Jean Acker. Acker, part Cherokee and a former vaudeville dancer and summer stock actress who only received small parts, had a love and sexual relationship with Metro Pictures star actress Alla Nazimova, who will be examined in the next chapter. Initially, the studio tried to launch her as an exotic star, but this failed. They then launched an all–American publicity campaign, complete with bathing suit shots. However, her career still did not catch on.

The actress soon tired of Nazimova's actions and attitudes. Madame Nazimova viewed sex as an interval of pleasure between her work and not for the forging of relationships. Consequently, Nazimova had begun a brief affair with a script girl during production of her movie *Stronger Than Death*. Meanwhile, Acker met another contract actress, Grace Darmond. The Canadian received her first contact in 1913 at the age of 16 and made many movies for smaller production companies throughout the 1920s. The beautiful blonde and Acker began an affair, then soon fought.

Smarting over her fight with Darmond, Acker went to a big Hollywood private party. Valentino, hurting over the recent death of her beloved mother, also attended the bash. The pair talked and commiserated together, forging a relationship. Two months later Valentino proposed to Acker. Reportedly because Acker remained upset from the split from her "girlfriend" Grace Darmond, she accepted his proposal of marriage.[51]

Two years later, with the release of the motion picture *The Four Horsemen of the Apocalypse*, Valentino became a star. Acker filed for divorce and the story received newspaper coverage across the country. This coverage of the proceedings revealed that the couple had a very unusual party after the wedding ceremony. Readers learned that the marriage ended at the private party after the wedding ceremony.

Mrs. Anna Karger testified that Jean Acker had not been a happy bride during the wedding reception party and that Acker came into her room following her marriage to Valentino and said, "I have made a mistake." Valentino explained that he was unable to find his bride when he awoke the morning after. The morning after the new bride and groom had not consummated their marriage, Acker called Valentino weeping. She said that she could not live this kind of life. The bride had passed the night with her friend, actress Grace Darmond. The actor then tried to see his new wife, but "she refused to see me. I could not see her alone; she was always accompanied by Miss Darmond." Acker said to him, "No, you go back like a good boy."

When Acker testified she indicated that during their brief marriage Valentino was not working. She felt great concern over the possibility that she would have him living off of her income. She referred to Valentino as a boy and confessed the cause of one of their arguments. "You see, he used the perfume out of my bottle. It was expensive perfume too." The large courtroom audience broke into titters. Darmond's testimony validated Acker's perspective on this "bathroom incident." Valentino's attorney asked Acker why her husband could not visit her on location but Grace Darmond stayed with Acker at the Lone Pine Hotel. "There were two beds in the hotel room," Acker responded.[52]

The Valentino-Acker private wedding party was unique. The party featured as the star a groom oblivious to his bride's whereabouts on his wedding night. He later enjoyed using his wife's perfume. His co-star was a bride crying tears of unhappiness at their private party and referring to her wedding as a mistake. The bride and her best friend spent the night of the party together. Months later, the bride would not make time to see her husband but spent time with her best friend. When questioned about this choice, the bride thought of bed with the mention of said girlfriend's name.

The emotional display by the principals of this wedding party differed from anything most readers previously encountered. Readers had personal experience with wedding parties, having been bride or groom, wedding party member or a friend or relative of the happy couple. They read media coverage of hundreds of other weddings of society people and local individuals. Yet the emotions of the Hollywood bohemians made the Valentino-Acker wedding party stand apart from even the most unusual of all other wedding parties. Acker was so highly attached to her friend Grace Darmond that their relationship appeared to feature same-sex interests.

The groom appeared unaware of his wife's whereabouts at the party and accepted not consummating his wedding. Both of these items raised the issue of whether he cared about having sex with his wife. Perhaps Acker wanted to generate more questions regarding Valentino's sexual interests during the trial. Her testimony, corroborated by Darmond's comments about the perfume bottle, indicated that Valentino had a bohemian attitude regarding adhering to masculine norms.[53] If he did not follow the norms for male behavior regarding cosmetics then he might not follow the norms regarding conjugal interests. The principals' gender attitudes and the emotions behind their sexual lives gave their Hollywood private party a farce-like unpredictability and drama that made it stand apart. The turnout at the courtroom demonstrated there was a large, eager audience for the show and the enjoyment of the crowd illustrated its success.

Only a few years later, Acker had left the movie industry and returned to the vaudeville stage. As the former wife of a big star, her appearance in a city received coverage in the press.

The former wife of Rudolph Valentino ... will appear at local big time house in about three weeks. She plays the San Francisco Orpheum first. In the meantime she will go to Catalina today to visit her old chum Grace Darmond, who is working on location.... The actress declares that she saw her former husband only once in New York, at a cafe, and then she didn't speak to him. So that's that.

Two weeks later, a gossip item observed that Grace Darmond finished her role and would take a trip to San Francisco to make personal appearances. These two items updated the story since the divorce trial. As one might have suspected after seeing the images, Acker and Valentino had no relationship whatsoever. However, Acker and Darmond maintained their relationship. Although she was not to appear in the Los Angeles vaudeville for three weeks, Acker arrived in the Hollywood area early. She then acted upon her arrangements to travel to spend time with Grace Darmond, who happened to be on a location shoot. When Acker went to San Francisco for her scheduled performances at its Orpheum Theater, Darmond arranged for a trip to San Francisco to make personal appearances.[54]

The circle around Nazimova provided the contemporary perspective on the veracity of the images of Acker and Darmond. Nazimova had discovered actress Patsy Ruth Miller at a Hollywood private party. Years younger than many of the people around her, Miller quickly joined the circle around Nazimova. While noting Acker's mannish style of dress, Miller did not know that Acker was a lesbian until hearing this information years later.

Another member of Nazimova's circle, cameraman Paul Ivano, stated that the image of Acker as a lesbian matched reality and that she and Darmond had a relationship as girlfriends. Ivano, born Ivanichevitcz to Russian parents who lived in Nice, France, came to Hollywood in 1919. He believed that the environment would help him to recuperate from the gassing he suffered while fighting in the French Army during World War I. Another of the circle, Dagmar Godowsky, stated that Acker telephoned her after marrying Rudy and said, "What in the world did I do? How could it happen? Will you help me? It was a terrible mistake."

Scholars agree with Ivano's assessment. Nazimova's biographer asserted that Acker had lesbian relationships with both Nazimova and Darmond. The author of a book on female stars who loved other women described Acker as having a romance with Nazimova but did not mention Darmond. The biographers of Valentino and of Valentino's second wife, Natacha Rambova, reached this conclusion as well. Acker died in 1978 and was buried in a Hollywood cemetery next to her long-term lover Chloe Carter.[55]

Miss Rambova starred with Valentino in another unusual wedding party less than a year after this divorce proceeding. As his breakthrough motion picture opened in the theaters, Valentino began the filming of *Camille* with Alla Nazimova and met the actress's friend, designer Natacha Rambova. A highly talented and ambitious woman, Rambova eventually saw value and a great deal that she liked in Valentino and accepted his marriage proposal. The pair and several friends departed for a wedding party in Mexico in mid–1922 and ran up against the law. Valentino and Acker won an interlocutory decree and their divorce would not take effect until March, 1923, so the romantic star faced charges of polygamy upon his return to Los Angeles.[56]

The coverage of the case against Valentino again revealed a private wedding party in which the central figures were Hollywood bohemians. At the hearing to determine whether to bring charges against Valentino, the couple's friends gave testimony that put the unique party on display. One referred to bridesmaid Alla Nazimova as a "strange [looking] lady," because of her wearing male clothing, a "bachelor" style analyzed in the next chapter. Dr. Floretta White of Palm Springs testified that after the wedding party Valentino slept in one room with actor and best man Douglas Gerard while the bride occupied another.[57]

The Valentino-Rambova private wedding party featured a bridesmaid in mannish attire and a bride and groom who willingly chose not to sleep together. The defiance of the usual man and wife behavior at a wedding party indicated the Hollywood bohemian nature of the participants. These odd figures and behaviors sold Hollywood through making this Hollywood private party so memorable and unlike any other affair readers might experience. Despite being aired in the news section rather than the gossip columns the story sold

Rudolph Valentino with his defense lawyers while on trial for bigamy, 1922 (courtesy the Academy of Motion Picture Arts and Sciences).

Hollywood without carrying scandal of a heinous variety similar to the Arbuckle case.

The Rudolph Valentino image that emerged from these parties formed the foundation of the star's off-screen image. This was part of the selling point of Hollywood's greatest romantic idol of the era. After their marriage, Rambova issued public statements that reinforced the perception of Valentino an unmasculine man, such as "He [Rudy] knows nothing whatever about business and that [she] manages everything." The party images, Rambova's comments, along with her series of "emasculating" costumes for Valentino, such as slave bracelets, all fueled the public's perception of the star during the mid–1920s.[58]

The pair created their own production company. Their critically and financially unsuccessful movies, debts, and other pressures added strain to their marriage. They opted for what they referred to as "a marital vacation" in the summer of 1925. When she returned from Europe, Natasha stated that they had a difference of opinion over whether she should continue her career and whether to have children.

Months later, they planned their divorce. Rudolph met her in Nice, France, as a friend for platonic lunch and dinner. In New York, the judge granted the pair a divorce on charges of desertion. Neither Rudy nor Natasha showed any concern or emotion and talked about their work. Natasha said she had no intention now of marrying again. Rudolph had not lived with his wife for years and had refused several times to resume conjugal relations. She preferred to live her own life, meeting her own expenses, and also denied that their marriage had ever been consummated.[59]

These images certainly played a significant role in prompting the famous *Chicago Tribune* editorial in which Valentino was blamed for the public presence of highly effeminate-acting men.[60] According to the observers of the city scene, Valentino's Hollywood sexual outlaw images were prevalent and powerful. The image shaped the behaviors of fans enough to prompt some of the males to adopt Valentino's style of clothing, slave bracelets, and masculine cosmetics in nightclubs across Chicago. While the editors objected to this presence and Valentino challenged the editors to a duel for their accusations, these Chicago nightclub prowlers clearly found Valentino's Hollywood sexual outlaw image useful for shaping their public presence and perhaps their romantic choices.

Only a few contemporaries offered comment on Natacha Rambova's interest and sexual behavior. George Cukor, the famous Hollywood director from the 1930s through the 1960s, established a very close friendship with Nazimova. This connection enabled him to insist that Natasha Rambova did have a love affair with the doyenne of Hollywood's lesbian circle from the late 1910s through the mid–1920s. Another person who began her career during the 1930s, costume designer Irene Sharaff, also made friends with Nazimova. Although she could not be certain she stated that "[Nazimova and Rambova] were both deeply involved with each other for a while, and they were both sexually free."[61]

The costume and art designer appeared in numerous books on Valentino and a biography of Nazimova, as well as in a biography of her own. Several of the biographers of the main figures in Rambova's life believe her to have held lesbian interests. Her own biographer disagreed, asserting that no tangible evidence of an affair with Nazimova or lesbian activities existed. He noted that in later years Natacha declared that she had a hatred of lesbians, generally because she disliked their adoption of mannish mannerisms. Nazimova's biographer stated that "sex never appeared to matter much to Rambova."

Rambova did not attempt to continue her career in Hollywood. She left for Europe shortly after Valentino's death. Almost ten years after her divorce from Valentino, she married a Basque, Alvaro de Urzaiz, but their marriage ended because she did not want children. In later life she became a noted scholar in Egyptology and religions. She died in June 1966 from dietary complications that resulted from her paranoid delusions that people poisoned her food.[62]

Valentino died in 1926 at age 31 from a perforated ulcer. The question of his sexual interests and behaviors has raged ever since. Patsy Ruth Miller and Nazimova reportedly viewed Valentino as "not the lady-killer type; the ladies killed him." According to Valentino's makeup artist, Mont Westmore, Valentino had an affair with actress Nita Valdi. His friend Paul Ivano claimed Rudolph had a love affair with actress Pola Negri after his divorce from Rambova.

Biographers and others advocated that the star held a variety of sexual proclivities. Rambova's biographer observed that Valentino was not homosexual. An interviewer of gay Hollywood males noted that Ramon Novarro told actor Cary Grant about his affair with Valentino. A recent biographer of Valentino described this affair as a passing sexual liaison for "The Sheik" but did claim that he gifted Novarro with an Art Deco dildo. Novarro's biographer asserted that we will never know if and what relationship the duo may have had; however there appeared to be no veracity to the dildo story.

Two of the more recent biographers of the movie idol radically disagree on this issue. David Bret argued that Valentino was gay by natural inclination and bisexual in early years through financial necessity. Valentino had sexual engagements with members of both sexes, including orgies in his place at Falcon Lair. He fell head over heels in love with Rambova, and during his early years in Hollywood had an intense love affair with Paul Ivano. Emily Lieder saw Valentino as a man who sought out strong women but who got along better with maternal women. He had an ambiguous, wounding sexual life.[63]

The famous *Chicago Tribune* editorial claimed that Rudolph Valentino's screen and publicity images offered the effeminate men in Chicago a figure to emulate. Other Hollywood private party images provided material for a different group to incorporate into their own everyday lives. Hollywood private parties also featured sexual outlaws whom women with homosexual interests could emulate. In Keane McGrath's 1932 novel *Hollywood Siren*, a tall redheaded girl walked over to a small group of people engaged in gossip at a party and presented new "dirt."

> Leona Chrisman and little Sue Nesbit had a peculiar party by themselves in one of the upstairs bedrooms at Sue's blowout last Wednesday night.... Well, you all know that Leona is "that way" about other girls, and I had suspected that she and Sue were having an affair for some time. I guess the liquor went to their heads a little more than usual that night, and they sneaked off by themselves before the rest of the party noticed. Leona's husband discovered them together. He dragged Leona out of that room by the hair of her head, and threw her into their car and took her home. "I'll bet he gets a divorce after that one." "I don't think he will," said one of the men. "He's been married to her for a long time and he must have found out her peculiarities by now."[64]

An outside observer writing on the Hollywood scene, McGrath offered the reader a typical private party scene. Readers could recognize from their own experience a small circle of party attendees engaged in conversation when a new person joined the group. However, the story that she told of the intense emotional expression of the two actresses and their sexually taboo actions removed the scene from most readers' realities. The scene revealed the existence of a secret love between a married and a single actress. The adulteress and homosexual held so intense a secret feeling for one another that they made love despite the presence of many people in Sue's house. Indeed, the performers' knowledge of the Hollywood private party's reputation as a place for romantic expression could have prompted Leona and Sue to host a party to begin with. The explicitness of the gossip about culturally taboo sexuality increased the titillation factor in the Hollywood private party image.

McGrath's scene also revealed to readers that Hollywood private parties offered industry people a place to learn about other industry people's affairs. It illustrated that industry people wanted to know about the private lives of others in Hollywood and that this knowledge titillated them. This validated these same interests within audience members and made it simpler for readers to "place" themselves within this situation.

The view of the Hollywood private party scene equated readers and Hollywood figures in their interest in celebrity culture and in discovering sexual outlaw activities within Hollywood locations. This equation rewarded audience members who took an interest in Hollywood's celebrities, its sexual outlaws and private parties because the image showed that the "in crowd" pursued it. This made the activity appear to be the hip thing to do. The non-judgmental response of these "in-crowders" illustrated the sophisticate's manner of viewing Hollywood sexual outlaws and presumably shaped the perspectives of the readers. An industry columnist of the era noted that gossip did not create problems in Hollywood:

> While there isn't a more gossipy town ... people here believe that everyone has a right to live his or her own life. While marriage and a home life is becoming the prevalent thing, no one is shunned for preferring something else.... The gossiping

is more of a pastime than anything else. As a matter of fact, there is very little criticism here of personal habits. It is a freeland in which persons are permitted to do as they please. As a result everything is done openly.[65]

This tidbit about gossipy Hollywood informed readers that in the movie colony all, including Hollywood bohemians, acted upon their sexual interests openly with little negative consequence. The community reacted with a lack of criticism and its gossiping served merely as a pastime. The lives of Chrisman and Nesbitt corroborated this. The actresses expressed sexual desire for females. Each maintained successful careers, earned significant incomes. Sue held the standing in the community to host a successful party (blowout) in the middle of the week. Both actresses were well known to be the topic of a conversation and to require no introduction among the gossiping people. The gossipers presumably liked the actresses because no one made a negative comment about them or their Hollywood bohemian behavior.

The degree of acceptance of different sexual interests and behaviors enabled married Hollywood bohemians to pursue their interests while attending the same party. In Tamar Lane's book, two successful movie stars who enjoyed an "open relationship" received regular invitations to the elite Hollywood parties. The pair appeared at the same party as Hollywood's biggest names and the three heartthrobs. Lane's choice of mentioning the twilight tandem among the names of contemporary motion picture stars probably made the tandem appear more realistic. It presumably prompted some readers to try to figure out who the living actors might be behind this fictional paring.

> Edgar Gray and Lydia Barnes, one of Hollywood's most unique screen couples, were busy making new conquests [at the party]. Edgar and Lydia had been married for several years but each took an extremely broad-minded viewpoint in regard to the heart affairs of the other. The only time they had ever seriously quarreled was when they both fell in love with the same girl.[66]

Like other Hollywood bohemians at private parties, this couple happily pursued their romantic interests. Readers could envision both Gray and Barnes, each driven by intense desire. The each stalked around this party like hunters looking for their conquests. The punch line, that these two fell in love with the same girl, added humor to the Hollywood private party image. The line also confirmed that the pair was successful in their taboo missions at Hollywood private parties. This image with the pair's adultery and Lydia's bisexuality confirmed the wild nature of the Hollywood private party by tying it to forbidden sexual behaviors. The piece provided enjoyment to a variety of readers, including spurring the desires of readers to want to be at a Hollywood private party in order to see a husband and wife act like this Barnes and Gray.

Despite the interests of readers, one novelist viewed Hollywood and its private parties very negatively. According to one Hollywood insider, not all Hollywood private parties and bearded couples were successful. As noted in the last chapter, John Dos Passos criticized the Hollywood industry for its promotion of the idolization of insignificant people. He lampooned the Latin Lover image Rudolph Valentino made famous with one of his characters in *The Big Money*.[67]

Cuban-born Antonio "Tony" Garrido was a highly effeminate man who married actress Margo Dowling (examined in the discussion of premiere parties in the previous chapter) years before they went to Hollywood. Garrido had big brown eyes and a smooth oval face of a very light brown. When Dowling observed his dark eyelashes "she kidded him and asked him what he put on his eyelashes to make them so black. He said it was the same thing that made her hair so pretty and golden...." Garrido defied gender norms. He used cosmetics like the men described in the *Chicago Tribune* editorial. He likened his use of them to the way in which a woman applies cosmetics "...to make oneself pretty and draw people's attention." Garrido accompanied his wife and her aunt to Hollywood, expecting to become a star. "If Valentino can do it, it will be easy for me."[68] He fell for Hollywood superficiality, becoming the lover of a phony Austrian count.

Dos Passos used the Hollywood private party to heighten his critique of Hollywood's superficiality and corruption. Garrido went to a secret underground Hollywood private party with the Count. The private party was a wild affair, with secret love, illegal drugs and death. Readers discovered the nature of the party along with Margo, who read a newspaper headline that a Hollywood extra was slain. Two sailors, stupefied from liquor or narcotics, were in custody after the police discovered them in an apartment house with Antonio Garrido, whose skull had been fractured. The phony count fled before the police arrived.[69]

Dos Passos depicted the private Hollywood party as a bad place. The attendees were lowlifes, not the usual Hollywood stars. They drank, consumed illegal drugs, and participated in violence. This Hollywood private party appeared as a dangerous place, he admonished readers. Dos Passos's depiction included the element of danger, presumably sparking fear, excitement, or both in the novel's readers. This enabled the readers to link these terrific emotions with the Hollywood private party, something they could not do with the image of high society's garden parties that appeared in magazines. Although critical of Hollywood, Dos Passos's party scene confirmed that Hollywood private parties were wild affairs. They appeared as places where a person could experience forbidden sexual behaviors, and this helped sell Hollywood private parties and Hollywood itself as a unique place where one could see the wildest of all behaviors.

As the images have shown, the Hollywood media depicted Hollywood private parties as having the best of everything. The Hollywood private party images matched media depictions of private parties in other locations for the splendor of their atmosphere, food and drink. However, Hollywood private parties surpassed all other affairs by putting the lovemaking of the culture's most romantic characters on display. The lovemaking enabled the Hollywood private party to seize the public's imagination.

These images Hollywood bohemians and their secret loves gave audiences more. The "secret" aspect to the love heightened the sense that the image revealed some of the mysteries about Hollywood private parties and their celebrity guests. This provided audiences with the belief that they now had insider knowledge about Hollywood's stars. It gave them the feeling that they were being included in on the Hollywood world. The titillation, forbidden pleasure, knowledge, and sense of being an insider of the Hollywood bohemians' secret loves distinguished the Hollywood private party from general Hollywood publicity and certainly from the depictions of parties in other cities.

The private Hollywood party provided audiences with an understanding of how Hollywood celebrities used their homes. Sometimes the images placed the house's size and splendor on display. Like many of the images of homes and their owners that appeared in the media, the Hollywood publicity images concentrated on displaying how the homes reflected the personality of their owners. The Hollywood publicity images focused on showing audiences a glimpse at the personality of Hollywood figures through leisure activities within a location that U.S. culture viewed as a highly private space offering sanctuary from the public world. The private party images associated the Hollywood celebrity home with a celebrity's personal behavior, particularly romance and sexuality. The images of Hollywood bohemians in star homes expanded on this association, presenting the chic engaged in forbidden pleasures in the Hollywood star home.

FOUR

The Hollywood Star Home
Chic Bachelor and Odd Bedfellow Digs

[Two reporters watch as Alla Nazimova enters a room in her house] dressed in blue suit mannishly tailored, feet in low-heeled oxfords. She wears no chiffons, no morbidities. She thinks, succinctly, as a man thinks. She speaks without evasions. She has a Peterish [sic] handshake.[1]

The Hollywood private party made the Hollywood celebrity home look like a glamorous fun house where all kinds of "naughty" activities occurred. The publicity increased audience members' interest in knowing more about celebrity homes in Hollywood. U.S. culture has idealized the home as the space where every person can live self-sufficiently. Homes are places where the owners can display their personality, their position in the community, and their purchases of expensive and high-quality things. Fans who maintained only a casual interest in the movie industry wanted to see celebrity homes to learn about these movie stars and their Hollywood world.

The studios knew that the audiences with the interest in star homes knew the place that the home held in U.S. culture. Hollywood publicity promoted the grandest and most splendidly furnished houses, but also homes that embodied the owner's personality. The Hollywood bohemian star homes usually had size and splendid decorations. They always expressed the star's personality by presenting clues about the gender and sexual interests of the celebrity. This thrilled audience members with the perception that they knew the celebrity more intimately. The hints about player personalities suggested that the star's romantic interests put them into a category of taboo people. This peek into the world of forbidden pleasure that came with the Hollywood bohemian image made the wondrous showplace of the Hollywood star home appear more exciting and more special than any home elsewhere in the United States.

The Hollywood star home images presented the home as a vital place in the culture. The home served as both the repository for the family and the realization of the American dream. Notable figures in the early American Republic perceived the home as the bedrock of the new nation. Thomas Jefferson promoted the National Survey, a system of land allotment that would preserve the virtuous republic by creating equal, independent homesteads as the nation expanded. John Adams and Alexander Hamilton consistently emphasized that the foundations of national morality lay in private families. All strove for a national housing style based on the repetition of simple forms in order to realize equality (at least among Caucasian males).

The generation born after the American Revolution viewed the home as the most effective place to pass down what they believed to be good values. They perceived that these values were necessary to make the nation the glorious republic. Beginning in the early 1830s, numerous schoolteachers, physicians, and judges instructed their fellow citizens on how to create good homes. Poets, writers, and composers of popular songs advocated that the home mirrored the moral and religious state of those who lived in it. Ministers and other religious figures pressed for houses to be buildings that maintained moral integrity by displaying a simple design and the family's moral associations. Ministers believed the home represented the most suitable place for moral teaching. The word "home" inspired a range of values in U.S. culture, including nostalgia, intimacy and privacy, domesticity, commodity, delight, austerity, comfort, and well-being.[2]

The country's top architectural minds and builders agreed with the role of the home in promoting proper values. Andrew Jackson Downing, who wrote three books on domestic architecture, argued for two types of beauty that each contained a component of morality. Downing argued that homes should express the owner's class, occupation, and background, but not so ostentatiously as to belittle the neighbors or aggrandize the children's manners. The principal American house in which to encourage these values and realize the appropriate look had been the detached rural or suburban single-family cottage for citizens of the middling sort.[3]

Alternative forms of housing emerged but none of them gained the status of being considered as proper homes. Tenement housing developed in the cities during the 1830s. Each building housed an average of 65 people by the 1850s. Despite offering the advantage of housing large numbers of families in single units, railroad tenements provided little sunlight or proper ventilation. As the century progressed, the dumbbell design provided improvements in these important areas. However, despite these technological and design improvements, housing reformers of the late nineteenth century perpetuated the belief that tenements were still improper environments for living. They claimed that this type of housing served as breeding grounds of crime, juvenile delinquency, prostitution, and disease.

During the mid-nineteenth century, upscale group housing emerged in the nation's cities. Apartment buildings offered housing to the urban elite. Apartments captured the fancy of many of these wealthy people because they incorporated several technological advances, such as elevators and hot water heating, as well as bathrooms in each unit. However, many people disliked apartments because they offered too little overall space in which to live. In addition, their thin walls and floors made residents uncomfortably aware of the neighbors. Most Americans believed that apartment buildings and any other kind of shared dwelling were aberrations of the model home that promoted promiscuity and wifely negligence of duties toward the home and her children.[4]

The culture's perceptions about proper housing and the home's role in the establishment of morality continued through the early decades of the twentieth century. Guidebooks stated that the home provided spiritual education for children and relaxation for men. Each detail of a dwelling revealed the personality and virtues of the family. Everyday phrases, such as "a man's home is his castle," indicated the culture believed in the man's right to own and rule in his home.

Wives and mothers blended in with the house itself in architectural books and popular culture since the mid–1800s, displaying those timeless qualities that suffused the rest of the home. In the twentieth century, advertisements and popular fiction pestered women readers about the appearance of their home, raising the questions of what the neighbors thought about her family's character. Along with selling a product, these items sold the ideal of home as moral guide for the family. They also carried the sexist attitude that it was the woman's role to make certain that the house provided the ability to raise her family with the culturally deemed proper values.

The preeminent American architect of the twentieth century, Frank Lloyd Wright, shared this view of the home. Wright designed prairie single-family detached houses to provide as many families as possible with their own home and the assurance of a place for them to build their moral status. The architect believed the quality of the home was all-important for the creation and maintenance of the state of family harmony.

Other builders and developers perceived the home similarly. Developers, who created most of the residences in the country, used uniform themes for suburban subdivisions to create a vision of harmony and community spirit. They filled former farmland and wilderness with single-family detached houses to fulfill the economic and cultural demands for housing. As they did this, these developers established the quintessential residential housing style in the twentieth-century United States. No other place in the country embodied this residential housing style better than Los Angeles.

Twentieth-Century City

Los Angeles set the standard for metropolitan development in the twentieth century. By 1930, single-family houses constituted over 94 percent of all dwellings in the city. The city became the country's twentieth-century city, and a variety of places in the United States used it as a model for their own development.[5] The Los Angeles metropolitan area grew dramatically between 1890 and 1940. Its population exploded from 50,000 people in 1889 to over 2.9 million in its metropolitan area by 1940. While migrants composed the majority of this growth, population growth also occurred when Los Angeles annexed neighboring towns and territories, including Hollywood.

The city underwent significant physical development to attract and support its population. One of the earliest included the harbor at San Pedro. This harbor gave Los Angeles deep-water capacity so that it could receive and send out ships. During the first decades of the twentieth century, Los Angeles spread pipelines carrying sewage and electricity into the newly annexed and developing sections. The Pacific Electric, known as "Big Red," provided trains that linked fifty communities in four counties (Los Angeles, Orange, Riverside, and San Bernardino) by 1910. This represented the height of mass transportation in Southern California. Property owners and businessmen soon organized programs to reconstruct the city's street system and eventually created the freeway system that supported automobiles, Los Angeles's residential dispersal and the city's car culture.[6]

While these changes shaped the physical layout of Los Angeles, the purchase of water rights from the Owens Valley sustained the growth of the city. The city acquired its aquatic lifelines despite the sacrifice of the natural environment and the battles with the Owens Valley farmers in the legislature and on the land itself. The Department of Water and Power (DWP) and the old city oligarchy battled over whether the hydroelectricity needed for irrigation, industry, and the lighting of the city at night ought to be under public or private control. With the support of the Chamber of Commerce and the Merchants and Manufactures Association, the DWP won referendums in Los Angeles, Burbank, and neighboring cities in 1925–1926 that created the Metropolitan Water District (MWD). After the legislature enacted a bill, the Metropolitan Water District became the largest non-federal government agency in the United States.[7]

As the quintessential United States city of the twentieth century, Los Angeles owed a significant portion of its expansion to effective advertising campaigns. Many of the newcomers who flooded the area from New England, Midwestern, and Southwestern farms arrived after hearing booster campaigns trumpet the promise of Los Angeles. Groups like the All-Year Club advertised Los Angeles as the place to offer middle-class horticulturists time for the finer things in life. Retirees and people searching for quiet Anglo-Saxon civilization constituted the majority of the early migrants. These people generally opposed the presence of the motion picture industry in their "Eden," because actors had a reputation as nomadic and promiscuous.

During the 1910s, the regularity of employment in the Hollywood movie industry enabled many performers and workers to settle permanently in Los Angeles. However, no single area of the city developed as the location for the big-name stars and their splendid houses. While Wallace Reid lived north of Hollywood Boulevard, Roscoe "Fatty" Arbuckle lived on West 5th Street and actresses Constance Talmadge and Lillian and Dorothy Gish lived on different portions of West 6th Street. This dispersal presumably discouraged companies from printing materials that sold star house tours to audience members. Few Hollywood homes of the era had the palatial size or flamboyant style that drew and held audiences' interests. A house of that stature, such as comedian Charles Chaplin's palatial house on top of a hill, was rare enough to even fascinate industry insiders, such as actress Miriam Cooper Walsh.[8]

Over the next two decades, Hollywood homes and the citizenry's attitude toward the movie industry changed greatly. In the 1920s and 1930s, an average of 350 people migrated daily to the 451 square miles that encompassed Los Angeles. The city grew in all directions, but the most lucrative areas proved to be in the city's north and west sections. These became the areas where the motion picture industry stars lived.

Promotional materials described Hollywood as "Los Angeles's Palatial Residential District." They claimed a homeowner could travel abroad for a year and return to discover his property had increased significantly in value during his absence. Wealthy motion picture industry celebrities moved into large houses in Los Angeles's canyons, hills and valleys. The stars forged the exclusive residential areas of Beverly Hills, Bel Air, Brentwood, and Malibu to the west and Los Feliz to the north. Up and coming people in the industry sought large, Mediterranean-style houses with arches in the construction to create the "right" image. These homes contained swimming pools, elaborate furnishings, and a household staff.

The Hollywood celebrity house images linked the stars' wealth to the cultural belief that everybody has a chance at the American dream. Maps with listings of star homes began to appear in fan magazines and other locations. The audiences wanted to see the homes of the stars and the industry actively promoted their interest with images that made those star homes appear more exciting than the houses of the country's tycoons and political elites.[9]

Palatial Mansions Across the U.S.

Hollywood homes competed with the mansions of the wealthy in other cities for media space and audience attention. Media outlets most frequently depicted the homes of wealthy and prominent Americans. The earliest publications of people and their houses appeared in books that featured Americans of notable achievements. Published in the 1850s, the books, *Homes of American Authors* and *Homes of American Statesmen*, promoted the role of humble homes in shaping the positive development of great Americans, including Nathaniel Hawthorne, George Washington, and Thomas Jefferson. Publishers continued printing new editions of these two books through the 1920s.

Other publications emerged that showed how homes forged the honest and clean lives of more specific groups of people. The categories of people ranged from classical music composers to Californians. On rare occasion a book featured the home of a little known person. One of these works presented the home of a religious and good "common folk" person. The story featured a maiden woman known to all her neighbors as an angel of mercy. The story of this good woman's house represented an effort on the part of the author and publisher to demonstrate the great reach of God's will and reinforce the importance of good character.[10]

Near the end of the nineteenth century, media images, particularly in magazine articles, portrayed houses and homes as serving a different purpose. Houses no longer were key to shaping the moral character of a great person. Instead they demonstrated the homeowner's high status in the community. Popular magazines regularly ran stories featuring people and their residences. Most of the articles described the mansions of the elite and nouveau riche in urban and suburban communities around the nation. These homes suggested palaces and manors of Old Europe, striving to present elegance and historical roots that demonstrated the class and importance of the owner. The owners favored for their residences architectural styles such as Second Empire, Romanesque, or Renaissance that carried connotations of power. Most significantly, these depictions of the social elite households presented spotlessness, order, and tranquility as the foremost personality traits and values of their owners.

In the early twentieth century, the way a house demonstrated status began shifting. The house's stylish echoes of the architectural past as the main interest lost out to two different factors. One method centered on the adoption of the modern. A few houses of the prominent moved toward newer architectural styles, such as Arts and Crafts. The sharp angles and repetitive linear forms distinguished these houses from the majority. These places also set their owners apart by creating the impression that innovation and adventure figured into their personalities. More frequently, media depictions of prominent people's homes involved showing them inside very large and expensive houses, demonstrating their ranking through the size and cost of their homes.[11]

The vast majority of magazine articles about houses during the first decades of the twentieth century featured males and married couples. Prior to 1918, approximately 93 percent of these articles featured society and businessmen and married couples. Among the few female representations, only one was a single woman. Between 1919 and 1941, the percentage of representations of women and houses climbed to 12 percent and over one-third of these women were single or identified by first names rather than their husbands' last names.

Several of these images featured women who worked in the entertainment field, particularly the motion picture industry. These articles about homes owned by women rarely discussed these women's attitudes or their position as homeowner. Some articles even established in the first sentence that the owner was a married woman. In one of these articles the woman homeowner receives scant mention while the piece described the actions of every man who enters the house, including something as mundane as sitting upon the large sofa in the back room. Most every article concerned itself with describing the design and decoration of the home and how it reflected the social status of the owner.[12]

Magazines also included regular sections that offered readers brief peeks at homes owned by people other than the wealthy. Magazines such as Ladies Home Journal and Delineator featured sections entitled, "Department of House Decoration" and "Home Building" that included short pieces or single pages with information about "average" homes. The pieces discussed interior decoration, home upkeep, and home maintenance. Accompanying photographs and drawings showed typical fireplaces, mantles, staircases, and decorations. However, they rarely included insight into the personalities of the homeowners or the influence of the house upon their lives.[13]

Depictions of houses and proper family life also appeared in pamphlets and bulletins that received wide-scale distribution through the efforts of organizations and associations. They did not present individual homes and homeowners, but did feature a vision of the house and home. The American Federation of Labor publications on issues such as the eight-hour day and women's protection laws promoted the male as the single-wage earner and the female as the housewife and mother. Associations involved with the woman's suffrage movement also printed broadsides that placed women in the home and valued her responsibilities for housekeeping, child rearing, and family morals.[14]

Hollywood's Everyday Homes

Articles and photographs featuring Hollywood homes appeared in a variety of magazines and newspapers, particularly with the increased focus on the private lives of motion picture people at the end of World War I. The depictions featured details about the interior and exterior of the homes, providing readers with the ability to imagine that they were visiting the house. Like the images of homes from other cities, the details about the home's style and décor demonstrated the owner's wealth and community status.

Hollywood star home images provided more than the details describing architecture and interior decoration. They presented the people inside the homes in much greater detail than any of these other images of houses. The details also provided insight into the owner's personality. The insight into the star's personality offered audience members the thrill that came with the belief that they shared an increased sense of intimacy with the Hollywood figure.

The vast majority of the stories about Hollywood houses described the homes of movie stars. The publicity wanted to use the house to show those parts of the star's personality that would appeal to the performer's fan base. An article on Paramount's "action" hero Jack Holt described the outside of the house more than the interior. The piece informed readers that the grounds around Holt's big, rambling house contained a tennis court, gardens, and a small playhouse set in a grove of eucalyptus trees for his three children. "There was a hospitable atmosphere about his California home which suggested that its owner came from down south.... Mr. Holt was fond of his home and he loves the real, the simple, the sane things of life.... His company, wife and children like him...." The article depicted Holt as a rugged, down-to-earth family man.

Actors Douglas Fairbanks and Mary Pickford composed the first family of Hollywood during the 1920s and early 1930s. The owners of one of the earliest and most frequently depicted Hollywood homes, the couple started the migration to Beverly Hills. Articles often described their enormous home as situated atop a climbing road, behind a white wall, a little like the Tuscan Hills. The theme that this Hollywood house presented the best of "civilization" continued in the descriptions of the house's interior, such as "...the rooms ... furnished with eighteenth-century treasures, with cabinets full of white jade, blond de chine and Waterford glass...."

These decorations demonstrated the couple's high status and good taste while providing hints about their personalities. Indeed, the reporter assured readers that their personalities were excellent, stating that the stars were so captivating that she needed to briefly stop the conversation so she could see Fairbanks's Chinese dressing room and Pickford's collection of Cinderella slippers.[15] These last items separated the couple's personalities and made each appear unique yet similar to the way their fans preferred to view each star.

Occasionally, the depictions of Hollywood homes featured the residences of unmarried stars. Like Hollywood house publicity for married stars, these articles also featured descriptions of the house's elegance and revealed some aspect of the star's personality. An article on Gloria Swanson's magnificent new home in Beverly Hills included a tour of the home that also displayed the "best of civilization" theme. The reporter, Adela Rogers St. Johns, showed appreciation for the beautiful art glass windows, peacock silks, velvet carpets, and gleaming silver and glass and linens. The reporter noted that this glamorous house matched Swanson's personality. She then assured readers that this glamour and her personality made Swanson a great lady, before describing the star's failed first marriage and subsequent divorce. The descriptions of Swanson's Hollywood homes illustrated that being married was not mandatory in Hollywood. In Hollywood, a woman who failed in her gender role as wife and homemaker remained a great lady and worthy of admiration rather than a failure in those roles the culture viewed as essential for a woman to fulfill.[16]

Images of women as owners of homes appeared more often in Hollywood house articles than in those from other cities. The movie industry offered women one of the few communities and businesses in which they could thrive during the era. Studios hired women as actresses, screenwriters, directors, editors, and artisans. Several positions provided women with careers and an income large enough to live independently, sometimes in great wealth.[17] The depictions of a few actresses, screenwriters, and a director within their homes featured decorations and activities that put these Hollywood bohemian personalities on display. These Hollywood bohemians, both on-screen performers and behind-the-scenes workers, formed a "bachelor chic" that gave star home images an association with lesbians and lesbian activities. This made these houses appear titillating, cool, and stylish. The images of the bachelor chic homes can be grouped into two clusters: homes of actresses and homes of behind-the-scenes creative people. The images of the homes of performers confirmed long-held perceptions of actresses as wild women.

On-Screen Chic: Playing It Their Way

The profession of actress had a tradition of sexual license and "immorality." This perception had such strength in the nineteenth century U.S. that many middle-class Americans forbade their daughters to join the profession.[18] Some publicity used this cultural "understanding" of actresses to promote the mystique of Hollywood star homes. One set of publicity items featured the star home of a famous stage actress who moved to Hollywood in the late 1910s. The actress's interviews while on Broadway presented her as exotic but did not focus on the clothes she wore around her house. These articles also did not provide descriptions of her style, which carried hints of lesbianism.

Contemporary publicity promoted Russian-born Alla Nazimova as a precocious child who spoke two languages fluently at age ten. The youngest sibling of an indiscreet mother and brutally violent father, Mariam Edez Adelaida Leventon lived in Switzerland after her parents divorced. Back in Yalta with her pharmacist father and stepmother, Adel, Alla now joined a conservatory in Odessa to expand her skills as a violinist. Her abilities enabled her to be accepted in a school in Moscow to continue her studies. After abruptly switching over to acting at 17 years old, Alla established herself as the leading woman at the Nemetti Theater Company in St. Petersburg. A world tour playing in *The Chosen People* brought Alla to the United States for the first time. The failed revolution in Russia informed her decision to stay in this new country, and she immigrated in 1905.

The Shuberts saw her perform in New York City's Russian theater. The theatrical magnates promised Nazimova a leading role if she learned the English language in six months. The Stanislavsky-trained actress achieved that goal and later became the leading interpreter of Ibsen on the Broadway stage. Nazimova had immediate success in motion pictures in Lewis J. Selznick's *War Brides* in 1916. Metro Pictures wanted her prestige, so the studio signed her to a contract. That contract granted Nazimova approval over the director, script, and leading man.

Nazimova ranked among the top stars in the annual *Photoplay* popularity poll for three years in the late 1910s. However, after three critical and financial failures and the only moderate box office success of her most recent movie, Nazimova and Metro ended their relationship acrimoniously. Nazimova seized the production and financial responsibilities for her next motion pictures.

The actress and her art director, Natacha Rambova, who was discussed in the preceding chapter, combined to make their vision of the movies. In 1921, they made *Camille*, starring Rudolph Valentino opposite Nazimova. Two years later they released *Salome*, based on the Oscar Wilde play. They produced an art film with Art Deco styling and the casting of drag queens among the ladies of Herod's court. The movie caused such a stir that newspaper articles detailed the responses the National Board of Review of Motion Pictures received to their questionnaire about *Salome*. The movies produced miserable box office returns. The actress sold her estate and returned to the stage for over a decade.[19]

During her early successful years Nazimova attracted a fair share of fan interest. The tabloid gossip columns suggested Nazimova's Hollywood bohemian status, stating that "[there are] rumors around that Nazimova has adopted trousers while lounging at the studio." The actress expanded upon that on various occasions. She met the media at the premiere for *Camille* in an opera cloak and short-cropped hair, dangling a long cigarette holder, and informed them, "I want to play a boy in my next picture." Nazimova's Hollywood bohemian panache most readily appeared in publicity pieces about her home.[20]

Befitting her position as movie star, Nazimova built herself a mansion. She named the place the "Garden of Allah," adding the "h" to her given name to associate it with the garden hostelry of sacred and profane love in Robert Hichens's 1904 novel *The Garden of Allah*. The star was an industry leader in the movement west of downtown Hollywood and the transformation of Sunset Boulevard into the Sunset Strip discussed in the nightlife chapter. She expanded her domicile, forming a development and operating company, and turned her homestead into a complex of villas. These twenty-five bungalows lined the largest swimming pool in Hollywood. Shaped like an eight on its side, the pool reminded Nazimova of the Black Sea of her homeland. These activities illustrated both the star's very strong business sense and her desire to exert control over her home and land.

Other aspects of her personality came out during this move. Nazimova showed her ambition and her desire to be a Hollywood bohemian. The actress maintained a mysterious relationship with her "husband" Charles Bryant during her years in Hollywood, while engaging in affairs with men as well as women. The Garden became known in the industry for the "8080 Club," a group of Nazimova's friends who met regularly at the star's home and enjoyed ribald activities. After Nazimova left Hollywood in the mid–1920s, her home-

Alla Nazimova enjoys the grounds at the Garden of Allah (Library of Congress).

stead became an apartment complex for many of the workers who came to Hollywood during the first years of the talkies.

Media descriptions of Nazimova in her house followed the pattern of describing the house's elegance and its reflection of its owner's personality. In his article for *Photoplay* magazine, reporter Herbert Howe described the home and décor using the "best of civilization" terms. Like other Hollywood home publicity, the piece described how the décor reflected Nazimova's personality. Howe mentioned the purple of great divans and the crystal lights reflected from a mirror laced with gold. He stated that the house "contrives to give the appearance of age and cloistered privacy. And that's a great piece of histrionism [sic] for a house in Hollywood."

The article featured information about Nazimova's use of her home. It also provided readers with a juicy surprise. As the head of her own production company, Nazimova decided that this type of publicity was beneficial to her image and would make her movies successful. Howe observed her masculine attire as he sat within the living room of Nazimova's house:

> "She enters whistling," I observed aloud. Nazimova made a move and twirled into the corner of a divan, drawing her feet up after. The effect was boyish, shining black hair cropped very short and parted on one side, a white Eton collar over a dark blouse, a short plaid skirt and flat-heeled brogues, and an abnormally long cigarette holder properly functioning.[21]

In this paragraph Howe shifted the focus from how the décor reflected the star's personality onto how Nazimova used her home. He revealed that the star wore men's clothing while lounging around her house. This information provided readers with insight into their favorite star. The adoption of men's clothing and a boyish style gave Nazimova a Hollywood bohemian status that made her stand apart from other actresses. Nazimova's player status gave her home the appeal of being a place where the owner acted upon taboo behaviors. Indeed, the reporter confirmed this sense of the star by noting that Nazimova had a dash of diablerie (wickedness) about her — that one could not precisely say that heaven was her home.[22]

In addition to her defiance of norms for female attire, newspaper coverage focused on revealing another of Nazimova's bohemian personality traits. These articles hinted at her preference for the company of women. Gossip columnists observed Nazimova's friendships with young actresses Jean Acker and Dagmar Godowsky. Acker, as we saw in the last chapter, had a love interest with fellow performer Grace Darmond.

Another columnist noted that Nazimova planned to leave the West Coast, the reporter claiming that Mademoiselle Natcha Rambova would probably accompany the star. Nazimova enhanced this perception with forthcoming comments about her friendships with young women. Nazimova told two interviewers that most of her friends were young girls. The star offered insight into her personality and these relationships. "They call me Peter and sometimes Mimi."

Nazimova's first nickname confirmed the reporter Hall's link of the actress to Peter Pan. This nickname strongly suggested a female behaving like a male. The latter nickname referred to the bohemian character of tragic love in the opera and play *La Boheme*.

Metro linked the star's personality and home in gossip regarding Nazimova and women at her home when the studio aimed to attack her after she split with it. One set of reports stated that the star's swimming pool, crowded with Hollywood ingénues, contained underwater lights. Other sources revealed that Nazimova regularly had pool parties at the Garden of Allah on Sundays, often with only women in attendance.[23] These Nazimova items featured the titillation of the release of information about the star's private affairs within the confines of her home.

Readers associated with the wealth and pleasure of Hollywood star homes. They also associated those homes with the ease and hedonism of wearing bathing suits and lounging around in a private back yard. These images turned Nazimova's star home into a spectacular place with the presence of female beauty, wealth, bodily pleasures, and hints of lesbianism and suggested that Nazimova had a Hollywood bohemian sexuality. Indeed, Nazimova and other Broadway theater people could not get over that Hollywood was either a one-night stand or a pleasure resort with the sky the limit.[24] Readers learned that Nazimova took advantage of this land of hedonism, bringing taboo behaviors into her star home.

Her Hollywood bohemian status did not stop Nazimova from enjoying a wildly successful time in Hollywood. The star obtained all the material and emotional advantages from being a big star. Nazimova owned a glorious estate and held other real estate interests. She had such fame that she was known by a single name, had a large number of friends in the industry, and owned her own production company until its movies' lack of success forced the company into bankruptcy.

She returned to the Broadway stage. A few years later, in 1938, Nazimova pushed director George Cukor, a leader in the industry's homosexual circles, to bring her back to Hollywood to serve as the technical advisor on the motion picture *Zaza*. She returned to a villa in the Garden of Allah with her longtime female companion Glesca Marshall and appeared in small character roles until her death in 1945.

A variety of Hollywood personalities from Nazimova's first and second periods in the movie industry commented on her sexual activities. As mentioned in the previous chapter, figures from Nazimova's second era, such as George Cukor, attested to her lesbian affairs. Another person familiar with the actress, photographer Cecil Beaton, confirmed of her affairs with screenwriter Mercedes De Acosta and actresses Marlene Dietrich and Greta Garbo. Although a teen during Nazimova's first time in Hollywood, Douglas Fairbanks Jr. also confirmed these affairs.

Testimony of the star's various sexual interests also came from two of her lovers. Cameraman Paul Ivano asserted his own amorous relationship with the Russian star. The most telling comment upon the star's love relationships comes from a woman who claimed to be one of Nazimova's lovers, Mercedes De Acosta. Her memoir, published in 1960, contained strong suggestions and clues to their relationship. The images of this screenwriter will be analyzed later in this chapter.[25]

Writers of the last decade have focused on Nazimova's sexuality. They dubbed her the doyenne of lesbians in Hollywood and observed her use of the term "sewing circle." Apparently the star used the term to describe a sapphic set that met at the Garden of Allah. Her biographer Lambert noted that Nazimova had affairs with men and women, ranging from Ivano to Acker. During the last decade and a half of her life, Nazimova forged a long-term relationship with a companion, Glesca Marshall, a performer on Broadway from 1927 to 1929.[26]

A few years after Nazimova's star faded, another actress on MGM's lot created such excitement in her movies that the public wanted to know about her home life. "One of her favorite amusements is throwing a huge medicine ball, weighing fifteen pounds or so. She would hurl it about her garden, flattening shrubs, flowers and bushes." Wilhelm Sorenson, the son of a Swedish millionaire, and English actor John Loder described the star's actions in masculine terms. "Garbo strides along like a man and fairly races over the ground," Sorenson stated. "She plays tennis like a man, too," added Loder. "Garbo was not at all domestic and never puttered around the house."[27]

In the mid–1920s, MGM signed a Swedish director and his protégé, an actress named Greta Louisa Gustafsson. The youngest of three, she formed an extremely close relationship with her father. She dealt with the double blow of his death and being forced to leave school to help support the family. As a fourteen-year-old she took a job that involved lathering males in a barber shop. She switched to a clerk position in a department store in Stockholm, Sweden. The store officials put her in a few of the filmed advertisements that they made to promote their products. A director saw these advertisements and discovered Greta.

Miss Gustafsson made one low-budget movie and received a big part in *Peter the Tramp* in 1922. Greta left her working-class family in Stockholm, Sweden, after winning a scholarship to the Royal Dramatic Theater training school during the early 1920s. While training, she met the renowned Finnish director Mauritz Stiller. Formerly a stage actor, Stiller left Finland for Sweden in the early 1910s and began screenwriting before turning to directing movies. At the Academy, Stiller taught Garbo to act for the movies. Impulsive, possessive and cruel on the set, he acted pompous off the lot as he staked a position of one of Sweden's top moviemakers by the early 1920s. He gave his new protégé a difficult time on and off the set. He also renamed her Greta Garbo.

In 1924, Louis B. Mayer came to Berlin seeking talent to bring back to Hollywood. When Mayer offered the director a contract, Stiller insisted upon bringing Garbo with him. Stiller struggled with a loss of control to the studio bosses and hierarchy. He continued to exert his influence over Garbo, getting her teeth fixed and hair coiffed. He also controlled what she said and in one zany story followed her to John Gilbert's mansion, reportedly disrupting the Gilbert-Garbo coupling for that night.

While Stiller barely completed two motion pictures as he fought with MGM executives, Greta also struggled to find a niche. MGM tried a range of things including bathing suit publicity shots as the studio executives struggled to find an image for her. After Garbo made a splash in her first motion picture, *The Torrent*, the shy actress insisted on not talking to the media. The MGM publicity department used this part of her personality to promote an image of Garbo as the Swedish Sphinx. The studio and media built upon this image of Garbo as mysterious. The actress made the transition into sound motion pictures and enjoyed nearly a decade of success.[28]

Garbo and her mannish clothes forged an image that the photographers wanted to capture. De Acosta, who also donned masculine styles, "...helped her friend Greta after a fan magazine photographer got shot of La Garbo emerging from her Hollywood Boulevard tailor. Now, her friend De Acosta emerges first as a lookout." A photograph caption screamed, "Garbo in pants!" imitating the way MGM's publicity department promoted the star's first talking picture. The item continued, "Innocent bystanders gasped in amazement to see Mercedes De Acosta and Greta Garbo striding swiftly along ... dressed in men's clothes."

The images associated the Hollywood streets with women that bent the conventions of gender. Their cross-dressing carried humor. It also may have indicated a pair of women who shared "same-sex interest"; perhaps the two women were a romantic couple themselves. The Hollywood streets acquired a reputation as wild and different. They were locations where readers "saw" people from the sexual underground.

Studio officials waited a few days after the release of the initial publicity. Then they issued a press release. This press release apologized under Garbo's name for inflicting her "trousered [sic] attitude" on hostesses and escorts. The release had an odd timing for an apology, coming out days later, after most people had forgotten the incident. The release almost seemed timed to remind people of the incident, generating the benefits of the original publicity again. In addition, it apologized not to the general public, but to certain people, who either worked in the hospitality industry or went out on the town with the star. The naming of these workers conveyed information to the reading public, informing them that Garbo affected her "trousered attitude" in Hollywood's nightclubs, restaurants and hotels. This provided the public with the joy of receiving additional information about the star, her activities and the way she dressed and looked while going about Hollywood. The apology also linked the Hollywood night world discussed in chapter one with a cross-dressing woman, adding to its cache.[29]

The image of Garbo out on the town was one of the few publicity pieces that emerged about the private, mysterious Garbo. The limited information about the star only enhanced the value of those images that did emerge. It also fueled an increased interest in her private activities and living circumstances. This intensified the allure and excitement associated with learning about Garbo's home.

Photoplay magazine commissioned Swedish writer Rilla Palmberg, who was writing a book about Garbo, to write articles on the actress's private life. Palmberg persuaded two friends of Garbo's to explain to her legion of fans how this elusive and alluring person lived when off screen. The stories of the athletic, outdoorsy star illuminated that Garbo stretched the culture's accepted behaviors for women. The actress was a Hollywood bohemian who cared more about "masculine" outdoor activities than "feminine" things like interior decoration. The actress created a vision of the glamorous on-screen romantic star whose off-screen personality made her star home appear more like the house of a male athlete.

Additional images of Garbo's house showed how the star used the interior while associating the star with more taboo behavior. Garbo enjoyed being with herself, but she also enjoyed having friends at her home. The article teased readers with alluring revelations that Garbo decorated her home with gifts from friends that carried suggestions of homosexual interest in her bedroom.

> Garbo had guests over for luncheons somewhat frequently. On one occasion, Sorenson gave Garbo a drawing of her in a trench coat, derby, and men's shoes. It had its basis in a Swedish folk-story that had an old man as its hero. The star framed the sketch and placed it on her favorite table beside her bed. Other friends knew she was fond of pansies and violets and often sent the flowers to her. A bunch of violets almost always appeared at the head of her bed.... When her manservant brought her [men's] shoes, the star laughed, "Just the kind for us bachelors, eh?"[30]

The presence of the violet was a well-known symbol for lesbianism during that era. This link blossomed with Edouard Bourdet's international success, *La Prisonnaire*. This play used violets to illustrate the presence of lesbianism. *La Prisonnaire* appeared in Europe and had a long run on Broadway as *The Captive* until the police closed it down in 1927. Over the next decades, many women would not purchase violets because of *The Captive*, even within sophisticated circles decades later. However, Garbo received them as gifts and kept a vaseful near her bed.[31]

The article claimed that the gifts represented Garbo's personality, with its Hollywood bohemian nature. Besides the violets, the drawing and story suggest that Garbo envisioned herself as a man. Her comment to the servant reinforced this perception. Indeed, his presence indicated that Garbo had a manservant rather than a housekeeper or female dresser, the type of help a woman would usually hire. She appeared to be more comfortable sharing her house with another "single man." Garbo probably forged a relationship with him similar to the one between a male master and his valet, appreciating his advice on common apparel. Adding the taboo homosexual interest to Garbo's adoption of "male" behaviors gave the star's Hollywood home the excitement of forbidden pleasures. The information about Garbo's Hollywood bohemian personality made a home that already drew public fascination into a sight like no other.

Unfortunately for the star, world events disrupted her as a market force. The start of World War II paralyzed the actress on both a professional and personal level. This war closed the European markets where Garbo's movies earned profitable box office returns. The studio tried to push her away from mystery and androgyny into a more straightforward character. However, Garbo, her friend and advisor screenwriter Salka Viertel, and George Cukor created the unqualified disaster of a movie known as *Two-Faced Woman* (1941). As a result of these changes, Garbo retired from the screen at the close of that year.

The contemporaries of the actress knew of Garbo's activities and found they meshed with her image. Barbara Stanwyck provided insight in an interview. "I heard that Dietrich, Greta Garbo, most of the girls from Europe swing either way. Then I found out it's true." Intrigued with this response the interviewer asked, "You found out...?" Stanwyck cried out, "Next!" Actress Agnes Moorehead, whose career in Hollywood began with the movie *Citizen Kane* in 1941, identified herself as a lesbian. She said in an interview, "Garbo, Gish, Dietrich, Jean Arthur, Kay Francis, Stanwyck, Bankhead, Del Rio, Janet Gaynor all enjoyed lesbian or bi relationships." Director Vincent Sherman noted that he could recognize homosexual women by their butch qualities, such as mannish suits and they way they walked around. He mentioned Dorothy Arzner and Greta Garbo as homosexual women. The star's close friend, director George Cukor, also confirmed the star's lesbian interests.[32]

Most of the biographers and others who have written about the Swedish star concur that the images represent Garbo's off-screen love interests. One quoted Garbo's reaction to Marie Dressler, a large, middle-aged actress.

> I will never forget her warm body, simple love, wisdom, and perceptive, friendly attitude toward me. She gave me the opportunity to meet other women and displayed great love for all her friends. She taught me not to be ashamed of this kind of love.

The actresses often left the *Anna Christie* set and went to Garbo's home together.

Dressler had fun with the supposed knowledge she had accumulated as Garbo's co-worker. In her second autobiography, Dressler analyzed Garbo as a lonely person. She promised readers to explode a Garbo myth that had been whispered and even shouted in certain quarters. She followed with an explanation that the Swedish star's feet were not big and unbeautiful.

One of the few biographies about the Canadian actress Dressler did not provide telling detail regarding the relationship between her and Garbo. However, she did express doubt about the intimate relationship. Dressler, who was over 60 years old when filming *Anna Christie* with Garbo, enjoyed and even preferred the company of women, including famous "bachelors." She met a 35-year-old divorcee, actress Claire Du Brey, in 1928. Du Brey played "vamps" in ten to fifteen silent films a year from 1917 to 1920 before getting cast in one to two small roles per year during the late 1920s. Dressler developed a highly emotional relationship with Du Brey. Their long-term companionship seemed validated when Du Brey described how nervous she and Dressler were at the opening of *Anna Christie*. The pair held hands so tightly that Dressler's ring was imprinted on Du Brey's finger for days.[33]

Presumably, a Garbo-Dressler affair did not occur. However, two scholars of lesbians in Hollywood and lesbian imagery in movies agree that the Swedish star had two great loves in her life: screenwriters Mercedes De Acosta and Salka Viertel. As noted earlier, the various images of De Acosta in Hollywood that emerged will be examined later in this chapter.

Salka Viertel arrived in Hollywood with her screenwriter husband Berthold and their three young sons. A theater actress who performed in Berlin and Vienna with noted companies, she reputedly had a love affair with a beautiful actress in her Düsseldorf, Germany, repertory company. When the family moved to the United States, the forty-year-old began working as a researcher and writer for MGM. She and Garbo shared a Middle European vitality and intellect. They spent a lot of time together and were greatly responsible for the cross-dressing and woman-to-woman love scene that appeared in *Queen Christina* (1933).[34]

The biographer for screenwriter Mercedes de Acosta viewed Viertel and de Acosta as rivals for Garbo's affection and attentions. He observed that the Viertels enjoyed an open marriage. They both pursued relationships with other people but at core remained steadfastly committed to each other and their marriage. De Acosta biographer Schanke argued that the marriage offered Garbo greater protection and boundaries for Salka's doting that the actress did not receive from the unrelenting Mercedes.[35]

A Garbo-Viertel affair lacked significant tangible evidence, according to two more recent biographers. Neither did they find similar proof for most of Garbo's reputed other love affairs. They agree that the star felt socially more comfortable around women and homosexual men. Paris concluded that after Stiller's death and the end of her affair with actor John Gilbert, Garbo moved on discreetly to women. The author found proof of only one lesbian affair that the actress had while acting in Sweden, years before coming to Hollywood. Paris observed circumstantial evidence for another three love affairs. Swenson observed that Garbo's male friends viewed Garbo as bisexual. Notwithstanding

Mercedes De Acosta's book, she concluded that little existing factual evidence accounted for Garbo's lesbian affairs. Swenson argued that what did survive were the images in the movies that offer some sense of Garbo holding such an interest. Those movie images do survive along with the press images described above, all of which might indicate Garbo's interest and attitudes if not account for her love affairs.[36]

While not a world-famous movie star like Nazimova or Garbo, comedienne Patsy Kelly received press coverage that described her home life. The Brooklyn-born Bridget Sarah Veronica Rose Kelly received the nickname from her brother Willie, who said she was always the patsy. The daughter of a garage foreman and housewife from Ireland, she moved with the family to Manhattan's Hell's Kitchen as a toddler. Being a wild child with little interest in school, Patsy drove her mother Delia crazy. She placed Patsy in Jack Blue's Dancing School to keep her off the streets of the rough neighborhood. Within a few years, the thirteen-year-old befriended the future movie star Ruby Keeler and became an instructor in pivoting and tapping.

Kelly's brother Willie brought his sister into contact with vaudevillian Frank Fay. Patsy's publicity is conflicting as to the way her brother brought the pair together. Regardless of these circumstances, a teenaged Patsy Kelly found herself playing the straight woman to a deadly ad-libber with an insouciant Irish charm. Fay soon discovered Kelly could match his ad libs and they often veered wildly from the script, to the amusement of their audiences. The verbal beating on stage and frequent firings and re-hirings lasted three years. After leaving Fay for the last time, Patsy landed several legitimate stage gigs.

As Patsy performed in *Three Cheers* on Broadway in late 1932, she caught the interest of Hal Roach. The producer of the short "three-reel" comedies that preceded the feature movie on a theater's bill, Roach saw the dynamic five-foot, three-inch, 136-pound Kelly as a match for his comedienne Thelma Todd. He convinced Kelly to give Hollywood a try.

The pair worked well together and established a friendship off screen as well. Kelly's success with Roach led to the major studios wanting her to play character roles in their movies. Her first feature movie was *Going Hollywood*, a movie about movie-making that will be examined for its Hollywood bohemian images in the next chapter. Kelly also found an old friend from New York City in Hollywood, female impersonator Jean Malin. As discussed in the nightlife chapter, Malin attended the dinner parties of Hollywood stars, and Kelly often accompanied him as his escort. The pair and Malin's roommate left the Ship Café after Malin's performance. Malin accidentally accelerated the car in reverse, and the trio plunged off the pier. Malin drowned, but Miss Kelly was rescued when lifeguards extricated her from the submerged machine.

Two years later, Kelly experienced another personal loss. Thelma Todd was murdered outside her café in late 1935. Patsy gained weight and sank into a depression. After regaining her composure, Kelly returned to the screen and continued to play the wisecracking friend in many motion pictures into the early 1940s. "The Queen of the Wisecrackers" suddenly disappeared from Hollywood in 1943, and for the next two decades she struggled professionally, surviving with the help of actress Tallulah Bankhead. Kelly appeared in a few television shows a year during the 1960s and returned to the screen in several small roles. She enjoyed a career revival with successful Broadway appearances in *No No Nanette* in 1971 and *Irene* in 1973. Kelly died of cancer in Woodland Hills, California, in 1981.[37]

Some images of Kelly offered readers insight that this character actress had a Hollywood bohemian personality. The comedienne defied the typical gender norms of the era in her activities. Articles informed readers that "[Kelly] was a wild kid who preferred boys and their sports to the namby-pamby amusements of other girls of her age and association." The tomboyish Kelly herself noted that she always had an interest in being a fireman and had her own baseball team and gang.

She also displayed this attitude with her lack of interest in certain pursuits associated with women. As a later article observed, "Clothes don't interest her. She claims that she doesn't look good even when she's all dressed up and that buying clothes is a waste of money for her." Another provided a physical description in order to deliver a punch line about her gender-crossing ways. "Patsy herself is no orchid.... She has a round face with a broad forehead and not very much chin. The amount of time Patsy spends worrying about her look amount to about ten minutes every other month. Between those times she can't be bothered." The stories on Kelly revealed that both in physical description and in her lack of interest in traditional female concerns, Kelly defied cultural prescriptions for a woman.[38]

An article on Kelly's star home provided information to her fans regarding Kelly, her personality and her home life. The image expanded upon the view of Kelly as defiant of the norms for women. The comedienne showed no interest in interior decoration, another area considered an activity and interest for women.

> Patsy lives, now, in a low white house in Beverly Hills. With her lives her friend, Wilma Cox, who was on the stage with her in New York. Wilma works occasionally in pictures on the Hal Roach lot. With them ... is a maid ... Patsy's house is all done, inside, in blue and white. Because blue and white are Wilma's favorite colors, not Patsy's....[39]

The article on Kelly's star home also offered readers insight into the character actress's living situation. As an actress in the motion picture industry, Patsy Kelly presumably had no financial need to have a roommate. Indeed, many successful actresses in Hollywood who were unmarried, such as Greta Garbo, lived alone. Having a housekeeper reinforced the idea that Kelly did not have a financial reason for having Wilma in her house. It was possible Kelly offered Wilma a place in her home because she was her friend.

Other facts from the article raised questions about the basis of the living arrangement being either financial or platonic. It would be rare to allow someone staying in the house for a brief period to make interior decorating decisions. These decisions reflected the friend's preferences, suggesting that the friend had a personal stake in this house. This revelation would lead many readers to wonder what type of relationship the two women could have had if Wilma's desires were so important to Patsy. The most logical conclusion to draw interpreted the pair as girlfriends and Hollywood bohemians, linking their home to a culturally taboo sexuality.

The article described other features in the house that revealed Kelly's personality and made her home appear more spectacular. "Patsy has a radio in every room of her house. She has made her large patio into a game room. There, besides the radio, are games of all kinds, a bar." The image noted that the comedienne cared about having entertainment and amusements in her home. She enjoyed having friends over to play, party and drink. She made that interest apparent in response to the usual question about marriage. Kelly stated, "Often Wilma and I have a few folks in for the evening, not picture folks very often. I like my life. I'm happy."[40]

The description of people enjoying home amusements made Kelly's star home appear as a place of fun and games. The house appeared more exciting because the people playing inside were a group of unmarried women who did not follow the clothing or behavior styles associated with women but instead wore men's clothing. This made Kelly's house appear to be the place where the chic bachelors came to play.

Gossip columns also offered readers insight into Kelly's friendships and the community of female homeowners in Hollywood. "Patsy Kelly and Helen Ainsworth went to actress Queenie Smith's Malibu beach house to help swish an extra coat of paint and be rewarded with a buffet supper."[41] This gossip item placed Kelly among her friends, women who exerted control over their house and environment. They chose to paint their house themselves rather than hire someone or have male friends do the work. The item created a unique scene of three Hollywood actresses who defied the norms for women as they painted and controlled their environments. The images of Kelly, like those of Nazimova and Garbo that preceded her, showed the actress in total control of her residence and environs.

Hollywood contemporaries of Kelly knew her to be a lesbian. Columnist Lee Graham observed that Kelly lost her position in Hollywood in 1943 because of her behavior. "Hollywood wouldn't forgive was that she went around with mannish women, wore slacks in public, cursed and swore, and told off color jokes at lesbian bars and clubs. They figured she was a scandal waiting to happen."[42]

Writers today also see a direct connection between these images of Kelly and her same-sex interests and actions. In his analysis of the impact of gays and lesbians on the movie industry, William Mann noted that Patsy Kelly and Wilma Cox lived openly as lovers. In his work on female stars who loved other women, Axel Madsen noted that the actress did not belong to the Hollywood sewing circle. However, he noted that Kelly was lesbian and included a small section describing Kelly's career and love life. During an interview in the early 1970s, Kelly heard the marriage question again, this time asking if she would have married a heterosexual. Slightly confused initially, Kelly rallied. "I'm a dyke. So what? Big deal." Only a work devoted solely to character actors merely mentioned that Kelly never married.[43]

Media depictions of Alla Nazimova, Greta Garbo and Patsy Kelly in their star homes presented the actresses in a manner that befitted their exalted status as Hollywood movie stars. The images expanded upon the usual star home publicity's discussions of home décor and household activities that provided revelations of about the star's personalities. The Hollywood bohemian star home images titillated audiences with the knowledge that these alluring and powerful women used their luxurious residences to defy the culture's norms for women and to pursue a taboo sexuality among a community of women.

The images revealed that in their star homes these actresses directed their off-screen lives. Nazimova demanded that a woman be viewed as a person first and foremost and insisted that she have the freedom to defy convention. "A woman living a creative life is bound, necessarily, to do things sometimes defiant to convention. In order to fulfill herself, she should live freely. Children bring fear and in that way arrest personal development." Nazimova's position regarding women's domestic role was unique even among women who identified themselves as feminists during the 1920s.[44]

Greta Garbo defied the cultural convention that women needed to marry. Beginning in the early 1930s, the press began asking the star when she would marry. One newspaper article noted that Garbo stated in a husky contralto, "No, I am not ever to marry." That did not stop the prying media.

As the highly private star aged, the issue of her marriage became more important to the media and their audiences. Reporters questioned Garbo about the time she spent with conductor Leopold Stokowski. A *Los Angeles Examiner* reporter ambushed Garbo in order to get an answer on this question. "No, no—I will not marry Mr. Stokowski. These rumors are absurd. I won't deny that Mr. Stokowski and I are very good friends, but as for marriage to him — no. That is out of the question." Caught by surprise, the star demonstrated how deeply she valued living at home as a "bachelor." She expressed her desire to live in the family of her choice rather than according to society's expectations.

Comedienne and character actress Patsy Kelly followed the defiance of convention in her own manner. As a comedienne, Patsy Kelly faced fewer questions regarding her unmarried status than a romantic star such as Garbo. Kelly took the opportunity the question provided to reveal her own interest and happiness. On another occasion she replied with humor, quipping, "No, I can't get up that early." She remained unmarried.[45]

These images of Nazimova and Garbo embodied the possibility that women could escape from men's erotic and economic control during the era and created a powerful anxiety in the culture. A small number of women writers during this era also sought to live more independently. They used feminist language in their writings to attack conventions. However, their efforts sparked personal attacks including images that depicted them as unnatural followed by criticism and the full brunt of social ostracism and legal censorship.[46]

These writers who pushed the culture's boundaries for women's behavior faced intense opposition. How were the Hollywood bohemian actresses received? Scholars have noted that an influential minority of the cosmopolitan chic during the 1920s and 1930s saw lesbianism as glamorous and alluring.[47] However, that was a very small number of people and not even influential enough to help protect the writers from their opponents. The media where images of the actresses appeared, such as fan magazines, sold to larger audiences in order to remain in business. The stories in their pages had to be things readers wanted to see and could not anger them or they would drop their subscriptions.

How did this larger audience of fans enjoy the images of these actresses? Did Nazimova's "flapper" images generate perceptions of allure among the readers or were they reading to emulate the cosmopolitan chic? Did Garbo's bachelor tossing a medicine ball have a proletarian strength that readers interpreted as chic like the powerful workers depicted in Works Progress Administration sponsored murals? Did Kelly or Nazimova's community of women appeal to a sexual fantasy for homosexually inclined women or heterosexually inclined males or for women who sought a platonic community as they may have had at their women's college or women's club? The Hollywood bohemian images' appearance in mass media suggested that the actresses had this range of appeal to the many audience members who followed their careers.

Behind the Scenes Chic: Making It Their Way

Female homeowners who worked as screenwriters and directors occasionally starred in movie publicity materials from Hollywood. Articles appearing in a wide range of newspapers and magazines offered readers details about the lives of a couple of screenwriters and a director. They revealed personalities that depicted these women as the behind-the-scenes "bachelor chic." These Hollywood bohemians lived in more modest residences that received less media attention than the actresses' homes. Still, the publicity depicted their homes as reflections of their personalities that promoted a belief among audience members that they gained a sense of intimacy with these celebrities. Their

Hollywood bohemian personalities maintained lifestyles that suggested a culturally taboo behavior that made their Hollywood homes appear spectacular.

Like actresses, women screenwriters in the motion picture industry sparked public suspicions about their sexuality. As career women who earned significant incomes, screenwriters faced questions about their attitudes toward their careers, motherhood, and family. A *Photoplay* magazine article realized the need to assure readers that the twelve important screenwriters were "regular" women. A caption noted, "These women were not temperamental 'artistes,' short-haired advanced feminists, not faddists [sic]...." This caption indicated that the readers of the motion picture fan magazines wanted to know about the top women screenwriters' romantic interests and these readers knew about these groups of people like the "artistes" who existed on the culture's margins.

Even Hollywood insiders who were critical of the movie industry and its ballyhoo followed this formula. F. Scott Fitzgerald in his last novel, *The Last Tycoon*, noted that successful screenwriter Jane Meloney received numerous labels, many focused on the private world of her sexuality. "The little blonde of fifty could hear the fifty assorted opinions of Hollywood ... a sentimental dope, the smartest woman on the lot, and of course, nymphomaniac, virgin, pushover, a Lesbian...."[48] The labels reflected the need for people, even within the movie industry, to categorize the woman screenwriter. While some of the labels might have been used to attack her, others appeared to be attempts to understand the wealthy writer. Readers would soon grapple with finding an appropriate label for two female screenwriters after the death of one of their husbands. The extensive coverage in a variety of newspapers of this bizarre love triangle during the late 1920s thrilled readers with its revelations about the private practices of female scribes of the screen.

The Los Angeles police visited screenwriter Beth Rowland at her Hollywood home to deliver the news that her husband, Peter Stratford, had died of tuberculosis. Peter was female, though he pretended to be a man. Rowland explained in the press that her marriage resulted from the love and respect that emerged during a two-year correspondence before Stratford declared "his" love for Rowland. The widow thought Stratford had only a few months to live, so she made her terms clear and accepted his proposal of marriage. Stratford settled in Niles, California, in an effort to ward off the disease, but his condition worsened. His declining circumstances led him to request that his wife establish a home with him.

Rowland left to be with her "husband." She described herself as a platonic wife, nurse, and homemaker to this fastidious gentleman. Then, Rowland discovered that her husband wrote endearing letters to her screenwriter friend Alma Thompson. Rowland requested that the letters stop and believed Stratford's "infidelity" released her from a continuing obligation to him. Shortly afterward, Stratford revealed "his" true sex, and Rowland decided to move to Hollywood and earn money for the two of them. However, Rowland discovered that Stratford continued corresponding with Miss Thompson and supposedly ended her relations with Stratford.[49]

Other figures in this drama of a triangular relationship questioned Rowland's descriptions of her home. J. A. McDonald, the former assistant manager of the nursery where Peter Stratford worked, observed that Peter had no problem moving plants and "...[Stratford] was a woman with no feminine attributes, loving horse races, masculine sports and talking like a man." Within less than two years, McDonald discovered Stratford's biological sex and agreed to keep the secret from the other employees. Was Stratford sickly or was he able to do physical labor? Since he did physical labor for over two years, then did he also want to engage in physical activities with Rowland? McDonald figured out Stratford's biological sex; why couldn't Rowland? Perhaps Rowland had figured him out and decided to form a household with this man.

Richard Rowland, Beth's only child from her first marriage, claimed his mother knew that Peter was a woman soon after the marriage. Beth Rowland explained to her son that she faced a terrible dilemma because she could not desert her physically disabled "husband" and so decided to stay with him.[50] Readers could combine Rowland's admission of her love for Stratford with her discovery of Stratford's female biology to believe that the Hollywood screenwriter loved Stratford regardless of her sex and enjoyed sharing a house with "him."

While an intriguing pairing, the Stratford-Rowland household soon became secondary in the media coverage. The focus of the tabloids became Stratford and the screenwriter Alma Thompson. Employed by a Hollywood studio, Thompson lived in a ranch house in Hollywood, where she engaged in the study of mysticism. Although she claimed to write to Stratford out of sympathy for his affliction, Thompson also sent Stratford secret rose petals. Stratford wrote that Thompson taught him Sufi beliefs and spoke to him with authority. Letters from Stratford to Thompson contained appeals for a deeper love, and Thompson's replies carried the salutations "Dearest Lamb" and "Dear Pedar." Stratford referred to Thompson as "my soul."[51]

These accounts linked revelations of Thompson's exotic personality to her home. The screenwriter used her home to explore her interest in mysticism. The Sufi spirituality that Thompson studied focused on sexuality. This knowledge provided readers with the idea that they went behind the closed doors of the screenwriter's house and gave them the chance to feel the titillation of having both little-known and sexual information.

Readers learned that Thompson pursued her Hollywood bohemian interests from her home. She exchanged deeply emotional letters with a person Thompson knew as the husband of her friend, fellow screenwriter Beth Rowland. Thompson might even have known Stratford to be a biological female if Rowland had confided in her, as many friends would have. Thompson actively engaged in an adulterous emotional affair with a person she believed to be a married man, or knew to be a woman living as a man. This Hollywood bohemian sexuality made Thompson's house spectacular. Thompson's home was a place where women practiced mysticism, where women defied the expectations for their sex and, most excitingly, where three women pursued a love triangle. Fittingly, Alma Thompson's one screen credit came a few years later for a feature entitled *I Loved a Woman* (Warner Bros., 1933).[52]

Another female screenwriter with few credits appeared in several publicity pieces throughout the 1930s. These pieces conveyed the image of Mercedes De Acosta as a Hollywood bohemian. The child of a political rebel from Cuba who fled to the United States and a woman descended from Spanish aristocracy, Mercedes de Acosta's mother called her Rafael. Her mother dressed her in male clothes and encouraged her to believe that she was a boy for several years. Her father worked as a highly paid steamship line executive but never warmed the heart of Mercedes, the last child among two surviving boys and five girls. The family resided in fashionable areas of New York City with Theodore Roosevelt and the William Vanderbilts as neighbors. The family continued to prosper, despite the suicide of her father, Ricardo de Acosta, when Mercedes was a teen.

While her elder sisters where decidedly elegant and fit well within New York City society, Mercedes caught much of her father's rebellious spirit. However, her sister Rita played a significant role in Mercedes's life as a symbol of high society and as a mentor. Mercedes's mother sent her off to a Catholic boarding school outside Paris to acquire femininity. Rita introduced Mercedes to luminaries of the arts and society. Under this tutelage Mercedes acquired skill that helped her as she mixed with Europe's nobles and European and American artists.[53]

The burgeoning playwright returned to New York City. She soon found herself amid the city's art world. De Acosta married painter Abram Poole in 1921, but the pair led separate lives and were divorced in 1935. Meanwhile her professional work as a playwright brought her small measures of success with productions in Paris and London as well as on Broadway. Her connections brought her to the attention of the studios and she signed a contract with RKO in 1930.[54]

Many personal contacts and independent wealth helped de Acosta overcome her tribulations with the movie studios. Theatrical producer and agent Elisabeth "Bessie" Marbury arranged for de Acosta to write at RKO studios on the latest Pola Negri feature in 1930. After RKO dropped that movie, Garbo eventually helped de Acosta obtain a position under Irving Thalberg at MGM. The screenwriter enjoyed a tumultuous professional relationship with the imperious, intuitive "boy wonder" of Hollywood. Their biggest battle centered on de Acosta's script for *Desperate*, a motion picture that would put Garbo in pants. While the actress would eventually don pants a year later in *Queen Christina*, Thalberg did not like either the attire or de Acosta's script.

A year later de Acosta tried again with a similar idea. She approached her friend with a screenplay for *The Life of Jehanne D'Arc*, but this time Garbo refused the script. Although the American Film Institute does not attribute any credits to de Acosta, she listed *The Shining Hour* (MGM, 1938) and *Camille* (MGM, 1936) as scripts to which she contributed.[55] The writer left Hollywood in 1942 and returned to New York City and the theatrical world.

The coverage of de Acosta illustrated the difference between theater and movie publicity. During the years de Acosta spent in the theatrical world, she

Mercedes De Acosta with her friend Theos Bernard, 1941 (courtesy Rosenbach Museum & Library, Philadelphia).

received a limited amount of publicity, and this material rarely resulted in descriptions of the writer's masculine attire. Within a year as a screenwriter in Hollywood, reporter Alma Whitaker visited de Acosta in her home. The reporter immediately offered a description of de Acosta in terms that revealed her Hollywood bohemian nature. Whitaker noted that de Acosta was in her late thirties and "affects the strictly tailored idea, even unto a genuine walking shoe."[56]

Hollywood columns expanded their disclosure of the private de Acosta. These articles informed readers that she established a residence different from other women screenwriters. The Whitaker article told readers that de Acosta lived alone in Hollywood while her husband stayed in New York City. "Miss de Acosta has taken a delightful house at Brentwood Heights, where she is ensconced with her servants and her dogs and she says her stay is indefinite. She also owns a home in New York and an apartment in Paris...." De Acosta appeared to have established a new "family" in Hollywood over which she ruled. The screenwriter expected a long, comfortable stay with them in her new, charming residence without her husband, whom she soon divorced.

Unlike the presentations of many other screenwriters, this depiction did not describe de Acosta's house in feminine terms. Stories featuring woman screenwriters made it a point to show that the screenwriters were still homemakers in their own house. This article, by contrast, stated that the screenwriter had servants who maintained the house.[57] The screenwriter created this life for herself in the hills of Los Angeles County, in an exclusive residential area north and east of Beverly Hills where stars like Gary Cooper and Shirley Temple lived.

The de Acosta house acquired a reputation as a place of sophistication and spectacular chic. Fellow screenwriter Anita Loos noted that she had dinner at Mercedes de Acosta's house and found other evidences of true sophistication in this new Hollywood.[58] A fan magazine article reinforced this sophistication by describing de Acosta as a woman who attained scholastic achievement. She achieved this at a time when few women in the country did so. "Miss d' Acosta [sic] is the author of a brilliant monograph on Benvenuto Cellini, XVI Century Italian artist and writer, and has been on the scenario staffs of several major studios for the past two years. She is a highly cultured and distinguished person."

The screenwriter tried to bring her Hollywood bohemian styling into her work life. A gossip piece noted that "Greta Garbo's 'best pal,' writer Mercedes de Acosta wrote what she thought was a marvelous role for GG.... At the last minute GG turned cool toward the script, Mercedes was offended and a long and loud behind closed doors discussion went on —for days...."[59] The role was as Joan of Arc, a cross-dressing woman with short boyish locks whose spiritual strength helped drive the English out of France in the fifteenth century.

De Acosta achieved fame and generated media interest during her time in Hollywood more from being a confidante and companion to several women in theatrical, artistic, and motion picture circles. Contemporaries knew her image and deduced that it signified a same-sex interest. Marlene Dietrich's daughter Mia Riva despised Mercedes and summed up her look as "[A] Spanish Dracula with the body of a young boy." Others remembered the screenwriter's long-term affair with actress Ona Munson in the late 1930s and into the 1940s.

The more compelling evidence for the depth of the same-sex relationships de Acosta had came from the people involved. In her memoir, published in 1960, de Acosta used code to explain the depth and loving extent of her relationships. She referred to her relationship with Munson as many years of friendship, then described her as "extremely pretty with eyes that touched [me] deeply." De Acosta mentioned that Marlene Dietrich bought her roses. The actress said that she came to see the screenwriter "because I just could not help myself." The screenwriter's limited, veiled suggestions in this book about her relationship with Greta Garbo were enough to infuriate the Swede.[60]

Documents in the collection of the screenwriter's papers strip the veil away. In the notes and telegrams that de Acosta kept from Marlene Dietrich, the actress revealed a tender attachment. One telegram contains an expression in French regarding de Acosta's tenderness. The note that accompanied a dressing gown contained the line, "I adore you forever and miss your hands." One undated correspondence from actress Ona Munson ended, "I love you, I love you, and shall only be 'home' when I am once more in your arms."[61]

The writers on Mercedes de Acosta all agree that she had several prominent loves within the motion picture circle. These female lovers included Alla Nazimova, Greta Garbo, and Marlene Dietrich. Her biographer noted that her affairs with prominent women began years before she arrived in Hollywood, with Nazimova and Isadora Duncan. However, he defined the relationship with Garbo as unpredictable. De Acosta's good friend Ram Gopal informed the screenwriter's biographer that all de Acosta did was dream Garbo. However, the actress feared having her life exposed, making for a problematic match. Perhaps this was so, but the screenwriter found the time to consummate a loving relationship with actress Dietrich as well. Eventually, the screenwriter's cloying emotionalism undid her relationships with both actresses.[62]

Like Alla Nazimova, de Acosta argued for the ability to defy the culture's expectations for a woman's romantic life. She told an interviewer, "Of course, I think matrimony is out of date. I don't approve of it at all.... Divorce ... should be unnecessary. And if matrimony were abolished it would be." Then, de Acosta added that she had no children, noting that she could "imagine how some mothers will feel about me."

The screenwriter and Hollywood bohemian challenged the prevailing family structure of the home. De Acosta did this during the 1930s when the culture strongly encouraged women to limit their aspirations to husband, family, and domesticity. She came across as everything the *Photoplay* magazine piece of ten years earlier denied the twelve women screenwriters were. Still, de Acosta faced no repercussions within or outside the industry as the result of expressing her opinions.[63] The outspoken screenwriter lived in Hollywood over the next decade with big stars Great Garbo and Marlene Dietrich among her circle of friends.

One peripheral member of the sewing circle made her living working in the predominantly male occupation of Hollywood director during the height of the studio era. Born in San Francisco in early 1900, Dorothy Arzner met motion picture industry personalities while waiting tables in the cafe her father bought when the family moved to Los Angeles. She abandoned her medical training and joined the ambulance corps in World War I. When she returned, Arzner decided that she wanted to work in Hollywood. She got work as a continuity supervisor with Alla Nazimova in 1919.

She met screenwriter William de Mille of the famous Players-Lasky Corporation. He helped her get a job at the subsidiary company, Paramount Pictures. She began as a typist, but worked her way up in the industry. At Paramount, Arzner built an association with successful director James Cruze, who raved about Arzner's work as a film editor. She became chief editor in the mid–1920s and pushed those in charge of the studio to make her a director.

Although she faced numerous struggles with studio heads, Arzner directed sixteen motion pictures that bear her credit. Among the most noteworthy were *The Wild Party* (Paramount, 1929), *Craig's Wife* (Columbia, 1936), and *Dance*

Dorothy Arzner-Marion Morgan Home (courtesy Department of Cultural Affairs, City of Los Angeles).

Girl Dance (RKO, 1940). Although poor health ended her career, the wealth she accumulated thorough wise investments enabled her to retire in comfort.[64]

The scholar Judith Mayne focused on some publicity images of the director in her book about Arzner. Mayne observed that the images wavered between describing Arzner's "mannish" attire and styles and granting the director "feminine" qualities. Reporters of the era, such as Herbert Cruikshank, presented the director's attire and tried to mitigate this with appeals to the culturally accepted feminine style. "She wears her clothes with a boyish ease, and despite an apparent distaste for the usual frills and frothy furbelows of femininity, there is a softness in the very severity of her apparel, which is very appealing." Hedda Hopper years later offered a suggestion about Arzner's gender attitudes. "Dorothy is the boyish type, wears her hair in a mannish cut, and favors men-tailored suits and low-heeled shoes."[65]

The reporters of the era exhibited less confusion over Arzner's Hollywood bohemian status when depicting the director within the studio. Columnist Grace Kingsley described Arzner's office as "a place as bare looking and businesslike as a man director's office would be." Gossip columnist Hedda Hopper gleefully reported that Arzner blushed because she did not know the period of her office furniture.[66] A third reporter likened Arzner to a man when she worked on the studio lot.

> To share even one characteristic with the great Napoleon is often the aim of men, but it is the real privilege of one woman in Hollywood, namely Dorothy Arzner, only woman director for Paramount. She resembles the great Corsican in her posture — that of standing with her hands clasped behind her back.[67]

The depictions of Arzner at home showed little ambivalence in describing how Arzner stretched the culture's norms for women. Articles in both *Time* and a fan magazine described Arnzer's home life. The article in *Time* noted that Arzner wore her mannish attire inside her home, which sat on a high hillside that afforded a tremendous view of the valley. The other asked Arzner to explain how she used her home. "Arzner announced that no one could expect her to be a little homemaker.... Her pet aversion is housework in any of its many phases. Dishes, perhaps, are the worst."[68] These presentations depicted Arzner as a woman who wore men's clothing, as a woman who exerted control over her home and as a woman who did not even feign an interest in supposed women's duties, such as household chores. The director Hollywood bohemian thus defied the cultural understanding of the women's role in the house, making Arzner's star home, different in the public's mind.

After images established the director's chicness, Arzner forthrightly addressed her living situation as a bachelor. One early item on the director noted that "Arzner is not married, nor is she engaged." A second piece was more direct about her intentions. "Dorothy is unmarried, and does not plan to marry." As her career reached its height, her choice appeared such a matter of fact that a writer stated, "Away from the camera Miss Arzner ... has never married."

The question of marriage offered the director an opportunity to express her philosophy. She considered herself to be defined not through her marital status but through her personal goals. Arzner declared that her biggest ambition involved "to be a successful woman," and also set as a goal to write a novel.[69] These images depicted Arzner as an independent woman homeowner who planned not to marry.

Contemporaries provided little information about the sexual activities of the director. One of the few instances involved the complaints of Paramount actress Esther Ralston. She wrote in her biography that she resented some of the "sexy scenes Arzner was asking me to do.... The photographing of my backside and the display of my legs just wasn't me!" After their work on the movie *Ten Modern Commandments*, the actress asked not to have to work with Arzner again after the director tried to get Ralston to sit on her lap between takes and insisted on patting and fondling me...."

Arzner's biographer and other Hollywood writers have confirmed that her images matched her sexual activities. Gavin Lambert noted that Arzner had an affair with actress Alla Nazimova when they worked on one movie together. Arzner biographer Judith Mayne emphasized that Nazimova nurtured the career of the younger Arzner and did not consider the relationship primarily sexual. Madsen and Mann both noted that Arzner had affairs with several actresses in Hollywood. They observed that the director formed her most significant relationship with Marion Morgan.

Morgan and her son left New Jersey for southern California in the 1910s. After forming

Dorothy Arzner sitting in Marion Morgan's lap (Library of Congress).

a dance company, Morgan also began working as a dancer and choreographer in the movie industry. She met Arzner on the set of *Man Woman Marriage* in 1921. Morgan and Arzner began an extensive professional partnership and moved in together in the house in the Hollywood Hills. They named their home "Armor," using their last names as actress Mary Pickford and actor Douglas Fairbanks used their surnames for the name of their home.[70]

Arzner and the bachelor chic screenwriters and actresses, as top personalities in the motion picture industry, made noteworthy copy. The women, the studio publicity machines, and the media each contributed to the shaping of the stories about women homeowners in Hollywood who lived as they wanted within their spectacular houses. These Hollywood bohemians differed dramatically from the flapper, the dominant image of the New Woman during the 1920s. The flapper enjoyed more sexual awareness and independence than any group of women had up to that time in the U.S. But much of her sexual gratification focused on pleasing males, and she usually left her job to marry and assume the position of wife and mother.[71]

Bachelor chic created images of women who developed rewarding careers for themselves and strove to improve them. The chic proudly defended their status as unmarried women, and even questioned the institution of marriage.

Bachelor Living in the United States

Images of bachelors and their living quarters occasionally appeared in the mass media during the late nineteenth and early twentieth centuries. Bachelors' rejection of settling down with a wife and kids and buying consumer goods to keep up with the Joneses prompted members of the middle classes to act hostile toward them. Most cultural observers believed bachelors came from the ranks of young men, homosexuals, sailors, and transient workers.

The cultural arbiters in the nineteenth century regarded bachelors warily. These monitors of middle class norms hoped that landladies at the places where bachelors rented rooms exerted social controls over these single males and their activities within their homes. However, in the late decades of the nineteenth century, the belief in this control declined. At the dawn of the twentieth century the bachelors had an established culture with their saloons, "improper conduct" in dance halls, prostitution in back rooms and flophouses. The U.S. cultural arbiters worried that bachelors would poison the mainstream with their culture and associated over-indulgence in the bawdy things.

Designers of living quarters for bachelors interpreted bachelorhood as a short period in a man's life. Fashionable bachelor apartments provided for sleeping and reading. They lacked private kitchens and laundries because the culture expected single men to take their meals at their clubs or with family or friends in private homes. In this way, the bachelors had some exposure to "home comfort" to combat fears that young men would become addicted to the independence of living outside the family structure. Sociologists confirmed the improperness of bachelor living, writing that children were important to all adults because they forced adults to plan and hope for the future and to consider other-directed action.[72]

Bachelors rarely appeared in the presentations of houses in the major periodicals of the era. Approximately two percent of the total images of homes depicted bachelors' residences. Only a few of these made the person's bachelor status the focus of the article. Even these articles catalogued the loneliness of living in a single room and eating bad food.

However, one image published in a magazine for people interested in home decoration made two bachelors' lives appear less bleak. A music arranger and a painter wanted a place near the city yet outside its noise and clutter. The reporter framed their story through the adage in *Poor Richard's Almanac* to "never take a wife until thou hast a house." The article detailed how "the boys" went about building their home. The piece described the colors and furnishings in the house while providing no quotations from either of the men or insight into their characters or relationship. The reporter perhaps offered a suggestion of the latter when he leafed through the bachelors' copy of the almanac and observed that the page containing the adage was not even cut.[73]

The few images in the mass media created the impression that most bachelors lived a difficult life without a real home. The culture expected them to marry a woman after a very short period of living alone, and the limited appearance of bachelor homes in magazines and other media of the day confirmed and reinforced that perspective. The images of Hollywood reflected but also challenged these expectations for bachelors.

The Bachelor Pad: Hollywood's Odd Bedfellows

The movie studios and the media did not create a lot of publicity about bachelors and their living spaces. Most of the depictions highlighted bachelors living extravagantly in luxurious residences. Like the other kinds of Hollywood publicity, these features also focused on the reflection of the celebrity's personality in the décor within his home.

A brief item in a gossip column informed readers that actor Douglass Montgomery rented an ultra-modern house with a swimming pool outside his bedroom window. He christened the place "The Vicarage," probably because he rented the place from someone else. This item linked a Hollywood heartthrob actor with a stylish and luxurious residence, attributing class and taste to him and the industry. The naming of the place provided readers with inside knowledge and the sense that they knew something more about this Hollywood heartthrob through this information about his home.[74]

Images of bachelors occasionally featured the homes of people who stretched conventional norms. A spread on director George Cukor's six-acre estate in West Hollywood centered upon "best of civilization" theme. The article likened Cukor's place to an Italian villa and offered detailed descriptions of its interior treasures. Readers learned that the bachelor Cukor loved to entertain, and his good friend, former actor Bill Haines, transformed Cukor's hillside cottage into an estate. Years before the publication of this piece on Cukor's house, many articles and gossip items hinted about Haines's homosexual interests. Only one year before this article appeared a scandal about Haines's homosexuality erupted in newspapers across the country.[75] This article on Cukor's house offered readers insight into the home and taste of this important director. It also offered readers information that he was unmarried and provided them with the opportunity to wonder about the director's romantic interests.

Very few Hollywood novels made a lifelong bachelor a main character. However, in Vicki Baum's *Falling Star* (1934), actor Oliver Dent had hard, luminous strength and supple, athletic shoulders. Despite the women clustered around him for attention, the star remained single. He shared his enormous home with his closest friend, Jerry, who served as Dent's secretary and confidant. The author described Jerry as soft and effeminate, with a girlish face and a little bracelet encircling his thin wrist. He attended the same college as Dent and talked Oxford slang with the star. He loved Dent furtively, abnormally.[76] Despite the use of this seemingly pejorative word, Baum did not have Dent or any other character express disdain or antagonism toward Jerry. Dent simply explained to an actress that "Jerry's not interested in the opposite sex." When the star grew sicker and was hospitalized, Jerry proved to be a true friend to Dent and stayed with the star until his death.

The novel featured many scenes within Dent's Hollywood star home. Descriptions of the rooms offered readers insight into how the home reflected Dent's personality. Dent's romances with starlets revealed the hidden secrets of a Hollywood star home. These romances between an unmarried man and various single and married females made the house exciting. Jerry's presence in the house gave the star home the additional titillation and cache of having a resident who practiced taboo sexual behaviors.

Although hardly charitable in her description of Jerry, Baum showed that Jerry had a place in the Hollywood community. Her book revealed this Hollywood bohemian to be a good man and the star's unyielding friend in life and death. The book left the possibility in the mind of the readers that Dent would leave his Hollywood home to Jerry. This would give the house a unique distinction as the house of a known homosexual.

Other Hollywood homes linked to a homosexual owner appeared in publicity materials. A recent book and article about MGM comedian William Haines discussed his homosexuality in the studio system of the 1920s and early

1930s. The book observed how the studio signaled Haines's homosexuality in order to appeal to a sophisticated urban audience.

The Staunton, Virginia, native left home as a young teen and ended up in New York City in the early 1920s. After winning a contest, Haines went to Hollywood where he met and fell in love with another performer, Jimmy Shields, who would be his life partner. He moved from character actor to star, his wisecracking persona making him the top male moneymaker in 1930. However, a variety of factors combined to end his movie career in the mid-1930s. Haines had already begun a second career as an interior decorator and would be very successful at it until his death from cancer on December 26, 1973.[77]

The publicity that carried hints about Haines's Hollywood bohemian status was but one part of the broader marketing of Hollywood through the use of nonconformist imagery. Early in his career, Haines described himself in an article as being photographically a cross between a prizefighter and a Broadway cake consumer.[78] Cake consumer referenced the slang term "cake-eater," which meant a self-indulgent or effeminate man. Soon after making it to the ranks of character actor, Haines played with his image, hinting at the potential for Hollywood bohemian status.

Several publicity pieces about MGM's star focused on his house and aesthetic taste. In the late 1920s, Haines opened up an antique shop on Sunset Boulevard. General interest magazines, such as *American Magazine*, included it on a map of tourist sites. Publicity pieces discussed Haines's antique shopping, his distinguished taste and even his lending pieces in his collection to the studios for use in movies. Hints about his Hollywood bohemian nature came across when Haines's interest in antiques and collecting art was contrasted with his disinterest in sports and other activities that generally held the interest of males.[79]

More obvious suggestions of Haines as a Hollywood bohemian appeared in fan magazine articles. A discussion among film folk was how a *Photoplay* article presented information about Haines. The piece reiterated Haines's interest in antiques, having one person state, "...he's kind of nuts on fancy furniture and antiques."

Among those gathered for conversation within the article, the one who knew him added another comment on Haines's house. The person noted that Haines went to "sleep on lace pillow slips in a bedroom that would make Clara Bow's look like a fireman's." This comment expanded upon Haines's defiance of gender boundaries. It carried the suggestion that his bedroom, the place where he engaged in sexual relations, reflected womanly tastes. The person who knew Haines well discussed the way the star ran his house and likened Haines to a housewife. Readers of the piece learned that Haines was a confirmed bachelor. "He has never been in love with any girl yet, and doesn't intend to."[80]

The Haines images shared characteristics with those of Ramon Novarro and Nelson Eddy discussed in the party chapters. Haines's declaration of no interest in falling in love with a woman left readers with a series of questions. How could they not wonder what this male star and the others discussed earlier did for their love lives? The declarations of these stars spurred the media to investigate the bachelor's personal activities.

Several articles appeared that tried to answer the question of love interests for bachelor male movie stars. One newspaper article on the presence of bachelors in Hollywood used Haines's star house and interest in decorating to describe his situation.

> Haines is protected with a mother complex. Besides, Bill goes in for house decoration, with a marked leaning toward feminine furnishings, so the girls are apt to regard Bill in the light of a sister, if you know what I mean. One can talk color, drapes, boudoirs, fancy bathrooms with Bill as an art decorator rather than as a gentlemen who might move in and share the charmed domesticity.[81]

This very funny item uses the Haines house as the vehicle to explain Haines's bachelor status. His interest and taste in interior decoration were labeled feminine and used to explain that women see him as a fellow "sister." The use of the phrase "if you know what I mean" immediately after the word sister clearly suggested that the writer intended for readers to look for seek a secondary meaning from the use of the word. The piece made Haines's star home stand out as the home of a male star with decidedly feminine interests and tastes. Haines's crossing of gender boundaries made him appear kindred to single women, if not unavailable to them because of his disinterest in being sexually involved with them. The suggestion of Haines's different sexual interest, his homosexuality, turned his star home into a rare experience of seeing inside a homosexual male's house.

A publicity department of a major studio decided that a photo spread of the interior of two bachelor stars' home would be a useful marketing device. In 1935, Randolph Scott and Cary Grant appeared in a publicity spread about their home in Santa Monica, California. Born in 1898 in Virginia, Scott was the sole son of his engineer father and mother from a wealthy tobacco family from North Carolina. After a stint serving with the U.S. Army during World War I, Scott attained an engineering degree. However, he also faced the disappointment of a severe back injury that cost him his ability to play college football.

Scott opted to move to Hollywood and explore his interest in acting. He joined the Pasadena Community Playhouse in 1929. His encounter with Howard Hughes on a golf course led to his entry into motion pictures. The path proved difficult until Paramount signed him and the studio moved him from Western actor to a romantic lead. When he opted out of the contract during the late 1930s, Scott began freelancing, playing heavies and heroes before launching a very successful career as a Western star after World War II. Through his movie production company, real estate, oil, and stock dealings, Scott became one of the richest men in Hollywood. The actor married twice. His first marriage, as the second husband of heiress Marion Du Pont, great-granddaughter of Éleuthère Irénée Du Pont de Nemours, failed miserably. The marriage ended in divorce after three years, in 1939. In 1944, Scott married Patricia Stillman and the pair then adopted two children. Scott died in 1987, leaving behind his second wife and three children.[82]

Archibald Leach grew up in a poverty-stricken home in Bristol, England. As a youngster, his mother, Elsie Kingdom Leach, imposed obsessive orderliness and frilly clothes upon him. His father, Elias James Leach, a pants presser, could not meet the middle-class aspirations of his wife. The pair's misery in their marriage carried the additional weight of a son who died in childbirth. Unbeknownst to Archie, his father had his mother institutionalized when Archie was ten.

Left mostly to care for himself, Archie ran away at 13 in 1917 and joined a traveling acrobatic troupe as a song-and-dance man. During the early 1920s he left on an engagement on the American vaudeville circuit with the Pendar Boys. After a few years of traveling the vaudeville circuit, Leach chose to stay in New York City. He struggled to make a living and according to the actor's most recent biographer, Grant acquired experience in escorting wealthy ladies around town. He also made friends with Australian George (John) Orry Kelly, a relationship that had the actor peddling Kelly's hand-painted ties in Greenwich Village. A few years later, Kelly's success as a costume designer resulted in Grant getting a part in the play *Golden Dawn*. The part led to a contract with theater producer Arthur Hammerstein, who sold Leach's contract to the Shuberts for three years into the early 1930s.

The movie studios took notice of the new actor. In his first screen test at Paramount's New York studios, Grant was not selected. Undeterred, he moved to Los Angeles in late October 1931 to break into the industry. A dinner party at the head of Paramount production chief B. P. Schulberg helped Leach secure a contract and a stage name, Cary Grant. After success in early motion pictures, particularly with Mae West, Grant's career foundered and he bought himself out of his Paramount contract. In 1937–1938, he revealed his knack for screwball comedy and charmed audiences until his retirement in 1966. Each of his four marriages ended in divorce, and Grant strove to keep his screen image as his public image until his death in 1986.[83]

The first publicity images containing information about Grant and Scott began after they became friends while filming the movie *Hot Saturday* in mid–1932. Press reports during the first two years described the actors' shared celebrity home and domestic life through phrases including, "Hollywood's twosome" and "the happy couple." The innuendos provided details about the two actors' personal lives which thrilled fans, making the actors appear to be two men sharing more than lodgings.

Other articles attempted to understand the actors' living arrangements in other ways, such as the need to reduce rental costs. These items noted that similar to other single men, the actors shared lodgings earlier in their lives when they struggled to make it in the arts. However, by 1935 they had little financial incentive to continue having roommates for this reason. Cary Grant's continued use of finances as the explanation for his living arrangement inadvertently revealed a deeper truth. "'Here we are,' Cary would say, leaning back in a chair, 'living as we want to as bachelors with a nice home at a comparatively small cost. If we got married, we would have to put up a front. Women — particularly Hollywood women — expect it.'"[84]

Cary Grant and Randolph Scott on their patio overlooking the Pacific Ocean (courtesy the Academy of Motion Picture Arts and Sciences).

Grant expressed that he and Scott lived as they wanted to: as bachelors, together within a nice home. The actor used the word "front" to mean that if he and Scott got married, the industry would require them to spend money and put on airs. However, his word choice had the double meaning: once they each married, Grant and Scott would be putting up a front that hid their desire to live together.

The pair continued their domestic relationship even after Grant's marriage to Virginia Cherrill in early 1934. Reporters noted, "The Grants and Randolph Scott have moved, all three, but not apart." Indeed, this choice for living arrangements appeared preplanned. An item from two weeks prior to Grant's marriage observed that Scott would not seek any permanent quarters until he heard from Grant. Innuendoes continued later that year. Shortly after Grant's divorce from Cherrill, an article proclaimed that Randolph Scott had moved back in with Grant. This article's title, "A Woman is Only a Woman," suggested that the two men formed a home life with one another that they probably could not have with a woman.[85] These items associated the actors' home with a forbidden sexuality, turning the place into an exotic experience.

There were few images of two men living together in popular culture, literature, or medical textbooks during this era. Many movies had strong male comradeship themes, but the men did not share a house. In these movies, a group of men bonded by accomplishing some "manly" act, such as going off to war or conquering the wilderness. Even the medical community members who wrote about their studies of homosexuals very rarely included case studies of two men who lived together. One of the few instances of an image of men living together appeared in Richard Meeker's *Better Angel*, a 1933 novel about homosexuals. Its protagonist Kurt stayed in effeminate David's apartment before Kurt decided to commit to his relationship with David.[86]

The Paramount publicity department shot over thirty photographs of Grant and Scott within different rooms of their Santa Monica beach house. The studio focused its interpretation of these pictures on the stars' personalities, bachelorhood, and use of the house. The caption stamped on the back of each photograph highlighted that the actors were two of filmland's most eligible bachelors who shared quarters but lived independent lives.

The studio believed that photographs of the actors using their swimming pool and sitting at their den bar revealed each man's physical attractiveness. The images also showed the men's fun-loving spirits within a luxurious and beautiful place. The studio presumably thought that the photographic series depicted each man as a swinging Hollywood bachelor. These images appealed to both heterosexually inclined women who appreciated the actors' looks, domesticity, or both, and to heterosexually inclined men, who saw the men living a fantasy "high life."

These groups were not the only people to whom the photographic series appealed. Other photographs in the series heightened the unusualness of their star home by illustrating the actors' Hollywood bohemian natures. In three photographs of the pair at the dining room table each man stared and smiled across the table at one another. In another set, Grant leaned over the seated Scott's shoulder and appeared to watch him write out a note or bill. The photographs demonstrated that the actors found the space and the homey atmosphere comfortable while they displayed a degree of shared intimacy with one another that people expected to find in a romantic heterosexual couple.

The photograph that depicted the end of this long day was the most suggestive that the actors were Hollywood bohemians sharing a loving relationship. Scott and Grant stood on their patio in the early evening. They appeared in silhouette, as Pacific Ocean waves crested behind them. Scott touched his lit cigarette against the cigarette dangling from Grant's mouth.

The presentation of two men smoking together appeared frequently in fiction during the era. However, these scenes occurred in bars, saloons, and other "masculine" spaces rather than in a space that the culture viewed as romantic. The interaction between the two men did not present them as a pair, isolated from everyone around them. One man rarely lit the other man's cigarette, and certainly did not lean forward to light a cigarette as it dangled from the other man's mouth. The image of a male and female couple lighting cigarettes within a beautiful night scene at home appeared most frequently in cigarette advertising since the mid–1920s. These images linked smoking cigarettes to romance.[87]

Scott and Grant appeared within that similar type of romantic setting. One lit the other's cigarette as the man lit a woman's cigarette for her in the advertisements and popular culture of the era. Scott gingerly touched the cigarette as it dangled from Grant's mouth, demonstrating a comfort with close physical proximity. This photograph hinted at a shared intimacy between the actors. This image took the viewer inside the actors' private dwelling and linked the house to a forbidden sexuality and pleasure. While depicting the taboo, it also showed that behavior in a remarkably touching and beautiful way that made the home even more memorable. This image also illuminated a type of coupling within a home that few readers would have seen, making this star home appear bohemian and highly unique. The actors' living arrangement lasted until early 1942 when they moved apart for the remainder of their lives.[88]

Contemporaries offered a split decision on whether the image and the reality match. Various family members deny the link. As Grant's third wife, Betsy Drake, said in a television interview with Turner Classic Movies, "I didn't have time to think about his homosexuality. We were too busy fucking." A few homosexual members of the industry disagreed. Director George Cukor said about a homosexual relationship between Scott and Grant: "Oh, Cary won't talk about it. At most, he'll say they did some wonderful pictures together. But Randolph will admit it to a friend." According to screenwriter Arthur Laurents, Grant was "at best bisexual."[89]

The most intriguing commentary on the relationship between the actors came from a studio employee based in New York City. Gean Harwood worked for twenty years at Paramount in New York City. Harwood made the transportation arrangements for stars and executives. He perceived Scott as Grant's "sidekick." While handling the pair's trip to Europe, Harwood noted their careful housekeeping and division of labor that he interpreted as implying a deep, ongoing relationship. The actors' glances at one another left the gay studio employee no doubt that they were more than just "friends."[90]

Biographers disagree on whether Grant was bisexual and the extent of his relationship with Scott. Marc Elliot, Charles Higham and Roy Moseley considered Grant to have been bisexual. Higham and Moseley claimed that Grant and Scott were seen kissing in a public parking lot outside a social function that both attended in the 1960s. Warren Harris included a strong inference that Grant was bisexual and that he and Scott had a long-term affair during the 1930s. Richard Schickel dismissed the question of Grant's homosexuality in a few pages. Graham McCann labeled the claims of Grant's homosexuality as rumors, and the citations in other works as "inconsistent." According to William J. Mann, photographer Jerome Zerbe spent "three gay months" in the movie colony taking many photographs of Grant and Scott, "attesting to their involvement in the gay scene."

Stars were not the only actors promoted as bachelors living in gorgeous Hollywood star homes. Publicity materials and newspaper articles appeared during the late 1930s featured the living arrangements of a bachelor who was famous as a character actor. Brooklyn-born Edward Everett Horton was the son of a press room printer for the *New York Times* and a mother who disapproved of the stage. He tried higher education but did not graduate from either Oberlin College or Columbia University. At the latter, he joined the drama club and moved into the professional ranks with a stock theater touring company.

After a stint in vaudeville, Horton moved to Los Angeles and managed the Majestic Theater with his brother George. He also performed in the city's theater companies and landed a role in the movie *A Front Page Story* in 1922. He moved from quirky leading men to comedy leads in many early 1920s motion pictures. During the 1930s and early 1940s, Horton played character roles, usually as the dear friend of the star. His jittery, befuddled, fussbudget characters remained bachelors and represented pansies (homosexual males) or sissy (effeminate) males.[91]

Most of the publicity about Edward Everett Horton's off-screen life created an image that was more complex than his screen roles. An undated Twentieth Century–Fox biography of the actor described his film characterizations as mousy, bumbling, and redundant. The piece then discussed the actor's off-screen personality in terms of his sexual behavior. "In private life Horton is a bachelor. 'Not confirmed,' he hastens to add, 'but it's the only thing I've known thus far.'" As they did with the bachelor chic actresses, fans wanted to know about the actor's sexual behavior in his private life. Similarly to bachelor chic character actress Patsy Kelly, Horton expressed his single status and offered a joke to please and placate fandom.

Other publicity pieces placed Horton's romantic life in the context of his domestic living arrangement and interest in interior decorating. This context revealed that Horton stretched the culture's conventions for being a man and showed that he was a Hollywood bohemian. Two different studios issued media releases that focused on these attributes to thrill readers and make his star home appear fascinating. Both provided readers with insight into Horton's home that showed Horton lived unconventionally.

The biography issued by Fox's Harry Brand and Paramount publicity piece focused on the actor's house. "He is unmarried. His mother shares his home in the San Fernando Valley.... He has spacious kennels for his eight dogs. A sunken garden, a swimming pool and lily ponds are among other attractions of his ranch home. The comedian is an ardent collector of antiques, with especial interest in English and early American furniture."[92] The references to the bachelor living with his mother and his interest in the typically feminine area of homemaking, as with Nelson Eddy and William Haines, turned the homeowner into a Hollywood bohemian and the house into something highly unusual.

Edward Everett Horton's ranch (Herald Examiner Collection, Los Angeles Public Library).

Paramount's publicity for the motion picture *Paris Honeymoon* (1939) tied both of the strands in the Horton imagery together. The piece created a celebrity image of an unmarried man who developed a deep affection for the collectibles that filled his house.

"Edward Everett Horton sank into his chair and heaved a heartfelt sigh of relief. Such members of *Paris Honeymoon* who heard it gathered around expecting something interesting to be said. 'Well,' he said with a blissful expression on his face, 'I've got my twins all set now.' 'But-but Mr. Horton,' [one] listener stammered, 'we didn't know you were married.' 'I'm not,' Horton snapped. There were gulps but no one said anything. 'I'm talking about my Adams twins,' he explained. The faces were blank. 'You know,' he said impatiently, 'my twin fireplaces.'"

Horton explained that Adams was an artist in creating fireplaces. Horton had found just the right space for the fireplaces in his home. Bing Crosby and others enjoyed the idea that Horton had added items to his collection, forcing himself to expand his house.[93] Readers might have enjoyed this also and enjoyed the sharing of a joke with Hollywood stars. The more obvious humor centered upon the misperception over Horton having children out of wedlock. An audience member with enough knowledge of Horton's personality could enjoy a chuckle over such a striking misperception. They could even feel a sense of superiority for having knowledge about the celebrity that his costars did not. The image of the house carried a uniqueness of ownership by a bachelor who constructed an idiosyncratic family, who treated his furnishings as others treat their children.

The image also promoted readers' empathy with Horton. Readers who valued the home as a commodity could enjoy Horton's fireplaces and antiques in general, as indicative of "good taste." Horton had the time and money to travel and purchase particular antiques. He had an unusual opportunity to create accurate styles for his rooms and give his home a significant sense of substance and elegance. These purchases enabled Horton to seem elegant and stylish and his home to appear uniquely bedecked in unusual, important commodities.

Most intriguingly, once Horton explained his comments, none of the listeners on the set questioned his vision of domesticity. Indeed, fewer homes had fireplaces because they lost their role as the primary heat source in the late 1800s. Many people felt their absence as if they lost a member of the family. Thus, readers could also understand Horton's attitude and might feel that way themselves. For homosexual readers, Horton's image and his valuing domesticity had greater resonance.

According to architectural scholar Aaron Betsky, the urge to collect and assemble objects mirrored an unseen self and was an important part of homosexual culture in this era.[94] The publicity piece accomplished several neat tricks. It made Horton and his home stand apart yet also made his thoughts and values familiar to the readers of the piece. The piece offered domesticity and nostalgia to the majority readership while also providing to a taboo minority group of readers an acknowledgment of their values as well.

Newspaper and magazine reporters described Horton's personality as having a mutually reinforcing relationship between his Hollywood bohemian status and his star home. A caption from a fan magazine noted that Horton was a bachelor who continued to maintain his solitude even after he built his home. A reporter on the quest to explain Hollywood bachelorhood found her explanation for Horton's marital status related to his star home. "Eddie Horton's system involves having the comradely platonic friendship idea down to a nicety.... He is fortified in this by owning a peculiarly comfortable home which functions all too satisfactorily minus a female."[95]

Another article described a Horton vacation from acting in terms of his domesticity. The piece noted that "he will conclude his domestic tour ... in the kitchen, where he and his mother will have a cup of tea and talk things over ... Edward is a bachelor and his mother is his confidant, his critic, and his pal." The personality of Horton that appeared centered on being a "mama's boy." Originally implying a coward or sissy, by the early twentieth century "mama's boy" meant an effeminate and homosexual man.[96] Horton's house appeared as a place where the actor expressed his personality, offering readers a glimpse at an unusual man.

Hollywood contemporaries appeared to interpret Horton's image as akin to his real world existence and probable homosexuality. Fred Astaire referred to Edward Everett Horton as being a pansy and not knowing it in a letter to his sister Adele. Intriguingly, he mentioned that he "had to be careful not to camp with him." As a long-time member of the theater and dance worlds, the actor encountered homosexuals and could recognize them. In two letters to Adele the dancer used the word "fagat" [sic] negatively, once thinking that after the filming of a scene he looked like a big "fagat."[97]

The two actors worked together on several motion pictures. They met on Astaire's second motion picture, *The Gay Divorcee*, in 1934 and would again play together in *Top Hat* the following year. Did the dancer enjoy going into the woods, breaking out the tents and camping? This type of camping did not seem very widespread Hollywood behavior. This use of the word also seems unlikely for a second reason. If this was what Astaire meant, then Horton, who was not aware of his same-sex interest, would not pose a threat to Astaire if the pair did go off into the woods together.

More likely, Astaire used the "camp" in a different manner—camp as a pose in exaggerated fashion with the effect of "ostentatious, exaggerated, affected, theatrical; effeminate or homosexual; pertaining to or characteristic of homosexuals," appeared in print twenty years earlier. In this way, Astaire expressed disappointment to his sister that he could not engage in play, using camp, because unlike other "pansies," Horton lacked the necessary self-awareness to have fun with Astaire.

The few writers about Horton have not reached a definitive conclusion about his homosexuality. Vito Russo's study focused on the depiction of homosexual men in movies. However, he asserted that men like Horton who played sissies on screen exhibited little consciousness of the behavior itself. Mann disagreed and asserted that most of the sissies were gay men. However, he could not find evidence of the male companion whom members of the Hollywood gay subculture linked with Horton.[98]

These bachelor Hollywood bohemians enjoyed every facet of the good life. They lived in glamorous locations with all the material things that their large salaries could buy. They had the love of good friends, their families, and their lovers. Like the bachelor chic, they also defied the culture's expectations about the formation of a proper household. Each of them ignored the imperative to get married. These men formed their own domestic arrangements. Horton viewed his antique furnishings as children. The intimacy between Grant and Scott made them appear similar to a husband and wife. The photograph series suggested that two men could live the heterosexual ideal family.

FIVE

Hollywood Behind the Scenes
Glamour and Mystery in the Workplace

Tall, twittering Gilbert Adrian ... inhabits an oyster-white office, works furiously chewing gum, deep in an overstuffed chair which is disconcertingly set on a dais to keep him from dripping paint on the oyster-white carpet.... At parties Adrian keeps a keen eye peeled for signs of dowdiness, can be convulsing about it afterwards. Of Tallulah Bankhead he once remarked: "She can wear one more silver fox than any other woman and still look underdressed...."[1]

Time magazine offered its readers MGM's fashion designer Adrian long before *People* featured Mr. Blackwell's "Worst Dressed List" and *Queer Eye for the Straight Guy* provided Carson Kressley with male fashion challenges. The power of the motion picture industry and the appeal of its products generated a great deal of interest in the activities on the studio lots. Despite the recognition of the mass production of movies inherent in Hollywood's nickname "The Dream Factory," Hollywood insiders and the media produced images that made the studios appear like no ordinary workplace. Hollywood studios held a glamour and mystery to which no factory floor or office cubicle could compare.

The glimpses "behind the scenes" of the movie industry allowed audiences into the studio doors. They let them in on the activities happening in this restricted, seemingly mysterious arena where glamorous movie stars plied their trade. Publicity pieces like this one featuring Adrian's office included descriptions that enhanced the glamour and mystery. These factors helped make the Hollywood behind-the-scenes workplace distinct from the locations where readers plied their trades. Hollywood bohemians like Adrian enhanced that sense of the area's uniqueness. Adrian's flitting and emotive nature, along with his wisecracks over the lack of style of the stars, added a taboo behavior. Combined with the aforementioned glamour and mystery, the taboo helped sell Hollywood, behind the scenes, as a very exciting and wild place.

Hollywood behind the scenes did not always appear in the media in this way. In the early years of moviemaking, the flamboyant surroundings and romances in dressing rooms rarely appeared in the behind-the-scenes publicity. Instead, the articles in movie magazines and the stories in Hollywood novels focused on the technology involved in making movies.

The columns in the daily newspapers and pieces in magazines like *Moving Picture World* and *Variety* told readers about the types of equipment used and how cinematic tricks made things appear as they did on the screen. Hollywood novels featured stories that found adventure and romance in the technology of making movies and the men who created the studios that made the movie industry into a giant business.[2] As with every trend and style, this approach ran its course. The readers, reporters and authors sought something new. By the early 1920s, behind-the-screen novels joined the newspaper gossip columns and feature sections in movie magazines in showing how stars and the other professionals behaved on the studio lots.

While Hollywood insiders and observers presented the new world behind the scenes of the movies, theater publicists and observers continued to provide images of backstage. The theater's backstage appeared in the mass media for over a generation before the emergence of Hollywood. Audiences enjoyed learning how a touring company created an explosion and other onstage phenomena. They also wanted to know what happened in the star's dressing room before and after the show. Like the behind-the-scenes images, the depictions of backstage at the theater provided a glimpse of the hidden activities that made the shows audiences loved possible.

The Backstage Life

The United States populace held a long and deep interest in the theater. Popular interest and participation in the theater's inner workings emerged well before the Civil War. Audiences experienced close interactions with performers and the theater generally because theatrical troupes performed in small cities and encampments, such as mining sites. Members of these theater companies interacted with town residents when they were not performing, providing audience members with knowledge regarding theatrical operations and the performers' personalities.[3]

With the development of the star system in the 1880s, audience attention increasingly focused on particular stars. These theater performers became celebrities. During the "golden age of American theater" in the 1880s and 1890s, more media devoted coverage to performers and performances as audiences sought more information about the people that they saw in the starring roles.[4] Theater performers carried with them the earlier reputation for immorality. Actresses in particular had a reputation as worldly-wise, self-sufficient, self-determining and hard-working. This reputation, coupled with the greater focus on stars, heightened interest in certain performers' behaviors behind the stage.

These factors helped form the perception that amorous activities occurred in theater actors' and actresses' dressing rooms.

Several novels and theatrical columns in daily newspapers during the nineteenth century presented information about the activities of the theatrical stars backstage. In the novels, the heroes were great actors and actresses bold and daring, who acted larger than life on stage. In the greenrooms backstage they held court with royalty, statesmen, and the very wealthy listening to every word. The less fortunate clamored outside the stage door with the overhanging lamp, wishing to get into the modern fairyland. These "Stagedoor Johnnies" waited in long rows, holding a bunch of orchids and a hansom cab for the women they loved or desired.[5]

These books provided readers with inside knowledge of stage life and the sense that they knew these performers more intimately. They made backstage appear worldly and glamorous. The theatrical backstage appeared to be an exciting place where the notable fraternized with individual actors and actresses who captivated everyone with their looks and charisma.

Presentations of backstage in the early twentieth century contradicted this vision of performers and of a glamorous theatrical life. These magazine articles did not provide information about particular celebrities. More significantly, these articles strove to eradicate from readers' thoughts the perception of the theater as a site for sexual behavior that the culture viewed as inappropriate. These articles depicted backstage as a workplace both crowded and unattractive. The stage door entrance existed within a dark, narrow alley that was nearly impossible to find. Inside, a surly, curt man, the griffin, sat with an ugly dog. A visitor would summon up the courage to ask to see a person or to hand him a note. The griffin returned each with a cold stare and the command, "Stay where you are."[6]

The article informed readers that most visitors traversed no farther into the behind-the-stage area. However, reporters aimed to reveal to their readers the secret and mysterious backstage life. They proceeded along a long hall containing an old upholstered sofa and into a space cluttered with props and other necessities of the theater. The dressing rooms appeared off to the side and did not fill the area with the frivolity and intrigue of visiting dignitaries. Small and cramped, dressing rooms usually had only enough furnishings for the performers to dress and apply their make-up. One observer spied the area and insisted that little sexual activity occurred in the dressing room. "Its quite positive ugliness, very evident discomfort, its narrow dimensions, its doubtful cleanliness, seemed to shut away all romance from its purlieus [sic]."[7]

The depictions of the theatrical life did more than make performers' environs appear unappealing. The images provided little information that would allow readers to feel that they knew the performers better. These articles referred to the chorus members as a group and did not describe any of their activities. Readers only learned that chorus members had cramped dressing rooms and low positions in the theatrical hierarchy. Chorus girls did not have to fear the approach of the manager or producer because they would not tempt her to transgress sexual propriety. "They are like business men who employ women in their offices ... [for] the far-off mother ... the managerial bugbear need cause her no uneasiness."[8] These references disrupted readers' ideas that the theatrical world was glamorous and full of romantic encounters. Instead, it made backstage appear more like a "regular" work environment.

These limitations on presentations held true for the vision of the backstage lives of stars. Stars generally behaved like congenial co-workers backstage, showing diplomacy and business sense, exchanging pleasantries with all the cast members and not risking these associations by lack of propriety.

Novels that included characters in the theatrical world reinforced the perception that theater stars and chorines were not sexual libertines. The title character of Theodore Dresier's novel *Sister Carrie* (1900) experienced no attempt at entering into an adulterous affair when she worked as a chorus member. As she advanced in the theatrical world, Carrie received letters offering love and fortune. Despite her loneliness, Carrie knew not to answer these men and felt resigned to her unglamorous backstage life.[9] The actresses in Hollywood did not face this alienation as they worked with many other performers in an environment that seemed at times like a fantasy world.

On the Studio Lots

Many of the people employed in the movie industry enjoyed working in the studios. Actor Jimmy Stewart liked the studio system because he felt like part of a family. Actor-dancer Fred Astaire observed that MGM was large and "...he loved the whole thing.... Dressing rooms are in a sort of garden and it was more like being on a vacation." Although the craftspeople engaged in battles with the studios and fellow unions throughout the era, some members and leaders appreciated their positions in Hollywood. Conference of Studio Unions president Herbert Sorrell, the most militant and pro-worker of all studio unions, noted that, "I went back to the studios. I like studio work."

The employees worked at elaborate facilities on expansive lots that replicated medieval fiefdoms. Hollywood showed audiences the studio grounds as microcosms of the world. "Warner Brothers studio has 39 miles of paved and lighted streets ... takes 15 minutes to 'visit' England, Germany, Italy, Spain, India ... Mexico and where-are-you-from ... San Francisco, New York, Havana, and Shanghai side by side on an artificial lake on the Burbank lot."[10] A person on the studio lot could see the world and find his or her neighborhood and would encounter both the familiar and the exotic. Thus, the visitor to this world would have everything as if in a dream.

The eight major and minor studios based their operations over the expanse of Los Angeles, from MGM's southern fiefdom in Culver City to Warner Bros. in the northern area of Burbank. The lots were enormous. United Artists had an 18.5-acre lot along Santa Monica Boulevard that contained huge soundstages and numerous buildings. Paramount Pictures Corporation's 35 acres included more than 70 structures, including 20 stages. The lots contained buildings for all the studio departments, facades of streets from all over the world, security forces, and gated entrances on nearly every side. Long-time actor Rod LaRoque observed, "The magnitude of the Los Angeles studios was a revelation to me. Some of the eastern studios were toyhouses [sic] in comparison."[11]

Like other factories, these enormous facilities produced an enormous amount of a single product. The studios created around 700 motion pictures yearly to fill the thousands of theaters over the world. They required numerous workers with a variety of skills, and the eight largest studios employed over 4,000 people in the late 1920s. During a single year in the late 1930s, these studios employed craftspersons who completed tens of thousands of work hours. Editors, cameramen, musicians, and others negotiated salaries and fringe benefits that placed them among the best-paid artisans and technicians in the world.

Hundreds of employees fit within a category the industry termed "the creative talents" (actors, directors, and screenwriters). Their earnings, which averaged between $10,000 and $48,000 annually during the midst of the Great Depression, aided in making filmmaking appear as a dream job within a dream factory. Since Horace Greely's famous editorial advice, "Go west, young man!" California has been viewed as a land of opportunity. The movie studios drew on this promise. Approximately 10,000 people a month invaded Hollywood to work in its movie business during the 1920s. A significant number of these people included homosexuals, establishing what one scholar dubbed "the great powder puff migration!"[12]

Many people wanted to see what happened inside the Hollywood studios. Over 1,600,000 tourists visited the studios annually in the hopes of entering them and seeing the work behind the scenes. "The studio gate has been regarded for years as an impenetrable barrier to those who desire to tread the same ground on which walk the dream children of the silver screen."[13]

Hollywood publicity materials played a very significant role in maintaining interest in Hollywood. These items provided the precious few glimpses of the variety of performers and artisans working on the stages to create the movies. This helped promoted the mystique of behind the scenes as a special place to a wide variety of audiences. This interest in the activities behind the scenes of an exotic work environment occurred during an era when most people toiled at routine jobs in sterile environs for fifty hours each week.

The majority of images behind the scenes in the motion picture industry featured stories about actors and actresses. The studios and media knew screen performers attracted audiences' attentions. The depictions revealed aspects of the star's personality to thrill audiences with the sense of increased intimacy and shaped the view of Hollywood as a glamorous and exciting place.

Most of these images of these performers in the studios ignored the difficulties, such as performers being bound to a single studio over a seven-year contract. The daily grind rarely received coverage. Actress Myrna Loy complained that MGM worked her to death, moving her from one picture to another without rehearsal, often without knowing what her part would be from scene to scene. Character actors complained about being restricted in their ability to be creative and act, noting that they were consistently typecast. All performers often waited hours under the hot lights filming scenes.

Occasionally they experienced brutal rehearsals before the director felt satisfied enough to have the actors check their make-up and hair before the final take. Between shots, performers waited endlessly. Actress Miriam Cooper noted that she had worked from nine A.M. to midnight and drank coffee to try to stay awake. "'Damn those slave drivers,' Wally [Reid] said half under his breath. 'They'll get their money's worth if they have to kill you to do it.' 'They're killing this set in the morning. We've got to keep going,'" Cooper told her fellow actor before he suggested that she visit the doctor, who would fix her up with something so that she would not feel tired.[14] This doctor provided illegal drugs. Reid's drug use appeared in images when Reid died in early 1923, but the scandal and subsequent drive to move the industry from Hollywood subsided.

Despite such trials and tribulations, performers found a great deal to enjoy about Hollywood behind the scenes. Star status provided a sense of creativity and power associated with realizing the pictures' success rested on their shoulders. Actor/dancer Fred Astaire noted that he "really liked the [Hollywood 'racket'] because it's important stuff nowadays and the work has charm and variety."

The stars enjoyed material support from the studios. Many stars had enormous dressing rooms ranging from rambling villas to luxury apartments on wheels. Mary Pickford's five-room stucco Norman cottage on the United Artists' lot came furnished with antiques and servants, while Marion Davies's 14-room villa parked at MGM and Warner Bros. during the 1920s and 1930s. Douglas Fairbanks, Sr., Charlie Chaplin, and their actor friends enjoyed a ritual steam bath at Fairbanks's office most afternoons.

Hollywood stars enjoyed more than splendid work environments on the studio lots. Many performers developed deep personal relationships with others while at work. Marlene Dietrich noted that her hairdresser Nelly Manley "...wept with me, hated my enemies, was my friend and personal 'guard.'" Robert Benchley enjoyed a similar feeling of closeness. He noted that the stage crew worked on all of Deanna Durbin's pictures so it was a very homey little group, one Big Family. Some performers enjoyed the opportunity to have shorter-term intimate relations. As screenwriter Anita Loos noted, "...every girl on the lot could have had her turn with Doug [Fairbanks Sr.] and most of them did." Clark Gable also had a large quotient of love affairs.[15] Hollywood insiders emphasized all of these features in their materials.

Stories from the Hollywood Lots

Hollywood publicity materials depicted three main characteristics behind the scenes. It appeared as a place where stars lived luxuriously, where workers formed a family environment, and where a man and woman could find romance. By the early 1920s, glimpses of "behind the scenes" Hollywood offered readers knowledge and titillation by providing private details about celebrities in a public forum. Magazine and newspaper articles constructed the understanding of the stars' glamorous working conditions with descriptions of dressing rooms filled with fabulous decorations that illustrated the stars' exquisite taste and their personalities. Other articles spurred the impression that Hollywood stars always had their every need met. Stories trumpeted that stars had their own personal hairdressers and make-up experts who knew every style, worked quickly, and responded immediately to a star's requests.[16]

Images of the behind-the-scenes "family" emerged from articles about actors celebrating special days on the set or bringing friends to the studio and having them quickly considered insiders. Stars and fellow studio personnel engaged in another family pastime of teasing. Universal star Eddie Polo saw a member of the press department waltz over and ask him if he had seen the story in print about the star's generosity. "'Did you see that swell piece of publicity,' the P. A. (press agent) queried. 'Oh,' Eddie replied, 'That wasn't publicity. That was the truth.'"[17]

The most frequent and popular images promoted the mystique of romance occurring between actors behind the scenes in Hollywood. Newspapers and magazines described budding real and imagined studio romances, with gossipy items such as Ramon Novarro receiving roses with a card signed Mata Hari from his co-star in that movie, Greta Garbo. One of the most popular works in the Hollywood novel genre, Henry Leon Wilson's 1922 novel *Merton of the Movies*, chronicled the budding love between the serious title character and comedienne "Flip" Montague on a silent movie set. Several of the earliest motion picture depictions of "inside" the Hollywood studios perpetuated the belief that performers found love within the studios.

The industry made a silent and early talking version of the aforementioned *Merton of the Movies. Show People* (MGM, 1928) was one of the most popular of the silent film depictions of behind-the-scenes Hollywood. The movie followed Peggy Pepper (Marion Davies) as a greenhorn who became a melodramatic star and then lost touch with her audience. However, she rediscovered her creative self, the benefits of family, and her love for a comedian Billy Boone (William Haines).[18] The gossip, novels, and movies all sent the message that behind-the-scenes Hollywood bred the best kind of love. However, stars interested in heterosexual lovemaking and conventionally constructed dressing rooms were not the only figures to appear in media materials.

Hollywood Bohemian Performers Behind the Scenes

A few Hollywood bohemians appeared in images that depicted stars luxuriating at the studio. One magazine article noted that Greta Garbo's dressing room was a large place where the reclusive actress frequently rested between takes. The piece placed readers inside the studio and offered them insight into a personal space that few people ever saw. According to the reporter, Garbo's three-room bungalow suffered from a masculine severity. The star's sense of decoration, as noted in the discussion of her star home in the last chapter, included a minimum of material objects and the maintenance of open space. Her decorations included items that hinted at her vision of herself as a bachelor.

The highly untypical decorations in Garbo's dressing room made behind the scenes seem very intriguing. The star's adoption of habits differed from what the culture thought of as proper for a woman. Her habits would have promoted an interpretation that the star was "gender inverted," a signal of homosexuality during this time period. As a dressing room, Garbo's place always had the potential to be a site where the star could engage in romantic liaisons. The forbidden nature of her sexual interests added an exotic appeal to Garbo's dressing room and made Hollywood behind the scenes much more exciting and unusual.[19]

Another actress who enjoyed luxury at the studio had a zany family and appeared to enjoy racy relationships as well appeared in MGM's movie *Bombshell* (1933). Jean Harlow played a fictional movie star named Lola Burns. Burns, known to her fans as the "Blonde Bombshell," had an image as a wanton woman who loved and left all sorts of men. The star Jean Harlow was known for her platinum blonde hair and alluring figure. The movie's story was based loosely on her real-life experiences.

Lola Burns enjoyed pampered treatment at her studio. She encamped in a large dressing room and many studio employees catered to her needs and whims. Burns also faced demands from every portion of her world. The actress needed to shoot retakes of her last movie because the Hays office believed they were too risqué. She had to cope with a crazy father and a freeloading brother and lately needed to juggle two jealous suitors.

Most importantly to Lola, she had to battle her studio to change her image. Despite being told by the studio publicist, Space Hanlon (Lee Tracy), that romantic scandal was what her adoring public wanted, Lola gave a "girl-next-door" interview to a matronly reporter. When the writer suggested that Lola might be more fulfilled if she were a mother, the actress believed the advice. Burns set about trying to attain marriage and motherhood, much to the consternation of the studio publicity department.[20]

Throughout the entire movie, the publicist undermined every one of the actress's efforts to develop her new image. While Lola tried to convince the adoption office of her suitability as a parent, Hanlon orchestrated anarchy to break out in Burns's house so that the representative would not support her application. Burns then tried to portray herself as ready for marriage. However, the publicist ran a story in the newspapers stating that Lola had another romantic tryst.

Bombshell offered a revelation regarding the activities within the studio and in the life of a movie star. The movie poked fun at the creation of star images and the assumed link between a star's image in the movies and their off-screen life. Most strikingly, the movie depicted a female movie star whose studio wanted her to appear to lead a Hollywood bohemian existence. The movie illustrated that a star who was a Hollywood bohemian could remain popular. In the view of the director Victor Fleming and screenwriters John Lee Mahin and Jules Furthman, a spectrum of audience members enjoyed the Hollywood bohemian antics and wanted to know the details about their favorite star's activities in Hollywood. The movie industry insiders behind *Bombshell* argued that the studio publicity departments actively promoted a star image of an actress as an unmarried woman having sex, sometimes with married men.

In the montage at the beginning of the movie, a series of different audiences were shown enjoying the Burns image. First, young and old commuters, housewives, and other people appeared on the screen eagerly reading a series of newspaper headlines that catalogued Burns's crossing the boundaries of sexual propriety. The reading public smiled over Burns's Hollywood bohemian activities.

The montage continued, showing other audience members identifying with Burns's "bad girl" image. Several women bought the cosmetics that Burns endorsed. Other men and women sat in a movie theater and enjoyed watching a love scene from Jean Harlow's previously released movie, *Red Dust*. The last audience members in the montage eyed Burns's image in the privacy of their own homes. A woman sat in her apartment dreamily thinking as *Photoplay* with Burns on the cover lay open on top of her breast. Two men also sat within their dark apartments looking at images of Burns in other magazines.

This wide range of the general public enjoyed a benefit from Burns's Hollywood bohemian image. The subway riders received a jolt of excitement into their lives from the wild stories. The women bought the cosmetics because they wanted to use the same products in order to have Burns's style. The men in the theater and at home imagined themselves in an embrace with Burns or being Harlow's co-star in the scene from *Red Dust*. The women envisioned themselves as Burns living a glamorous, decadent life. Did the woman who dreamt while the image of Burns lay across her chest imagine herself being with Burns romantically? Could Lola Burns's image as a sexually adventurous woman have factored into this woman's dreams about being her or being with her? To this wide variety of people, the Burns Hollywood bohemian image made Hollywood behind the scenes appear to be a very vibrant, exciting workplace.

The critics generally praised the movie, which was called adroit, markedly clever, and one of the best comedies of life in Hollywood. Reviewers praised the performances as well. Lola was considered a temperamental star who dabbled in everything, including her personal relationships. They enjoyed the publicist character. They relished the way he humorously used Lola's pseudo-relationships and his imagination to grab any front-page headlines that he could. The public expressed mixed reactions. While doing well in the big cities on the first week, the movie did not prove to have lasting box-office power.

The movie grossed excellent box office receipts in the mid-sized and smaller cities throughout the country,[21] allowing audiences to view Lola Burns as a sexy, wild woman. Yet by having Burns attempt to change this image, the movie made it easier for audiences to like and accept her. Burns became the "good bad woman," an obvious fantasy figure for many males. This woman would also be a fantasy figure for those females who wanted to play this part in their own lives or perhaps only through identifying with a character such as Lola Burns.

The depiction of highly sexed star actresses behind the scenes in Hollywood appeared years earlier in Jim Tully's novel *Jarnegan*. Actress Velma worried that Jarnegan would give away the starring role in his next picture. "No, I won't," the director responded. "I'll make the 'Seven Foolish Virgins' next and give you all a part." Velma whispered to him, "Where will you get virgins in Hollywood?" [Jarnegan responded] "We'll use a few leading men — and Charlie Chaplin."[22]

This joke centered upon actors and actresses being Hollywood bohemians. The inference about actresses noted that like Lola Burns, they violated the cultural proscription against unmarried women having sex and married women committing adultery. The joke added another wallop: Hollywood actors could play women. Two probable interpretations emerge. The first centered on the notion of major male Hollywood stars who were effeminate enough to play virgin women. The second interpretation centered on the male stars' homosexuality that kept them from having sexual intercourse with women, thus making them what was commonly understood as "virgins." The jibe at Chaplin made fun of his tendency to marry very young women. The exchange between Velma and Jarnegan created the impression of Hollywood bohemians, including wanton women, homosexual males, and straight men who married young girls, running around studio lots. All of these people made studio lots into wild places where readers would meet people engaged in every type of forbidden sexual pleasure.

Casting couches were only one environment on the studio lots. Hollywood bohemians also turned the soundstages into wild places. Warner Bros'. *Show Girl in Hollywood* (1930) told the story of Dixie Dugan, played by Alice White, a musical comedy star who was whisked off to become a movie star in Hollywood. Based on a story by J. P. McEvoy and directed by Mervyn LeRoy, the movie provided an accurate view of how early silent movies were made while showing Dixie's travails and her encounters with fading movie star Donna Harris (Blanche Sweet).[23]

Dixie Dugan wandered around the studio lot in a trance because she felt so upset over her recent failure to find employment. She approached a soundstage. The red warning light glowed, signaling that the filming of a movie was in progress. Dugan opened the door and walked in. She did not see the crew shooting a scene in a gangster movie. An actor seated behind a desk in a skyscraper argued with the man in a white fedora at his right. The man at the desk stood and lunged at his enemy. The man in the white fedora overpowered his enemy and pushed him toward the open window. The director of the scene sat behind the cameras with his assistant. Excited over the action in the scene, the director tapped the leg of his assistant director. When the directors looked back at the scene they were filming, Dixie Dugan walked in from behind the window and looked over at the two actors who were in the middle of wrestling. The director got up out of his chair and yelled at Dugan.

> "Hey, hey, get away from that window. What's the matter with you. Don't you know you're spoiling my scene. Here I am rehearsing this scene all day and you walk in on the set." The director turned to his assistant. "Throw her out!" The assistant escorted Dixie off the set. The director turned to his actors. "Now Mr. Blanton and Mr. Harvey, don't act so effeminately." The director's eyes flared wide and he pursed his lips and grabbed at the knot of his tie. One actor looked stoically then when the director's back was turned both actors said, "Yes, Mr. Smith."[24]

Viewers saw how a movie was filmed and the positions of the various people on the set during shooting. As Dugan destroyed the illusion of being in the top floor of the skyscraper by walking into the background, she provided audiences with additional knowledge about movie sets and the process of filming a movie. Dugan also provided a laugh by being disruptive and by displaying the flimsy nature of the supposed outside of the building.

Dugan's entry into the scene sparked the director of the gangster movie to reconsider how the scene he was filming was proceeding. The makers of *Show Girl in Hollywood* did not show Dixie Dugan, the star of their movie, being escorted out of the soundstage. Instead, they stayed with characters that never appeared anywhere else in *Show Girl in Hollywood* and were unimportant to the movie's plot line. The moviemakers chose to stay with the director and actors to show the viewers of *Show Girl in Hollywood* something they believed to be important. The scene featured the director yelling that his actors' behavior on the stage set suggested effeminacy and homosexuality. The director added to his point and the humor of the situation by imitating an effeminate or homosexual man.

This scene from *Show Girl in Hollywood* added humor to the movie. The scene also commented on Hollywood. Audiences laughed at the theatrics of the director and the unexpected events that occurred on the stage set. The director's comments suggested the presence of effeminate and homosexual males on the stage sets and studio lots of Hollywood. On these stage sets of Hollywood behind the scenes, people made a show of themselves and discussed private topics including taboo gender and sexual behaviors. Even when not present, Hollywood bohemians remained on the minds of Hollywood's workers and turned behind the scenes into a funny, risqué place.

The reviewers of *Show Girl in Hollywood* viewed the picture as a moderately amusing program with much studio atmosphere. That studio atmosphere "is perhaps the chief reason why fans will care for the picture." The movie box office totals revealed very mixed results. While doing well in its first week on Broadway, in San Francisco and in Kansas City, *Show Girl in Hollywood* flopped in Pittsburgh, Portland Oregon, Boston, and St. Louis.[25]

Other Hollywood materials indicated that performers discussed taboo sexual behaviors on the stage sets behind the scenes in Hollywood. One scene from *Reckless Hollywood* took place on a studio lot. The scene placed readers in a conversation amongst extras as they waited for shooting to resume on the set. A former female star told another extra, "People out here they're Mr. and Mrs. God according to their sex, and you can't even be sure of *that* [emphasis mine] in this town."

This comment offered readers the thrill of being placed behind the scenes. They also received the chance to learn from an insider about Hollywood's movie stars. As a former star, this extra knew about the big-name movie industry people because she used to be friends with and attended events with many of them. She informed readers that Hollywood's big stars either did not act like the culture expected males and females to act, engaged in forbidden sexual behaviors, or both. The two industry reporters placed Hollywood bohemians at the center of the behind-the-scenes world. Those bohemians made that world appear distinct by making it the place to see beautiful people who held forbidden impulses.

The authors of *Reckless Hollywood*, Dorothy Loubou and Harmony Haynes, worked as movie industry reporters and published this book in 1932. Their novel included a prefatory note stating that many of the "fictional" characters would be recognizable to those knowledgeable about 1920s and early 1930s Hollywood. Readers engaged in the game of guessing who Mr. and Mrs. God might be referring to in the real Hollywood of the day. The two reporters not only created a show of the Hollywood stage set but turned reading their book into a game with the reward of "discovering" knowledge about Hollywood celebrities.

Another novel that came out that same year featured one of those beautiful Hollywood bohemians. The character was one of those actors who became the extras' topic of conversation on the soundstage in *Reckless Hollywood*. *Screen Star* showed readers a big star who acted upon taboo impulses with people that he met on the studio lot. Author Jack Preston, a pseudonym for a figure about town named John Preston Buschlen, described Actor Tony Deveraux as almost too handsome for a man, with hypnotic and insolent eyes. Deveraux had a girlfriend who was also a movie star. While not married, the pair made love, thus violating the cultural standard to wait until marriage before engaging in intercourse.

Certainly, both Deveraux and his girlfriend were Hollywood bohemians. However, Deveraux was even more of a bohemian. His girlfriend arrived at Deveraux's place and discovered that his dalliances also included male lovers.[26] The scene promoted the studio lot as a place where a suave male heartthrob met actresses with whom he could have a romantic and sexual relationship. More intriguingly, the lot appeared as a location where an attractive man met other men with whom he could have romantic and sexual relations. The sex between an unmarried male and female and Deveraux's bisexuality transformed the studio lot into an exotic locale where major stars engaged in decadent pleasures.

The male heartthrob character in the novel illustrated the differences between the Hollywood novels and other literature of the era. The depictions of Hollywood bohemians in Hollywood novels and adulterers and people with homosexual interests in other literature and pulp fiction were significantly different. Deveraux would have faced ruin and felt tortured in the other literature of the era. However, in *Screen Star*, a Hollywood novel, he escaped relatively unscathed. Deveraux lost his star actress girlfriend when she discovered him in bed with a man. He also had to battle with the studio after this discovery. Yet the star remained composed and confident in himself and his abilities. Near the end of the book, he retained his career and appeared with other big-name stars at a charity dinner.

Hollywood's stars were not the only performers who exhibited their forbidden desires behind the scenes. A reporter snuck behind the scenes with a few Warner Bros. and Twentieth Century Pictures office employees to the place where chorus girls relaxed amongst themselves. The girls talked in slang. They gave names to everything they encountered on the studio stage sets. To the chorus girls, the studio was the "factory," the camera was a "blinker," and earning overtime was "drawing a winner." They also gave names to the people that they worked with on the job. The girls called the chorus boys "creampuffs" and "campers." Creampuffs were effeminate-acting chorus boys who had a softness not associated with normative masculinity.[27] Campers were people who used camp humor, which during this era was associated with homosexual men.

The article gave readers access into studio employees' private scene on the lot. This provided the readers with the impression that they were receiving special information. Their slang gave their behind-the-scenes world pizzazz and their words for the chorus boys told readers that Hollywood behind the scenes was no ordinary workplace.

Behind the scenes one saw chorus boys who displayed their Hollywood bohemian effeminate and homosexual behavior on the stage sets. The chorus boys sold that behind-the-scenes world as a workplace you could only find in Hollywood. Hollywood publicity distinguished behind the scenes from Broadway backstage publicity by giving the chorus girls personality. But it also made behind the scenes into a wildly different place from the Broadway stare readers encountered in theater publicity and in the Hollywood movies about backstage, including *Forty-Second Street* and *The Gold Diggers of 1933*.

By the early 1940s, the depiction of actors, actresses, and choirboys who behaved like Hollywood bohemians behind the scenes changed. As with the closing of female impersonator nightclubs and the steering of private partiers like Nelson Eddy into marriage, the depiction of Hollywood bohemians behind the scenes became rare and less positive. One of the few images of them behind the scenes during 1940 showed that heartbreak awaited them.

A female star of spectacles and costume dramas in Ann Bell's novel *Lady's Lady* (1940) experienced a broken heart. The star, Lotus, fell deeply in love with Bunny, a woman she picked from among hundreds of extras while filming a scene in a movie. After they slept together, Bunny showed no interest in a romance, which caused the star to plead for renewed affection.

> My heart is aching. Whenever I close my eyes, I can see you in my imagination with other girls. I had planned and hoped never to have any more heartaches, but the way I feel about you is pitiable. I would give my life to be with you this very moment, just to feel you near me, to drift in the dreamland of heavenly bliss for only a few minutes. I would be happy if you would allow me to be with you once again ... but regardless of anything and everything, I wish and am longing to hear your voice again. Darling, may I?[28]

The scene turned the soundstage into a meat market. A star could walk around the stage and exchange glances with hundreds of extra girls until finding the right one for her. The star exhibited little fear that one of these extra women or other studio workers might object to her Hollywood bohemian activities. While Bunny might not have wanted to pursue the relationship beyond one night, she responded to the star's letter. Bunny made it clear that Lotus could have chosen a different girl and fulfilled her romantic desires.

Secretaries might work at a job and meet a man they wanted to marry. They would usually not have the wealth and celebrity that came with being in a relationship with a Hollywood star. At the Hollywood behind-the-scenes workplace, an unheralded extra girl could find romance with a wealthy, popular actress. This two-female love affair offered the extra girl a Cinderella opportunity. She could marry a person she loved and live a happy, healthy, wealthy life. The romance made Hollywood behind the scenes one of the only places where a person could fulfill that fantasy romance outside of the movies themselves.

The images of stars, chorus girls and boys, and extras provided audiences with glimpses into the dressing rooms, soundstages, and studio lots where the people with whom audiences identified on and off screen made the movies. While reminding audience members that the lot served as the stage for the filming of movie spectacles, the images enabled these readers and viewers to "know" the mysteries of the performers' private lives behind the scenes.

The Hollywood bohemians revealed the spectacularly hidden elements on the studio lots. They showed that several actors and actresses engaged in homosexuality and adultery, turning behind the scenes into a private playground where even the forbidden occurred. Performers in front of the cameras were not the only people working behind the scenes in Hollywood. Many people labored at the crafts that made the filming of movie scenes possible. Some of these professions descended from the backstage crews of the legitimate theater. Magazine articles and syndicated newspaper columns described the work and workers who toiled behind the curtain to make the theater come alive.

Backstage Crew

Images of theatrical artisans rarely appeared in nineteenth-century publicity and novels about the stage. Few artisan professions existed within the theater prior to the late nineteenth century. Performers put on their own make-up and they often purchased their own costumes. Slowly, theaters, particularly in New York City, realized the cost benefits that they would accrue through purchasing the wardrobes themselves. They began hiring workers to alter the costumes, store them, and eventually design them. Meanwhile, the creators of props evolved from a single jack-of-all-trades person into a small group of carpenters and prop men who also served as stagehands.

The numbers and importance of these crafts grew. With the growth of realism in theatrical productions during the first two decades of the twentieth century, designers of stage scenery and clothing became increasingly important. The workers soon realized their influence and strove to obtain a better work environment. The majority of the stagehands unionized with the International Alliance of Theatrical and Stage Employees by the mid–1910s. They received additional attention and credit in playbills and within the pages of theatrical trade publications. General interest magazines began to include both articles that discussed their work and interviews that featured these men.[29]

These magazine images of the theatrical backstage only occasionally provided depictions of the theater artisans. The articles observed that most theaters had a scenic artist and a crew of electricians, a boss carpenter and stagehands. However, these articles did not personalize this information by discussing or quoting individual workers. Readers learned highly general details about the people in these professions. These articles described scenic artists as well-dressed men of the world. Meanwhile, the stagehands and carpenters had unfriendly dispositions. They spent their down time sitting around arguing about sports under a bunch-light during the theatrical performances.[30]

A few articles in magazines during the late 1910s focused upon explaining backstage through the discussion of one artisan position. One group of these pieces informed audiences about the techniques involved in performing particular theatrical effects. However, these articles rarely discussed individual stagehands and their lives. A second set of articles focused on the evolution of the specific craft, such as scenic art in American theater. These pieces provided a general description of the activities involved in performing the job. Occasionally, these articles provided brief descriptions of the person's looks and training for their position.[31]

Neither of these types of behind-the-scenes articles presented the personalities of these artisans of the stage. The missing details about the people who worked as artisans and the environment where they toiled denied the backstage any color or élan. The backstage appeared to be a place unpopulated by interesting characters and undefined as a space. Hollywood publicity and the people writing Hollywood novels and the scripts of movies about Hollywood strove to make Hollywood arts and crafts jobs and the workers performing them appear exciting.

Hollywood Arts and Crafts

The craft world behind the scenes in the movie industry grew increasingly complex and exciting over the first two decades of the studios centralization in Hollywood. In the early silent film days decisions about furnishing sets usually involved the director, a carpenter, and a prop man. Increased motion picture production and demand for realism made the need for specialists to accomplish behind-the-scenes tasks apparent to the studios.

Many of the artisan professions developed during the late 1910s and early 1920s. The workers who created the sets, fashions, and cosmetic styles seen on movie screens also engaged in private activities behind the scenes in Hollywood. While not as frequently depicted in Hollywood as performers, these images offered audiences peeks at people who they otherwise never saw. The images highlighted the same three things they did with the performers behind the scenes. They used glamour, familial feeling, and sexual escapades to present behind the scenes as a magical work environment, different from backstage or any other workaday world.

Motion picture artisans engaged in their pre-production or production tasks within specific locations on the enormous studio lots. Set decorators worked within the art department and on the stage sets to create the sets' scenic décor. These workers also synchronized these sets with the action and made certain the colors of sets and costumes complemented each other. Hairdressers and make-up artists toiled in one big room with three-double-mirrored tables. They began work on the stars and hundreds of other performers very early in the morning.

Although certain performers cooperated in creating their best looks, the make-up professionals insisted on their expertise in creating the glamorous styles. The glamorous fashions emerged from the visions and activities occurring in places such as the concrete mausoleum that housed ladies' wardrobe at Paramount. This sat atop men's wardrobe, which had shoes, shirts, uniforms, and fixing shops. Over 180 people worked in wardrobe at MGM in the late 1930s, operating metal spray-dying machines and the sewing and beading equipment.

During and after production, stars went with publicity people to the photography studios. The top photographers produced an average of 300 negatives daily to capture the excitement and emotion in a motion picture scene or personality with a single exposure. Photographers' star images graced the theater lobbies and fanzines, presenting the sex and earnestness that together spelled glamour.[32]

Hollywood publicity materials included stories and articles that promoted individual studio artisans as well as their work. A story about the head of Warner Bros'. flower department explained that the floral beauty and style notable in this studio's Hollywood productions depended upon the work of Joe Trusty and his staff. Trusty studied scripts and planned flowers to match sequences (e.g. summer flowers for summer sequences), and his staff created vibrant imitations of flowers for "long shots."

Another piece of publicity featured art directors. This article explained that the beautiful towns and buildings that appeared on the screen emerged because of the creativity of studio art directors and their departments. The article noted that Columbia's Lionel Banks and his staff created everything from enormous skyscrapers to historical Tucson, Arizona, that had a significant impact on making the movie. Thus, the piece demystified this portion of behind the scenes for readers.[33]

Items suggested that many artisans experienced the type of familial closeness that many actors mentioned they experienced behind the scenes. The wardrobe chief at Warner Bros. heaped lavish praise on his clothing designer, Orry Kelly. He noted that Kelly and wardrobe supervisor Miss Twas McKenzie worked together, then with the director and star, to make the creations that appeared on screen. The head of the script department at Twentieth Century–Fox, Kathleen Ridgway, "...is the boss and office mother of 150 girls—secretaries, stenographers, mimeograph operators and script distributors...."

Not only did Ridgeway keep the women working in harmony, but she was "on call" 24 hours a day to scores of executives, producers, writers, directors, and department heads.

Despite these pressures, the studio functioned like a big family so that "Kathleen knows practically everybody on the lot, and they all call her by her first name—from janitors to executives." Mary Eicks served as the traffic dispatcher for the drivers of more than 150 units of rolling stock, including camera cars, buses, trucks, sound units, and limousines. Her office handled from 500 to 1,000 calls daily. The men liked taking orders from this woman because Eicks had a role in their close-knit group, as she was "a regular guy" to all of them.[34]

The depictions of artisans fueled the belief that romance regularly occurred off-screen. Items in gossip columns occasionally noted dates between performers and artisans. When romances blossomed into marriages, articles described their glamorous weddings, such as the ceremony that occurred within a mission between actress Dolores Del Rio and MGM art department director Cedric Gibbons. Whether a fabulous wedding or a short-term relationship, these images presented information about private affairs while cementing the notion that behind the scenes with artisans had its mysteries, glamour, family bonding and romance.

Several of these professions, including interior designers and make-up artists, had reputations for attracting certain employees. Several of the jobs behind the scenes appealed to men who did not adopt culturally defined masculine behaviors and heterosexual interests. During the early twentieth century, interior design groups such as C.R. Ashbee's Guild offered a homosexual and effeminate community. This continued in Hollywood. During congressional testimony in the 1940s, the head of Columbia's Scene Art Department, Thomas Cracraft, noted that "...his scenic artists were rather peculiar creatures." The committee counsel stated, "I think we can look at you and say that."[35] Hollywood materials put the men in these professions and other effeminate and homosexual, male, temperamental artistes on display.

Temperamental Artistes Behind the Scenes

A temperamental artiste appeared with other electricians in an impromptu skit in *Going Hollywood* (MGM, 1933). Unhappy teacher Sylvia Bruce (Marion Davies) left her job at a private school and ingratiated herself with the producer of crooner Bill Williams's (Bing Crosby) new movie on a train to California. Befriended by an out-of-work actress, Jill Baker (Patsy Kelly), Sylvia used her connection to get them both work on the Williams movie. At the dinner break, Jill told Sylvia to watch the three electricians who were ready to perform in front of fake microphones for the other artisans and small-time actors on the set.

The first man imitated a boxing announcer, then introduced "...the new heavyweight champion of the world ... Kate Smith." A tall, fey man in the middle of the trio exaggerated his eyes and pursed his lips as he mouthed, "When the Moon Comes Over the Mountain." Upon concluding he said, "Hello, this is little Katie, and I'm going to sing a song for all those people down at the nudist colony. You're an old smoothie." After the last man faked more announcing, the first introduced the fey man as the tenor Morton Downey. He pretended to sing as the third Radio Rogue stated, "And you're still suffering, people. This is Tony Twice speaking and you know who's singing, umm? Why that's Morton Downey's nephew, Up-side Down-ey."[36]

MGM suggested to exhibitors that they market *Going Hollywood* with catch phrases including, "It's Hollywood Through A Keyhole — Its Glamour, Its Loves, Its Melody!"[37] The promotion promised audiences revelation of mysteries. It also boasted that the movie showed behind-the-scenes contained glamour and romance.

If the promotional material was accurate, then audiences for the movie got inside the studio. When audiences for the movie looked, they saw that Hollywood behind the scenes was a place where people knew each other and had fun performing. The soundstage scene revealed that effeminate males worked in Hollywood as electricians. These Hollywood bohemians were friends with other electricians and had fun with them putting on a show for other behind-the-scenes workers.

Noted screenwriter Donald Ogden Stewart originally conceived the idea of depicting behind the scenes as familial in *Going Hollywood*. Stewart viewed the scene as a group of extras gathered around a piano during the lunch break watching Sylvia imitate the star of the film within the film, Lilly Yvonne (Fifi D'Orsay). A later script positioned electricians, prop boys, and extras eating lunch around the piano. Jill asked Mike to do his "radio" act. The script directed Mike to imitate Kate Smith perfectly naturally, without stepping forward and staging a number. By late September, the scene simply stated that the Radio Rogues go into their act.[38] Stewart's version focused on depicting the soundstage as a family where some members put on a show. Stewart injected Hollywood humor based on putting impressions into the scene. At first, the humor centered on the lower workers making fun of the star, but he changed the scene to have the humor come from a man imitating a well-known female singer.

The Three Radio Rogues, Jimmy Hollywood, Ed Bartell, and Henry Taylor, had a long vaudeville career. This would be the first of the few motion pictures that the trio made during the 1930s. The group's scene in *Going Hollywood* was the vaudeville comedy section that occurred in most of the musical comedies within the Hollywood-on-Hollywood movies. The vaudeville style cared more about a joke than the need to maintain narrative consistency. Often, these comedy scenes included sexual ambiguity that fluctuated from scene to scene depending upon the comic potentials of each situation. It was not unusual for the humor to center on same-gender sexuality.[39]

The Three Radio Rogues' version of Stewart's scene greatly embellished upon the original idea. By expanding the part for the Radio Rogues, the moviemakers increased the role of the artisans behind the scenes. The troupe made fun out of radio programming. Commercial radio programming had started in the early 1920s and developed stars like Kate Smith and Morton Downey. The Rogues imitated the experience of turning the radio dial, moving from boxing to two different orchestras with pop singers. The trio played on the inability to see the performers on the radio, from staging a fake boxing match to using a man to perform as a woman singer.

The troupe presented the insight into the electrician's Hollywood bohemian status in two comedic ways. Ed Bartell's female impersonation included exaggerating the rolling and batting of his eyes and the pursing of his lips. As noted earlier in the soundstage scene from *Show Girl in Hollywood*, these actions were considered signs of a homosexual male in the era. This understanding was ubiquitous enough for a motion picture censor on another movie to label these actions "too pansyish." He requested their removal from the movie before he gave his approval for its release. The troupe also engaged in word play on the identity of other singer the trio imitated, Morton Downey. The joke named the representation "Upside Downey," implying a reversal and inversion and the suggestion that the movie's female impersonator shared this inversion. The group added this hint of homosexuality, enhancing the perception of the artisan performer as Hollywood bohemian. Their addition also made the stage set behind the scenes as a place where a bohemian could be found and a place where he could be seen revealing his interest in forbidden pleasures.

The scene revealed behind the scenes as a familiar workplace where workers put on shows for themselves. The presence of the Hollywood bohemian created a show within that show. This second show was spectacular because it featured culturally taboo behaviors of a man acting like a woman and expressing his homosexuality humorously. Audiences and critics enjoyed the humor. The picture, which cost nearly one million dollars to produce, earned its producing studio, Cosmopolitan, a healthy profit. The reviews were fair, with *Variety* noting that the Three Radio Rogues "are cleverly spotted in such a way that their number is a break both for themselves and the picture." Obviously, the exposure of this electricians' taboo romantic activities met the audience's expectations as they peered through the keyhole into Hollywood behind the scenes.[40]

Other Hollywood materials offered peeks behind the scenes that showed temperamental artistes working in other movie industry professions. In the novel *Reckless Hollywood* the behind-the-scenes character worked in a studio art department. The novel suggested that the worker's Hollywood bohemian attitudes shaped his work in the movie industry.

> Petty went over to Bob Bates' table [at Sebastian's Cotton Club]. He had been on the make for the tall, lean and beautiful actor Perry at Faith Hope's party. Bates was a kid who did clever sketches in Aubrey Beardsley manner. They greeted

each other happily. He teased her about being a foolish virgin. She said she wouldn't introduce Dan to him "...because you'll try to steal him from me. You're dangerous." When she returned to her table, Dan became jealous, then raged that she disgraced him by standing in the middle of the room talking to a fairy.[41]

Readers learned that some sketch artists in the Hollywood studios were homosexual Hollywood bohemians. Bates sought males for sexual encounters at a party and a nightclub. He acted on his interests without particular concern for other people's reactions. Readers wondered how the sketch artist behaved on the lot. Did he behave like some of the stars and find willing partners in locations behind the scenes? Was he involved with one of the Hollywood bohemian male actors? The scene revealed secrets about the sketch artist but raised mysteries about what kind of activities went on behind the scenes, making that environment more exciting and intriguing.

This depiction of a sketch artist implied that his player nature enabled him to influence the movies. Sketch artists prepared preliminary versions of the approximately thirty sets that appeared in every motion picture. When turned into movie stage sets, these settings from the sketch artist's drawings created a sense of place. The sets also allowed spectators to feel that they were within an environment so that they would not have their attention distracted from the characters and the story.

The description of Bob Bates noted that the sketch artist's reputation and style reminded movie people of designer Aubrey Beardsley. Beardsley enjoyed membership in theatrical and homosexual circles in London during the 1890s. Bates's adoption of Beardsley's style meant that he brought some theatricality and hints of homosexual love to the movies. Behind the scenes in Hollywood was now made more mysterious because it served as a place where a sketch artist like Bates expressed his homosexual interests at work as he created glamorous movie sets seen in the movies. A critic noted that Hollywood bohemian actress Alla Nazimova and set designer Natacha Rambova used Beardsley's designed in the Nazimova-financed *Salome* in 1923.[42]

Other temperamental artistes brought new technologies as well as new styles to Hollywood. Still photographers played significant roles in creating Hollywood's glamour. They created the portraits of the stars that filled the movie magazines and fired the imaginations of countless movie fans. Keane McGrath's *Hollywood Siren* (1932) featured a still photographer named Leslie Beaumont. McGrath used references to the psychiatrists of the day to reveal the character's player interests.

> A slightly built young man with golden hair and Greek-features, Carmen enjoyed Leslie Beaumont's cultured ways and his taking her to museums and talk of books. Little by little she began to observe peculiarities of his nature, such as a high-pitched feminine laugh when excited, his love of jewelry and his choice of delicate pastel shades for his ties and socks. Slowly it dawned on her

that he was one of the third sex. She enjoyed not having to keep her barriers up with him and her cursory studies of Freud and Krafft-Ebing gave her a more humanitarian view of his affliction. His splendid mind equipped with a first class education from Oxford furnished a mine of information for her. He'd found neither the business world nor the social life of England to his liking and had cultivated his artistic abilities. He drifted to America and after many hardships he had at length achieved his success in color photography.[43]

Industry still photographers formed a select guild, with approximately 90 working within their studios on the lots. Insiders such as Fred Astaire observed their Hollywood bohemian natures. Astaire labeled Cecil Beaton an English "fagat" [sic] and quipped that Beaton disliked Clare Booth Luce's voice probably because it was the same as his. Whether actors such as Astaire liked it or not, these photographers were the bosses within their photography studios. The photographers behaved as they wanted in their behind-the-scenes workspaces. The Hollywood bohemian photographer with his taboo sexual interests turned the photographer's studio that many readers knew from their own experiences of having photographs taken into an exotic locale.

The depiction of Beaumont's player nature and professional skills made him appear uniquely qualified to work in Hollywood. The artistic abilities that he cultivated and the temperament that kept him out of the business and social worlds of England fit well within Hollywood behind the scenes. Beaumont's artistic abilities helped him create the photographs of the glamorous lifestyles that promoted public worship of movie stars. His skills in color photography became increasingly valuable as studios saw full-color advertisements as a major marketing device to attract attention to their features. His work, like the elegant portraits of the male movie stars that emerged from the work of photographers such as George Hurrell, established the legitimacy of male nude or seminude glamour in photographs. These male star photographs expanded homoerotic possibilities in all of photography.[44]

The scene with Beaumont illuminated that the photographer shared his elegance and culture around the studio. This was particularly true in his relationship with the actress Carmen. This sharing resulted in the pair developing a deeply caring relationship that resembled certain family relationships, such as between an older brother and his sister or between two cousins. Actresses fondly described their relationships with the still photographers. Myrna Loy noted that George Hurrell, Laszlo Willinger, and Ted Allan were great and spent a lot of time working with performers to create the best images.

Clarence Bull, MGM's portrait artist, developed this relationship with bohemian Greta Garbo. At first he thought her shy and quiet for their first three hours of shooting. He believed his diffidence at their first meeting allowed Garbo to think he was a kindred spirit. They developed a longtime friendship. Actresses had professional reasons to develop close relationships with the still photographers. The industry was aware that "...glamour and publicity are tied to getting good pictures. This makes the still photographer one of the most important people in town."[45] The homosexual men who held this vital position made Hollywood behind the scenes exciting because they expressed their taboo interests and sexuality on the lot with their star actress friends.

Temperamental artistes who helped create Hollywood glamour appeared in a couple of Hollywood on Hollywood movies in the mid–1930s. Their forbidden interests were obvious to other behind-the-scenes workers in the movie. Like the artistes that appeared in the Hollywood novels, these movies observed the significant impact the artisans' Hollywood bohemian nature had on their work. *Something to Sing About* (Grand National, 1937) provided audiences with thrills by placing its audience in a producer's office.

Studio executive B. O. Regan, publicity man Hank Meyers, and their new star Terry Rooney (Jimmy Cagney) awaited the arrival of a trio of department heads. Easton from make-up, studio stylist Mr. Davianai, and drama coach Mr. Blaine entered. They stood at the far end of Regan's enormous office. The producer introduced them to Rooney. Quickly, the producer demanded that each of his artistes assess Rooney's physical features and explain how they would shape him into a movie star. Mr. Easton, played by actor Dwight Frye, spiced up the scene with his Hollywood bohemian attitude.[46]

> Easton took out a monocle and stepped forward and examined the Cagney character. He reaches up to the forehead of Rooney and breathlessly said, "The hairline. Gracious." His eyes bulged out and his voice rose. "It belongs on an entirely different face, Mr. Regan." "Well, fix it," Regan barked. Easton frowns and pouts. "Hmmph. So easily said." His eyes again bulged out as he tossed his head back. With a slight wiggle to his torso he turned his back to Regan and walked back to stand beside his fellow artisans.[47]

The boss's office was an area of behind the scenes that audiences would be familiar with from their own lives. However, few viewers had a boss with an office of the size and décor of this one. The movie then expanded upon those environmental differences, adding a character to sell Hollywood as a very different place. Few audience members witnessed an employee behave as they wanted in their boss's office. The Easton character put in his monocle and became something to watch. He added words and mannerisms that brought the showiness and humor of a homosexual male to the office. The make-up artist "stole" the scene, thrilling viewers with a look at a taboo person and etching in viewers' minds the zaniness of the Hollywood producer's office.

A second scene from *Something to Sing About* also focused on how Hollywood built stars. This scene showed the key role Hollywood artisans played in that process. Rooney worked with the drama coach, who tried to change his speech, then went to the stylist, who wanted him to wear different clothes. The would-be star entered the make-up area. Rooney seated himself in the barber shop chair. While Easton, clad in white smock, stood behind him, Rooney practiced his lines. Easton whined that Rooney was annoying him, but the actor did not stop. "When I look at that hairline I could almost cry," Easton winced, prompting Rooney to smirk. Easton grabbed a toupee off a mannequin and tried to persuade Rooney to wear the widow's peak, but the actor refused.

The scene introduced viewers to another area behind the scenes. Easton's effeminate mannerisms made the make-up room appear especially memorable. According to studio figures of the era, the scene was truthful. Director Vincent Sherman stated that there was a general feeling that the make-up artist was a homosexual occupation. He and others could tell that these men would have homosexual interests "...by their feminine delicacies and gracefulness in the way that they walked and the way that they used their hands."[48]

The make-up department scene revealed to viewers the mystery behind the make-up artists' creation of stars' glamorous looks. The scene suggested that the artisan's Hollywood bohemian nature helped in the creation of glamour. Earlier, in the producer's office, Easton's homosexuality helped him assess the actor's looks. Now his abilities went toward giving the actor a successful look. Easton persisted in trying to put a toupee on Rooney to give him a widow's peak style. This hairstyle was linked to MGM romantic star Robert Taylor.

Part of a movie artisan's job involved providing artifice in motion pictures. One of the methods that they used to accomplish this involved drawing attention to their costume as a product itself. Easton's sense of camp (a homosexual cultural style of the era) presumably informed his ability to "play." Easton's sense of play would be to put part of a look associated with a famous actor on another actor. Thus, the make-up artist had both personal and professional motivation to believe that a new romantic male star could find success with a look similar to the romantic male then in vogue. The critic for the *New York Times* found this aspect of the movie accurate and humorous. He wrote that "...the movie was an amusing, sardonic and frolicsome piece.... The best of the film is the satirizing of the Hollywood star-building methods."[49] The scenes with the Hollywood bohemian helped sell the movie and Hollywood itself.

Despite the satirical take on the movie industry, *Something to Sing About* showed that the make-up artist got along with other people in behind-the-scenes Hollywood. Both scenes suggested that Easton shared a type of family with the other department heads. In the first scene, the three men waited together before entering the producer's office. The trio sympathized with each other's plights in having to turn Rooney into a star. After each had a frustrating time attempting to transform Rooney, the three artisans went to the soundstage to watch Rooney perform in a fight scene. The designer whispered to the men and each agreed that they wanted the new star to take a punch. When the stunt man actually hit Rooney, the trio smiled.[50] *Something to Sing About* showed the artisans shared a unity similar to a family group, accepting and even enjoying each other's character behind the scenes in Hollywood.

Another motion picture about the movie industry revealed that some costumers were also Hollywood bohemians, linking forbidden sexuality to another area behind the scenes. Screenwriters Jerry Wald and Maurice Leo established that the dress designer in *Hollywood Hotel* (1937) would have homosexual interest. Production Code Administration (PCA) reviewers noticed the homosexuality of this character and passed this information on to their boss, Joseph Breen. In his letters to Warner Bros. studio chief Jack Warner, Breen warned that there must be no "pansy" flavor to any of the stylist's actions or dialogue.

By September, the PCA found the revisions they requested for other scenes acceptable. However, Breen's letter again protested that there must be no suggestion of a "pansy" in the characterization of the male dress designer. Two months later, Breen happily advised Jack Warner that *Hollywood Hotel* seemed satisfactory from the standpoint of the production code. Interestingly, there was little change in the characterization of the designer between Wald and Leo's first script and the depiction in the motion picture almost a year later.[51]

The movie took viewers into a place where the female star received a fitting. The image suggested that a circus atmosphere prevailed in the area, with the effeminate stylist constituting one portion of the zaniness. Early in the movie, the star actress Mona Marshall, stood while being fitted for a dress as gossip columnist Louella Parsons (playing herself) began to interview her. The dress designer (Curt Bois), in a pinstriped suit, carnation in the lapel and cigarette holder dangling from his mouth, walked about Mona as she stood on a podium.

"Please, everybody. Quiet, my nerves, I'm going mad," Mona said, unintentionally sounding hammy. "Mona darling, the dress is so gorgeous, I can't stand it." The dress designer swooned over the dress. He leaned back, hand on his chest. "Oh, do you really think so, Butch?" "Really.... If your fans don't collapse on the sidewalk when you walk into that theater tonight," his voice rose, "I'll tear it to pieces." He fluttered around and fussed over the dress while Mona answered one of Louella's questions.

A shoe salesman held up a pair. "I can have these dyed any color you wish, Miss Marshall." She tried to answer but the designer flitted over to the shoe man. "No, no, no, no. Am I the designer, or am I the designer!" Mona conceded. The designer opened his coat and ran a hand down his torso. "I want her feet practically on the ground — nothing but jewels." His eyes grew large and he stared down at the man. The man gave him a confused gaze.

> While a man requested that Mona sign a radio contract, Mona's personal secretary, Miss Jones, walked in. After a subtle insult at Mona, Jones picked up a pair of shoes and told the shoe man, "You better dye these and send a pair of black ones too." The designer stood at Jones's side. "You mean you want black ones too. Why don't you get her a pair of skates while you're at it? I want a pair of very high-heeled shoes," he pointed his cigarette holder in a highly animated fashion. Jones dropped the shoes and said to the designer, "What are you going to wear them with?"[52]

An interview and a fitting would ordinarily occur at different times. The movie combined them in order to save time in telling its story. Still, the scene offered its audience a look behind the scenes at a dress fitting. They saw the fitting of a movie star with the wardrobe woman pinning the dress and the shoe man toting several choices into the room. The designer oversaw the entire activity.

The behaviors of the characters made the dress fitting memorable and helped market Hollywood as a unique place. The star acted like a prima donna. She basked in the attentions of all the people in the room while she asked for their reassurances. As distinctive as the star was, the dress designer made the scene. The designer was as elegantly dressed as the star, adding a carnation and a cigarette holder for good measure. His flourishes with his hands and other mannerisms gave him a distinctive air. The secretary's comment regarding the shoes signaled that the designer was a homosexual. With this declaration, the designer gave viewers of the scene the titillation of sexual revelation and the unique experience of seeing a taboo person.

The scene linked the designer's Hollywood bohemian nature with glamour. The designer created a gown for the actress to accentuate her womanliness and elicit envy and adoration from her fans. Like the make-up artist in *Something to Sing About*, this Hollywood bohemian artisan wanted to play with

Curt Bois as the dress designer posing with actress Mona Marshall (Lola Lane) while she is fitted by a seamstress (played by Georgie Cooper). A radio representative (played by John Harron) wants her to sign a contract in *Hollywood Hotel* (Warner Bros., 1937) (courtesy George Eastman House Motion Picture Department Collection).

the star's looks. He promoted a camp style through helping the female star portray her life as theater and herself as an exaggeration of femininity. Hollywood studio stylists, such as Howard Greer, noted that they designed with exaggerated femininity in mind. He enjoyed Hollywood's over-emphasis on clothes and its precociousness and juvenile manners with every curve and muscle proudly emphasized.[53] Butch enjoyed these same things and his experience of wearing women's clothes, hinted at by Mona's secretary, enabled him to easily place himself in the actress's shoes, and other apparel.

Hollywood Hotel received strong critical and spectator response. Critics writing for both the trade magazines and newspapers gave the movie positive reviews. The film earned good returns at the box office, although they did not reach the success that *Film Daily* had predicted. The reviewer for *Film Daily* also noted, "Marshall, Fuzzy, Callaghan, and dress designer score with their comedy."[54]

A similar view of dress designers emerged from a novel by another movie industry insider one year later. Jane Allen's 1938 Hollywood novel, *I Lost My Girlish Laughter*, brought her readers inside a successful studio. There readers found a jaded publicity director and a naive secretary/narrator. The book also included two different Hollywood bohemians, a lecherous studio executive and an effeminate studio stylist. Allen was the pseudonym of Silvia Schulman, who served as producer David O. Selznick's personal secretary during the mid–1930s. The novel contained many of Schulman's experiences with the producer and his company. Selznick unsuccessfully attempted to prevent Orson Welles from broadcasting the novel on CBS radio but did stop MGM from using its screen rights to create a movie from the book. While several reviewers praised the novel as humorous and filled with highly provocative details, none of these reviews mentioned the stylist.[55]

After featuring behind-the-scenes locations throughout the book, the author brought the studio business to an area hospital. Producer Sidney Brand developed "sympathy" pains while waiting for his wife to give birth. He checked himself into his own hospital room. Members of the studio staff crowded around Brand's bed as they planned the filming of their new production. Eric of wardrobe entered the hospital and said "yoo-hoo" to Madge (Brand's personal secretary), who was waiting outside. The pair entered Brand's room.

> "Mr. Brand ... Mr. Brand." It was Eric waving frantically. "I've simply got to get an okay on these sketches and get back to the studio." "Alright Eric. Let's see them." Eric flitted over to the bed and spread out his portfolio. Sidney Brand turned pages carelessly and looked out the door at nurses strutting past. He said he didn't like them. "You can't tell me that a dame in the jungle's going to wear a Chanel creation...." "But Mr. Brand, this is exotic.... This is exciting. You know perfectly well that illusion can be preserved only by covering the form." Here Eric made a few passes down his own divine form. "...I want every woman in the audience to itch to be in the jungle with nothing on like Tarn and I want every man to get hot." Jim (the publicist) broke in. "Mr. Brand wants you to raise a

wholesale libido!" "Swell word Jim, that's just what I mean.... You'll have plenty of time in the American sequence to do a Schraparelli." "But there are fashions even in the jungle, Mr. Brand. A woman is a woman no matter what or where...." "Okay true, just so long as you keep conscious of the fact that she is a woman I'll be satisfied. But to hell with illusions." Eric appeared injured. "But Mr. B...." "Good-bye Eric." Eric shrugged his shoulders eloquently but gathered up his sketches and departed.[56]

Brand's hospital room was no place for the sick or even the weary. The producer and the studio staff conducted business as if they were on the studio lot. The two Hollywood bohemians turned what was already a nutty scene into a crazy situation. Brand lusted after the female nurses. His lustfulness and other energies were so intense that he drove Madge out of the room. The dress designer added his giddiness and flamboyance and brought the menagerie inside this hospital room to a fevered pitch.

The scene illustrated that Hollywood bohemian attitudes shaped the making of movies. In his role as the producer of the movie that they were planning, Brand had both professional and personal reasons behind how he wanted to dress the star. Brand put a jungle scene in the motion picture because the location would allow him to justify to the censors placing a woman in skimpy clothes. Besides attracting viewers, Brand included the scene to please his own lustful appetite for females.

The designer's gender and sexual attitudes led to his focus on glamour. Eric's approach to his work, influenced by his lack of sexual interest in women, prompted him to want to dress the female star in the latest fashions regardless of the location of the scene. Eric intended to preserve the illusion of the form of the female star. In his view this highlighted the purpose of the woman star, to be an alluring, distant and glamorous figure on which to display clothes. He thought that this was as exotic and exciting for the audience as it was for him. To Eric, a woman was a woman, a person who wore great clothes. Brand agreed that a woman was a woman. In his interpretation, a woman was a sexual object for males. The department heads realized that the stylist could not understand Brand's perspective on this issue. The publicist tried to help the stylist understand through making the producer's view very obvious, but to no avail.

How were readers to interpret Eric's inability to understand his boss's view? Could Eric have been so naïve and have lived such a sheltered life that he did not understand Brand's base motivations? Maybe Eric did understand but feigned ignorance in order to express his perspective? Like the designer in *Hollywood Hotel*, Eric promoted camp in his motion picture work. Eric wanted to put the actress into gowns that highlighted her figure and prompted fans to want to collapse on the sidewalk in front of her. Or, similar to the makeup artist, Eric expressed camp in his work through his use of artifice. Eric's intention to place the female star in a glamorous evening gown within the middle of the jungle created an incongruity between the female star, "the object," and the jungle, "the context." This incongruity was so extreme that it was funny. If Eric wanted the star dressed his way he would make his argument while being naïve to Brand's position to avoid a confrontation with his boss.

A studio stylist who was a Hollywood bohemian appeared in newspaper and magazine articles that offered readers glimpses behind the scenes. Warner Bros'. irascible chief designer George Orry Kelly, a native of Kiama, Australia, was born on New Year's Eve of 1897 to middle-class Irish emigrants. The town originally served as a primary supplier of lumber and later rock to Sydney; its increased transportation routes to Sydney made the area a desirable location for vacations.

Known as Jack, Kelly attended local public schools and helped out in his father's tailoring business by hand-painting ties and shawls for the customers. He studied art and design. After an initial foray into banking, Kelly soon began to act upon his longtime interest in the stage, which required leaving his native country and heading for the big theater areas in the English-speaking world: London and New York.[57]

Neither of these theater capitals proved a fertile place for this tall, smart, and impeccably dressed young man's dreams of becoming an actor. He obtained small parts and places in the chorus. This first attempt came to an end with word of his father's illness. Upon returning home, he opened his own clothing shop in Sydney. His father's death prompted Orry Kelly to try New York City again.

In the beginning of the roaring 1920s, Kelly still rarely obtained performing positions. However, he found work in the city's clothing industry and selling his own painted ties. He began receiving commissions to paint murals for restaurants, department stores, and wealthy socialites. These displays led to work designing costumes and sets in vaudeville and on Broadway. Orry Kelly moved to Hollywood in 1930, when his friend Archie Leach, known in Hollywood as Cary Grant, showed Kelly's sketches to Warner Bros'. executives. Jack Warner asked to meet the designer and hired him on a conditional basis.[58]

Several images of Orry Kelly indicated that his experience behind the scenes appeared similar to the depictions of Hollywood bohemian artisans in fiction. Similar to the fictional photographer Leslie Beaumont, Orry Kelly cultivated his artistic abilities as a teen, which helped him in Hollywood. Kelly spent most of his boyhood years drawing and designing and following an absorbing interest in everything connected with the stage.[59] He won his job at Warner Bros. with flattering sketches in miniature of actresses Kay Francis and Ruth Chatterton wearing his creations.

Like the fictional studio stylists, Orry Kelly focused on promoting glamour. "Kelly likes long evening dresses because they are becoming and dignified." The designer summarized his view of Hollywood when he arrived in the early 1930s and sounded like fellow designer Adrian. "In Hollywood there was ... a great deal of very bad taste.... Ladies' hats looked like something caught in a revolving door.... And everything in sight — from clothing to upholstery — simply dripped with beads!"

Orry Kelly developed similar relationships to the ones that the fictional artisans had. Like Beaumont, he developed close friendships with actresses.

> In a lovely Colonial house, set in a high-walled garden in the Los Feliz Hills, Orry Kelly ... lives alone among the paintings achieved by his own clever hands — and the priceless collection of porcelain cats which have come to him

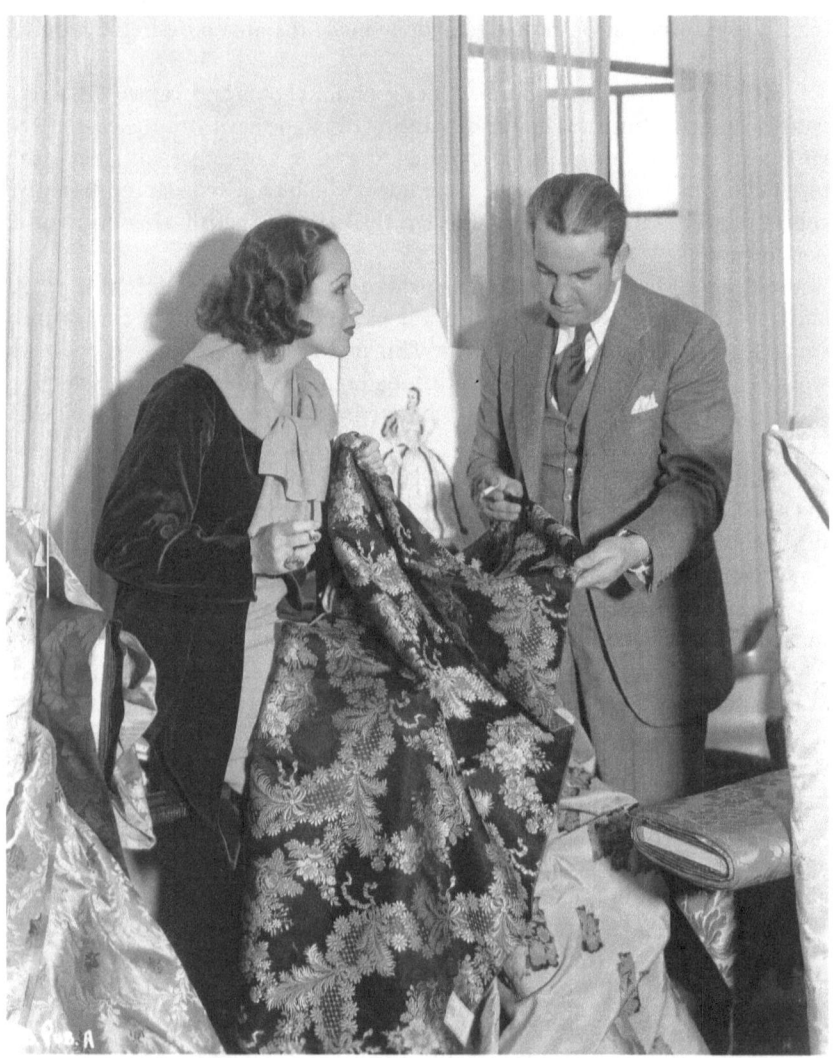

Orry Kelly and actress Dolores del Rio looking over fabrics, 1935 (courtesy George Eastman House Motion Picture Department Collection).

from friends, including Marion Davies, Lady Mendl, Perc Westmore, Cary Grant, Barbara Hutton, and Norma Talmadge.[60]

Orry Kelly's interactions with other artisans behind the scenes showed a similarity to the family relations the artisans established in the movies *Going Hollywood* and *Something to Sing About*. Orry Kelly observed that the entire design department needed to function like a dependable group on numerous occasions. "One fitting is about all any star has time to take. Sometimes a costume must be designed, fitted and sewn in one day. They work on it in shifts, people sewing all night." He noted that he worked at Warners' studio twelve years without ever having trouble with any of his principals and retained a close relationship with the studio family head. "Jack Warner still invites me home to Sunday dinner; a gesture rare, indeed, in this town."[61]

The depictions of this noted stylist provided readers with a view of Orry Kelly's behind-the-scenes professional life. These images showed this his work life shared many similarities with the fictional depictions of Hollywood bohemian artisans. Yet none of these views presented Orry Kelly as a Hollywood bohemian directly. One of the few images of Orry Kelly's private activities featured the designer at home.

> Orry Kelly has a lovely home on a hill in Hollywood, with a fine collection of lovely antiques. Here his constant companion is "Stymie" a Sealyham dog which he adores. Mr. Kelly's mother is naturally looking forward to seeing her son again — she has already been to America twice to stay with him. She says he is still very quiet and modest, and that most of what she knows of his work she learnt not from him, but from his friend, Milton Owen, a former stage manager for J. C. Williamson, Ltd., who now lives in Hollywood.[62]

The designer lived in similar circumstances to the Hollywood bohemian bachelor/odd bedfellows described in the last chapter. Besides being unmarried, Orry Kelly maintained a collection of antiques similar to Edward Everett Horton. The living arrangement in his house appeared similar to that of Orry Kelly's friend, Cary Grant. As we described in the star homes chapter, Grant shared a beach house with fellow actor Randolph Scott. Readers learned that Orry Kelly had a man in his life who enjoyed a relationship and proximity close enough to the designer that he spoke to the designer's mother on a regular basis. That man also had a significant enough knowledge of Orry Kelly's life that he could satisfy her with insight into her son.

Readers of this article would seek the most obvious explanation for Owen speaking with Orry Kelly's mother regularly and having insight into Orry Kelly's life. Their conclusion would be that the pair lived in the same house. This enabled Owen to answer the telephone when Mrs. Kelly called her son. His knowledge came from an intimate relationship with Orry Kelly. Two adult men without financial need living together and possessing intimate knowledge of one another created the impression that the Warner Bros. dress designer was another artisan Hollywood bohemian.

Contemporaries of Orry Kelly believed his life matched his image. Actress Shelley Winters arrived in Hollywood in the early 1940s. She made friends with clothing designer Jean Louis and with Orry Kelly because he had been the dress designer on movies that she made. She had a party for her husband, who had to leave town. Everyone drank a lot, chased a live turkey on the street, and jumped into a swimming pool with their clothing on. Orry Kelly wore Shelley's sister's babushka on his head. Winters's husband snapped and opened the front door while announcing, "All right, everybody ... out! I didn't do eighty bombing missions in order to have a bunch of fairies in my house!" Winters defended her friends and later passed on her husband's apology for being "an intolerant bastard."[63]

A recent biographer of actor Cary Grant provided details regarding the dress designer's life in both New York City and Hollywood. According to Eliot, Grant (then Archibald Leach) met the sophisticated, extremely effeminate, and openly and unabashedly gay Orry Kelly. They soon moved into an apartment together in Greenwich Village. The pair became lovers for a short time before they fought over career differences. The main difference appeared to be that despite being seven years younger, Grant wanted to be the main earner of the money. After two years of not speaking, Grant called Orry Kelly, who invited

Movie industry dress designers at a fashion review in February 1941. Left to right, Orry Kelly, Bernard Newman, Travis Benton, Edith Head, Adrian, and Irene (Herald Examiner Collection, Los Angeles Public Library).

Grant to join him in the circle of gay Broadway. From there Grant got a role in the show *Golden Dawn* and shortly thereafter a contract with a William Morris agent. The biographer focused less on the designer after his arrival in Hollywood. He noted that Grant and Orry Kelly met on the set of the movie *Arsenic & Old Lace* but did not stay in touch.

A few of the earlier biographers of Cary Grant, notably Charles Higham and Ray Moseley, have provided details about Orry Kelly's life. They confirm that the two men had an amorous relationship in New York City. They also detail that the pair maintained limited contact once in Hollywood.[64]

Mann's book on the influence of gays and lesbians in Hollywood provided details on Orry Kelly's life in the studios. He noted that the pair had an encounter during the filming of *Arsenic & Old Lace*. According to set decorator George James Hopkins, the movie had a limousine with the painted title "Queen for A Day." Grant quipped, "Your limousine is waiting outside." Orry Kelly did not accept the comment well at all.

Images of craftsmen and artisans in Hollywood novels, newspapers, and movies took audiences behind the scenes in Hollywood. This environment featured locations ranging from the particular to Hollywood, like sound sets, to those familiar to audiences, like photography studios. The images provided readers with the thrill of "getting inside" this closed world. Hollywood bohemian artisans also enhanced this sense of behind the scenes as a special world. They turned soundstages, offices, and other places around the lot in memorable locations by adding taboo people and forbidden sexual pleasures. This made Hollywood behind the scenes more enjoyable than backstage at any theater or those factories and offices where other people worked.

The Hollywood bohemian images of performers embodied glamour and elegance with the clothes they wore. The artisans forged that glamour and elegance with the styles that they created. Both of these groups reinforced the belief that Hollywood behind the scenes teemed with elegance and style. The relations they forged amongst themselves and with other members of the studio on stage sets, within departments, and at homes during parties convinced audiences that the Hollywood off-screen world functioned both like a family and as a hotbed of romance.

Unlike the depressed, alienated images of homosexuals that appeared on stage and in pulp fiction, Hollywood bohemians thrived behind the scenes. The performer and artisan lived and worked in the larger community and incorporated their subculture's humor and styles into Hollywood's movies. The artisans, behind the scenes, could take advantage of a place that needed their special skills. Presumably this spurred a migration of people like Leslie Beaumont, Orry Kelly, and others to work behind the scenes and live in the dream factory. But dreams can not last forever.

Before the end of the 1940s, groups of movie people made trips to testify before Congress in Washington, D.C. These people explained Hollywood, its workers, and their politics to congressional committees investigating the movie industry. Clarence Thompson was a squeaky-voiced man whom fellow members of the local Painter's Union considered womanly who may have come to Hollywood to enjoy the dream. Hollywood offered the chance to paint scenes, which required artistic skills, and behind the scenes, a place for Hollywood bohemians.

By the mid–1940s, Thompson found himself embroiled in a labor and ideological battle in Hollywood.[65] Under continued questioning from the congressional committee investigating labor in the movie industry, the head of Columbia's Scene Art Department, Thomas Cracraft, noted that "...his scenic artists were rather peculiar creatures." The Congressional committees probing Hollywood lifestyles signaled that the transition from the era of humorous and talented gender inverts to the decades of the lavender menace had begun in earnest.[66]

Conclusion
Hollywood Bohemians Today

Between 1917 and 1941 Hollywood solidified its position as the center of the production of motion pictures. The big five and little three studios certainly accomplished industry domination through vertical integration and factory production methods. But they also used Hollywood Hoopla, the continual promotion of movie products, movie stars and people, and the movie industry and its town. These factors in the industry's success are well known.

This book has illustrated that the media making the hoopla contained images of adulterers, cross-dressers, and homosexuals. These images showed stars and other movie people toying with crossing the boundaries of culturally acceptable gender and sexual interests and activities. These Hollywood bohemians associated the taboo and pleasure of experiencing the forbidden with specific places in Hollywood. Readers of Hollywood novels and entertainment-reporting organizations' articles saw the Hollywood bohemians make Hollywood nightclubs, parties, and star homes into special places with wild and crazy activities and people. Hollywood-on-Hollywood movie audiences watched the bohemians' presence turn Hollywood behind the scenes into a spectacle. Moviegoers and readers enjoyed these spectacles while these displays helped these audience members distinguish Hollywood spaces from media depictions of similar places that existed throughout the country.

A few scholars have examined a small amount of the Hollywood bohemian publicity. Their sole focus has been some of the images that appeared in newspapers and fan magazines that hinted at homosexuality. They attributed the existence of these images to the "open secret" nature of Hollywood or to the presence of gays and lesbians in the industry.

However, this book has illuminated that the Hollywood bohemians were a much larger and more significant phenomenon. Neither of the proposed factors can explain the amount of Hollywood bohemian images and the inclusion of adulterers in addition to homosexuals and cross-dressers. Neither factor can account for the bohemians' presence in all Hollywood materials nor for the creation of some of the images by the studios themselves.

The Hollywood bohemians also formed an integral part of Hollywood's self-definition. For over twenty-five years the studios put them in the movies that they made about their industry. Gossip columnists, magazine, and newspaper reporters alluded to their presence in their syndicated columns and feature articles. The movie industry's screenwriters and other observers of moviedom put them in their Hollywood novels. Like other studio publicity of the era, the Hollywood bohemians confirmed that Hollywood was a place to achieve success and personal fulfillment.[1] Hollywood bohemians attained material success. But they also demonstrated that Hollywood guaranteed people the ability to achieve their dreams and be happy, even if some of their interests and activities surpassed the boundaries of social acceptability.

Hollywood's self-definition exerted a significant influence on the general public. It helped explain why so many people and organizations described Hollywood as a sinful city. The Hollywood bohemians' appearance in movies, books, and articles about the movie industry showed that the industry promoted images that defied and eroded traditional values. That enhanced the view of Hollywood as a business that had a dangerous influence upon the culture.[2] The Hollywood bohemians indicated that the movie industry and its community generally accepted this view of itself. In addition, this view provided ammunition to those people who held this perspective.

Why would moviedom promote images that would generate a strong negative response from these groups? There would have to be an advantage that outweighed these obvious negatives. This advantage involved expanding Hollywood as a place for tourism. The presentation of the Hollywood bohemians illustrated the existence of links among mass-produced culture, sexual imagery, and the marketing of urban environments in history. The book *How to Sin in Hollywood* demonstrated this linkage and the belief that tourists had an interest in seeing this unconventional sexuality.

There were a few other instances in which commentators created works that reflected other cities in this same way. The author of *How to Sin in Hollywood* created a similar book for San Francisco a year earlier. The photographer Gyula Halasz, better known as Brassai, took photographs of the Paris underworld of nightclubs and other locations. His images helped build upon the French capital's reputation for raciness when they appeared in the book *Paris after Dark* in the mid–1930s. These instances occurred sporadically in San Francisco, Paris and other cities. Only Hollywood figures regularly exploited the connection among these three items and incorporated the sexual and gender non-conventional into its self-definition and the public understanding of the city.

After a quarter of a century, circumstances in U.S. culture changed and Hollywood changed with them. The number of Hollywood bohemians that appeared in the media during the early 1940s declined significantly. During 1940–1941, the few Hollywood bohemians that did appear received "harsher" depictions. The United States' preparations for and eventual entry into World War II figured prominently in this decline and change in the treatment of Hollywood bohemians. Even before the U.S. entered World War II, the movie industry sought to diminish its focus upon the Hollywood spectacle in its publicity.

The materials emerging in this era promoted Hollywood's similarity to other American locales in fighting the good fight. With the country's entry into the war, the federal government created the Office of War Information to oversee the motion picture industry's output. They located their department in the center of Hollywood. The government wanted the motion picture industry to align itself with the rest of the nation and present material promoting conventional cultural values and placed an agency in the media capital to monitor the movie industry and ensure its cooperation.

Other developments in the culture and industry made the Hollywood bohemians less useful to the industry. The understanding of what defined one of the largest groups of Hollywood bohemians had changed by the early 1940s. More people and institutions across the culture accepted the definition of homosexual as a person romantically attracted to a person of their biological sex. Fewer accepted the view of homosexual as a person who embodied the traits of the opposite gender. This change made the Hollywood bohemian depictions of men acting feminine or women acting masculine make less sense and be less interesting to audience members.

The absence of gender reversal and play in the images of homosexuals removed part of the humor of the image. This made the player images less useful to the entertainment industry. In addition, Hollywood bohemians lost a part of their usefulness because the unique effects that the images generated among audiences would diminish with their continued use. Much like any item, the player appeared less distinct and spectacular after continued use. Furthermore, the movie industry had solidified Hollywood's position as one of the world's preeminent cultural capitals by the early 1940s. Hollywood embodied urbanity, sophistication, and spectacle in the United States culture and indeed around the world. The studios had succeeded in creating the vision of Hollywood.

During the years that they appeared, the Hollywood bohemians were remarkable. They illustrated the possibility of not following the norms and still living successful lives. The Hollywood bohemians stand out as upbeat depictions of adulterers, homosexuals, and people who did not behave according the "proper" roles for men and women. The bohemians earned enormous salaries, owned fancy homes, and worked on the most important motion pictures. They held high community standing, had friendships and lovers at work and home, and expressed themselves in their work and amongst their peers. The bohemians forced people to see boundary crossers and to understand that they can live excellent lives.

They provided some audience members with another powerful gain. Members with adulterous and homosexual inclinations saw others who had the same feelings. These audiences gained the understanding that they were not alone in their behaviors. Hollywood bohemians offered audience members a small space for expressing their own fantasies and needs. The Hollywood bohemians provided these viewers with the knowledge that a vibrant group of people of untraditional behavior existed in one of the most glamorous places in the world.[3] Not only did they exist, they did well for themselves there. The influence this had on an audience member's life was immeasurable.

Previous studies of adulterous, homosexual and gender-crossing images in media noted that the figures suffered as a consequence of their behavior. These observers discovered that adulterers, homosexuals, and others rarely appeared, as magazines, literature, and motion pictures ignored their existence. In the instances when the news media included these figures, newspapers, magazines and later television documented their arrest and their pitiful lives. Fictional media sources featured these figures' renunciation of their previous selves, or their descent into suicide and death. Scholars argued that the images appeared in the media to serve as a warning about going too far over the line of acceptable behavior.

The emergence of sexual liberation and gay and lesbian political and social movements sparked slow changes in media images. The representations of people with different sexual behaviors received grudging acknowledgment in the news media. Fictional media in the late 1960s and early 1970s showed them as objects of pity or in need of support. Eventually, homosexuals began appearing as surprise characters on 1970s television sitcoms. Depictions of adulterers and other nonconformists began to appear more regularly in the media.

Finally, the market forces in the media over the last twenty years brought a variety of changes in the imagery. The media aimed at the mainstream market included a few programs, movies, and books featuring homosexual, adulterous or gender-bending characters. While depicted as a professional and personally successful characters, they generally appeared as nonsexual. The development of niche markets and narrow casting has sparked media aimed at gay, lesbian, bisexual and those with a variety of sexual interests. These characters now figure prominently in novels, have feature roles in motion pictures, and starring parts in television dramas and sitcoms. The Hollywood bohemians are the forerunners of the homosexual and adulterous images seen today.

The Hollywood bohemians have impacted the media market in additional ways. The bohemians in the Hollywood-on-Hollywood materials, with their focus on supplying audiences with information about celebrity personal lives, blazed the path followed today. Current news, magazines, and entertainment programs have become the predominant creators of the images. With current culture's greater latitude for the discussion of the sexual and personal, the media and publicists provide audiences with ever-increasing information about the romantic and sexual interests of celebrities and public figures.

Unlike the more traditional publicity materials from the studios, the Hollywood bohemians stretched the boundaries of acceptable images in their era. As such, the bohemians were one of the earliest occasions that a mass media industry featured exotic figures in their entertainment. The bohemians represented people and behaviors on the edge of cultural acceptance. They appeared new, exciting, daring, and associated the industry with these attributes. These attributes enabled the images to attract and maintain audiences for the movie industry. Audience members, particularly the young adults and teens, enjoyed the bohemians because the new and exciting placed them on the "cutting edge." The mass media of today follows suit, using association with the risqué, exciting, and cutting edge to draw audiences.

The Hollywood movie industry recognized the audience for and the appeal of presenting cutting-edge sexual images. Sets of images that pushed the boundaries of what was culturally acceptable have emerged in popular entertainment ever since. Today, movie studios, television and cable stations, and recording industry push this envelope in their effort to appear sophisticated and win market share. The Hollywood bohemians encouraged and exploited this market decades ago, helping to establish the commonplace in our contemporary society. As key figures in developing this market, the Hollywood bohemians figure prominently in the cornerstone tension of today's United States: finding the balance between the individual's desire for freedom in personal morality and the society's need for order.

Chapter Notes

Introduction

1. *Los Angeles Evening Herald and Express*, 17 December 1935, A-9; 31 December 1935, A-1; 8 January 1936, 2.
2. Anita Loos, "Hollywood Now and Then," from *Fate Keeps on Happening* (New York: Dodd, Mead, 1984), pp. 153–161, quoted in James Parris Springer, "Hollywood Fictions: The Cultural Construction of Hollywood in American Literature, 1916–1939," (Ph.D. diss., University of Iowa, 1994), p. 4; Michel Foucault, *The History of Sexuality: An Introduction, Volume 1* (New York: Random House, 1978), pp. 32–35; Richard de Cordova, *Picture Personalities: The Emergence of the Star System in America* (Urbana: University of Illinois Press, 1990), pp. 140–143; Joshua Gamson, *Claims to Fame: Celebrity in Contemporary America* (Berkeley: University of California Press, 1994), pp. 35, 66–68; Richard Schickel, *Intimate Strangers: The Culture of Celebrity* (Garden City, NY: Doubleday, 1985).
3. The examination of a broad scope of media aids that process of discovering widely-held cultural attitudes and beliefs. This range of material allows this book to capture the gamut of audiences interested in Hollywood. The audiences include fans of a particular genre, such as Cain's drama or Hollywood novels; people who enjoy Hollywood materials movies, novels, and newspapers on an occasional basis; and the Hollywoodphillic, such as the regular reader of *Photoplay* or of Louella Parsons's column. Figures from *Variety* determined the box office status of these movies. Most of these audience members could recognize these images of nonconformist gender and sexuality. Culture studies scholars of audience analysis observe that most consumers view mass-produced media within interpretive communities. These communities share similar interpretive frameworks that help individuals understand the media images they experience. The community would provide assistance to group members so that all audience members would understand the nonconformist representations. Equally as important, producers of news and entertainment rely upon mass appeal and continuing purchase of their product. Thus, articles, characters, and stories must be understandable to the largest possible audience. The dailies and tabloids that discussed the taboo topic of homosexuality used code words and phrases that would have been obvious and enjoyable enough for the largest number of audience members to maintain and expand the newspaper's circulation. Denis McQuail, *Audience Analysis* (Thousand Oaks, CA: SAGE Publications, 1997), pp. 17–20; Simon Michael Bessie, *Jazz Journalism: The Story of the Tabloid Newspaper* (New York: E. P. Dutton, 1938).
4. In 1929, the New York Special Sessions Court overturned a lower court ruling Radclyffe Hall's *The Well of Loneliness* obscene because it "idealized and extolled perversion." Over 100,000 copies of the book sold between the decision in April and the beginning of 1930. The decision offered the publishing world the ability to print books with homosexuality as a theme. Felice Flanery Lewis, *Literature, Obscenity and Law* (Carbondale: Southern Illinois University Press, 1976), pp. 109–111; William H. Short, *A Generation of Motion Pictures: A Review of Social Values in Recreational Films* (New York: National Committee for the Study of Social Values in Motion Pictures, 1928); Paul Boyer, *Purity in Print: The Vice-Society Movement and Book Censorship in the United States* (New York: Scribner's, 1968).
5. Jeannette Foster, *Sex Variant Women in Literature* (New York: Vantage Press, 1956), pp. 343–349; Jane Rule, *Lesbian Images* (Garden City, NY: Doubleday, 1975); Roger Austen, *Playing the Game: The Homosexual Novel in America* (Indianapolis: Bobbs-Merrill, 1977), pp. 20–30, 69–72; James Gifford, *Dayneford's Library: American Homosexual Writing, 1900–1913* (Amherst: University of Massachusetts Press, 1995), pp. 10–47; Lillian Faderman, *Odd Girls and Twilight Lovers: History of Lesbian Life in Twentieth-Century America* (New York: Columbia University Press, 1991), pp. 65, 100–102; Bessie; Helen MacGill Hughes, *News and the Human Interest Story* (Chicago: University of Chicago, 1940); Edward Alwood, *Straight News: Gays, Lesbians and the*

News Media (New York: Columbia University Press, 1996); Jonathan Katz, *Gay American History: Lesbians and Gay Men in the U.S.A.* (New York: Avon Books, 1976); Lisa Duggan, "The Trials of Alice Mitchell: Sensationalism, Sexology, and the Lesbian Subject in Turn-of-the-Century America," *Signs* (Summer 1993), pp. 791–814; Gary Alan Fine, "Scandal, Social Conditions, and the Creation of Public Attention: Fatty Arbuckle and the 'Problem of Hollywood,'" *Social Problems*, v. 44, No. 3 (August 1997), pp. 297–317; William J. Mann, *Wisecracker: The Life and Times of William Haines, Hollywood's First Openly Gay Star* (New York: Viking, 1998), chs. 6 & 7; Kenneth Anger, *Hollywood Babylon* (San Francisco: Straight Arrow Books, 1975).

6. Janet Steiger, *Bad Women: Regulating Sexuality in Early American Cinema* (Minneapolis: University of Minnesota Press, 1995); Lea Jacobs, *The Wages of Sin: Censorship and the Fallen Woman Film, 1928–1942* (Madison: University of Wisconsin Press, 1991); Vito Russo, *The Celluloid Closet: Homosexuality in the Movies* (New York: Harper & Row, 1981); Andrea Weiss, *Vampires and Violets: Lesbians in Film* (New York: Penguin Books, 1993); pp. 22–28; David Lugowski, "Queering the (New) Deal: Lesbian and Gay Representation and the Depression-Era Cultural Politics of Hollywood's Production Code," *Cinema Journal* 38 (Winter 1999).

7. Richard Dyer, *The Matter of Images: Essays on Representations* (London: Routledge, 1993). See Russo, Faderman and Michael Bronski notes in his book *Culture Clash: The Making of Gay Sensibility* (Boston: South End Press, 1984) for consideration of derision and psychological effects. The stereotypes indicated that the culture needed to make the boundaries fast, firm, and separate because in reality gender and sexual behavior was more capable of crossing the boundaries than the dominant value system wanted to admit.

8. Ann Douglas, *Terrible Honesty: Mongrel Manhattan in the 1920s* (New York: Farrar, Straus, and Giroux, 1995); Henry F. May, *The End of American Innocence: A Study of The First Years of Our Own Times, 1912–1917* (New York: Alfred A. Knopf, 1959); Robert Wiebe, *The Search for Order, 1877–1920* (New York: Hill and Wang, 1967); William R. Taylor, ed., *Inventing Times Square: Commerce and Culture At the Crossroads of the World* (Baltimore: Johns Hopkins University Press, 1996), pp. 120–132, 290; Tino Balio, *The Grand Design: Hollywood as a Modern Business Enterprise, 1930–1939*, Vol. 5, *History of the American Cinema*, ed. Charles Harpole (New York: Scribner's, 1993), pp. 31–32, 76; Sheila Rothman, *Woman's Proper Place: A History of Changing Ideals and Practices, 1870 to the Present* (New York: Basic Books, 1978); Juliann Sivulka, *Soap, Sex and Cigarettes: A Cultural History of American Advertising* (Belmont, CA: Wadsworth Publishing, 1998), pp. 140–160; *New York County District Attorney Scrapbooks*, v. 319–330 (1921–1927) New York City Municipal Archives; *New York Times*, 27 May 1921; Roy Rosenzweig, *Eight Hours for What We Will* (New York: Cambridge University Press, 1983); Lauren Rabinovitz, *For the Love of Pleasure: Women, Movies and Culture in Turn-of-the-Century Chicago* (New Brunswick, NJ: Rutgers University Press, 1998); William E. Leuchtenburg, *The Perils of Prosperity, 1914–1932* (University of Chicago Press, 1993), p. 178; Douglas Gomery, *The Hollywood Studio System* (London: Macmillan, 1986), p. 15; Warren I. Susman, *Culture as History: The Transformation of American Society in the Twentieth Century* (New York: Pantheon Books, 1984), p. xix; Benjamin McArthur, *Actors and American Culture, 1880–1920* (Philadelphia: Temple University Press, 1984), pp. 163–165.

9. Sharon R. Ullman, *Sex Seen: Emergence of Modern Sexuality in America* (Berkeley: University of California Press, 1997); Douglas; Vern L. Bullough, *Science in the Bedroom: A History of Sex Research* (New York: Basic Books, 1994); Lynn Duminel, *The Modern Temper: American Culture in the 1920s* (New York: Farrar, Straus and Giroux, 1995); de Cordova, 140–143; Gamson, pp. 35, 66–68.

10. Alwood; Bessie; Springer; Anthony Slide, *The Hollywood Novel* (Jefferson, NC: McFarland, 1995); Christopher Ames, *Movies About the Movies: Hollywood Reflected* (Lexington: University of Kentucky Press, 1997).

11. Vanessa P. Schwartz, *Spectacular Realities: Early Mass Culture in Fin-de-Siecle Paris* (Berkeley: University of California Press, 1998); Debbie Ann Doyle, "'The World's Playground': Tourism and Mass Culture in Atlantic City," (Ph.D. diss., American University, 2003).

12. Joe Laurie, *Vaudeville: From Honky-Tonks to the Palace* (New York: Holt, 1953), pp. 90–92; "At the Theater," *Los Angeles Herald*, 11 February 1900, p. 13; Geraldine Maschio, "Effeminacy or Art? The Performativity of Julian Eltinge," *Journal of American Drama and Theatre* 10 (Winter 1998), pp. 31–32; Ullman, pp. 51–61; Kaier Curtin, *We Can Always Call Them Bulgarians: Gay Men and Lesbians on the Stage* (Boston: Alysion Books, 1976); Samuel L. Leiter, ed., *The Encyclopedia of the New York Stage, 1920–1930* (Westport, CT: Greenwood Press, 1985); *The Encyclopedia of the New York Stage, 1930–1940* (Westport, CT: Greenwood Press, 1989); Marybeth Hamilton, "When I'm Bad, I'm Better": *Mae West, Sex, and American Entertainment* (New York: HarperCollins, 1995), ch. 4. Actress Mae West twice tried to bring groups of "fairies" to the Broadway stage, drawing condemnation and/or official repression. The theater establishment refused to offer West's play, *The Drag*, a stage in February 1927. New York City officials removed her 1928 play, *The Pleasure Man*, from the boards on its opening night.

13. Mark Dawidziak and Paul Bauer, *Jim Tully, Writer: Drifters, Grifters, Bruisers, and Stars* (Tucson, AZ: Dennis McMillan Publishing, forthcoming 2004); Charles Willeford, "Jim Tully: Holistic Barbarian," *Writing and Other Blood Sports* (Tucson, AZ: Dennis McMillan Publishing, 2000).

Chapter One

1. Sadie Thompson was a South Seas island trollop who was confronted by a fire-and-brimstone preacher in *Rain* (MGM, 1932). The movie was based on Somerset Maugham's story of the same title, which also became a highly popular play during the early 1920s and the subject of a 1928 film starring Gloria Swanson as Sadie Thompson. *Hollywood Reporter*, September, 1932 in Tichi Wilkerson and Marcia Borif, *The Hollywood Reporter: The Golden Years* (New York: Coward-McCann, 1984), p. 48.

2. Madelon Powers, *Faces Along the Bar: Lore and Order in the Workingman's Saloon, 1870–1920* (Chicago: University of Chicago Press, 1998), pp. 2–5; Hughes, pp. 11–13; Paul G. Cressey, *The Taxi-Dance Hall: A Sociological Study in Commercialized Recreation and City Life* (Chicago: University of Chicago Press, 1932), p. 3; Lewis Erenberg, *Steppin' Out: New York Nightlife and the Transformation of American Culture, 1890–1930* (Westport, CT: Greenwood Press, 1981), p. 22; Lawrence J. Levine, *Highbrow/Lowbrow: The Emergence of Cultural Hierarchy in America* (Cambridge, MA: Harvard University Press, 1988); Leonard Harry Ellis, "Men Among Men: An Exploration of All-Male Relationships in Victorian America," (Ph.D. diss., Columbia University, 1982), pp. ii-xii; George Chauncey, *Gay New York: Gender, Urban Culture and the Making of the Gay Male World, 1890–1940* (New York: Basic Books, 1994); Norman Clark, *Deliver Us from Evil* (New York: W. W. Norton, 1976); Kevin J. Mumford, *Interzones: Black/White Sex Districts in New York and Chicago in the Early Twentieth Century* (New York: Columbia University Press, 1997).

3. Cressey, p. xiii; Kathy Peiss, *Cheap Amusements: Working Women & Leisure in Turn-of-the-Century New York* (Philadelphia: Temple University Press, 1986); Frederic Cople Jaher, "Style and Status: High Society in Late Nineteenth-Century New York," in Frederic Cople Jaher, ed., *The Rich, the Well Born and the Powerful: Elites and Upper Classes in History* (Urbana: University of Illinois Press, 1973), pp. 262–264, 277; Bessie, pp. 55–57. In the 1882–1883 season, the *New York Tribune* devoted coverage to 849 weddings, 205 dinner parties, 301 receptions and 61 theatrical and musical parties. May King Van Rensselaer, *The Social Ladder* (New York: Henry Holt, 1924), p. 199; Erenberg, p. 43; McArthur, pp. 70–71.

4. Erenberg, pp. 40–55.

5. Ibid, pp. 113–114.

6. Ibid, pp. 117–137.

7. Edwin O. Palmer, *History of Hollywood* (New York: Garland, 1938), pp. 99–200; Bruce T. Torrence, *Hollywood: The First Hundred Years* (New York: Zoetrope, 1982), p. 87; David Yallop, *The Day the Laughter Stopped: The True Story of Fatty Arbuckle* (New York: St. Martin's Press, 1976), pp. 78–87; City Directory of the United States, Segment IV, *Los Angeles City Directory*, p. 1917.

8. Margaret Tante Burk, *Are the Stars Out Tonight: the Story of the Famous Ambassador and Coconut Grove* (Los Angeles: Round Table West, 1980), pp. 45–47; Jim Heimann, *Out With the Stars: Hollywood Nightlife in the Golden Era* (New York: Abbeville Press, 1985), pp. 5–10; *Los Angeles City Directory*, 1917; Susan Struthers, "Resident recalls 'Old Hollywood,'" *Hollywood History File*, International Gay and Lesbian Archives; Ralph Block, *The Zoned Quest*, Box 9, Ralph Block Collection, Manuscript Division, Library of Congress. Other unimpressed figures included screenwriter Anita Loos, Box 1, Folder 12, Mugar Library Special Collections Department, Boston University, hereafter BU, and Ben Hecht, Ben Hecht Papers, autobiography, Manuscript Division, Library of Congress, hereafter LC; Postcard of Cafe Nat Goodwin, *Los Angeles Restaurant and Nightclub File*, Academy of Motion Picture Arts and Sciences, hereafter AMPAS; Miriam Cooper Walsh, "Raoul Walsh," Letters & Writings: Drafts & Typescripts folder, Miriam Cooper Walsh Papers, Manuscript Division, LC.

9. *Los Angeles Evening Herald and Express*, 30 July 1918, sec. II, p. 3; Vale, p. 28.

10. F. Michael Moore, *DRAG! Male and Female Impersonators on Stage, Screen and Television: An Illustrated World History* (Jefferson, NC: McFarland, 1994), pp. 95–99; Joan M. Vale, "Tintype Ambitions—Three Vaudevillians in Search of Hollywood Fame," (M.A. thesis, University of San Diego, 1985), pp. 15–22.

11. Martin Banham, ed., *The Cambridge Guide to Theatre* (New York: Cambridge University Press, 1992); Anthony Slide, *The Encyclopedia of Vaudeville* (Westport, CT: Greenwood Press, 1994); Laurence Senelick, *The Changing Room: Sex, Drag and Theater* (New York: Routledge, 2000), pp. 250, 307–323.

12. During the 1910s, Hollywood turned to proven theatrical bohemians to star in films, but most failed because they proved too old, too unfamiliar to the mass audience, and too theatrical in acting style. Foreign stars included Emil Jannings and Marlene Dietrich. The industry also put many vaudeville comedians in motion pictures when sound technology became part of most motion pictures. Additionally, the industry attempted to make stars out of successful athletes and singers, including Babe Ruth, Sonja Henie, Johnny Weissmuller, and Johnny "Scat" Davis. Garth Jowett, *Film: The Democratic Art* (Boston: Little, Brown, 1976), pp. 55–56; Benjamin McArthur, pp. 200–203; Donald Spoto, *The Blue Angel: The Life of Marlene Dietrich* (New York: Doubleday, 1992); Henry Jenkins, *What Made Pistachio Nuts: Early Sound Comedy and the Vaudeville Aesthetic* (New York: Columbia University Press, 1992).

13. *Los Angeles Times*, 19 May 1915, sec. III, p. 4.

14. This suggestion of same-gender sexuality was bolstered in other gossip items that offered readers "insight" into Eltinge's personality. Gossip columnist Grace Kingsley joked, "It is hinted that a good many of Mr. Eltinge's forthcoming

picture productions will have nothing at all to do with skirts—that is, skirts as a term applied to Eltinge's wardrobe..." Eltinge formed a partnership in 1918 with independent producer Fred Balshofer to put several of his famous roles on celluloid. Balshofer had strong connections, including a motion picture distribution deal with Metro Studios. However, their first production, an anti-Kaiser story, proved ill-timed as the Armistice arrived and the major studios declined to release a motion picture it felt would lose money. Most of the glamour drag female impersonators did not want to be mistaken for a woman off-stage, yet this representation of Eltinge reveals that he appeared to court this. His comment about looking unusually beautiful in his saucy hat is noteworthy for its revelation that Eltinge notes how beautiful he appears as a woman. *Los Angeles Times*, 6 October 1918, sec. III, pp. 1,19; *Variety*, 25 January 1918, p. 46; Anthony Slide, *The Vaudevillians: A Dictionary of Vaudeville Performers* (Westport, CT: Arlington House, 1994), pp. 44–47; *Moving Picture World*, 17 August 1918, p. 969; *Los Angeles Times*, 26 April 1918, sec. II, p. 3.

15. *Photoplay*, v.14, No. 6, November 1918.
16. Senelick.
17. Clark; Chauncey; Erenberg, pp. 238–240.
18. Hughes, pp. 20–24; Cleveland Amory, *Who Killed Society?* (New York: Harper & Brothers, 1960), p. 136; Erenberg, p. 243.
19. Hamilton, pp. 93–97;
20. Amory, p. 147. Among the works on slumming include David Levering Lewis, *When Harlem Was in Vogue* (New York: 1982), p. 165; Erenberg, pp. 240–250; Hamilton, pp. 93–98; Chauncey, pp. 311–323. Two good sources on discussing Los Angeles's gambling and prostitution areas are Ivan Light, "From Vice District to Tourist Attraction: The Moral Career of American Chinatowns, 1880–1940," *Pacific Historical Review* 43 (1974), pp. 367–394, and Bruce Henstell, *Sunshine & Wealth: Los Angeles in the Twenties and Thirties* (San Francisco, Chronicle Books, 1984); Laurence Senelick, "Lady and the Tramp: Drag Differentials in the Progressive Era," cited in Thomas A. Bolze, "Female Impersonation In the United States, 1900–1970," (Ph.D. diss., State University of New York at Buffalo, 1994), pp. 162–163.
21. *New York Times*, September 30, 1926, p. 23; *Variety*, February 4, 1927, p. 8; *American Mercury* 10 (March 1927), pp. 373–375. See the Hamilton book for a detailed discussion of the situation on Broadway. Historians of entertainment in the United States during the early 1920s observed a decline in interest in female impersonators. The performers, who tried to trick audiences into believing that they were really females, provided cheap lessons in etiquette, bearing, cosmetics, and clothing for women. Their routines proved useful in addressing the culture's fear of the burgeoning women's movement and helped to contain the potential of the new "powerful woman" image. However, changes occurring after World War I, their usefulness in that role ended. Bolze, pp. 140–156; Robert C. Toll, *On With the Show: The First Century of Show Biz in America* (New York: Oxford University Press, 1976), pp. 240–256; *Los Angeles Times*, 13 February 1921, sec. III, p. 15.

22. Actress Mae West twice tried to bring groups of "fairies" to the Broadway stage, drew condemnation and/or official repression. The theater establishment refused to offer West's play, *The Drag*, a stage in February 1927. New York City officials removed her 1928 play, *The Pleasure Man*, from the boards on its opening night. Chauncey, pp. 333–354; Curtin; Hamilton, Ch. 4.
23. Bolze, pp. 220–240.
24. Lewis Erenberg, "Impresarios of Broadway Nightlife," in William Robert Taylor, ed., *Inventing Times Square: Commerce and Culture at the Crossroads of the World* (New York: Russell Sage Foundation, 1991), pp. 159–175; Otis Ferguson, "Breakfast dance, in Harlem," *New Republic*, February 12, 1936, pp. 15–16.
25. Mildred Adams, "The City of Angels Enters Its Heaven," *New York Times*, 3 August 1930, sec. V, p. 7; Hentsel, pp. 8–15; Kevin Starr, *Material Dreams: Southern California through the 1920s* (New York: Oxford University Press, 1990), pp. 94, 290–340; Leo Rosten, *Hollywood: The Movie Colony—The Moviemakers* (New York: Harcourt, Brace, 1941), pp. 5, 371; Palmer, p. 236; Neal Gabler, *An Empire of Their Own: How the Jews Invented Hollywood* (New York: Crown, 1988), pp. 36–42, 63–64, 104–154; *Los Angeles City Directory*, 1927, pp. 2330–2335, 1933, 2637–2643; Writers' Program of the Work Projects Administration, pp. 232–233; *Sandborn Fire Insurance Maps of Los Angeles, 1919–1950*, v. 20; David Ehrenstein, interviewed by author, West Hollywood, California, 15 January 2000.
26. Burk, pp. 25–39; Robert S. Sennett, *Hollywood Hoopla: Creating Stars and Selling Movies in the Golden Age of Hollywood* (New York: Watson-Guptill Publications, 1998), pp. 86–89; Anthony Slide, "The Regulars," article in the Hollywood Community MFL, NC 2812 folder, New York Public Library, hereafter NYPL; unidentified clipping, Patsy Kelly folder, NYPL; Heimann, pp. 23–37.
27. Untitled article in Cinema: Hollywood folder MWEZ, pp. 14, 280 at NYPL; "Protest West Hollywood's Alleged Vice," *Los Angeles Evening Herald*, 20 June 1933, sec. B-1.
28. Christopher Finch and Linda Rosenkrantz, *Gone Hollywood* (Garden City, NY: Doubleday, 1979), pp. 215–219; *Los Angeles Times*, 11 December 1939, sec. II, 11; Slide, "The Regulars," Heimann, pp. 43–47; Sennett, pp. 86–91.
29. Heimann, pp. 40–42; Burk, pp. 20–30; *Los Angeles Times*, 19 January 1920, sec. II, p. 22; *Los Angeles Times*, undated article; Writers' Program of the Work Projects Administration, p. 238.
30. Neal Gabler, *Winchell: Gossip, Power, and Culture of Celebrity* (New York: Alfred A. Knopf, 1994), p. 158.
31. *Los Angeles Times*, 14 September 1930, p. 22; 13 September 1931, sec. III, p. 25; 27 October 1940, sec. IV, p. 9; 27 June 1937, sec. IV, p. 5; 3 Feb-

ruary 1935, sec. II, p. 1; *Los Angeles Evening Herald*, 2 January 1921; Herman Hover, "It Happened at Ciro's," *Motion Picture Magazine*, December 1950, p. 70, in Hollywood — Sunset Strip file, AMPAS; *Los Angeles Times*, 6 September 1931, p. 8.

32. Irene Mayer Selznick, *A Private View* (New York: Alfred A. Knopf, 1983), pp. 168–172; Rudy Behlmer, Memo to David O. Selznick (New York: Avon Books, 1972), p. 132.

33. "The big men came in [to the Derby] and casually nodded to unimportant folk. In-betweeners rated a quick smile and a vague, 'H'yuh." Top notchers received an enthusiastic back slapping, 'Old boy-old-boy!'" Jimmy Fidler, "Jimmy Fidler in Hollywood," *Los Angeles Times*, 29 May 1939, sec. II, p. 14; Heimann, pp. 44–49.

34. *What Price Hollywood?* Dir. George Cukor. Perf. Constance Bennett, Lowell Sherman, and Neil Hamilton. RKO, 1932.

35. The teaser campaign of what was happening behind the picture studios proved alluring to customers. Eastern and Midwestern and far western cities provided strong box office returns. However, it did poorly in southern cities like Louisville and Birmingham. *Motion Picture Herald*, 18 June 1932, p. 35; *Film Daily*, 22 June 1932, p. 4; *Variety*, 28 June 1932, pp. 8–10; 12 July, 1932, pp. 6–8; 19 July 1932, p. 24; 26 July 1932, p. 7; 16 August 1932, pp. 8, 21, 46.

36. Herbert Cruikshank, "Director Dorothy: The One Woman Behind the Stars," *Motion Picture Classic* 30, (September 1929), p. 76; *Los Angeles Times*, 18 September 1927, sec. III, p. 15; 9 February 1936, sec. III, p. 2; 9 June 1935, sec. III, p. 3; 16 August 1936, sec. III, p. 2;

37. *Photoplay*, XLIII, No. 5, April 1933, p. 8; XLIII, No. 6, May 1933, p. 10.

38. Katharine Hepburn, *Me: Stories of My Life* (New York: Ballantine Books, 1991); Howard Greer, *Designing Male* (London: Robert Hale, 1952), pp. 216–220.

39. William J. Mann, *Kate: The Woman Who Was Hepburn* (New York: Henry Holt, 2006).

40. Joel Lobenthal, *Tallulah! The Life and Times of a Leading Lady* (New York: HarperCollins, 2004); http://home.hiwaay.net/~oliver/tbbiography.htm.

41. David Bret, *Tallulah Bankhead: A Scandalous Life* (New York: Robson Books/Parkwest, 1996); http://www.awhf.org/bankhead.html; http://home.hiwaay.net/~oliver/tbsquabfarm.htm; "The Squab Farm," *New York Times*, 14 March 1918, p. 11.

42. Lobenthal; *http://home.hiwaay.net/~oliver/tbstage.htm*; *Los Angeles Times*, 18 October 1931, p. B11.

43. *Los Angeles Times*, 18 October 1931, p. B11; *Los Angeles Evening Herald*, 15 November 1932 sec. B-4. Tip Poff, "That Certain Party," 8 August 1933, p. A1; 13 August 1933, p. A1.

44. Oliver, Phillip. "Tallulah: A Passionate Life." *http://home.hiwaay.net/~oliver/tbskin.htm*; May 3, 2002. 5/10/2007; Robert Benchley Collection, Box 11, Folder 3, Letter dated 6/29/36 Mugar Library, BU.

45. Denis Brain, *Tallulah Darling: A Biography of Tallulah Bankhead* (New York: Macmillan, 1980); Lobenthal; Bret; Alabama Women's Hall of Fame, *http://www.awhf.org/bankhead.html*; Axel Madsen, *The Sewing Circle: Hollywood's Greatest Secret: Female Stars Who Loved Other Women* (Citadel, 1995), pp. 112–116, 188;

46. Marlene Dietrich and Attanasio, Salvator [Translation] (1989). *My Life* (Weidenfeld & Nicolson, 1989); Maria Riva, *Marlene Dietrich* (New York: Knopf, 1993).

47. As the contracts of both director Josef von Sternberg and Dietrich approached their end, most of the studio's executives wanted to break up this pairing. Dietrich's last motion picture in 1932, *Blonde Venus*, earned unenthusiastic reviews and lackluster box office returns. The top executives released von Sternberg and strove to get Dietrich into another picture before her contract expired. Dietrich rebelled over von Sternberg's absence and spoke of returning to Germany, but Paramount sued the star for irreparable loss due to its inability to proceed with filming of *The Song of Songs*. The star agreed to act in the motion picture two days later and received a new five-year contract. *Los Angeles Times*, 2 January 1933, sec. II, p. 2; Grace Kingsley, "Hobnobbing In Hollywood," *Los Angeles Times*, 25 January 1933, sec. 2; Spoto, pp. 100–102.

48. Jimmy Starr, "Football Season Past, Film Folk Turn Toward Polo," *Los Angeles Evening Herald and Express*, 5 January 1933, sec. B-4; Harrison Carroll, "Stars, Designers Advocate Figure to Match Styles," 22 March 1933, sec. B-5; Grace Kingsley, "Hobnobbing In Hollywood," *Los Angeles Times*, 6 January 1933; Finch and Rosenkrantz, p. 273.

49. Paramount Collection, Press Sheets, August 1, 1933-July 31, 1934, AMPAS; Rachel Bowlby, *Just Looking: Consumer Culture in Dreiser, Gissing and Zola* (New York: Methuen, 1985), pp. 10–13; Edward Schallert, "Warblers Ripe for Comeback," *Los Angeles Times*, 1 February 1933, sec. II, p. 5.

50. *Hollywood Party MPP*, AMPAS. Letter from James Wingate to E. J. Mannix, June 23, 1933, *Hollywood Party MPP*, AMPAS.

51. Mercedes de Acosta, *Here Lies the Heart*, (New York: Reynal, 1960), pp. 235–243; Madsen, p. 208.

52. Riva, pp. 111–197; Diana McLellan, *The Girls: Sappho Goes to Hollywood* (New York: St. Martin's Press, 2001); Madsen.

53. As one industry columnist stated, "The truth about that masculine attire which Marlene Dietrich affects these day is this. She liked wearing that sort of clothes — trousers. Paramount objected. Marlene insisted on trotting about in pants. Finally they gave up. 'Oh well,' sighed Paramount, 'then we'll make a cult of it — exploit Marlene in men's clothes.'" That Dietrich's image was alluring is confirmed by contemporaries. See *Los Angeles Times*, 25 January 1933, sec. II, p. 7. Film

fashion scholar Patty Fox notes, "Wearing blatantly man-tailored clothes appealed to the subliminal urges in both men and women. On a purely visual level, menswear on a woman, especially this woman, was incredibly sensual." Rebecca Bell-Metereau, *Hollywood Androgyny* (New York: Columbia University Press, 1985), pp. 103–105; Josef von Sternberg, *Fun In a Chinese Laundry* (New York: Macmillan, 1965), p. 247; Patty Fox, *Star Style: Hollywood Legends as Fashion Icons* (Los Angeles: Angel City Press, 1995), p. 52; "Hollywood Tourists Accommodated," *New York Times*, 22 March 1936, sec. IX, p. 4.

54. Moore, pp. 84–85; Slide, *The Encyclopedia of Vaudeville*, p. 374; Chauncey, pp. 239, 314–338.

55. M. Alison Kibler, *Rank Ladies: Gender and Cultural Hierarchy In American Vaudeville* (Chapel Hill: University of North Carolina Press, 1999), pp. 163–169.

56. *Los Angeles Evening Herald and Express*, 24 September 1932, sec. A-7; 7 April 1933, sec. B-6; 25 January 1933, sec. B-3; *Los Angeles Times*, 13 January 1933, sec. I, p. 6. Bud Schulberg's Hollywood novel *What Makes Sammy Run?* (1941) uses "swish" to describe an effeminate man and a homosexual. "If ... that fat swish lets the producer know he did all the writing, you're dead." *Oxford English Dictionary*.

57. *Modern Screen*, March 1933. See http://www.queermusicheritage.us/jun2004jm.html

58. *Los Angeles Evening Herald and Express*, 24 September 1932, sec. A-7; 7 April 1933, sec. B-6; 25 January 1933, sec. B-3; *Los Angeles Times*, 13 January 1933, sec. I, p. 6.

59. Alma Mater, "Hollywood Lowdown," *Broadway Brevities*, 11 April 1932, p. 10; "Hollywood Stays," *Hollywood Magazine*, May 1933, p. 38, cited in Ronald Gregg, "Gay Culture, Studio Publicity, and the Management of Star Discourse: The Homosexualization of William Haines in Pre-Code Hollywood," *Quarterly Review of Film and Video* 20 (April-June, 2003), p. 87.

60. Katz; http://www.imdb.com/name/nm0401729/; Grace Kingsley, "Hobnobbing in Hollywood," *Los Angeles Times*, 14 December 1932, p. A16.

61. William Haines and Joan Crawford attended another quaint new spot with an equally "wicked" show. "After releasing *The Song of Songs*, Marlene Dietrich, attired in her mannish clothes, Brian Aherne and Rouben Mamoulien went to the Club New Yorker." William Mann, *Wisecracker*, pp. 184, 364; *Los Angeles Evening Herald and Express*, 21 April 1933, sec. B-4; 17 December 1935; *Los Angeles Times*, 2 January 1933, sec. III, p. 8.

62. www.queermusicheritage.us; Arizona to Broadway at http://www.imdb.com/title/tt0023764/; Double Harness at http://www.imdb.com/title/tt0023960/; Turner Classic Movies "This Month," Double Harness at http://www.tcm.com/thismonth/article.jsp?cid=159636&mainArticleId=159623.

63. The female impersonators in Hollywood, unlike their brethren in other United States cities and different "exotic other" performers such as "New Negros," were able to transcend their position as "other." Certain performers identified with the female impersonators. Some Hollywood figures, including actor Dan Dailey, borrowed gowns and other female attire from studio wardrobes to wear on nights out on the town. Others borrowed the idea. Hamilton, 48. For a discussion of the history of the theater see Curtin and Nicholas de Jongh, *Not in Front of the Audience: Homosexuality on Stage* (London: Routledge, 1992); Boze Hadleigh, *The Vinyl Closet: Gays in the Music Industry* (San Diego: Los Hombres Press, 1991), pp. 225–229; Robert Benchley letter of June 29, 1936. Robert Benchley Collection, Box 11, Folder 3, Mugar Library Special Collections Department. Tallulah is actress Tallulah Bankhead mentioned earlier in the chapter as a woman who occasionally donned masculine attire (drag). Bill Haines is the actor whose biography is noted in footnote 42. Jerry Zeibe was the "strikingly handsome and flirtatious" photographer and socialite who was a lover of both Cary Grant and Randolph Scott. David Ehrenstein, *Open Secret: Gay Hollywood 1928–1998* (New York: William Morrow, 1998), pp. 29–30.

64. Personal relationships among female impersonators and some of the syndicated columnists who reported on nightlife also presumably developed. This may account for the degree of publicity the female impersonators received. In the first version of *A Star Is Born* (1937), Franklin Pangborn brought "pansy" behavior to his role as a motion picture industry gossip columnist. His character twice flicked his hand behind his ear, raised his voice such that he chirped effeminately, and changed the word divine to "devoon" as he crooned it. The representation suggested that some columnists enjoyed playing with gender conventions and might even hold same-gender sexual interest. The *Los Angeles Evening Herald and Express*'s syndicated columnist Harrison Carroll had the reputation of being a "grandmother" among performers in Hollywood. Perhaps his same-gender sexual interest influenced the somewhat extensive coverage that he devoted to female impersonators in the Hollywood nightclubs. *A Star Is Born*, dir. William Wellman, perf. Janet Gaynor. Fredric March, Adolphe Menjou. Selznick International, 1937. Actress Shelley Winters referred to Carroll as the grandmotherly type in her book, *Shelley: Also Known As Shirley* (New York: Ballantine Books, 1980), pp. 250–265.

65. Moore, p. 84; Brooks Peters, "Gay Deceiver," *Out Magazine*, December 1998.

66. John Zneimer, *The Literary Vision of Liam O'Flaherty* (Syracuse, NY: Syracuse University Press, 1970), pp. 30–32.

67. Liam O'Flaherty, *Hollywood Cemetery* (London: Victor Gollancz, 1935), pp. 38–45.

68. Over the years people needing assistance with women's clothing knew that Julian Eltinge had the reputation for dispensing recommendations for the most becoming women's wear. *Los*

Angeles Times, 16 December 1932, Billy Rose Theater Collection, Folder MWEZ 7394.

69. *Los Angeles Evening Herald and Express,* 23 May 1933, p. 1. This article details how six Hollywood "male chorus dancers" were arrested for appearing in public in women's clothes.

70. O'Flaherty, pp. 80–91; 270–288.

71. Zneimer, pp. 125–126; A. A. Kelly, *Liam O'Flaherty: The Storyteller* (London: Macmillan, 1976), p. 116.

72. "Books of the Day," *London Times,* 19 November 1935, p. 8.

73. *Variety* predicted that the craze in Hollywood ended in 1933, *Variety,* November 21, 1933, p. 59. Historian George Chauncey also believes that most of the spark in the pansy craze diminished with the passing of the ordinance law barring cross-dressing in local night clubs and bars in 1933, although he observes that the craze continued for two more years before either the discovery or enforcement of the ordinance led to the demise of the clubs. Chauncey, p. 321. *Los Angeles Evening Herald and Express,* 11 September 1935, sec. B-1; Starr, *Material Dreams,* pp. 156–161. A former president of the Water and Power Commission, the organization that controlled Los Angeles's water and hydroelectric resources, Baumgartner held sway as a significant figure in the "Power Bureau," one of the city's two power brokers age.

74. The vast majority of homosexual areas of major cities in the United States, such as in Chicago or San Francisco, existed in these areas. *Creating a Place for Ourselves: Lesbian, Gay, and Bisexual Community Histories,* Brett Beemyn, ed. (New York: Routledge, 1997).

75. *Sandborn Fire Insurance Maps of Los Angeles, 1919–1950,* v. 3, 7, 9, 11, Geography and Maps Division, LC; *Los Angeles Times,* 3 May 1933, sec. II, p. 1; 4 May 1933, sec. II, p. 1; Eshref Shevky and Marilyn Williams, *The Social Areas of Los Angeles: Analysis and Typology* (Berkeley: University of California Press, 1949), pp. 68–89, appendix C-E.

76. Chauncey, pp. 304–328; Julian B. Roebuck and Wolfgang Frese, *The Rendezvous: A Case Study of an After-Hours Club* (New York: Free Press, 1976), pp. 4–7; Kimmel, pp. 124–125.

77. There is a significant amount of scholarship on how the various groups of citizens viewed the city as the site for corruption. Christine Stansell, *City of Women: Sex and Class in New York, 1789–1860* (Chicago: University of Chicago, 1982), observes that Protestant reformers interpreted New York as filled with sin, and that the concentration of vice appeared in working-class neighborhoods. Kevin Starr, *Inventing The Dream: California Through the Progressive Era* (New York: Oxford University Press, 1985), pp. 88–95, observes that in the twentieth century many of the settlers in southern California saw the East as declining area filled with undesirable foreigners. They viewed southern California as a suburban land of sunshine and "the new Eden of the Saxon home seeker." Resolution to City Council of August 12, 1935, Number 2780 (1935) Council Files, Los Angeles City Archives. Ordinance Number 75,626 is noted in October 10, 1935 letter from Raymond L. Chesbro, City Attorney.

78. Harry Levette, "Thru Hollywood," *The Chicago Defender,* 24 July 1937, p. 11; 22 January 1938, p. 18.

79. Jack Lord and Lloyd Hoff, *How to Sin in Hollywood* (Hollywood? CA, c. 1940), p. 39.

80. The image can be interpreted as a precursor to the butch-femme lesbian couple. Butch-femme coupling among lesbians in the 1930s is featured in Elisabeth Lapovsky Kennedy and Madeline D. Davis, *Boots of Leather, Slippers of Gold: The History of a Lesbian Community* (New York: Routledge, 1993). Heimann, p. 161; Lord and Hoff, p. 38.

81. Kingsley Widmer, *Nathanael West* (Boston: Twayne Publishers, 1982), pp. ix–xvi; Robert Van Gelder, "A Tragic Chorus," *New York Times,* 21 May 1939, sec. VII, pp. 6–7; *Los Angeles Times,* 28 May 1939, sec. III, p. 6. Robert van Gelder argued, "...The combination of climate, cheap living and the entertainment industry have concentrated in Los Angeles too many shoddy minds and people who have energy without rational purpose." The Los Angeles critic observed that West satirized the millions who make bad movies possible. "They will one day forge a mediocre–minded revolution unless something happens to stop the revolution at its source—Hollywood."

82. Nathanael West, *The Day of the Locust* (New York: Random House, 1939; repr., New York: Bantam Books, 1975), p. 96. Diane C. Bonora, "The Hollywood Novel of the 1930s and 1940s," (Ph.D. diss., State University of New York at Buffalo, 1983), examined *The Day of the Locust* and four other Hollywood novels that appeared between 1930 and 1950 for their similarities and differences regarding the interpretation of Hollywood's artificiality and immorality and the industry's shaping of manhood and womanhood. Bonora observed that West's Hollywood figures faced disrupted love and marriages because of the industry's artificiality. Women dominated both the action and the men in West's book. Faye Greener used her body to influence men. Joan Schwartzen dominated Tod at a party. Maybelle Loomis was the stereotypical stage mother over her son Adore. Bonora states that the female impersonator was the only favorably presented "woman."

83. *Dictionary of Literary Biography* vol. 9 (Detroit: Gale Publishing, 1991), p. 125. As scholars Leo Charney and Vanessa Schwartz have argued motion pictures were the fullest expression of this modernity. Motion pictures expanded Impressionism and photography by using technology to stage actual movement. For millions, they became a primary mode for the representation of the reality of modern life. This increasing tendency to understand the "real" only through its representations was a crucial aspect of modernity. Leo Charney and Vanessa Schwartz, eds., *Cinema and*

the *Invention of Modern Life* (Berkeley: University of California Press, 1995), pp. 2–10. George Milburn, "The Hollywood Nobody Knows," *Saturday Review of Literature*, 20 May 1939, p. 14; Edmund Wilson, "Hollywood Dance of Death," *New Republic*, 26 July 1939, p. 339.

84. *Los Angeles Times*, 20 January 1940, sec. II, p. 1; Number 1976 (1940), Council Files, Los Angeles City Archives.

85. *Los Angeles Examiner*, 17 January 1940, Julian Eltinge Biography Files, AMPAS; "Application of Julian Eltinge to operate as a female impersonator at the *Hollywood Rendezvous*," 16 January 1940, *The Official Minutes of the Board of Police Commissioners of the City of Los Angeles*, 2 January 1940 to 28 June 1940; Vale, pp. 38–40.

86. *American Film Institute Catalog of Motion Pictures produced in the United States, 1931–1940*, p. 1003; Moore, pp. 108–109; *Variety*, 1 May 1940; Slide, *The Vaudevillians*, p. 47; Anthony Slide, *The Best of Rob Wagner's Script* (Metuchen, NJ: Scarecrow Press, 1985), p. vii.

Chapter Two

1. Finch and Rosenkrantz, 266–267. The promotion was the brainchild of Sid Grauman, Hollywood exhibitor par excellence and a homosexual.

2. The images surrounding Valentino will receive analysis in the next chapter. See Gaylyn Studlar, *The Male Masquerade*, for a discussion of the issue of males as objects of display.

3. Mary Cable, *Top Drawer: American High Society from the Gilded Age to the Roaring Twenties* (New York: Atheneum, 1984), chapter 8.

4. Robert Darton, *The Great Cat Massacre and Other Episodes in French Cultural History* (New York: Basic Books, 1984), in Chandra Mukerji and Michael Schudson, *Rethinking Popular Culture: Contemporary Perspectives in Cultural Studies* (Berkeley: University of California Press, 1991), pp. 97–119. These parties drew highly formalized media coverage, as the press tracked activities from certain areas of the party and the reporting of the event followed a similar pattern over the years.

5. Cable, Amory.

6. Kathryn Allamong Jacob, *Capital Elites: High Society in Washington DC after the Civil War* (Washington, D.C.: Smithsonian Institution Press, 1995), p. 18.

7. *Ibid.*, pp. 22–23, 43; *New York Times*, March 4, 1853; March 5, 1853; March 4, 1857; March 5, 1857; *Washington Evening Star*, March 1–6, 1861.

8. Betty Boyd Carol, *First Ladies* (New York: Oxford University Press, 1987), pp. 13–33. Most balls received little more than passing mention in several newspapers through the ball for Franklin Pierce in 1853. *New York Times*, 5 March 1853, p. 1; 5 March 1861, p. 1; 5 March, 1873, p. 1; 5 March 1897, p. 3; *Los Angeles Evening Herald*, 5 March 1897, pp. 1, 5; *Los Angeles Times*, 5 March 1885, pp. 1, 3; 5 March 1889, pp. 1, 4.

9. *Los Angeles Times*, 5 March 1905, pp. 1, 5, 10; *Outlook* (March 13, 1909), p. 576; *Los Angeles Evening Herald*, January-March 1921; *Los Angeles Evening Herald and Express*, 4 March 1929, sec. A-11; 21 January 1941, sec. A-1. I read these newspapers for other years as well and found very little description of the presidential balls.

10. Ronald Brownstein, *The Power and the Glitter: The Hollywood-Washington Connection* (New York: Pantheon Books, 1990).

11. Many of the attendees were politicians, actors, and actresses and were thus regularly before the public eye. These figures realized that to "go public" involved coming under the gaze of others and having their image negotiated by the audiences' and media's definitions. In reaction to this media coverage and the resultant diminishment of their control over their images, politicians and actors developed a routine to manage their relations with the press. Many of these public figures consciously organized their public display. They adopted a public personality (persona) that they constructed to intentionally highlight the presence of particular aspects of themselves and to exclude or limit the display of other facets. These ambitious public figures, with the assistance of public relations experts who developed during this era, used clothes, words, and image control to make their personas appealing. Leo Braudy, *The Frenzy of Renown: History of Celebrity* (New York: Vintage, 1986), pp. 12, 490–496; Gamson, pp. 27–33.

12. Brett L. Abrams, "The Hollywood Test Case: Organized Labor's 'Assumption' into Corporate Liberalism," (MA thesis, Northeastern University, 1992); The Academy of Motion Picture Acts and Sciences offers a history of itself at the website *www.oscars.org*.

13. Sennett, *Hollywood Hoopla*, p. 29.

14. Gabler, *An Empire of Their Own*.

15. Ray Milland, *Wide-Eyed in Babylon: An Autobiography* (New York: William Morrow, 1974), p. 119; Tante Burk, pp. 3–21; Gabler, *An Empire of Their Own*, pp. 250–252; Sennett, p. 87; Anthony Holden, *Behind The Oscars: The Secret History of the Academy Awards* (New York: Penguin Books, 1994), pp. 90–93.

16. "Events In Hollywood: Voting on Annual Motion Picture Awards," *New York Times*, August 31, 1930, p. X4; Mordant Hall, "The Screen," *New York Times*, November 12, 1931, p. 30; Chapin Hall, "Pictures and Bohemians In Hollywood," *New York Times*, May 22, 1932, p. X3; "Coming to Local Stages," *Washington Post*, March 5, 1933, p. S6; "A New Movie Queen," *Washington Post*, March 19, 1934, p. 8.

17. "On the Hollywood Front," *New York Times*, November 27, 1932, p. X5; Holden, pp. 35–49; Emmanuel Levy, *And the Winner Is...: The History and Politics of the Oscar Awards* (New York: Ungar, 1987), pp. 2–24. The sponsoring organization, the Academy of Motion Picture Arts

and Sciences, initially served management efforts to resolve labor issues among the studios' "creative" talents: writers, directors and performers. During its second year the Academy negotiated the first standard contract for a talent group, covering the freelance actors and actresses. However, with the deepening of the Depression, the Academy's handling of the producers' attempt to institute a substantial pay cut led to the perception that the Academy was a producer-ruled body. Having alienated many within the talent groups and the studios themselves, the Academy struggled to remain viable. Under Frank Capra's leadership, the organization switched its focus away from labor and studio politics. *Hollywood Reporter*, 11 November 1931, p. 2 in Academy Awards Files, Clipping Folder, AMPAS.

18. *Hollywood Reporter; Los Angeles Times; New York Times.*

19. *New York Times,* 11 November 1931, p. 26; 28 February 1941, p. 1; *Los Angeles Evening Herald and Express,* 17 March 1934, sec. A-3; 6 March 1936, sec. A-3; 28 February 1941, sec. B-1.

20. *Los Angeles Times,* 10 November 1931, sec. II, 9; *Los Angeles Evening Herald and Express,* 10 November 1931, sec. A-12; *New York Times,* 11 November 1931, p. 26.

21. *Hollywood Reporter,* 11 November 1931, p. 2; 6 March 1936, p. 2; 24 February 1939, p. 3; 1 March 1940, pp. 1, 3 in Academy Awards Files, Clipping Folder, AMPAS; *Los Angeles Evening Herald and Express,* 6 March 1936, sec. A-3; *Los Angeles Times,* 11 March 1938, sec. II, p. 1; 28 February 1941, sec. II, p. 1; Richard Schickel, *Intimate Strangers.*

22. Fox; Fred Davis, *Fashion, Culture, and Identity* (Chicago: University of Chicago Press, 1992).

23. Cable, pp. 192–201. The major metropolitan dailies and tabloids usually devoted a page or two to society news that included weddings, balls, waltzes, and dinner parties. Articles in magazines appeared in the Readers' Guide to Periodical Literature under the categories balls (parties), dancing, dinners and dining, garden parties, masquerades, parties, and entertaining. Over the period of this study, the other categories produced fewer as entertaining increased in the number of representations. Still, a significant number of these articles contained little information about actual parties and often focused on providing advice about having parties. Amory, pp. 160–162; *Los Angeles Times,* June 1906; July 1907, April 1912. *Los Angeles Evening Herald,* January 1903; February 1903; June 1909; September 1911. These pages included different types of stories, describing society folks attending school performances, musical presentations of their children, or local theater, particularly Shakespeare.

24. Jacobs, pp. 35, 90–91, 110–111, 169–170. *The Washington Post,* August 11, 1879, p. 1; August 12, p. 3; August 13, p. 2; August 14, p. 1; August 15, p. 2; August 19, 1879, p. 1; *New York Times,* August 10, 1879, p. 7; August 12, 1879, p. 1; August 19, 1879, p. 1.

25. *Los Angeles Times,* June 1919; July 1921; September 1929; March 1935; and December 1940, particularly 3 July 1921, sec. III, p. 3, and 17 September 1929, sec. II, p. 6; *Los Angeles Evening Herald and Express,* May 1919; January 1922; March 1931; January 1932; June 1934; and January 1940, especially 4 January 1922, sec. B-5, 7 January 1932, sec. B-7, and 6 January 1940, sec. B-12. On occasion, the descriptions included more details regarding the dresses worn by the bridesmaids, or noted that the entertainment at a dance or gala included an up-to-date cabaret or play that preceded the dance.

26. "To a Debutante," *The Century* (February 1888); "A Debutante in New York Society," *North American Review* (August 1888), pp. 239–240.

27. Four articles appeared in the *Readers' Guide to Periodical Literature* under the Society heading and the Newspaper Society column heading between 1890–1899. While over 60 articles under the Society heading appeared between 1905 and 1909, only six appeared between 1915 and 1918 and nine between 1925 and 1928.

28. "Life Goes to a Mass Debut," *Life* (September 30, 1940), p. 99; Michelle Thurgood Haynes, *Dressing Up Debutantes: Pageantry and Glitz in Texas* (Oxford, Eng.: Berg, 1998), chapters 3 & 4.

29. A. Etheridge, "Christmas Cotillion," *Ladies Home Journal* (December 1907), p. 9; A. W. Morrison, "For a garden party," *Delineator* (September 1904), pp. 440–441; Josephine Grenier, "Garden Party," *Harper's Bazaar* (August 1903), pp. 733–735; "The White House as Social Treadmill," *Literary Digest* 94, (August 20, 1927), pp. 35–36; Maude Parker Child, "Diplomatic Entertaining: The Pomps and Pitfalls of Foreign Society," *The Saturday Evening Post* (May 16, 1925), pp. 16, 178–179.

30. "A Ball at Delmonicos," *The Galaxy* (April 1874), pp. 513–528; Cable, pp. 135–145; May King Van Rensselaer, *The Social Ladder* (New York: Henry Holt, 1924), pp. 198–212;

31. Cable, pp. 135–145; "Gay and Glittering Beaux Arts Ball," *Literary Digest* 122 (December 5, 1936), p. 30; "Architects Ball; Chicagoans cavort as their favorite myth," *Life* (February 5, 1940), pp. 80–82; "Rhode Islanders mourn end of summer at Fisherman's ball," *Life* (October 14, 1941), pp. 120–123. These descriptions of the costuming probably illustrated changes in societal norms, such as the proper dress for women, rather than a transgression of those norms.

32. Finch and Rosenkrantz, p. 154; Gabler, *An Empire of Their Own,* pp. 250–252; *Photoplay* (May, 1931), p. 30; *Los Angeles Times,* 5 May 1935, p. B7; 19 April 1936, sec. IV, p. 12.

33. *Los Angeles Times,* 28 January 1936, p. 8.

34. Sennett, pp. 169–171; Gabler, *An Empire of Their Own,* pp. 100–101; Douglas Gomery, *Shared Pleasures: A History of Movie Presentation in the United States* (Madison: University of Wisconsin Press, 1992); Herbert Howe, "Hollywood in a High Hat," *Photoplay* (August, 1925), p. 29; Melrose Gower, "Hollywood Bestows A Dowry of Ballyhoo

on Its Celluloid Children," *RKO Press Release*, 5 March 1938, in Premieres and Previews File, AMPAS; Harold A. C. Sintzenich, "Diary for 1927," November 12, 1927 entry, Harold A. C. Sintzenich Collection, Manuscript Division, LC; Erik Barnouw, "The Sintzenich Diaries," *The Quarterly Journal of the Library of Congress* (Summer/Fall, 1980), p. 321.

35. Donald Dewey, *James Stewart* (Atlanta: Turner Publishing, 1987), p. 181; Sennett, pp. 50–51. The gossip columnists and studio publicists played this game to such a degree that contemporaries complained. Fabricated romances created when legmen (publicists) see anything remotely romantic and report back. "Spare us from Momoulian and Garbo, Niven and Loretta Young, [Jimmy] Stewart and Norma Shearer, Crawford and Cesar Romero, Irene Harvey and Taylor ... Enough. Also ridiculous." Unidentified clipping, Cinema: Hollywood Gossip folder, NYPL. *Los Angeles Times*, 17 May 1936, sec. IV, p. 11; 14 March 1937, sec. II, p. 8; 4 February 1940, sec. IV, p. 8; *Los Angeles Evening Herald*, 9 January 1922, sec. B-3; *Los Angeles Times*, 23 November 1930, p. 30; 17 May 1936, sec. IV, p. 11; 4 February 1940, sec. IV, p. 8; *New York Times*, 6 December 1936, sec. XII, p. 9.

36. *Hollywood Party*. Dir. Roy Rowland. Perf. Jimmy Durante, Stan Laurel, and Oliver Hardy. MGM, 1934. This motion picture is available on video. The script of the motion picture is in the MGM Script Collection at the Cinema and Television Library, University of Southern California.

37. Young's lines highlighted the number and variety of manufactured looks and behaviors in Hollywood and particularly focused upon the hair color of the women entering the party. In Hollywood, women used dye and makeup to create hairstyles and change facial shapes. The changes illustrated that in Hollywood, women, especially actresses, adapted their femininity to suit their career purposes. Thus femininity was not a natural item that every woman had but an activity that the person performed. Similarly, male actors could develop a set of behaviors and looks so that people would perceive them as masculine. Off-screen, particularly at industry private parties, these Hollywood bohemians could adopt a different set of behaviors, act less masculine, and challenge the idea that every man naturally behaved masculinely by acting like "pansies." The partygoers viewed the Hollywood bohemians' adoption of gender mannerisms similarly to the women who manufactured their on-screen looks. Like those women, the Hollywood bohemians could attend the party. This view of the flexible and consciously adopted nature of femininity appeared in contemporary psychological literature in Joan Riviere's 1929 essay, "Womanliness as Masquerade." This psychologist argues that femininity is an act that a woman can adopt at will. Even the most masculine of women can act the feminine role when they choose. This suggests that gender is a nature that is flexible and can be consciously adapted.

38. The movie might have been even more disruptive of traditional romantic standards. The Studio Relations Committee mandated that the producing studio, MGM, eliminate four sexually suggestive lines from the script. Letter from James Wingate to Mannix of September 5, 1933, *Hollywood Party MPP*, AMPAS. The party at the house represented Hollywood's attempt to display its superiority to another important cultural medium of the era, the radio. Young played a radio announcer who presented the Hollywood party event to the millions of radio listeners. However, this scene revealed the limitations of the radio. Because the medium lacked a visual element, the audience learned only what the announcer chose to tell them and the announcer's words could mislead them. The scene demonstrated that Hollywood's images of its parties were more truthful than radio's because they took audience members "inside" and gave them audio and visual access.

39. *New York Times*, 26 May 1934, p. 12; *Variety*, 29 May 1934, pp. 9, 11; 5 June 1934, pp. 9, 10; 12 June 1934, pp. 8–10. With the help of an advertising campaign, the movie did a big $17,500 in New York City and completed its second week with an acceptable box office return. The movie generated good trade from cities including Cincinnati and San Francisco. Although *Hollywood Party's* earnings of $9,000 in Chicago qualified it for only a one-week stint, this proved better than the movie's light business in Kansas City, the weak earnings in Indianapolis, and the brutal return from Pittsburgh.

40. *Los Angeles Evening Herald*, 23 January 1933, sec. A-10.

41. Katz, pp. 538–539.

42. *Los Angeles Times*, April 16, 1933, II, p. 6; Ephraim Katz, *The Film Encyclopedia* (New York: Putnam's, 1979), pp. 538–539.

43. Allan R. Ellenberger, *Ramon Novarro* (Jefferson, N.C.: McFarland, 1999), pp. 30–50; *Los Angeles Times*, 2 February 1930, p. 22.

44. *Variety*, 6 January 1926; *Los Angeles Times*, 3 August 1926, p. A11; 24 January 1930, p. A11.

45. *Photoplay*, April 1925, pp. 55–59, 142.

46. *Los Angeles Times*, 11 February 1933, p. A7; 30 June 1934, p. 7.

47. *Washington Post*, 1 July 1928, p. A3; 29 September 1929, p. A4; *Los Angeles Times*, 10 April 1932, III, p. 15.

48. *Los Angeles Examiner*, 20 February 1934; *Los Angeles Times*, 16 April 1933, sec. II, p. 6; 4 August 1935, p. A1; Ellenberger, pp. 110–129. Mann, *Wisecracker*, p. 227; *Photoplay*, April 1925, p. 142. Scholar Michael Bronski notes in his book *Culture Clash: The Making of Gay Sensibility* (Boston: South End Press, 1984), reproductions of the statue were a fixture in gay households of this era, p. 46. "Ramon Novarro's Christmas Spirit," *Silver Screen* (December, 1931), pp. 20, 66 argued his devotion to his mother kept him from marrying.

49. *Los Angeles Times*, 26 July 1937, p. A4; Ellenberger, pp. 133–146.

50. Myrna Loy and James Kotsilibas-David,

Myrna Loy: Being and Becoming (New York: Alfred A. Knopf, 1987); Michael G. Ankerich, Broken Silence: Conversations with 23 Silent Film Stars (Jefferson, N.C.: McFarland, 1993); Ellenberger; William J. Mann, Behind the Screen: How Gays and Lesbians Shaped Hollywood (New York: Viking, 2001), pp. 96–100.

51. Warren G. Harris, Clark Gable: A Biography (New York: Aurum Press, 2002); Lyn Tornabene, Long Live the King: A Biography of Clark Gable (New York: Putnam Books, 1976); Jane Ellen Wayne, Clark Gable: Portrait of a Misfit (New York: St. Martin's Press, 1993).

52. Ibid.; Katz, pp. 460–461; Samantha Barbas, Movie Crazy: Fans, Stars, and the Cult of Celebrity (New York: Palgrave, 2001), pp. 151–154.

53. Los Angeles Times, 28 July 1935, p. A1; 15 November 1935, p. 20; 5 January 1936, p. C8.

54. Los Angeles Times, 2 February 1936, p. C1; 29 April 1936, p. 15; 19 July 1936, p. C1; Washington Post, 20 June 1937, p. T3.

55. "Movie 'Celebs' Show Off at a Premiere and Party for Marie Antoinette," Life, 25 July 1938, p. 44 in Premieres and Previews File, AMPAS.

56. Katz, pp. 730–731; Mann, pp. 219–221, Finch and Rosenkrantz, pp. 234–235.

57. Los Angeles Times, 4 August 1935, III, p. 5; 5 January 1936, III, p. 1; 23 February 1936, IV, p. 6; 31 May 1936, IV, p. 8; 8 November 1936, IV, p. 8; 26 September 1937, IV, p. 10; 31 December 1939, IV, p. 4; Edward Doherty, "Can the Gable-Lombard Love Story Have a Happy Ending?" in Photoplay Treasury, ed. Barbara Gelman (New York: Crown, 1972).

58. Wayne; Harris, pp. 144–145.

59. Alfred Kazin, "Dos Passos and the 'Lost Generation,'" in ed. Allen Belkind, Dos Passos, the Critics and the Writer's Intention (Carbondale, IL: Southern Illinois University Press, 1971), pp. 15–19; Townsend Ludington, John Dos Passos: A Twentieth Century Odyssey (New York: E. P. Dutton, 1980), pp. 330–331, 352–358; John Dos Passos, The Big Money (New York: New Amsterdam Library, 1989), pp. 426–430.

60. "A Private Historian," Time, v. 28, no. 7, August 10, 1936, p. 51; New York Times, August 16, 1936.

Chapter Three

1. Nina Putnam, Laughter Limited (New York: George Duran, 1922), pp. 115–123.

2. Duncan Aikman, "Hollywood Assumes the Grand Manner," New York Times, 8 March 1931, sec. V, pp. 11–18.

3. Edwin Schallert, "Star Invasion Starts New Boom at Malibu," Los Angeles Times, 4 June 1933, II, p. 3. Homeowners included directors John Stahl, David Butler, William Le Baron, and Frank Capra, actors Alexander Kirkland, George Raft, Norman Foster, Stephen Gooson, and studio executives Jack Warner and Bud Schulberg.

4. Cable, pp. 136–140; Jacob.

5. Cable; Los Angeles Times, 7 April 1912, sec. III, p. 3; Los Angeles Evening Herald, 15 February 1903, sec. III, p. 1.

6. Josephine Grenier, "Garden Party," Harper's Bazaar, 37 (August 1903), pp. 733–735; Nathalie Schenck, "Everybody Enjoys a Garden Party," Ladies Home Journal (June 1921), p. 74; Claire Wallis, "A Valentine Party in Five Reels," Ladies Home Journal (February 1921), p. 144; Leah F. Collins, "An Ellis Island Party," Pictorial Review, 30 (May 1929), p. 55; Elaine, "A Spanish Party for Gay Madrid," Good Housekeeping, 77 (March 1924), p. 90; Phyllis Pulliam, "The Progressive Dinner Party," Good Housekeeping, 88 (May 1929), p. 96; Elaine, "Famous Folks Valentine Party," Good Housekeeping, 100 (February, 1935), p. 110.

7. Sophie Kerr, "Twenty Years of Dinner Parties," Saturday Evening Post (September 21, 1935), p. 30; Cable, p. 112; "Life Goes to a Party," Life (January 3, 1938); author interview with Sarah Tapper, Curator of Collections, Decatur House Museum, March 6, 2003.

8. John Hay, The Bread-Winners (New York: Harper & Brothers, 1883), cited in Cable, p. 107; Francis Biddle, The Llanfear Pattern (New York: Scribner's, 1927), cited in Cable, pp. 108, 113; Many of James's novels included parties that he depicted similarly.

9. Edith Wharton, The House of Mirth (New York: Scribner's, 1905).

10. F. Scott Fitzgerald, The Great Gatsby, 1925 reprint (New York: Banton, 1974); Thomas Wolfe, The Party at Jack's, ed. Suzanne Stutman and John L. Idol, Jr. (Chapel Hill: University of North Carolina, 1995), pp. v–xxiii; 139–200; Robert S. Kennedy, The Window of Memory: The Literary Career of Thomas Wolfe (Chapel Hill: University of North Carolina, 1962), pp. 345–354.

11. Los Angeles Times, 29 December 1935, sec. IV, p. 2; 30 August 1936, sec. IV, p. 8; 7 October 1934, sec. II, p. 1; 16 August 1936, sec. III, p. 2; 2 July 1939, sec. III, p. 2; Myrna Loy and James Kotsilibas-David, pp. 90–96; "A Stitch in Big Time," and unidentified clipping of 3 May 1933 in Woolf: Edgar; Allan Clipping, NYPL; Aljean Harmetz, The Making of The Wizard of Oz (New York: Delta, 1977), pp. 46–47; Finch and Rosenkrantz, 234–235; Howe, "Hollywood in a High Hat," pp. 29–30.

12. Finch and Rosenkrantz, p. 234; Tay Garnett, with Fredda Dudley Balling, Light Your Torches and Pull Up Your Tights (New Rochelle, NY: Arlington House, 1973), p. 206; Los Angeles Times, 25 August 1935, sec. III, p. 9; 25 August 1935, sec. III, p. 9; "January 2nd," Anita Loos Collection, Box 1, Folder 10, Mugar Library, BU.

13. The three trials received detailed coverage in metropolitan dailies from late 1921 through 1922. The scandal is discussed in Richard Koszarski, An Evening's Entertainment: The Age of the Silent Feature Picture, 1915–1928. Vol. 3, History of the American Cinema, ed. Charles Harpole (New York: Scribner's, 1990).

14. Fine, pp. 297–317; Lisa Duggan, "The

Trials of Alice Mitchell: Sensationalism, and the Lesbian Subject in Turn-of-the-Century America," *Signs* (Summer 1993), pp. 791–814.

15. Richard Rodgers and Lorenz Hart, "Hollywood Party," *Hollywood Party* (MGM, 1934).

16. Recently, a couple of writers (Mann and Ehrenstein) have observed the discussion of nonconformist gender and sexuality in gossip columns. However, neither focused their work on how these images enhanced the Hollywood party mystique or demonstrated the possibility of living successfully outside the culture's romantic standards. Stuart Timmons, *The Trouble with Harry Hay: Founder of the Modern Gay Movement* (Boston: Alyson Publications, 1990), p. 71; Jack Levin and Arnold Arluke, *Gossip: The Inside Scoop* (New York: Plenum Press, 1987), pp. 28–31.

17. David Nasaw, *The Chief: The Life of William Randolph Hearst* (New York: Houghton Mifflin, 2000), chapters 3, 6, 7; Louis Pizzitola, *Hearst Over Hollywood: Power, Passion, and Propaganda in the Movies* (New York: Columbia University Press, 2002), chapter 2.

18. Pizzitola, pp. 1–16; "President's Bible," *Time*, 15 August 1927, www.time.com/time/magazine/article/0,9171,730920-3,00.html, 06/20/2007.

19. Fred Laurence Guiles, *Marion Davies* (McGraw-Hill, 1972), pp. 1–55; Pizzitola, chapter 7.

20. Guiles; Pizzitola.

21. *Los Angeles Times*, 1 September 1929, p. 19; *Washington Post*, 23 November 1931, p. 2; *New York Times*, 17 March 1932, p. 16.

22. *Los Angeles Times*, 4 October 1932, p. 1; *Chicago Daily Tribune*, 7 October 1932, p. 3.

23. *Los Angeles Times*, 23 September 1932, p. A4; 7 February 1934, p. A4; 20 July 1934, p. A4; http://en.wikipedia.org/wiki/Bonus_Army, 06/20/2007.

24. Pizzolta, pp. 220–260, 390–391; Guiles, pp. 193–195, 335–350; *New York Times*, 6 August 1928, p. 1.

25. *Chicago Daily Tribune*, 6 January 1931, p. 7; *New York Times*, 22 January 1931, p. 18.

26. Pizzitola, pp. 347, 390–391.

27. *Citizen Kane*. Dir. Orson Wells, perf. Orson Wells, Joseph Cotten, and Dorothy Comingore. RKO, 1941.

28. Nasaw; Guiles; Pizzitola; *Los Angeles Times*, 15 August 1951, p. 1; 15 March 1981, p. L9; *Chicago Daily Tribune*, 21 September 1961, p. 18.

29. Dawidziak and Bauer; Charles Willeford, "Jim Tully: Holistic Barbarian," *Writing and Other Blood Sports* (Tucson, AZ: Dennis McMillan Publications, 2000).

30. Jim Tully, *Jarnegan* (New York: Albert and Charles Boni, 1926), pp. 180–193.

31. *Ibid*, pp. 250–265.

32. Frederick Lewis Allen, *Only Yesterday: An Informal History of the 1920s* (New York: Blue Ribbon Books, 1931); Paula S. Fass, *The Damned and the Beautiful: American Youth in the 1920s* (New York: Oxford University Press, 1979).

33. "Miss Millay's 'Wayfarer' and Other Works of Fiction," *New York Times*, 19 September 1926, sec. V, p. 22; Will Cuppy, "A Roughneck in Art," *New York Herald Tribune*, 19 September 1926, sec. VII, p. 15; W. B. "Jim Tully and Jarnegan," *Boston Evening Transcript*, 20 October 1926, sec. VII, p. 4.

34. *Chicago Daily Tribune*, 4 July 1932, p. 10; 14 November 1937, p. G2; *Chicago Defender*, 23 July 1932, p. 5; *Los Angeles Times*, 2 October 1932, p. B16; Barry Monush, *Encyclopedia of Hollywood Film Actors: From the Silent Era to 1965 Vol. 1*, (New York: Applause Theatre & Cinema Books, 2003), pp. 738–740.

35. Monush, pp. 811–812; *Chicago Daily Tribune*, 29 January 1930, p. 3; *Los Angeles Times*, 25 September 1927, p. 11; 7 February 1931, p. A2; Denny Jackson, biography of Loretta Young at imdb.com; Joe Morella and Edward Z. Epstein, *Loretta Young: An Extraordinary Life* (New York: Delacorte Press, 1986), pp. 3–41.

36. *Los Angeles Times*, 21 August 1933, p. A9; 24 September 1933, p. A1; 16 November 1933, p. 7; 29 November 1933, p. A7; 16 December 1933, p. A7; 21 January 1934, p. A1; 8 February 1934, p. 13; 15 April 1934, p. A1; 22 May 1934, p. 13; 28 May 1934, p. A9; 15 June 1934, p. A, 15; 14 August 1934, p. 19.

37. *Chicago Daily Tribune*, 12 August 1934, p. D5; 13 October 1937, p. 23; *Los Angeles Times*, 2 December 1934, p. A1.

38. Mann, *Kate*, pp. 317–318; David Bret, *Joan Crawford: Hollywood Martyr* (New York: Carroll & Graf Publishers, 2006), p. 115.

39. Wayne; Morella and Epstein, pp. 70–74; Bill Davidson, *Spencer Tracy: Tragic Idol* (New York: E. P. Dutton, 1987), p. 61.

40. D. L. M., "Laughter Limited," *Boston Evening Transcript*, November 4, 1922, sec. V, p. 2; *Springfield Republican*, October 29, 1922.

41. Tamar Lane, *Hey Diddle Diddle* (New York: Adelphi Press, 1932), p. 140.

42. *New York Times*, January 13, 1924, III, p. 10; Nancy Brooker-Bowers, *The Hollywood Novel And Other Novels About Film, 1912–1982* (Garland Publishing, 1985), p. 52; Interview with biographer Mark Dawidziak with author, February 27, 2003.

43. Sharon Rich, *Nelson Eddy: The Opera Years* (New York: Bell Harbour Press, 2001); Henry Cory Baxter, "A Voice, a Phonograph and BRAINS," *Silver Screen* (May, 1935), p. 56; Katz, p. 373. Eventually, the studio perceived that his public display of romantic non–conformity invited a publicity backlash and successfully forced Eddy to marry.

44. *Los Angeles Times*, 10 October 1934, sec. II, p. 3; 29 December 1935, sec. IV, p. 2; 30 January 1937, sec. IV, p. 11; 15 August 1937, sec. IV, p. 10. Actor Basil Rathbone (known for playing Sherlock Holmes) and his wife Ouida Rathbone gave parties that were command performances, with lavish dinners and champagne flowing like the conversation of the illustrious guests. Joan Fontaine, *No Bed of Roses* (New York: William Morrow, 1978), p. 118. For example, at Jack Oakie's "come as your favorite star" soiree, Eddy could mix with homosexually active actors Rod La Rocque, Edmund Lowe, Eric Blore, Cary Grant,

William Haines, Edward Everett Horton, Cesar Romero, Randolph Scott, screenwriter Edgar Allen Woolf, and studio dress designer Bernard Newman. *Los Angeles Times,* 31 March 1937, III, p. 10. Boze Hadleigh's *Hollywood Gays* (New York: Barricade Books, 1996). The discussion of Woolf appears in Harmetz. Madsen, *The Sewing Circle,* p. 18.

45. Helen Fay Ludlam, "The Romantic Nelson Eddy," *Silver Screen* (July 1936), pp. 26, 55.

46. Howard Sharpe, "The Private Life of Nelson Eddy," *Photoplay,* 50 (August 1936), p. 86.

47. *Los Angeles Times,* 9 May 1937, sec. III, p. 1.

48. Anita Loos Collection, Box 1, Folder 5, Mugar Library, BU; Mann, *Behind The Screen,* p. 154; Sharon Rich, *Sweethearts: The Timeless Love Affair—On-Screen And Off—Between Jeannette MacDonald and Nelson Eddy* (New York: Bell Harbour Press, updated ed., 2001).

49. *Random House Historical Dictionary of American Slang A-G,* ed. J. E. Lighter (New York: Random House, 1994), p. 115; Barry Paris, *Garbo: A Biography* (New York: Alfred A. Knopf, 1995), pp. 249–252; Kenneth Anger, *Hollywood Babylon I* (San Francisco: Straight Arrow Books, 1975), p. 171; Boze Hadleigh, *Bette Davis Speaks* (New York: Barricade Books, 1996), p. 130; Madsen, *The Sewing Circle,* pp. 52–53. The aforementioned instance of Nelson Eddy and Anne Franklin followed the style known as contracting with a "beard." Among the actors and actresses who formed successful versions of these partnerships were Edmund Lowe and Lilyan Tashman and Charlie Farrell and actress Virginia Valli. Some actresses forged tandems with artisans, including Janet Gaynor with studio stylist Adrian and Dolores Del Rio with MGM's art department head, Cedric Gibbons.

50. Emily Leider, *Dark Lover: The Life and Death of Rudolph Valentino* (New York: Farrar, Straus and Giroux, 2003), pp. 50–110; David Bret, *Valentino: A Dream of Desire* (New York: Carroll & Graf Publishers, 1998), pp. 3–40; Katz, pp. 1181–1182; Internet Movie Database, *http://www.imdb.com/title/tt0010103/;* Jon C. Hopwood, mini-biography of Clara Kimball Young, Internet Movie Database, *http://www.imdb.com/name/nm0949403/bio.* American Film Institute, *Silent Film Catalog, http://www.afi.com/members/catalog/Detail View.aspx?s=1&Movie=17452&bhcp=1; New York Times,* 1 December 1919, p. 9; David Bret, pp. 34–48

51. Gavin Lambert, *Nazimova: A Biography* (New York: Alfred A. Knopf, 1997), pp. 201–223; Madsen, *The Sewing Circle,* pp. 99–100; *New York Times,* 12 August 1917, p. X7; 31 August 1919, p. 46; Frank Fob, "Grace Darmond Biography, IMDb; *http://us.imdb.com/name/nm0201472/bio; Washington Post,* 27 June 1915, p. SM2; 26 June 1921, p. 46; Bret, pp. 34–48.

52. *Los Angeles Evening Herald,* 23 November 1921, sec. A-5; 26 November 1921, sec. A-7; *Los Angeles Times,* 26 November 1921, sec. II, p. 9.

53. Roughly a year after Acker's divorce from Valentino, readers of industry gossip columns discovered the latest on these actresses. Acker brought her vaudeville show to the West Coast and visited Darmond on location on Catalina Island for a few days. She left to begin a two-week stay in San Francisco. Darmond finished her part in the motion picture and departed on a personal appearance tour. Darmond went to San Francisco the final weekend of Jean Acker's stay in that city. *Los Angeles Times,* 6 June 1923, sec. II, p. 11; 22 June 1923, sec. II, p. 9.

54. *Los Angeles Times,* 6 June 1923, sec. II, p. 11; 23 June 1923, sec. II, p. 9.

55. Lambert, pp. 217–218; Bernard Rosenberg and Harry Silverstein, *The Real Tinsel* (London: Macmillan, 1970), p. 260; Madsen, pp. 98–100; Leider, pp. 98–103; Bret, pp. 34–35, 206; Michael Morris, *Madame Valentino: The Many Lives of Natacha Rambova* (New York: Abbeville Press, 1991), p. 76.

56. *Los Angeles Evening Herald,* 20 May 1922, p. 1.

57. *Los Angeles Times,* 3 June 1922, sec. II, p. 1; 4 June 1922, p. 12; 6 June 1922, sec. II, p. 5; *New York Times,* 16 May 1922, p. 10.

58. "Wedded and Parted," *Photoplay,* December 1922, pp. 58–59, 117; Gaylyn Studlar, *This Mad Masquerade: Stardom and Masculinity in the Jazz Age* (New York: Columbia University Press, 1996).

59. *Washington Post,* 21 August 1925, p. 3; 11 November 1925, p. 3; *New York Times,* 10 January 1926, p. 20; 20 January 1927, 1, p. 27;

60. *Chicago Tribune,* 18 July 1926, sec. I, p. 10. The editorial follows: "We personally saw two 'men'—as young lady contributors to the Voice of the People are wont to describe the breed—step up, insert coin, hold kerchief beneath the spout, pull the lever, then take the pretty pink stuff and pat it on their cheeks in front of the mirror.... It is time for a matriarchy if the male of the species allows such things to persist. Better a rule by masculine women then by effeminate men.... How does one reconcile masculine cosmetics, sheiks, gloppy pants, and slave bracelets with a disregard for law an aptitude for crime more in keeping with the frontier of half a century ago than a twentieth century metropolis? ... Down with Decatur, up with Elinor Glyn. Hollywood is the national school of masculinity. Rudy, the beautiful gardener's boy, is the prototype of the American male. Hell's bells. Oh, sugar."

61. Lambert, pp. 235–245.

62. Lambert; Bret; Morris; Leider.

63. *Ibid.*

64. Keane McGrath, *Hollywood Siren* (New York: William Godwin, 1932), pp. 120–121.

65. *New York World Telegraph,* June 5, 1934, in NYPL, Billy Rose Collection, Folder MWEZ+ n.c. 6785.

66. Lane, p. 141.

67. Townsend Ludington, *John Dos Passos: A Twentieth Century Odyssey* (New York: E. P. Dutton, 1980), pp. 330–331.

68. John Dos Passos, pp. 201–205, 400–420.
69. Ibid., p. 431.

Chapter Four

1. Unidentified clipping in Alla Nazimova file, Lesbian Herstory Archives, Brooklyn, New York.
2. Drew McCoy, *The Elusive Republic* (New York, 1982); David P. Handlin, *The American Home: Architecture and Society, 1815–1915* (Boston: Little, Brown, 1979), pp. 4, 11–30; Gwendolyn Wright, *Building the Dream: A Social History of Housing in America* (Cambridge, MA: MIT Press, 1981), pp. 21–25, 75–80; Witold Rybczynski, *Home: A Short History of an Idea* (New York: Viking Books, 1986).
3. Handlin, pp. 40–44; Wright, pp. xvi, 80–84.
4. Handlin, pp. 199–213. As urban planner Raymond Unwin wrote, "[The multiple dwelling] was the most difficult with which to assimilate any sense of home, and absolutely the most miserable type of place in which children can be raised." Raymond Unwin, "Discussion," *Proceedings of the National Conference on City Planning*, 3 (1911): pp. 110–111; Wright, pp. 11–145.
5. Wright, pp. 149–211. The editorial board of *Architectural Record* complained that apartment buildings proved deleterious to the important role of woman maintaining the home. "A woman who lives in an apartment hotel has nothing to do … Her personal preferences and standards are completely swallowed up in the general public standards of the institution. She can not create that atmosphere of manner and things around her own personality, which is the chief source of her effectiveness and power." Roger Sherwood, *Modern Housing Prototypes* (Cambridge, MA: Harvard College, 1978), pp. 29–30; Handlin, pp. 17, 307–308; Mike Davis, *City of Quartz: Excavating the Future in Los Angeles* (New York: Vintage Books, 1992), pp. 26–29; Sam Bass Warner, *The Urban Wilderness: History of the American City* (Berkeley, University of California Press, 1972). The Greenes viewed the ultimate bungalow as a "cathedral in wood," and the masses could buy small but stylish imitations in "do-it-yourself" kits that created democratic bungalows. These kits promoted the old ideals of equality and the repetition of simple forms in housing.
6. Starr, *Inventing the Dream*, pp. 70–72; Eshref Shevky and Marilyn Williams, pp. 27–35; Scott L. Bottles, *Los Angeles and The Automobile: The Making of the Modern City* (Berkeley: University of California Press, 1987).
7. Starr, pp. 45–50, 156–163.
8. Starr, *Inventing the Dream*, p. 64; McArthur, pp. 70–71; *Los Angeles City Directory*, 1917. The residences of stars were gleaned from the alphabetical listing of residents in the first section of the directory. Certain stars, including Charles Chaplin, did not provide their home addresses. Miriam Cooper Walsh, "Chapter VIII," in Lectures & Writings: Drafts & Typescripts folder, Miriam Cooper Walsh Papers, Manuscript Division, LC.
9. Henstell, pp. 13–22; Norman M. Klein and Martin J. Schiesl, eds., *Twentieth Century Los Angeles: Power, Promotion and Social Conflict* (Claremont, CA: Regina Books, 1990), pp. 1–27; Shevky and Williams; Irene Mayer Selznick, *A Private View* (New York: Alfred A. Knopf, 1983), pp. 65–77; Christopher Finch and Linda Rosenkrantz, pp. 5–7, 70–75, 143–144; Larry May, *Screening Out the Past: The Birth of Mass Culture and the Motion Picture Industry* (Chicago: University of Chicago Press, 1980), pp. 220–235. Maps listing the locations of star homes appeared in various locations including *Photoplay*, November 1938, and from private sources, such as a Souvenir Map and Guide to Starland Estates and Mansions issued in December 1937. These and other maps appeared in the Cinema: Hollywood folder, NYPL.
10. William Edward Schenck, *Aunt Fanny's Home and Her Talks About God's Work* (Philadelphia, PA: Presbyterian Board of Publication, 1863).
11. Handlin, pp. 20–21. Among the books with these stories were: *Famous American Homes* (New York: Home Insurance, 1939); Elbert Hubbard, *Little Journeys to the homes of the Great: Famous Women* (New York: World Publishing, 1928). The former included statesman such as John Marshall and Andrew Jackson and inventors including S.F.B. Morse and Robert Fulton. The latter contained writers from Elizabeth B. Browning and Jane Austen to Mary W. Shelley. Mary Cable, *Top Drawer: American High Society from the Gilded Age to the Roaring Twenties* (New York: Atheneum, 1984), pp. 85–90, 150–152.
12. Prior to 1918, 204 of 228 articles featured men or married couples while 438 of 498 did so between 1919 and 1941. This survey of the literature came from the Architecture–Domestic and Country Homes and Country Houses sections of the *Readers' Guide to Periodical Literature* between the years 1880 and 1941. This survey of literature reduced the number of representations of entertainment houses because it omitted film fan magazines. However, this sample enables us to understand what the larger reading public encountered. Handlin, pp. 360–361; "West Indian Colonial Invades the Deep South," Norma Talmadge home, *House and Gardens* (February, 1935), p. 26; Mary J. Linton, "'The Hedges' The Home of Miss M. G. B. Clapp, Nantucket," *The House Beautiful* (November 1925), pp. 550–554; Verna Cook Salomonsky, "The Little White House, Margaret Owen home, *House Beautiful* (October 1932), pp. 224–228; Wolfe, "Modified Colonial in Iowa; home of the Misses Wolfe," *American* (November 1936), pp. 41, 69.
13. *Ladies Home Journal*, see August 1917, p. 59 for example. *The Delineator*, see January 1926, v. 108, #1 for example.
14. See pamphlet collection, American Federation of Labor–Congress of Industrial Unions, George Meany Memorial Archives, Silver Spring,

MD. "Women In The Home," Woman Suffrage Association Collection, 1848–1921, Rare Book and Special Collections Division, LC, Washington, D.C.

15. Delight Evans, "The Man Uncomfortable," *Photoplay* (November 1922), pp. 30–31, 111; Anne O'Hare McCormick, "Searching for the Mind Behind Hollywood," *New York Times Magazine*, 13 December 1931, pp. 4–5.

16. Adela Rogers St. Johns, "Gloria! An Impression," *Photoplay* (September 1923), pp. 28–29, 104–105.

17. Wendy Holliday, "Hollywood's Modern Women: Screenwriting, Work Culture and Feminism, 1910–1940," Ph.D. diss. New York University, 1995, pp. 3–10.

18. Greenberg, p. 320; Tracy Davis, *Actresses As Working Women: Their Social Identity in Victorian Culture* (London: Routledge, 1991), pp. 18–19, 71; Donald Dewey, *James Stewart: A Biography* (Atlanta: Turner Publishing, 1996), p. 181.

19. A collection of biographical materials and press clippings from Alla Nazimova's stage career are in the Alla Nazimova Collection, LC, Washington, D.C. Starr, *Material Dreams*, pp. 216–217; *Washington Post*, 31 July 1921, p. 48; Lambert, pp. 11, 178–192, 230–279; 362–385; *New York Times*, 6 August 1922, p. 80; *Washington Post*, 31 July 1921, p. 48.

20. "Pajama Charge Denied by Actress," *Los Angeles Evening Herald*, 22 November 1920, sec. B-8; Lambert, p. 248. Nazimova's hairstyle, coupled with her choice of clothing, creates a highly gender-crossing image that surpassed the normative New Woman visage. Ishbel Ross, *Taste in America: An Illustrated History of the Evolution of Architecture, Furnishings, Fashions, and Customs of the American People* (New York: Thomas Y. Cromwell, 1967), pp. 180–182; Simmons, pp. 160, 168–169.

21. Herbert Howe, "A Misunderstood Woman: She's Addressed as Madame Nazimova, but one thinks of her as Naz," *Photoplay* (April 1922), p. 119.

22. *Ibid.*, pp. 24–25.

23. *Los Angeles Evening Herald*, 15 March 1920, sec. B-6; Grace Kingsley, "Flashes," *Los Angeles Times*, 20 April 1921, sec. III, p. 4; 18 July 1920, sec. III, p. 15; Lambert, pp. 220–222.

24. Thoreau Cronyn, "The Truth About Hollywood," *New York Herald*, March 19-April 2, 1922.

25. Lambert, pp. 176, 230–236; Bret, pp. 34–49; Mercedes De Acosta, *Here Lies the Heart* (New York: Reynal, 1960).

26. Madsen, pp. 14, 98–99, 117; Lambert, pp. 10–11; Bret, Morris.

27. Rilla Palmborg, *Photoplay*, "The Private Life of Greta Garbo" (September 1930), p. 40; Palmborg, (October 1930), pp. 39, 143.

28. Two of the strongest biographies of the Swedish star are Barry Paris, *Garbo: A Biography* (New York: Alfred A. Knopf, 1995), pp. 374–385, and Karen Swenson, *Greta Garbo: A Life Apart* (New York: Scribner's, 1997); Dale O'Connor, "IMDb Mini-Biography — Greta Garbo" at *http:// www.imdb.com/name/nm0001256/bio*; John Wakeman, editor, "World Film Directors, Volume One, 1890–1945" (New York: H.W. Wilson, 1987), pp. 1063–1069; Madsen, *The Sewing Circle*, pp. 30–37.

29. *Los Angeles Evening Herald and Examiner*, 11 May 1932, p. B5; Madsen, pp. 93–94.

30. Palmborg, (October 1930), p. 142.

31. Curtin, pp. 40–50.

32. Boze Hadleigh, *Hollywood Lesbians* (New York: Barricade Books, 1994), pp. 192, 208; Vincent Sherman, telephone interview with the author, 26 January 1998; Patrick McGilligan, *George Cukor: A Double Life* (New York: St. Martin's Press, 1991), pp. 108, 167.

33. Madsen, p. 134, as quoted in Antonio Gronowicz, *Garbo: Her Story* (New York: Simon and Schuster, 1990), p. 311; Betty Lee, *Marie Dressler: The Unlikeliest Star* (Lexington, KY: University of Kentucky Press, 1997), pp. 170–195; Marie Dressler, *My Own Story* (Boston: Little, Brown, 1934), pp. 251–252.

34. Andrea Weiss, *Vampires and Violets: Lesbians in Film* (New York: Penguin Books, 1993), pp. 30–40; Madsen, pp. 21–23, 54–57, 82–83, 135.

35. Robert A. Schanke, *That Furious Lesbian: The Story of Mercedes de Acosta* (Southern Illinois University Press, 2003), pp. 103–118.

36. Barry Paris, pp. 223–259; Karen Swenson, pp. 249–275, pp. 490–494.

37. Anthony Slide, *The Vaudevillians: A Dictionary of Vaudeville Performers* (Westport, CT: Arlington House, 1994), p. 169; Katz, p. 646; David Ragan, *Who's Who In Hollywood 1900–1976* (New Rochelle, NY: Arlington House Publishers, 1976), pp. 221–222; *Los Angeles Times*, 17 December 1935, p. 10; *Washington Post*, 13 October 1935, SM3; 4 July 1940, p. 11. Mann, *Behind The Screen*, pp. 138, 146; *Hollywood Studio Magazine*, February 1982.

38. "It Comes Out Here," *Silver Screen* (March, 1936), p. 58; Hall, p. 32; *Los Angeles Times*, 17 December 1935, p. 10. *Oxford English Dictionary*, v. XVIII, p. 212. In *Royal Elsmere* (1888), Mrs. Humphrey Ward writes, "As a rough tomboy of fourteen, she had shown Catherine ... a good many uncouth signs of affection." The phrase "uncouth signs of affection" connotes "aberrant" sexual behavior. Since the character is a boyish-behaving woman, the affection is most likely woman-loving-woman. *New York World Telegram*, 12 October 1935, Kelly, Patsy (actress) folder, NYPL; unidentified newspaper clipping from 12 August 1941 in Kelly, Patsy (actress) folder, NYPL;

39. Gladys Hall, "'Tis the Likes of the Kelly You'll Be After Liking Now!" *Motion Picture Magazine* (January 1937), p. 104.

40. *Ibid.*

41. *Los Angeles Times*, 22 March 1936, sec. IV, p. 6.

42. Hadleigh, *Hollywood Lesbians*, pp. 62–68.

43. *Ibid.*, Mann, pp. 138–139; Madsen, p. 188; David Quinlan, *The Illustrated Encyclopedia of Movie Character Actors* (New York: Harmony Books, 1985), pp. 147–148.

44. Unidentified clipping in Alla Nazimova file, Lesbian Herstory Archives; Anne Frior Scott, *Natural Allies: Women's Associations in American History* (Urbana: University of Illinois Press, 1991), pp. 141–150. Feminist advocates wrote that children resulted in complicating factors for career women. Some offered compromise solutions, not fully offsetting the professional and salary risks and other issues that this path entailed. Most career advocates supported the gender norms of wife and mother, and these advocates viewed women's jobs especially promising when this work stemmed from or aimed to improve family life. Most creative women argued that being a mother helped their creative energy and provided grist for their mill. Nancy Cott, *The Grounding of Modern Feminism* (New Haven: Yale University Press, 1987), pp. 197–201.

45. *New York Daily News*, 20 June 1940 in Kelly, Patsy (actress) folder, NYPL. Both performers' ideas about marriage moved against the trend for both women and men during the first decades of the twentieth century. The proportion of women who never married dropped from ten to six percent between the generations who came of age between 1895–1915 and those who came of age between 1917–1939. The average age at which women married dipped from twenty-four years to twenty-two and a half.

46. Carroll Smith-Rosenberg, "Discourses of Sexuality and Subjectivity: The New Woman, 1870–1936," in *Hidden From History: Reclaiming the Gay and Lesbian Past* (New York: North American Library, 1989), pp. 276–280; Norma Fain Pratt, "Culture and Radical Politics: Yiddish Women Writers in American, 1890–1940," in ed. Lois Scharf and Joan M. Jensen, *Decades of Discontent: The Women's Movement , 1920–1940* (Westport, CT: Greenwood Press, 1983), pp. 142–144.

47. Inness, p. 37; Cott, pp. 159–162.

48. "How Twelve Famous Women Scenario Writers Succeeded," *Photoplay* (August 1923), p. 31; F. Scott Fitzgerald, *The Last Tycoon* (New York: Scribner's, 1941), p. 36.

49. "Woman Lived As Man, Wed to One of Her Sex," *New York Times*, 4 May 1929, p. 40; "Writer Blamed Pity For Affair," *Los Angeles Times*, 4 May 1929, sec. II, p. 2.

50. "Dying 'Man' Proves Woman," *Los Angeles Times*, 3 May 1929, p. 2; "Tells Mother Romance With Woman Poser," *Los Angeles Evening Herald*, 4 May 1929, sec. A-1.

51. "Writer Blamed Pity For Affair," *Los Angeles Times*, 4 May 1929, sec. II, p. 2; "Bare Loves of 'Man' Found to Be Woman," *Los Angeles Evening Herald*, 3 May 1929, sec. A-1.

52. *American Film Institute Catalog of Motion Pictures produced in the United States, 1931–1940*, Patricia King Hanson, executive editor (Berkeley: University of California Press, 1993), p. 1003.

53. Madsen, pp. 39–41; Schanke, pp. 3–23.

54. de Acosta, pp. 212–227, 240–245, 316–318; Paris, pp. 257–264; Axel Madsen, *Forbidden Lovers: Hollywood's Greatest Secret—Female Stars Who Loved Other Women* (New York: Carol Publishing Group, 1996), pp. 9, 21–26, 66–79; Mia Riva, *Marlene Dietrich* (New York: Alfred A. Knopf, 1993).

55. de Acosta, pp. 206–222; Madsen, pp. 41–42; Swenson, pp. 273–275, 327–329; Introduction of Mercedes de Acosta during speaking engagement. Box 5 folder 3, Mercedes de Acosta Collection, Rosenbach Museum, Philadelphia.

56. The lack of mention of her clothing appeared in a *Philadelphia Public Ledger* piece of April 12, 1925, in an unidentified clipping of May 8, 1928, and in most of the New York newspaper reviews for her plays. The article on the Lucy Stone League appeared in the *New York Sun*, February 27, 1922, de Acosta Collection, Box 5, Folder 3, Rosenbach Museum; Alma Whitaker, "Change Her Name? Well, Mercedes Just Refuses," *Los Angeles Times*, 27 December 1931, sec. III, p. 7. In a review column, a theater critic made the following observation: "The actor who played the Moor, although highly accomplished, was physically unsuited to the part. He looked just like Mercedes d'Acosta [sic], which is a very good way to look, but not when one is acting Othello ... When Othello flounced off the stage it was only for an instant that one found oneself saying, 'Well, I never knew Mercedes d'Acosta [sic] had such a temper.'" *Los Angeles Examiner*, 31 May 1932 de Acosta Collection, Box 5, Folder 4, Rosenbach Museum.

57. Whitaker, "Change Her Name?" p. 7; Holliday, pp. 330–331.

58. *Movie Classic*, undated, presumably late 1932, de Acosta Collection, Box 17, Folder 4, Rosenbach Museum. The screenwriter's status as a scholar illustrated both the gains women made and the limitations they faced in academia in the middle of the twentieth century. Most professional women in the 1930s worked as nurses and elementary and secondary school teachers. Within academics, women were confined to the lowest ranks of the professoriate and usually channeled into areas unofficially deemed women's work, including nutrition and home economics. Only a few notable women emerged as highly accomplished researchers and writers. Cott, pp. 215–222; Ware, pp. 79–81; Notes, Box 1, Folder 10, Anita Loos Collection, Mugar Library, BU.

59. *The Hollywood Reporter*, January 1935, cited in Tichi Wilkerson and Marcia Borif, *The Hollywood Reporter: The Golden Years* (New York: Coward-McCann, 1984), p. 78.

60. Riva; Mann, *Behind the Screen*, pp. 136–137; de Acosta, pp. 230–278.

61. De Acosta Collection, Box 12, Folder #1, Dietrich Correspondence, 1932–1933, Telegram, 10 October 1932, Note, 6 November 1932, Note, 11 May 1933; Box 10, folder #18, Munson to De Acosta (undated).

62. Schanke; Madsen; Mann.

63. Whitaker, "Change Her Name?" p. 7. As a gender role, the position of mother dramatically influenced the opportunities that women have had to enter the cultural, political, and social worlds

in the United States. During this era opponents of women's involvement in these worlds used motherhood to deny women the opportunity to enter those realms. As noted earlier, an ideology of motherhood enabled some women to enter these worlds during the Progressive era, if their activities stayed within those areas where the ideology could justify women's involvement. Susan Ware, *Holding Their Own: American Women in the 1930s* (Boston: Twayne Publications, 1982).

64. Judith Mayne, *Directed by Dorothy Arzner* (Bloomington: Indiana University Press, 1994), pp. 13–30.

65. Herbert Cruikshank, "Director Dorothy: The One Woman Behind the Stars," *Motion Picture Classic* (September 1929), p. 76. Other instances include: *Photoplay* (December 1933), p. 24, Dorothy Arzner Biography File, AMPAS; Hedda Hopper, *Los Angeles Times*, 21 February 1937, sec. III, p. 3; *Los Angeles Times*, 18 September 1927, sec. III, p. 15.

66. *Los Angeles Times*, 18 September 1927, sec. III, p. 15; 21 February 1937, sec. III, p. 3.

67. Mayne, p. 160.

68. *Time*, 12 October 1936, p. 32; Cruikshank, p. 76.

69. *Los Angeles Times*, 18 September 1927, sec III, p. 15; 17 April 1927, sec. III, p. 2; *Time*, 12 October 1936, p. 32.

70. Lambert; Madsen, pp. 136–146; Mann, pp. 59–74; Mayne, pp. 20–55.

71. The idea for a contestation of stories forming lesbian identities and media representations of the "mannish lesbian" appeared in Duggan, "The Trials of Alice Mitchell"; Cott, pp. 155–165; Mary Ryan, "The Projection of a New Womanhood: Movie Moderns in the 1920s," in ed. Scharf and Jensen. Depictions of New Women in mass culture, such as Hollywood movies, showed them desiring to escape work and winning retirement through the prompting of love and trusting submission to her man.

72. Chauncey, pp. 75–86; Paul Groth, *Living Downtown: The History of Residential Hotels in the United States* (Berkeley: University of California Press, 1994), pp. 107, 216–218, 290–292; Richard Plunz, *A History of Housing in New York City: Dwelling Type and Social Change in the American Metropolis* (New York: Columbia University Press, 1990), pp. 50–60; Wright, p. 141. The placement of elevators in hotels and apartment houses removed a significant physical limitation and the cultural stigma of living within a multiple-floor dwelling.

73. Sidney Wahl Little, "Off Campus; new home in which a bachelor college professor finds life again worth living," *American Home* (November 1936), pp. 86–89; L. Morris, "Bachelors' paradise in the Druid hills," *American Home* (February 1938), p. 19.

74. *Los Angeles Times*, 8 April 1934, sec. II, p. 2.

75. "Keeping Bachelor's Hall: George Cukor's house, West Hollywood," *Country Life* (June 1937), pp. 52–57; Mann, *Wisecracker: The Life and Times of William Haines*, offers detailed descriptions of the articles and the El Porto scandal. The article from *The New York Times*, June 3, 1936, p. 46, noted that Haines and a companion Jimmy Shields were beaten and that 19 other friends had been guests at a party Haines threw; all the guests were males. One example came from the *Los Angeles Times* in 1932. Reporter Alma Whitaker asked why Bill Haines had not married. Whitaker offers her readers a complex answer, observing that he remains a bachelor because factors within his identity convince women to view him as a fellow "sister," and not as a romantic and sexual interest.

76. Vicki Baum, *Falling Star* (Garden City, NY.: Doubleday, Doran, 1934), pp. 5–7, 80–83. It is arguable that Dent would have married his flame, actress Donka, but the studio kept her working on their picture and lied about the time of Oliver's death.

77. The book is William Mann's *Wisecracker*, which has been cited earlier in this chapter. Ronald Gregg, "Gay Culture, Studio Publicity, and the Management of Star Discourse: The Homosexualization of William Haines in Pre–Code Hollywood," *Quarterly Review of Film and Video* 20: pp. 81–97, 2003.

78. *Photoplay*, September 1924, p. 45.

79. "The star-spangled manors of Hollywood," *The American Magazine*, May 1932, pp. 24–26.

80. Harry Lang, "A Melancholy Wisecracker," *Photoplay*, May 1931, pp. 58, 108.

81. *Los Angeles Times*, April 10, 1932, III, p. 15.

82. Tony Thomas, *Hollywood and the American Image* (Westport, CN: Arlington House, 1981); Katz, p. 1300; Mark Eliot, *Cary Grant: A Biography* (New York: Three Rivers Press, 2004); Robert Nott, *The Films of Randolph Scott* (Jefferson, N.C.: McFarland, 2004).

83. Katz, pp. 499–500, 1030; Beverly Bare Buehrer, *Cary Grant: A Bio-Bibliography* (New York: Greenwood Press, 1990); Eliot, p. 400; Warren G. Harris, *Cary Grant: A Touch of Elegance* (London: Sphere, 1988); Charles Higham and Roy Moseley, *Cary Grant: The Lonely Heart* (New York: Harcourt Brace Jovanovich, 1989); Richard Schickel, *Cary Grant: A Celebration* (New York: Applause Books, 2000).

84. Several of these extraordinary images hinted at homosexual interest between them. Several biographers of Grant and writers about homosexual Hollywood during the studio era noted that photographs with the two sharing a luncheon at their dining table and harmonizing at the piano are suggestive of this interest. Most significantly, while many of these writers believed that the photographs came from a subrosa source, in fact, Paramount controlled the copyright and offered newspapers and magazines reproduction rights. Vincent Sherman, *Studio Affairs* (Lexington, KY: University of Kentucky, 1996); Dale Edwards, "Has Cary Grant Gone High Hat?" 1939, in MWEZ + n. c. 17, 956, Grant, Cary. Billy Rose Theater Collection, NYPL.

85. Mann, pp. 230–233; *Los Angeles Evening Herald and Examiner*, 12 January 1934, sec. B-6; *Los Angeles Times*, 21 April 1935, sec. II, p. 2.

86. Russo, pp. 70–72; Richard Meeker [Forman Brown] *Better Angel* second ed., Boston: Alyson Publications, 1995. Paramount packaged the sexuality of these actors in these photographs. The studio had been struggling to create the image for each of the actors. Grant had not done a motion picture recently, and Paramount was struggling to find roles that were appropriate for him. Scott had recently taken his first lead in a motion picture that was not a Western. This motion picture, *So Red the Rose* (1935), was a lavishly budgeted affair that needed a great deal of publicity.

87. Cary Grant and Randolph Scott photographs, Paramount Pictures Collection, Box 2, folder 11 and folder 12, AMPAS; Sivulka, pp. 166–168; Jackson Lears, *Fables of Abundance: A Cultural History of Advertising In America* (New York: Basic Books, 1994), p. 181.

88. The publicity approach exemplified in the Grant-Scott photographs had little precedent among the major motion picture studios. Few male stars had representations of themselves made that displayed their bare torsos. One of the few examples of a fan magazine depicting a male star's bare torso involved actor Reginald Denny. The *Photoplay* photographs from 1923 depicted Denny in a prize fighting pose and in his swimming clothes for his new *The Leather Pusher* series. The caption on the boxing image noted that Denny almost took up boxing as a profession, while the swimming photograph's caption noted that he possessed a physique second to none and held a lot of swimming titles. The Grant-Scott photographs, their poses and settings, could not be directly linked to either actor's then current screen roles. "His name is 'Reggie' But he packs a Wallop," *Photoplay* (June 1923), p. 28.

89. Turner Movie Classic interview in *Cary Grant: A Class Apart*; Hadleigh, *Hollywood Gays*, pp. 240–242; Arthur Laurents, *Original Story by Arthur Laurents: A Memoir of Broadway and Hollywood* (New York: Applause Theater Book Publishers, 2001), p. 131.

90. Gean Harwood, *The Oldest Gay Couple In America: A 70-Year Journey Through Same-Sex America* (New York: Carol Publishing Group, 1997), pp. 30–35.

91. Katz, p. 578; Russo, pp. 31–36; Barrios, p. 143; Douglas Macaulay, *Great Character Actors* at http://www.dougmacaulay.com/kingspud/sel_by_actor_index_2.php?actor_first=Edward.Everette&actor_last=Horton.

92. Twentieth Century–Fox undated Edward Everett Horton biography and Paramount Edward Everett Horton biography of October 1938, Edward Everett Horton biography file, AMPAS; Edward Everett Horton clipping file, Billy Rose Collection, New York Public Library (NYPL).

93. Paramount Press Release, c. 1939. Edward Everett Horton biography file, AMPAS.

94. Handlin, pp. 478–479; Aaron Betsky, *Queer Space: Architecture and Same-Sex Desire* (New York: William Morrow, 1997), p. 6.

95. *Silver Screen* (August 1935), p. 42; *Los Angeles Times*, 10 April 1932, sec. III, p. 15.

96. *Boston Post*, 19 May 1940, Horton Clipping File, NYPL; Lester V. Berrey and Martin Van Den Bark's *American Thesaurus of Slang* (New York: Thomas Y. Cromwell, 1953);Vern L. Bullough, *Science In the Bedroom: A History of Sex Research* (New York: Basic Books, 1994), p. 89; *The Complete Psychological Works of Sigmund Freud*, ed. Anna Freud, trans. James Strachey (London: Hogarth Press, 1957), Vol. 11, pp. 95–100; vol. 18, pp. 106–110; Havelock Ellis, *Studies in the Psychology of Sex, Sexual Inversion* (New York: Random House, 1937), pp. 94, 108, 111; George Henry, *Sex Variant: A Study of Homosexual Patterns* (New York: Paul B. Hoeber, 1948), pp. 147, 223; Dyer, pp. 62–63. By the 1940s, the film noir genre of motion pictures used these images of homosexual males. "Waldo in *Laura* (1944) is the epitome of the homosexual male in film noir. His room is full of neatly arranged, over-fussy objects d'art and he is revealed to have obsessions with clothes, wines, gossip and the arts."

97. Adele Astaire Collection, Box 1, Fred Astaire Letters, Mugar Library, BU.

98. Russo, pp. 35–36; Mann, *Behind the Screen*, pp. 128–132.

Chapter Five

1. "Cinema," *Time*, 1 July 1940, p. 36.

2. Barbas, ch. 12–18; Springer, pp. 10–12.

3. Lawrence J. Levine, *Highbrow/Lowbrow* (Cambridge, MA: Harvard University Press, 1988), pp. 2–20. Since the early 1820s English actors had faced suspicions of aristocratic leanings among numerous Americans. Performers like Edmund Kean precipitated antagonism from audiences in the United States when they refused to perform for small audiences. In 1849, English actor William Charles Macready could not perform in *Macbeth* over audience members who protested his aristocratic demeanor and his identification with the wealthy gentry. He was persuaded to perform again and completed it under great duress. Protesters outside the Astor Place Opera House in New York City threw stones and attempted to storm the entrances but were stopped by the bullets from militia. At least twenty-two people were killed and over 150 wounded.

4. McArthur, pp. 3–10; Davis, *Actresses As Working Women*, pp. 15–17, 70–74; Toll, pp. 6–11; David Nasaw, *Going Out: The Rise and Fall of Public Amusements* (New York: Basic Books, 1993), pp. 10–16. The explosion of touring productions during the "golden age" expanded the interest in behind the scenes of the theater. Touring productions rose from 50 to over 500 between 1880 and 1900 and, despite high ticket prices, brought more people in contact with the theater.

5. Charles Belmont Davis, "Behind the Scenes," *Outing*, 49 (March 1907), pp. 705-706.
6. Simultaneously, there appeared to be a decline in the interest in backstage. While nearly ten articles appeared on this subject during the first decade of the new century, the articles emerged at half that rate for the next two decades before stopping in the late 1920s. Louise Closser Hale, "The Inside Life of the Stage," *Bookman*, 24 (March, 1907), pp. 54-58.
7. Franklin Fyles, "Behind the Scenes," *Ladies Home Journal* (March, 1900), p. 10; "The Spectator," *Outlook* 107 (August 8, 1914), p. 875.
8. Davis, pp. 712-714; Hall, p. 60; Hale, p. 559.
9. Hale, p. 556; "The Spectator," p. 876; Theodore Dresier, *Sister Carrie* (1900 repr., ed. Donald Pizer, (New York: W.W. Norton, 1970).
10. *Warner Brothers Press Release* undated, Studios — Early Days file, AMPAS.
11. Writers' Program of the Work Projects Administration, *Los Angeles: A Guide to the City and Its Environs* (New York: Hastings House, 1941), pp. 242-43; *Los Angeles Evening Herald*, 25 July 1921, sec. B-3; Harold A. C. Sintzenich, "Diary for 1927," January 7, and January 11, 1927 entries, Harold A. C. Sintzenich Collection, Manuscript Division, LC.
12. Douglas Gomery, *The Hollywood Studio System* (London: Macmillan, 1986), pp. 2-15; *Motion Picture Almanac 1929* (New York: Quigley Publishing, 1929), pp. 60-62; Rosten, pp. 374, 382-383; Motion Picture Editors Local 776, "Historical Review of Basic Wages, 1928-1972," IATSE Local 776 files, Los Angeles, CA; Dewey, pp. 138-142; Fred Astaire, letter to Dolly, August 9, 1933, Box 1, Fred letters folder, Adele Astaire Collection, Mugar Library Special Collections Department, BU; Testimony of Herbert Sorrell, *Jurisdictional Disputes In The Motion-Picture Industry*, Vol. 3., 1844; Springer, pp. 53, 135. The quip belongs to historian Vanessa Schwartz.
13. *Los Angeles Times*, 10 September 1939, sec. III, p. 3; *New York Times*, 22 March 1936, sec. IX, p. 4.
14. Ronald Davis, *The Glamour Factory: Inside Hollywood's Big Studio System* (Dallas: Southern Methodist University Press, 1993), pp. 103, 114-115, 240-243; Thomas Cripps, *Hollywood's High Noon: Moviemaking and Society Before Television* (Baltimore: Johns Hopkins University Press, 1997), pp. 14-147; Loy and Kotsilibas-David, pp. 83-150; Elsa Lanchester, *Herself* (New York: St. Martin's Press, 1983), pp. 153-165; Michael B. Druxman, *Basil Rathbone: His Life and Films* (New York: A.S. Barnes, 1975), pp. 11-13; Miriam Cooper Walsh, *Letters & Writings: Drafts & Typescripts* folder, Miriam Cooper Walsh Papers, Manuscript Division, LC. Unfortunately, Reid used these narcotics too often and thereafter died of a heart attack related to drug use.
15. Fred Astaire, letter to Dolly, August 9, 1933, Mugar Library; Douglas Fairbanks, Jr., *The Salad Days* (New York: Doubleday, 1988), p. 105; Finch and Rosenkrantz, pp. 88-89, 224; Marlene Dietrich, pp. 100-103; Robert Benchley, letter of November 14, 1940, Box 11, Folder 7, Mugar Library. Durbin starred with Judy Garland in a musical short in 1936 and Universal signed her after MGM chose to keep Garland over Durbin. Her wholesome sweetness and bubbling personality as well as her excellent singing voice enabled her to be a top box-office attraction from the late 1930s through the early 1940s. Katz, p. 367; Anita Loos, Box 1, Folder 12, 22; Box 1, Folder 18, Anita Loos Collection, Mugar Library.
16. *Woman's Home Companion*, August, 1940, cited in Finch and Rosenkrantz, p. 91; *Los Angeles Times*, 28 July 1935, II, p. 1.
17. *Los Angeles Times*, 8 June 1941, IV, p. 7; 1 February 1931, p. 20; *Los Angeles Evening Herald*, 30 July 1918, sec. II, p. 3.
18. Henry Leon Wilson, *Merton of the Movies* (Garden City, NY: Doubleday, Page, 1922); *Los Angeles Times*, 24 January 1932, sec. III, p. 16; *Show People* (MGM, 1928).
19. *Modern Screen*, March 1931, cited in Finch and Rosenkrantz, p. 91.
20. Victor Fleming, *Bombshell* (MGM, 1933).
21. Mordaunt Hall, "The Screen," *New York Times*, October 21, 1933, p. 11; Mordaunt Hall, "Passing Broadway Pictures," October 29, 1933, sec. X, p. 3; Rush, "Bombshell," *Variety*, October 24, 1933, pp. 17, 31; October 31, 1933 through December 26, 1933, pp. 8-12.
22. Tully, pp. 195-196.
23. *American Film Institute Catalog of Motion Pictures produced in the United States, 1931-1940*, Patricia King Hanson, executive editor (Berkeley: University of California Press, 1993), p. 2905.
24. *Show Girl In Hollywood*. Dir. Mervyn LeRoy; Perf. Alice White, Jack Mulhall, Blanche Sweet; Warner Brothers, 1930. The director symbolized the homosexual male in two ways, by making enlarged eyes and touching his tie at the knot. This latter was a reference to the cultural stereotype of a homosexual male having an enlarged adam's apple.
25. Laud, "Show Girl in Hollywood," *Variety*, May 7, 1930, p. 8; May 14, 1930, p. 8; May 21, 1930, p. 8; May 28, 1930, p. 10; June 4, 1930, p. 8; June 11, 1930, pp. 10, 25.
26. Brooker-Bowers, p. 52; Haynes Loubou, (pseud.), *Reckless Hollywood* (New York: Amour Press, 1932), pp. 106-120; Jack Preston, *Screen Star* (Garden City, NY: Doubleday, Doran, 1932), pp. 8-12. The screenwriter/narrator's "a" to modify the boyfriend instead of a "the" or "his" suggested that Mr. Deveraux had more than one boyfriend.
27. Philip Schueler, *Los Angeles Times*, March, 24, 1935, II, p. 1; Lester V. Berrey and Melvin Van Den Bark, *American Thesaurus of Slang* (New York: Thomas Y. Cromwell, 1953), p. 360.
28. Ann Bell, *Lady's Lady* (New York: House of Field, 1940), p. 88.
29. Bobbi Owen, *Costume Design on Broadway: Designers & Their Credits, 1915-1985* (New York: Greenwood Press, 1987), pp. xiii-xv; *Stage Design Throughout the World Since 1935* (New York: The-

atre Arts Books, 1957), pp. 29–30; Louis B. Perry and Richard S. Perry, *A History of the Los Angeles Labor Movement, 1911–1941* (Berkeley: University of California Press, 1963), pp. 318–321, in the Hollywood Strikes Collection, Southern California Studies for Social Research; Sheldon Cheney, *The Theatre: Three Thousand Years of Drama, Actions & Stagecraft* (New York: Tudor Publishing, 1929), pp. 490–527.

30. Davis, p. 706; Hale, pp. 60–61.

31. Lionel Josaphare, "The Property Man," *Harper's Weekly*, September 12, 1912, p. 14; B. Matthews, "Evolution of scene-painting," *Scribner's Magazine*, July 1915, p. 82; "Groping toward a new scenic art in the American theater," *Current Opinion*, May 1919, pp. 301–302; C. Meltzer, "Stage decoration," *Arts and Decoration*, April 1920, pp. 408–409.

32. Davis, pp. 208–210; Mike Steen, *Hollywood Speaks! An Oral History* (New York: Putnam's, 1974), pp. 277–280; For one example of a make-up artist getting the better of an actor who questioned his work, see Mike Steen, pp. 269–271; Greer, pp. 147–218; Harmetz, pp. 236–238; Clarence Sinclair Bull, *The Faces of Hollywood* (South Brunswick, NJ: A. S. Barnes, 1968), pp. 70–80; Sennett, pp. 159–160.

33. *Los Angeles Times*, 27 August 1939, sec. III, p. 3; 1 October 1939, sec. III, p. 3.

34. Herman Politz, Director of Wardrobe at Warner Brothers, *Los Angeles Herald Examiner*, 21 May 1932, sec. A-6; *Los Angeles Times*, 20 August 1939, sec. III, p. 3; 3 September 1939, sec. III, p. 3.

35. Kevin Brownlow, *Hollywood: The Pioneers* (New York: Alfred A. Knopf, 1979), pp. 80–100; Aaron Betsky, *Queer Space: Architecture and Same-Sex Desire* (New York: William Morrow, 1997), p. 86; Testimony of Thomas A. Cracraft, *Jurisdictional Disputes in the Motion-Picture Industry*, Vol. 1., pp. 715–717; Kathy Peiss, *Hope in a Jar: The Making of America's Beauty Culture* (New York: Henry Holt, 1998), pp. 158–160.

36. *Going Hollywood*. Dir. Raoul Walsh; Perf. Marion Davies, Bing Crosby, and Fifi D'Orsay; MGM, 1933; *AFI Catalog*, p. 790; *Going Hollywood* script in MGM script Collection, USC. Morton Downey had a popular radio show in the early 1930s, broadcast from his supper club.

37. Press Book, *Going Hollywood*, (MGM, 1933), Press Book Collection, AMPAS.

38. *Going Hollywood* script of 22 August 1933, in MGM script Collection, USC; 29 September 1933.

39. *Variety*, 26 December 1933, p. 10; Jenkins.

40. Gerald Gardner, *The Censorship Papers: Movie Censorship Letters from the Hays Office, 1934 to 1968* (New York: Dodd, Mead, 1987), pp. 37–3, 137–138; *American Film Institute Catalog of Motion Pictures produced in the United States, 1931–1940*, p. 790. The picture earned strong box office returns in Oregon, Kansas City, St. Louis, New Orleans, Boston, Pittsburgh, Washington, D.C., and Chicago. *Variety*, 26 December 1933, p. 6 through 16 January 1934, p. 23. The scene resumed the movie's commentary on radio. Earlier in the movie Sylvia fell in love with Bill's voice on the radio. The power of her emotional bond and the revelation that the school where she taught banned radios because they supposedly promoted destructive values acknowledged the importance of radio as a cultural medium. The attitude of the school linked the radio and motion picture industries as Hollywood also faced arguments from cultural critics who claimed that its pictures corrupted the values of citizens. The Radio Rogues section allowed the motion picture to draw a distinction between these industries and put the Hollywood on top. As in the party at Schnarzan's scene from *Hollywood Party* discussed in Chapter III, the Radio Rogues show revealed the illusions and dissimilitude of radio. After all, the image showed that there was no boxing match and that a man imitated Kate Smith. At least with the movies the audience member could see these lies. The scene allowed Hollywood to compare favorably to the radio in a second way. The performance revealed that radio's behind the scenes was small, had few employees, and did not contain the number of spaces of glamour and fantasy that *Going Hollywood* revealed existed behind the scenes on a studio lot.

41. Loubou (pseud.), pp. 139–141.

42. Robert Langenfeld, "Beardsley in Time," and Brian Reade, "Beardsley Re-Mounted," in *Reconsidering Aubrey Beardsley* (Ann Arbor, MI: University Microfilm Press, 1989), pp. 5, 110; Linda Zatlin, "Felicien Rops and Aubrey Beardsley: The Naked and The Nude," in *Reconsidering Aubrey Beardsley*, pp. 184–187; *New York Times*, 1 January 1923, p. 18.

43. Keane McGrath, *Hollywood Siren* (New York: William Godwin, 1932), p. 82.

44. *Los Angeles Times*, 17 January 1937, sec. III, p. 4; Fred Astaire to Dolly, Monday, Adele Astaire Collection, Box 1, Fred Letters Folder, Mugar Library, BU; Fred E. Basten, *The Lost Artwork of Hollywood* (New York: Watson-Guptill Publications, 1996), pp. 46–47; May, pp. 97, 130–145; Allen Ellenzweig, *The Homoerotic Photograph: Male Images From Durieu/Delacroix to Mapplethorpe* (New York: Columbia University Press, 1992), p. 92.

45. Loy, p. 118; *Los Angeles Times*, 2 July 1939, sec. III; 16 December 1945, sec. III, p. 1.

46. *American Film Institute Catalog of Motion Pictures produced in the United States, 1931–1940*, Patricia King Hanson, executive editor (Berkeley: University of California Press, 1993), pp. 1994–1995. The studio, Grand National, was attempting to become an important producer of films. They signed Warner Brothers' star Jimmy Cagney to a multi-picture deal and brought in well-established songwriter and director Victor Schertzinger to direct this musical. The studio spent the equivalent of a major studio's budget for a respectable feature motion picture, approximately $750,000. *Variety's* reviewer considered it a first-class comedy and good entertainment. Gregory William Mank,

James T. Coughlin, and Dwight D. Frye, Jr., *Dwight Frye's Last Laugh* (Midnight Marquee Press, 1997). Dwight Frye came from the Broadway stage to Hollywood and established himself as a top character actor in the early 1930s in horror films. He played in a wide variety of adventure, horror, and mystery motion pictures until the late 1930s. Biographer Gregory Mank notes that a refreshing change of pace was the role of a gay hairdresser in *Something to Sing About*.

47. *Something to Sing About*. Dir. Victor Schertzinger; Perf. James Cagney, Evelyn Daw, and William Frawley; Grand National, 1937, reel 1.

48. Ibid., reel 2; Vincent Sherman, interviewed by author by telephone, 26 January 1998. Sherman came to Hollywood in the early 1930s as an actor, but turned to screenwriting later in the decade. He began directing in 1939 and spent most of the rest of his three decade career with Warner Brothers. The testimony of many people alleged that the make-up artists had the reputation of being a highly temperamental group. Davis, pp. 226–227.

49. *Hollywood and History: Costume Design in Film*, ed. Edward Maeder (Los Angeles: Thames & Hudson, 1987), pp. 49–52; *New York Times*, 7 July 1940, sec. VII, p. 6; *New York Times*, 16 February 1941, sec. VII, p. 10; Jack Babuscio, "Camp and the Gay Sensibility," in ed. David Bergman, *Camp Grounds: Style and Homosexuality* (Amherst: University of Massachusetts Press, 1993), pp. 21–25; Sarah Elizabeth Berry, "Screen Style: Consumer Fashion and Femininity in 1930s Hollywood," (Ph.D. diss. New York University, 1997), pp. 11–14; Charles Affron and Mirella Jona Affron, *Sets in Motion: Art Direction and Film Narrative* (New Brunswick, NJ: Rutgers University Press, 1995), pp. 36–37. The Affrons argued that designers influenced motion pictures in three ways. These ways included denotative, helping to define a character's status, punctuation, making a statement about the character, and embellishment, adding a cinematic element. *Variety*, 1 September 1937, p. 22; *New York Times*, 21 September 1937, p. 29.

50. *Something to Sing About*, reel 3.

51. Breen to Warner letters. These begin in June 29, 1937 and end in November 20, 1937. Production Code Administration Files, *Hollywood Hotel*, AMPAS; *Hollywood Hotel* (Warner Brothers, 1937), Warner Brothers Script Collection, Cinema and Television Library, University of Southern California.

52. *Hollywood Hotel*. Dir. Busby Berkeley; Perf. Dick Powell, Rosemary Lane, and Lola Lane; Warner Brothers, 1937; *Hollywood Hotel* script.

53. Greer, pp. 147–156.

54. *Film Daily*, 27 December 1937, p. 8; *Variety*, 22 December 1937, p. 16; *New York Times*, 13 January 1938, p. 17. Curt Bois started on the stage in his native Germany as a young child. He matured into a cabaret star, but with the rise of National Socialism in 1933, he emigrated. After a brief stop on Broadway, he joined many compatriots in Hollywood. He established a reputation as a fine character actor. Katz, p. 136.

55. Slide, p. 22; *Saturday Review of Literature*, 14 May 1938, p. 6; *New York Times*, 22 May 1938, sec. VI, p. 7.

56. Jane Allen (pseud.), *I Lost My Girlish Laughter* (New York: Random House, 1938), pp. 98–101.

57. Joel Greenberg, "Kelly, Orry George (1897 – 1964)," *Australian Dictionary of Biography*, Volume 14, (Melbourne, Australia: Melbourne University Press, 1996), pp. 614–615; Garry Maddox and Alexa Moses, "Australian Oscar Champ You've Never Heard of," *Sydney Morning Herald*, 23 March 2002 at http://www.smh.com.au/articles/2002/03/22/entlexoscar23.htm; Mann, p. 230.

58. W. Robert La Vine, *In a Glamorous Fashion: The Fabulous Years of Hollywood Costume Design* (New York: Scribner's, 1980), pp. 219–221; Vincent Sherman, *Studio Affairs: My Life as a Film Director* (Louisville: University of Kentucky Press, 1996), p. 76. Kelly took on the name Orry-Kelly and formed one of the notable actress-designer combinations with Bette Davis. Each acted as a catalyst upon the other. He enjoyed combustible relations with actresses throughout his years and used his temperament to win battles over budgets with studio executives. His wit and good humor made him a regular at parties. Warner Brothers director Vincent Sherman developed a friendship with Kelly and listened to his many stories. La Vine, p. 221; Winters, pp. 128, 221–227; *Los Angeles Times*, 8 December 1935, sec. III, 11; p. 8, June 1941, sec. IV, p. 7; *New York American*, 2 August 1936 in Cinema: Hollywood Entertaining folder at NYPL.

59. *New York Sun*, 4 January 1938, Orry Kelly Clippings folder, NYPL; Orry-Kelly, "Star dressing," *New York Journal American*, 8 December 1945, Orry Kelly Clippings folder; Winters, pp. 221–227; Laura Benham, "A Scout on the Fashion Trail," undated clipping, Orry Kelly Clippings folder; "Gowns by Orry Kelly," undated clipping, Orry Kelly Clippings folder, NYPL.

60. *New York Journal American*, 8 December 1945, Orry Kelly Clippings folder, NYPL.

61. *New York Sun*, 10 April 1935, Orry Kelly Clipping folder; *New York Journal American*, 8 December 1945.

62. "Gowns by Orry Kelly," Orry Kelly Clippings folder, NYPL.

63. Winters, pp. 127–131.

64. Eliot; Higham and Moseley; Mann, *Behind the Screen*.

65. Testimony of Herbert Sorrell, *Jurisdictional Disputes in the Motion-Picture Industry*, Vol. 1., pp. 2121–2123.

66. Testimony of Thomas A. Cracraft, *Jurisdictional Disputes in the Motion-Picture Industry*, Vol. 1., pp. 715–717. As to the artistic skill of scenic artists, Cracraft stated during his testimony that "[the scenic artist] is truly an artist. I wouldn't want him to paint my house."

Conclusion

1. Lary May, *Screening Out the Past: The Birth of Mass Culture and the Motion Picture Industry* (Chicago: University of Chicago Press, 1980).

2. Springer; Gregory Poe, "Disinfecting Hollywood: 'Dirt' and the Cultural Logics of American Film Censorship, 1900–1935," (Ph.D. diss., University of Kansas, 1995); Francis Walsh, *Sin and Censorship: The Catholic Church and the Motion Picture Industry* (New Haven: Yale, 1996); Gregory Black, *Hollywood Censored: Morality Codes, Catholics and the Movies* (Cambridge, Eng.: Cambridge University, 1994).

3. As noted in the introduction there are many books that discuss images in every form of mass media.

Bibliography

Books and Articles

Allen, Frederick Lewis. *Only Yesterday: An Informal Account of the Nineteen-twenties*. New York: Harper & Row, 1931.

Allen, Jane. [Silvia Schulman and Jane Shore]. *I Lost My Girlish Laughter*. New York: Random House, 1938.

Altman, Diana. *Hollywood East: Louis B. Mayer and the Origins of the Studio System*. New York: Birch Lane Press, 1992.

Alwood, Edward. *Straight News: Gays, Lesbians and the News Media*. New York: Columbia University Press, 1996.

American Film Institute Catalog of Motion Pictures produced in the United States, 1931–1940. Patricia King Hanson, exec. ed. Berkeley: University of California Press, 1993.

Ames, Christopher. *Movies About the Movies: Hollywood Reflected*. Lexington: University of Kentucky Press, 1997.

Amory, Cleveland. *Who Killed Society?* New York: Harper & Brothers Publishers, 1960.

Anderson, Christopher. *Hollywood TV: The Studio System in the Fifties*. Austin: University of Texas Press, 1994.

Anger, Kenneth. *Hollywood Babylon*. San Francisco: Straight Arrow Books, 1975.

———. *Hollywood Babylon II*. San Francisco: Straight Arrow Books, 1975.

Ankerich, Michael G. *Broken Silence: Conversations with 23 Silent Film Stars*. Jefferson, NC: McFarland & Co., Inc., Publishers, 1993.

Austen, Roger. *Playing the Game: The Homosexual Novel in America*. Indianapolis: Bobbs-Merrill Company, Inc., 1977.

Bacall, Lauren. *By Myself*. New York: Alfred A. Knopf, 1979.

Bach, Steven. *Marlene Dietrich: Life and Legend*. New York: William Morrow & Co., Inc., 1992.

Bailey, Beth L. *From Front Porch to Back Seat: Courtship in Twentieth-Century America*. Baltimore, MD: Johns Hopkins University Press, 1988.

Bailey, Paul. *Song Everlasting*. Los Angeles: Westernlore Press, 1946.

Balio, Tino, ed. *The American Film Industry*. (Revised Edition). Madison: University of Wisconsin Press, 1985.

———. *The Grand Design: Hollywood as a Modern Business Enterprise, 1930–1939* Vol. 5, History of the American Cinema, Charles Harpole, ed. New York: Charles Scribner's Sons, 1993.

———. *United Artists: The Company Built by the Stars*. Madison: University of Wisconsin Press, 1976.

Bankhead, Tallulah. *Tallulah: My Biography*. New York: Harper & Brothers, Publishers, 1952.

Barrios, Richard. *Screened Out: Playing Gay in Hollywood from Edison to Stonewall*. New York: Routledge, 2003.

Basten, Fred E. with Robert Salvatore, and Paul A. Kaufman, *Max Factor's Hollywood: Glamour, Movies, and Makeup*. Los Angeles: General Publishing Group, 1995.

Baum, Vicki. *Falling Star*. New York: Doubleday, 1934.

Baxter, John. *Hollywood in the Thirties*. London: A. Zwemmer Ltd., 1968.
Beaty, Frederick L. *Ironic World of Evelyn Waugh: A Study of Eight Novels*. Northern Illinois University Press, 1992.
Behlmer, Rudy, ed. *Memo From: David O. Selznick*. New York: Avon Books, 1972.
Behlmer, Rudy, and Tony Thomas. *Hollywood's Hollywood*. Secaucus, NJ: The Citadel Press, Inc., 1978.
Belfridge, Cedric. *Promised Land: Notes for a History*. London: Gollancz, 1938.
Bell, Ann. *Lady's Lady*. New York: House of Field, Inc., 1940.
Bellamy, Ralph. *When the Smoke Hit the Fan*. Garden City, NY: Doubleday & Co., Inc., 1979.
Bell-Metereau, Rebecca. *Hollywood Androgyny*. New York: Columbia University Press, 1985.
Benson, Susan Porter. *Counter Cultures: Saleswomen, Managers and Customers in American Department Stores, 1890–1940*. Urbana: University of Illinois Press, 1986.
Berger, Maurice, Brian Wallis, and Simon Watson, eds. *Constructing Masculinity*. New York: Routledge, 1995.
Bergman, David, ed. *Camp Grounds: Style and Homosexuality*. Amherst: University of Massachusetts Press, 1993.
Bernstein, Matthew. *Walter Wanger, Hollywood Independent*. Berkeley: University of California Press, 1994.
Berry, Sarah Elizabeth. "Screen Style: Consumer Fashion and Femininity in 1930s Hollywood." Ph.D. diss., New York University, 1997.
Berube, Allan. *Coming Out Under Fire: The History of Gay Men and Women in World War II*. New York: Plume, 1990.
Bessie, Simon Michael. *Jazz Journalism: The Story of the Tabloid Newspaper*. New York: E. P. Dutton & Co., Inc., 1938.
Betsky, Aaron. *Queer Space: Architecture and Same-Sex Desire*. New York: William Morrow & Co., Inc., 1997.
Bingham, Dennis. *Acting Male: MasculinitiesIn the Films of James Stewart, Jack Nicholson, and Clint Eastwood*. New Brunswick, NJ: Rutgers University Press, 1994.
Black, Gregory. *Hollywood Censored: Morality Codes, Catholics and the Movies*. Cambridge, U.K.: Cambridge University, 1994.
Bonora, Diane C. "The Hollywood Novel of the 1930's and 1940's." Ph.D. diss., State University of New York at Buffalo, 1983.
Borton, Elizabeth. *Pollyanna in Hollywood*. Boston: L. C. Page, 1931.
Bogle, Donald. *Dorothy Dandridge: A Biography*. New York: Armistad Press, 1997.
Bolze, Thomas A. "Female Impersonation in the United States, 1900–1970." Ph.D. diss., State University of New York at Buffalo, 1994.
Bordwell, David, Janet Staiger, and Kristin Thompson, *The Classical Hollywood Cinema: Film Style and Mode of Production, 1917–1960*. New York: Columbia University Press, 1985.
Bowlby, Rachel. *Just Looking: Consumer Culture in Dreiser, Gissing and Zola*. New York: Methuen, 1985.
Bradley, Edwin M. *The First Hollywood Musicals: A Critical Filmography of 171 Features, 1927 Through 1932*. Jefferson, NC: McFarland & Co., Inc., Publishers, 1996.
Brandeis, Madeline. *Adventure in Hollywood: A Story of the Movies for Girls*. Coward-McCann, 1937.
Brandt, Allan M. *No Magic Bullet: A Social History of Venereal Disease in the United States Since 1880*. New York: Oxford University Press, 1985.
Braudy, Leo. *The Frenzy of Renown: Fame and Its History*. New York: Vintage Books, 1986.
Bret, David. *Joan Crawford: Hollywood Martyr*. New York: Carroll & Graf, Publishers, 2006.
_____. *Valentino: A Dream of Desire*. New York: Carroll & Graf Publishers, 1998.
Brett, Philip, and Elizabeth Wood and Gary C. Thomas, eds. *Queering the Pitch: The New Gay & Lesbian Musicology*. New York: Routledge, 1994.
Breward, Christopher. *The Culture of*

Fashion: A New History of Fashionable Dress. Manchester: Manchester University Press, 1995.

Brian, Denis. *Tallulah, Darling: A Biography of Tallulah Bankhead*. New York: Macmillan Publishing Co., Inc., 1972.

Bronski, Michael. *Culture Clash: The Making of Gay Sensibility*. Boston: South End Press, 1984.

Brooker-Bowars, Nancy. "The Hollywood Novel: An American Literary Genre." Ph.D. diss., Drake University, 1983.

Brownlow, Kevin. *Hollywood: The Pioneers*. New York: Alfred A. Knopf, 1979.

———. *The Parade's Gone By*. New York: Alfred A. Knopf, 1969.

Bull, Clarence Sinclair. *The Faces of Hollywood*. South Brunswick, NJ: A.S. Barnes & Co., 1968.

Bullough, Vern L. *Science in the Bedroom: A History of Sex Research*. New York: Basic Books, 1994.

Buehrer, Beverly Bare. *Cary Grant: A Bio-Bibliography*. New York; Greenwood Press, 1990.

Burk, Margaret Tante. *Are the Stars Out Tonight: The Story of the Famous Ambassador and Cocoanut Grove*. Los Angeles: Round Table West, 1980.

Burroughs, Edgar Rice. *The Girl from Hollywood*. New York: The Macaulay Co., 1923.

Burton, Humphrey. *Leonard Bernstein*. New York: Anchor Books, Doubleday, 1994.

Cable, Mary. *Top Drawer: American High Society from the Gilded Age to the Roaring Twenties*. New York: Atheneum, 1984.

Cain, James M. *Serenade*. New York: Vintage Books, 1937.

Carey, Gary. *All the Stars in Heaven: L. B. Mayer's MGM*. New York: E. P. Dutton, 1981.

Carnes, Marc C., and Clyde Griffen, eds. *Meanings for Manhood: The Construction of Masculinity in Victorian America*. Chicago: University of Chicago Press, 1990.

Cassini, Oleg. *In My Own Fashion: An Autobiography*. New York: Simon & Schuster, 1987.

Castle, Terry. *The Apparational Lesbian: Female Homosexuality and Modern Culture*. New York: Columbia University Press, 1993.

Cavin, Susan. *Lesbian Origins*. San Francisco: Ism Press, 1985.

Ceplair, Larry, and Steven Englund. *The Inquisition in Hollywood: Politics in the Film Community, 1930–1960*. Berkeley: University of California Press, 1979.

Charney, Leo, and Vanessa Schwartz, *Cinema and the Invention of Modern Life*. Berkeley: University of California Press, 1995.

Chauncey, George. *Gay New York: Gender, Urban Culture and the Making of the Gay Male World, 1890–1940*. New York: Basic Books, 1994.

Chester, George, and Lilian Chester. *On the Lot and Off*. New York: Harper & Brothers Publishers, 1924.

Chierichetti, David. *Hollywood Costume Design*. New York: Harmony Books, 1976.

———. *Mitchell Leisen: Hollywood Director*. 1973; reprint, Los Angeles: Photoventures Press, 1995.

Clarke, Donald Henderson. *Alabam'*. New York: Vanguard, 1934.

Clarke, Graham, ed. *The Portrait in Photography*. London: Reaktion Books, Ltd., 1992.

Coben, Stanley. *Rebellion Against Victorianism: The Impetus for Cultural Change in 1920s America*. New York: Oxford University Press, 1991.

Cohan, Steven, and Ina Rae Hark, eds. *Screening the Male: Exploring Masculinities in Hollywood Cinema*. New York: Routledge Press, 1993.

Cole, Lester. *Hollywood Red: The Autobiography of Lester Cole*. Palo Alto, CA: Ramparts Press, 1981.

Cook, Bruce. *Dalton Trumbo*. New York: Charles Scribner's Sons, 1977.

Cott, Nancy. *The Grounding of Modern Feminism*. New Haven: Yale University Press, 1987.

Couvares, Francis. "Introduction: Hollywood, Censorship and American Culture." *American Quarterly* 44 (December 1992): 509–524.

———. "Hollywood, Main Street and the

Church: Trying to Censor the Movies Before the Production Code." *American Quarterly,* 44 (December 1992), pp. 584–616.

Cowan, Tom. *Gay Men and Women Who Enriched the World.* Los Angeles: Alyson Publications, 1986.

Crawford, Patricia, and Sara Mendelson. "Sexual Identitites in Early Modern England: The Marriage of Two Women in 1680," *Gender & History,* 7 (1995), pp. 362–377.

Cressey, Paul G. *The Taxi-Dance Hall: A Sociological Study in Commercialized Recreation and City Life.* Chicago: University of Chicago Press, 1932.

Cripps, Thomas. *Hollywood's High Noon: Moviemaking and Society Before Television.* Baltimore: The Johns Hopkins University Press, 1997.

Crowther, Bosley. *The Lion's Share: The Story of an Entertainment Empire.* New York: E. P. Dutton, 1957.

Curtin, Kaier. *We Can Always Call Them Bulgarians: The Emergence of Gays and Lesbian on the American Stage.* Boston: Alyson Press, 1987.

Curtis, James. *James Whale.* Metuchen, NJ: The Scarecrow Press, Inc., 1982.

Czitrom, Daniel J. *Media and the American Mind: From Morse to McLuhan.* Chapel Hill: University of North Carolina Press, 1982.

_____. "The Politics of Performance: From Theater Licensing to Movie Censorship in Turn-of-the-Century New York," *American Quarterly,* 44 (December 1992).

Daily, Jay E. *The Anatomy of Censorship.* New York: Marcel Dekker, Inc., 1973.

Dardis, Tom. *The Man Who Wouldn't Lie Down.* New York: Charles Scribner's Sons, 1979.

Davidson, William. *Spencer Tracy: Tragic Idol.* New York: E. P. Dutton, 1987.

Davis, Bette with Michael Herskowitz. *This 'n That.* New York: G. P. Putnam's Sons, 1987.

Davis, Fred. *Fashion, Culture, and Identity.* Chicago: University of Chicago Press, 1992.

Davis, Roland L. *The Glamour Factory: Inside Hollywood's Big Studio System.* Dallas: Southern Methodist University Press, 1993.

Davis, Tracy C. *Actresses as Working Women: Their Social Identity in Victorian Culture.* London: Routledge, 1991.

Dawidziak, Mark, and Paul Bauer. *Jim Tully, Writer: Drifters, Grifters, Bruisers, and Stars.* Tucson, AZ: Dennis McMillan Publishing, 2004.

de Acosta, Mercedes. *Here Lies the Heart.* New York: Reynal & Co., 1960.

De Cecco, John P., and Michael J. Shively. "From Sexual Identity to Sexual Relationships: A Contextual Shift," *Journal of Homosexuality,* 9 (1984), pp. 1–25.

de Cordova, Richard. *Picture Personalities: The Emergence of the Star System in America.* Urbana: University of Illinois Press, 1990.

de Jongh, Nicholas. *Not in Front of the Audience: Homosexuality on Stage.* London: Routledge, 1992.

D'Emilio, John. *Sexual Politics, Sexual Communities: The Making of the Homosexual Minority in the United States, 1940–1970.* Chicago: University of Chicago Press, 1983.

_____, and Estelle Friedman. *Intimate Matters: A History of Sexuality in America.* New York: Harper & Row, Publishers, 1988.

de Grazia, Edward. *Girls Lean Back Everywhere: The Law of Obscenity and the Assault on Genius.* New York: Randon House, 1992.

_____, and Roger K. Newman. *Banned Films: Movies, Censors and the First Amendment.* New York: R R Bowker Co., 1982.

DelGaudio, Sybil. *Dressing the Part: Sternberg, Dietrich, and Costume.* Rutherford, N.J.: Fairleigh Dickinson University Press, 1993.

De River, Joseph Paul. *The Sexual Criminal — A Psychoanalytical Study.* Oxford, Eng: Blackwell Scientific Publications, 1949.

Dewey, Donald. *James Stewart: A Biography.* Atlanta: Turner Publishing Inc., 1996.

Dietrich, Marlene. *Marlene.* Trans. Salvator Attanasio. New York: Grove Press, 1987.
Donaldson, Frances. *P. G. Wodehouse: A Biography.* New York: Knopf, 1982.
Donati, William. *Ida Lupino: A Biography.* Lexington: The University Press of Kentucky, 1996.
Dos Passos, John. *The Big Money.* New York: Harcourt Brace, 1936.
Dowd, Douglas E. *Thorstein Veblen.* New York: Washington Square Press, Inc., 1966.
Druxman, Michael B. *Basil Rathbone: His Life and Films.* New York: A.S. Barnes & Co., 1975.
Dubbert, Joe. *A Man's Place: Masculinity in Transition.* Englewood Cliffs, NJ: Prentice-Hall, Inc., 1979.
Duggan, Lisa. "From Instincts to Politics: Writing the History of Sexuality in the U.S." *The Journal of Sex Research,* 27 (February 1990), pp. 95–109.
_____. "Making It Perfectly Queer." *Socialist Review* (January 1992), pp. 11–31.
_____. "The Trials of Alice Mitchell: Sensationalism, Sexology, and the Lesbian Subject in Turn-of-the-Century America." *Signs* (Summer 1993), pp. 791–814
Dulles, Foster Rhea. *A History of Recreation: America Learns to Play.* New York: Appleton-Century-Crofts, 1965.
Dumenil, Lynn. *The Modern Temper: American Culture and Society in the 1920s.* New York: Farrar, Straus & Giroux, 1995.
Dunaway, David King. *Huxley In Hollywood.* New York: Harper & Row Publishers, 1989.
Dyer, Richard. *The Matter of Images: Essays on Representations.* London: Routledge, 1993.
Edelman, Robert, and Audrey E. Kupferberg. *Angela Lansbury: A Life On Stage & Screen.* New York: Birch Lane Press, 1996.
Edmonds, Andy. *Hot Toddy: The True Story of Hollywood's Most Sensational Murder.* New York: William Morrow & Co., 1989.
Eels, George. *Hedda and Louella.* New York: G. P. Putnam's Sons, 1972.

Ehrenstein, David. *Open Secret: Homosexuality in Hollywood, 1928–1998.* New York: William Morrow & Co., Inc, 1998.
Eisner, Lotte H. *Murnau.* Berkeley: University of California Press, 1973.
Ellenberger, Alan R. *Ramon Novarro: A Biography of the Silent Film Star, 1899–1968.* Jefferson, N.C.: McFarland & Co., Inc., 1999.
Ellenzweig, Allen. *The Homoerotic Photograph: Male Images From Durieu/Delacroix to Mapplethorpe.* New York: Columbia University Press, 1992.
Ellis, Havelock. *Sexual Inversion.* London: Macmillan, 1897.
Ellis, Leonard Harry. "Men Among Men: An Exploration of All-Male Relationships in Victorian America." Ph.D. diss., Columbia University, 1982.
Erenberg, Lewis. *Steppin' Out: New York Nightlife and the Transformation of American Culture, 1890–1930.* Westport, CT: Greenwood Press, 1981.
Ernst, Morris, and Pare Lornetz. *Censored: The Private Life of the Movie.* New York: Cape and Smith, 1930.
Ewing, Elizabeth. *History of Twentieth Century Fashion.* London: B.T. Batsford Ltd, 1974.
Eyman, Scott. *Mary Pickford: American's Sweetheart.* New York: Donald I. Fine, Inc., 1991.
Faderman, Lillian. *Chloe Plus Olivia: An Anthology of Lesbian Literature from the Seventeenth Century to the Present.* New York: Viking, 1994.
_____. *Odd Girls and Twilight Lovers: A History of Lesbian Life in Twentieth-Century America.* New York: Columbia University Press, 1991.
Fairbanks, Douglas, Jr. *The Salad Days.* New York: Doubleday, 1988.
Famous American Homes. New York: The Home Insurance Co., 1939.
Fass, Paula S. *The Beautiful and the Damned: American Youth in the 1920s.* New York: Oxford University Press, 1979.
Ferguson, Ann. "Is There a Lesbian Culture." In *Lesbian Philosophies and Culture,* ed. Jeffner Allen. Albany, NY: State University of New York, 1990.

Ferris, Lesley., ed. *Crossing the Stage: Controversies on Cross Dressing.* London: Routledge, 1993.

The Film Daily Year Book of Motion Pictures, 1930–1949. New York: Film Daily, Annual.

Finch, Christopher, and Linda Rosenkrantz. *Gone Hollywood.* Garden City, NY: Doubleday and Co., 1979.

Fine, Gary Alan, and Sherryl Kleinman. "Rethinking Subculture: An Interactionist Analysis." *American Journal of Sociology,* 85 (1979), pp. 1–21.

Finler, Joel W. *The Hollywood Story.* New York: Crown Publishers, Inc., 1988.

Fitzgerald, F. Scott. *The Last Tycoon.* New York: Charles Scribner's Sons, 1941.

Fontaine, Joan. *No Bed of Roses.* New York: William Morrow & Co., Inc., 1978.

Fordin, Hugh. *The World of Entertainment: Hollywood's Greatest Musicals.* New York: Doubleday & Co., Inc. 1975.

Fox, Patty. *Star Style: Hollywood Legends as Fashion Icons.* Los Angeles: Angel City Press, 1995.

Franzen, Patricia. "Spinsters and Lesbians: Autonomous Women and the Institution of Heterosexuality, 1890–1920 & 1940–1980." Ph.D. diss., University of New Mexico, 1990.

French, Philip. *The Movie Moguls: An Informal History of the Hollywood Tycoons.* Chicago: Henry Regnery Co., 1969.

Friedman, Andrea. "Prurient interests: Anti-obscenity campaigns in NYC, 1904–1945." Ph.D. diss., University of Wisconsin at Madison, 1995.

Friedrich, Otto. *City of Nets: A Portrait of Hollywood in the 1940s.* New York: Harper & Row Publishers, 1986.

Friskopp, Annette, and Sharon Silverstein. *Straight Jobs, Gay Lives: Gay and Lesbian Professionals, The Harvard Business School and the American Workplace.* New York: Simon & Schuster, 1995.

Gabler, Neal. *An Empire of Their Own: How the Jews Invented Hollywood.* New York: Crown Books, 1988.

Gale Research Company. *Dictionary of Literary Biography,* Volume 9, Part II. Detroit: Gale Research Company, irregular.

Gamber, Wendy. *The Female Economy: The Millinery and Dressmaking Trades, 1860–1930.* Urbana: University of Illinois Press, 1997.

Gamson, Joshua. *Claims to Fame: Celebrity in Contemporary America.* Berkeley: University of California Press, 1994.

Garber, Marjorie, *Vested Interests: Cross-Dressing and Cultural Anxiety.* New York: Routledge, 1992.

Gardner, Gerald. *The Censorship Papers: Movie Censorship Letters from the Hays Office, 1934–1968.* New York: Dodd, Mead and Co., 1987.

Garnett, Tay, with Fredda Dudley Balling. *Light Your Torches and Pull Up Your Tights.* New Rochelle, NY: Arlington House, 1973.

Gatiss, Mark. *James Whale: A Biography or the Would-be Gentleman.* London: Cassell, 1995.

Gifford, James. *Dayneford's Library: American Homosexual Writing, 1900–1913.* Amherst: University of Massachusetts Press, 1995.

Gilman, Sander L. *Difference and Pathology: Stereotypes of Sexuality, Race, and Madness.* Ithaca, NY: Cornell University Press, 1985.

Gomery, Douglas. *Shared Pleasures: A History of Movie Presentations in the United States.* Madison: University of Wisconsin Press, 1992.

_____. *The Hollywood Studio System.* London: Macmillan, 1986.

Gordon, Rose, and Ione Reed. *Stunt Girl.* Hollywood, CA: George Palmer Putnam, 1940.

Gorman, John. *Hollywood's Bad Boy.* Hollywood, CA: Eugene V. Brewster Co., 1932.

Gorman, Paul R. *Left Intellectuals and Popular Culture in Twentieth-Century America.* University of North Carolina Press, 1996.

Graham, Carroll, and Garrett Graham. *Queer People.* 1930; reprint: Carbondale: Southern Illinois University, 1976.

Grant, Barry Keith, ed. *Film Genre Reader.* Austin: University of Texas Press, 1986.

Green, Benny. *P.G. Wodehouse: A Literary*

Biography. New York: Rutledge Press, 1981.

Greenberg, David F. *The Construction of Homosexuality*. Chicago: University of Chicago Press, 1988.

Greer, Howard. *Designing Male*. London: Robert Hale Ltd., 1952.

Griffith, Richard. *The Talkies: Articles and Illustrations from a Great Fan Magazine, 1928–1940*. New York: Dover Publishing Inc., 1971.

Groth, Paul. *Living Downtown: The History of Residential Hotels in the United States*. Berkeley: University of California Press, 1994.

Guilaroff, Sydney. *Crowning Glory: Reflections of Hollywood's Favorite Confidant*. Santa Monica, CA: General Publishing Group, 1996.

Guiles, Fred Laurence. *Marion Davies*. New York: McGraw-Hill Book Company, 1972.

Gunn, Fenja. *The Artifical Face: A History of Cosmetics*. New York: Hippocrene Books, Inc., 1973.

Hadleigh, Boze. *Bette Davis Speaks*. New York: Barricade Books, 1996.

_____. *Hollywood Gays*. New York: Barricade Books, 1996.

_____. *Hollywood Lesbians*. New York: Barricade Books, 1996.

_____. *The Vinyl Closet: Gays in the Music Industry*. San Diego, CA: Los Hombres Press, 1991.

Hall-Duncan, Nancy. *The History of Fashion Photography*. New York: Alpine Book Co., 1974.

Hamilton, Marybeth. *"When I'm Bad, I'm Better," Mae West, Sex, and American Entertainment*. New York: Harper Collins, 1995.

Handel, Leo A. *Hollywood looks at its audience: a Report of film audience research*. Urbana: University of Illinois, 1950.

Handlin, David P. *The American Home: Architecture and Society, 1815–1915*. Boston: Little, Brown, and Co., 1979.

Haney, Robert, W. *Comstockery in America: Patterns of Censorship and Control*. New York: Da Capo Press, 1974.

Haralovich, Mary Beth. "Motion Picture Advertising: Industrial and Social Forces and Effects." Ph.D. diss. University of Wisconsin, 1984.

Harmetz, Aljean. *The Making of The Wizard of Oz*. New York: Delta, 1977.

Harris, Warren G. *Cary Grant: A Touch of Elegance*. New York: Doubleday, 1987.

Harwood, Gean. *The Oldest Gay Couple in America: A Seventy Year Journey through Same-Sex America*. New York: Carol Publishing Group, 1997.

Hastings, Selina. *Evelyn Waugh: A Biography*. Boston: Houghton Mifflin Co., 1994.

Hay, Peter. *MGM — When the Lion Roars*. Atlanta: Turner Publishing Inc., 1991.

Hayes, Michael Thurgood. *Dressing Up Debutantes: Pageantry and Glitz in Texas*. New York: Berg, 1998.

Hayne, Donald, ed. *The Autobiography of Cecil B. De Mille*. Englewood Cliffs, N.J.: Prentice-Hall, Inc., 1959.

Hecht, Ben. *A Child of the Century*. New York: Simon & Schuster, 1954.

Heimann, Jim. *Out with the Stars: Hollywood Nightlife in the Golden Era*. New York: Abbeville Press, 1985.

Heins, Marjorie. *Sex, Sin and Blasphemy*. New York: The New Press, 1993.

Heisner, Beverly. *Hollywood Art: Art Direction in the Days of the Great Studios*. Jefferson, N.C.: McFarland & Co., Inc., 1991.

Henry, George W. *Sex Variants: A Study of Homosexual Patterns*. New York: Paul B. Hoeber, Inc., 1948.

Henstell, Bruce. *Sunshine & Wealth: Los Angeles in the Twenties and Thirties*. San Francisco: Chronicle Books, 1984.

Hepburn, Katharine. *Me: Stories of My Life*. New York: Alfred A. Knopf, 1991.

Higgenbotham, Evelyn B. *Righteous Discontent: The Women's Movement in the Black Baptist Church, 1880–1920*. Cambridge, Havard University Press, 1993.

Higham, Charles. *Sisters: The Story of Olivia de Havilland and Joan Fontaine*. New York: Coward-McCann, Inc., 1984.

_____, and Roy Moseley. *Cary Grant: The Lonely Heart*. New York: Harcourt Brace Jovanovich, 1989.

Hoffman, Judy. "The Discourse of 'Special Effects' Cinematography in the Silent American Cinema," *Post Script* Vol. 10, No. 1.

Hoffman, Richard J. "Clio, Fallacies and Homosexuality." *Journal of Homosexuality*, 10 (1984), pp. 45–53.

Holden, Anthony. *Behind the Oscar: The Secret History of the Academy Awards.* New York: Plume Books, 1994.

Hopper, Hedda, and James Brough. *The Whole Truth and Nothing But.* Garden City, N.Y.: Doubleday & Co., Inc. 1962.

Horrocks, Roger. *Male Myths & Icons: Masculinity in Popular Culture.* New York: St. Martin's Press, 1995.

Hubbard, Elbert. *Little Journeys to the Homes of the Great: Famous Women.* New York: World Publishing Co., 1928.

Hughes, Helen MacGill. *News and the Human Interest Story.* Chicago: University of Chicago, 1940.

Hughes, Rupert. *Souls for Sale.* 1922; reprint: New York: Garland Publishing Inc., 1978.

Hyde, H. Montgomery. *The Trials of Oscar Wilde.* New York: Dover Publishers, Inc., 1962.

Isherwood, Christopher. *Prater Violet.* New York: Random House, 1945.

Jablonski, Edward. *Harold Arlen: Happy with the Blues.* Garden City, N.Y.: Doubleday & Co., 1961.

Jacobs, Lea. *The Wages of Sin: Censorship and the Fallen Woman Film, 1928–1942.* Madison: University of Wisconsin Press, 1991.

Jansen, David A. *P. G. Wodehouse: A Portrait of a Master.* New York: Continuum, 1981.

Jauss, Hans Robert. *Aesthethic Experience and Literary Hermeneutics.* Translated by Michael Shaw. Minneapolis: University of Minnesota Press, 1982.

Jenkins, Henry. *What Made Pistachio Nuts: Early Sound Comedy and the Vaudeville Aesthetic.* New York: Columbia University Press, 1992.

Jowett, Garth. *Film: The Democratic Art.* Boston: Little, Brown & Co., 1976.

Kaiser, Charles. *The Gay Metropolis, 1940–1996.* Boston: Houghton Mifflin, 1997.

Katz, Ephraim. *The Film Encyclopedia.* New York: G.P. Putnam's Sons, 1979.

Kelly, A. A. *Liam O'Flaherty: The Storyteller.* London: The Macmillan Press, Ltd., 1976.

Kennedy, Elisabeth Lapovsky, and Madeline D. Davis. *Boots of Leather, Slippers of Gold: The History of a Lesbian Community.* New York: Routledge, 1993.

Kerr, Paul, ed. *The Hollywood Film Industry.* London: Routledge & Keegan Paul, 1986.

Kerr, Sophie. *Love Story Incidental.* New York: Rinehart & Co., Inc., 1946.

Kimmel, Michael. *Manhood in America: A Cultural History.* New York: The Free Press, 1996.

Kirkpatrick, Stanley D. *A Cast of Killers.* New York: E. P. Dutton, 1986.

Kitch, Caroline. "Changing Theoretical Perspectives on Women's Media Images: The Emergence of Patterns in a New Area of Historical Scholarship." *Journalism and Mass Communication Quarterly* v.74 (Autumn 1997).

Koszarski, Richard. *An Evening's Entertainment: The Age of the Silent Feature Picture, 1915–1928.* Vol. 3, *History of the American Cinema*, Charles Harpole, ed. New York: Charles Scribner's Sons, 1990.

Kuhn, Annette. *Cinema, Censorship and Sexuality, 1909–1925.* London: Routledge, 1988.

Kwolek-Folland, Angel. *Engendering Business: Men and Women in Corporate Office, 1870–1930.* Baltimore: Johns Hopkins University Press, 1994.

Lambert, Gavin. *Nazimova: A Biography.* New York: Alfred A. Knopf, 1997.

Lanchester, Elsa. *Herself.* New York: St. Martin's Press, 1983.

Lane, Tamar. *Hey Diddle Diddle.* New York: The Adelphi Press, 1932.

Langenfeld, Robert. *Reconsidering Aubery Beardsley.* Ann Arbor, MI: University Microfilm Press, 1989.

Lasch, Christopher. *Haven In a Heartless World: The Family Besieged.* New York: Basic Books, Inc., 1977.

Latham, Aaron. *Crazy Sundays: F. Scott*

Fitzgerald in Hollywood. New York: Viking Press, 1970.

Laurents, Arthur. *Original Story by Arthur Laurents: A Memoir of Broadway and Hollywood*. New York: Applause Theater Book Publishers, 2001.

Laurie, Joe, Jr. *Vaudeville: From the Honky-Tonks to the Palace*. New York: Henry Holt & Co., 1953.

Lavine, W. Robert. *In a Glamorous Fashion: The Fabulous Years of Hollywood Costume Design*. New York: Charles Scribner's Sons, 1980.

Lears, Jackson. *Fables of Abundance: A Cultural History of Advertising in America*. New York: Basic Books, 1994.

Lee, Betty. *Marie Dressler: The Unlikeliest Star*. University Press of Kentucky, 1997.

Leff, Leonard J., and Jerold Simmons. *The Dame in The Kimono: Hollywood, Censorship and the Production Code from the 1920s to the 1960s*. New York: Grove Weidenfeld, 1990.

Leiter, Samuel L., ed. *The Encyclopedia of the New York Stage, 1920–1930*. Westport, CT: Greenwood Press, 1985.

_____, ed. *The Encyclopedia of the New York Stage, 1930–1940*. Westport, CT: Greenwood Press, 1989.

Levin, Jack, and Arnold Arluke. *Gossip: The Inside Scoop*. New York: Plenum Press, 1987.

Levy, Emmanuel. *And the Winner Is... The History and Politics of the Oscar Awards*. New York: Ungar, 1987.

_____. *George Cukor, Master of Elegence*. New York: William Morrow & Co., 1994.

Lewin, Ellen, ed. *Inventing Lesbian Cultures in America*. Boston: Beacon Press, 1996.

Lewis, David Levering. *When Harlem Was in Vogue*. New York: 1982.

Lewis, Felice Flanery. *Literature, Obscenity and Law*. Carbondale: South Illinois University Press, 1976.

Leyda, Jay, ed. *Voices of Film Experience, 1894–Present*. New York: Macmillan Publishing Co., 1977.

Lichter, S. Robert, Linda Lichter, and Stanley Rothman. *Watching America*. New York: Prentice Hall Press, 1991.

Light, Ivan. "From Vice District to Tourist Attraction: The Moral Career of American Chinatowns, 1880–1940," *Pacific Historical Review*, 43 (1974), pp. 367–394.

Lipovetsky, Gilles. *The Empire of Fashion: Dressing Modern Democracy*, trans. Catherine Porter. Princeton: Princeton University Press, 1994.

Little, Elizabeth A. "The Female Sailor on the Christopher Mitchell: Face and Fantasy." *American Neptune* 54 (4) 1994: 252–258.

LoBrutto, Vincent. *By Design: Interviews with Film Production Designers*. Westport, CT: Praeger, 1992.

Lord, Jack, and Lloyd Hoff. *How to Sin in Hollywood*. Hollywood, CA, c.1940.

Lott, Eric. *Love and Theft: Blackface Minstrelsy and the American Working Class*. New York: Oxford University Press, 1993.

Loy, Myrna, and James Kotsilibas-David. *Myrna Loy: Being and Becoming*. New York: Alfred A. Knopf, 1987.

Lubou, Haynes. [Dorothy Loubou and Harmony Haynes]. *Reckless Hollywood*. New York: Amour Press, Inc., 1932.

Lugowski, David. "Queering the (New) Deal: Lesbian and Gay Representation and the Depression-Era Cultural Politics of Hollywood's Production Code," *Cinema Journal*, 38, No. 2, Winter 1999, pp. 3–35.

Madden, David. *James M. Cain*. Pittsburgh: Carnegie Mellon University Press, 1987.

Maddow, Ben. *Face: A Narrative History of the Portrait in Photography*. New York: New York Graphic Society, 1977.

Madsen, Axel. *Forbidden Lovers: Hollywood's Greatest Secret—Women Who Loved Other Women*. New York: Carol Publishing Group, 1996.

_____. *Stanwyck*. New York: HarperPaperbacks, 1994.

Maeder, Edward, ed. *Hollywood and History: Costume Design in Film*. Los Angeles: Thames & Hudson, 1987.

Maltby, Richard. "'To Prevent the Prevalent Type of Book': Censorship and Adaptation in Hollywood, 1924–1934." *American Quarterly,* 44 (December 1992), pp. 554–583.

_____, and Ian Craven. *Hollywood Cinema: An Introduction.* Oxford, U.K.: Blackwell, 1995.

Mank, Gregory William, James T. Coughlin, and Dwight D. Frye, Jr. *Dwight Frye's Last Laugh.* Midnight Marquee Press, Inc., 1997.

Mann, William J. *Behind The Screen: How Gays and Lesbians Shaped Hollywood, 1910–1969.* New York: Viking, 2001.

_____. *Kate: The Woman Who Was Hepburn* (New York: Henry Holt, 2006).

_____. *Wisecracker: The Life and Times of William Haines, Hollywood's First Openly Gay Star.* New York: Viking, 1998.

Marc, David, and Robert J. Thompson. *Prime Time, Prime Movers: from I Love Lucy to L.A. Law: America's Greatest TV Shows and the People Who Created Them.* Boston: Little Brown, 1992.

Marcus, Eric. *Making History: The Struggle for Gay and Lesbian Equal Rights 1945–1990.* New York: Harper Collins, 1992.

Marshall, P. David. *Celebrity and Power: Fame in Contemporary Culture.* Minneapolis: University of Minnesota Press, 1997.

Martin, Albert Harry. *Done Gone Hollywood.* Hollywood, CA: Martin Publishing Co., 1930.

Marion, Frances. *Minnie Flynn.* New York: Boni & Liveright, 1925.

Marx, Arthur. *Goldwyn: A Biography of the Man Behind the Myth.* New York: W. W. Norton & Co., 1976.

Maschio, Geraldine. "Effeminacy or Art? The Performativity of Julian Eltinge." *Journal of American Drama and Theatre,* 10 (Winter 1998).

Matzen, Robert D. *Carole Lombard: A Bio-Bibliography.* New York: Greenwood Press, 1988.

May, Henry F. *The End of American Innocence: A Study of the First Years of Our Own Times, 1912–1917.* New York: Alfred A. Knopf, 1959.

May, Lary. *Screening Out the Past: The Birth of Mass Culture and the Motion Picture Industry.* Chicago: University of Chicago Press, 1980.

Mayne, Judith. *Directed by Dorothy Arzner.* Bloomington: Indiana University Press, 1994.

McArthur, Benjamin. *Actors and American Culture, 1880–1920.* Philadelphia: Temple University Press, 1984.

McCambridge, Mercedes. *The Quality of Mercy: An Autobiography.* New York: Times Books, 1981.

McEvoy, J. P. *Society.* New York: Simon & Schuster, 1931.

McFadden, Margaret T. "'America's Boy Friend Who Can't Get a Date': Gender, Race and the Cultural Work of the Jack Benny Program, 1932–1946," *Journal of American History* (June 1993), pp. 110–135.

McGilligan, Patrick. *George Cukor: A Double Life.* New York: St. Martin's Press, 1991.

McGrath, Keane. *Hollywood Siren.* New York: William Goldwin, Inc., 1932.

McQuail, Dennis. *Audience Analysis.* Thousands Oaks, CA: SAGE Publications, 1997.

Meade, Marion. *Buster Keaton: Cut to the Chase.* New York: Harper Collins, 1995.

Mellencamp, Patricia. *High Anxiety: Castastrophe, Scandal, Age and Comedy.* Bloomington, IN: University of Indiana Press, 1992.

Melosh, Barbara. *Engendering Culture: Manhood and Womanhood in New Deal Public Art and Theater.* Washington, DC: Smithsonian Institution Press, 1991.

Meyer, Richard. "Rock Hudson's Body," Diana Fuss, ed. *Inside/Out Lesbian Theories/Gay Theories.* New York: Routledge, 1991.

Meyers, Warren B. *Who Is That? The Late Late Viewers Guide to the Old Old Movie Players.* New York: Personality Posters, Inc., 1967.

Milland, Ray. *Wide-Eyed in Babylon: An Autobiography.* New York: William Morrow & Co., Inc., 1974.

Miller, Ruth. *That Flannigan Girl.* New York: William Morrow & Co., 1939.

Minnelli, Vincente. *I Remember It Well.* Hollywood, CA: Samuel French, 1974.

Moews, Daniel. *Keaton: The Silent Features Close Up.* Berkeley: University of California Press, 1972.

Moore, F. Michael. *DRAG! Male and Female Impersonators on Stage, Screen and Television: An Illustrated World History.* Jefferson, NC: McFarland & Co., Inc., Publishers, 1994.

Morella, Joe, and Edward Z. Epstein. *Loretta Young: An Extraordinary Life.* New York: Delacorte Press, 1986.

Morgan, Michael. [Cecil E. Carle and Dean M. Dorn] *Nine More Lives.* New York: Random House, 1947.

Morris, Michael. *Madam Valentino: The Many Lives of Natacha Rambova.* New York: Abbeville Press, 1991.

The Motion Picture Almanac, 1930-1949. New York: Quigley Publication Co., annual.

Mukerji, Chandra, and Michael Schudson, eds. *Rethinking Popular Culture: Contemporary Perspectives in Cultural Studies.* Berkeley: University of California Press, 1991.

Mumford, Kevin J. "Homosexual Changes: Race, Cultural Geography and the Emergence of the Gay." *American Quarterly,* 48 (September 1996), pp. 395-414.

_____. *Interzones: Black/White Sex Districts in New York and Chicago in the Early Twentieth Century.* New York: Columbia University Press, 1997.

Mungo, Ray. *Palm Springs Babylon: Sizzling Stories from the Desert Playground of the Stars.* New York: St. Martin's Press, 1993.

Nasaw, David. *The Chief: The Life of William Randolph Hearst* New York: Houghton Mifflin Co., 2000.

_____. *Going Out: The Rise and Fall of Public Amusements.* New York: Basic Books, 1993.

National Museum & Archive of Lesbian and Gay History, ed. *The Gay Almanac.* New York: Berkley Books, 1996.

_____. *The Lesbian Almanac.* New York: Berkley Books, 1996.

Newton, Esther. *Cherry Grove, Fire Island: Sixty Years in America's First Gay and Lesbian Town.* Boston: Beacon Press, 1993.

Nollen, Scott Allen. *Boris Karloff: A Critical Account of His Screen, Stage, Radio, Television and Recording Work.* Jefferson, N.C.: McFarland & Co., Inc., 1991.

O'Flaherty, Liam. *Hollywood Cemetery.* London: Victor Gollancz Ltd., 1935.

Oller, John. *Jean Arthur: The Acress Nobody Knew.* New York: Limelight Editions, 1997.

Oppenheimer, George. *The View from the Sixties: Memories of a Spent Life.* New York: David McKay, Co, Inc., 1966.

Parish, James R. *Hollywood Character Actors.* New Rochelle, NY: Arlington House Publishers, 1978.

Parish, James R., and Michael R. Pitts. *Hollywood On Hollywood.* Metcheun, NJ: The Scarecrow Press, Inc. 1978.

Parris, Barry. *Garbo: A Biography.* New York: Alfred A. Knopf, 1995.

_____. *Louise Brooks.* New York: Alfred A. Knopf, 1989.

Parrish, Robert. *Growing Up in Hollywood.* New York: Harcourt Brace Jovanovich, 1976.

Parsons, Louella. *The Gay Illiterate.* Garden City, NY: Doubleday, Doran & Co., Inc., 1944.

Pascoe, Peggy. *Relations of Rescue: The Search for Female Moral Authority in the American West, 1874-1939.* New York: Oxford University Press, 1991.

Peiss, Kathy. *Cheap Amusements: Working Women & Leisure in Turn-of-the-Century New York.* Philadelphia: Temple University Press, 1986.

_____. *Hope in a Jar: The Making of America's Beauty Culture.* New York: Henry Holt and Company, 1998.

_____, Christina Simmons, and Robert A. Padgug, eds. *Passion & Power: Sexuality in History.* Philadelphia: Temple University Press, 1989.

Perry, Stella G. S. *Extra-Girl.* New York: Frederick A. Stokes Co., 1929.

Pittitola, Louis. *Hearst Over Hollywood: Power, Passion, and Propaganda in the Movies.* New York: Columbia University Press, 2002.

Pizer, Donald. *Dos Passos' U.S.A.: A Critical Study*. Charlottesville: University Press of Virginia, 1988.

Plunz, Richard. *A History of Housing in New York City: Dwelling Type and Social Change in the American Metropolis*. New York: Columbia University Press, 1990.

Ponce de Leon, Charles Leonard. "Idols and cons: Representations of Celebrity in American Culture, 1850–1940." Ph.D. diss. Rutgers University, 1992.

Powers, Madelon. *Faces Along the Bar: Lore and Order in the Workingman's Saloon, 1870–1920*. Chicago: University of Chicago Press, 1998.

Preston, Jack. [John Preston Buschlen]. *Screen Star*. New York: Doubleday, Doran & Co., 1932.

Prindle, David F. *The Politics of Glamour: Ideology and Democracy in the Screen Actors Guild*. Madison: University of Wisconsin Press, 1988.

Putnam, Nina Wilcox. *Laughter Limited*. New York: George H. Doran Company, 1922.

Quinlan, David. *The Illustrated Encyclopedia of Movie Character Actors*. New York: Carroll & Graf Publishers, 1985.

Rabbes, Henry H. *Hollywood Episode*. Philadelphia: Dorrance & Co., 1946.

Rader, Paul. *Big Bug*. New York: Fleming H. Revell Co., 1932.

Ragan, David. *Who's Who in Hollywood 1900–1976*. New Rochelle, NY: Arlington House Publishers, 1976.

Rapf, Joanna E., and Gary L. Green. *Buster Keaton: A Bio-Bibliography*. Westport CT: Greenwood Press, 1995.

Rapping, Elayne. *The Looking Glass World of Nonfiction TV*. Boston: South End Press, 1987.

Rhodes, Gary Don. *Lugosi: His Life in Films, on Stage, and in the Hearts of Horror Lovers*. Jefferson, NC: McFarland & Company, Inc., 1997.

Rice, Elmer. *A Voyage to Purilia*. New York: Cosmopolitan Book Corporation, 1929.

Rich, Sharon. *Nelson Eddy: The Opera Years*. New York: Bell Harbour Press, 2001.

_____. *Sweethearts: The Timeless Love Affair—On-Screen and Off—Between Jeannette MacDonald and Nelson Eddy*. New York: Bell Harbour Press, updated 2001.

Richardson, Diane. "The Dilemma of Essentiality in Homosexual Theory." *Journal of Homosexuality*, 9 (1984), pp. 79–90.

Riva, Maria. *Marlene Dietrich*. New York: Alfred A. Knopf, 1993.

Robinson, David. *Hollywood in the Twenties*. London: A Zwemmer Ltd., 1968.

Robinson, Edward G. with Leonard Spigelgass. *All My Yesterdays: An Autobiography*. New York: Hawthorn Books, Inc., 1973.

Rosenberg, Bernard, and Harry Silverstein. *The Real Tinsel*. London: The MacMillan Co., 1970.

Rosenbloom, Nancy. "Between Reform and Regulation: The Struggle Over Film Censorship in Progressive America, 1909–1922," *Film History*, 1987 1(4).

_____. "In Defense of the Moving Pictures: The People's Institute, The National Board of Censorship and the Problem of Leisure in Urban America," *American Studies*, 1992.

Rosenstein, Jaik. *Hollywood Leg Man*. Los Angeles: The Madison Press, 1950.

Rosmanith, Olga. *Picture People*. London: John Long, Ltd., 1934.

Ross, Ishbel. *Taste in America: Illustrated History of the Evolution of Architecture, Furnishings, Fashions, and Customs of the American People*. New York: Thomas Y. Cromwell Co., 1967.

Rosten, Leo. *Hollywood: The Movie Colony—The Moviemakers*. New York: Harcourt, Brace and Company. 1941.

Rothman, Ellen K. *Hands & Hearts: A History of Courtship in America*. New York: Basic Books, 1984.

Rothman, Sheila. *Woman's Proper Place: A History of Changing Ideals and Practices, 1870 to the Present*. New York: Basic Books, 1978.

Rule, Jane. *Lesbian Images*. Garden City, NY: Doubleday & Co., Inc. 1975.

Russo, Vito. *The Celluloid Closet: Homosexuality in the Movies*. New York: Harper & Row, 1981.

Ryan, Donald. *Angel's Flight*. New York: Boni & Liveright., 1927.
———. *A Roman Holiday*. New York: The Maculay Co., 1930.
Rybczynski, Witold. *Home: A Short History of an Idea*. New York: Viking Books, 1986.
St. Dennis, Madelon. *The Death Kiss*. New York: The Fiction League, 1932.
St. Johns, Adela Rogers. *The Skyrocket*. New York: Cosmopolitan, 1925.
Sandman, Peter M., David M. Rubin, and David B. Sachsman. *Media: An Introductory Analysis of American Mass Communications*, 3rd Ed. Englewood Cliffs, N.J.: Prentice-Hall, Inc., 1981.
Sands, Pierre Norman. *A Historical Study of the Academy of Motion Picture Arts and Sciences (1927–1947)*. New York: Arno Press, 1973.
Schanke, Robert A. *Shattered Applause: The Lives of Eva Le Gallienne*. Carbondale: Southern Illinois Press, 1992.
Scharf, Lois. *To Work and to Wed: Female Employment, Feminism and the Great Depression*. Westport, CT: Greenwood Press, 1980.
Scharf, Lois, and Joan M. Jensen, eds. *Decades of Discontent: The Women's Movement, 1920–1940*. Westport, CT: Greenwood Press, 1983.
Schatz, Thomas. *The Genius of the System: Hollywood Filmmaking in the Studio Era*. New York: Pantheon Books, 1988.
Schickel, Richard. *Cary Grant: A Celebration*. New York: Applause Books, 2000.
———. *Intimate Strangers: The Culture of Celebrity*. Garden City, NY: Doubleday & Co., Inc., 1985.
Schudson, Michael. *Discovering the News: A Social History of American Newspapers*. New York: Basic Books, Inc., 1978.
Schulberg, Budd. *What Makes Sammy Run?* New York: Random House, 1941.
Schwartz, Nancy L., and Sheila Schwartz. *The Hollywood Writers' Wars*. New York: Alfred A. Knopf, 1982.
Schwarz, Judith. *The Radical Feminist of Heterodoxy: Greenwich Village, 1912–1940*. Norwich, VT: New Victoria Publishers, 1986.

Schwarz, Vanessa R. *Spectacular Realities: Early Mass Culture in Fin-de-Siecle Paris*. Berkeley: University of California Press, 1998.
Schwerdt, Lisa M. *Isherwood's Fiction: The Self and Teaching*. New York: St. Martin's Press, 1989.
Scott, Anne Frior. *Natural Allies: Women's Associations in American History*. Urbana: University of Illinois Press, 1991.
Seidman, Steven, ed. *Queer Theory/Sociology*. New York: Blackwell Publishers Ltd., 1996.
Selznick, Irene Mayer. *A Private View*. New York: Alfred A. Knopf, 1983.
Sennett, Robert S. *Hollywood Hoopla: Creating Stars and Selling Movies in the Golden Age of Hollywood*. New York: Watson-Guptill Publications, 1998.
Sennett, Ted. *Warner Brothers Presents*. New Rochelle, N.Y.: Arlington House, 1971.
Shand-Tucchi, Douglass. *Boston Bohemia: Ralph Adams Cram, Life and Architecture, 1881–1900*. Amherst: University of Massachusetts Press, 1995.
Sheehy, Helen. *Eva Le Gallienne: A Biography*. New York: Alfred A. Knopf, Inc., 1997.
Sherman, Vincent. *Studio Affairs: My Life as a Film Director*. Louisville: University of Kentucky Press, 1996.
Sherwood, Roger. *Modern Housing Prototypes*. Cambridge, MA: Harvard College, 1978.
Short, William H. *A Generation of Motion Pictures: A Review of Social Values in Recreational Films*. New York: National Committee for the Study of Social Values in Motion Pictures, 1928.
Sivulka, Juliann. *Soap, Sex and Cigarettes: A Cultural History of American Advertising*. Belmont, CA: Wadsworth Publishing Co, 1998.
Sklar, Robert. *Movies-Made America: A Cultural History of American Movies*. New York: Vintage Books, 1975.
Slide, Anthony. *The Best of Rob Wagner's Script*. Metuchen, NJ: The Scarecrow Press, Inc., 1985.
———. *The Hollywood Novel*. Jefferson, NC: McFarland & Co., Inc., 1995.

_____. *The Vaudevillians: A Dictionary of Vaudeville Performers*. Westport, CT: Arlington House, 1982.

Smith-Rosenberg, Carroll. *Disorderly Conduct: Visions of Gender in Victorian America*. New York: Oxford University Press, 1985.

Snyder, Robert W. *The Voice of the City: Vaudeville and Popular Culture in New York*. New York: Oxford University Press, 1989.

Spacks, Patricia Meyer. *Gossip*. New York: Alfred A. Knopf, 1985.

Spatz, Jonas. *Hollywood in Fiction: Some Versions of the American Myth*. Paris: Mouton, 1969.

Sperber, Ann, and Eric Lax. *Bogart*. New York: William Morrow & Co., Inc., 1997.

Spoto, Donald. *The Blue Angel: The Life of Marlene Dietrich*. New York: Doubleday, 1992.

_____. *The Dark Side of Genius: The Life of Alfred Hitchcock*. Boston: Little, Brown & Co., 1983.

Sprague, Gregory A. "Male Homosexuality in Western Culture: The Dilemna of Identity and Subculture in Historical Research." *Journal of Homosexuality*, 10 (1984).

Springer, John Parris. "Hollywood Fictions: The Cultural Construction of Hollywood in American Literature, 1916–1939." Ph.D. diss., University of Iowa, 1994.

Stacey, Jackie. *Star Gazing: Hollywood Cinema and Female Spectatorship*. London: Routledge, 1994.

Staiger, Janet. *Bad Women: Regulating Sexuality in Early American Cinema*. Minneapolis: University of Minnesota Press, 1995.

Stansell, Christine. *City of Women: Sex and Class in New York, 1789–1860*. Chicago: University of Chicago, 1982.

Starr, Kevin. *Inventing the Dream: California Through the Progressive Era*. New York: Oxford University Press, 1985.

_____. *Material Dreams: Southern California Through the 1920s*. New York: Oxford University Press, 1990.

_____. *The Sixth Man*. Garden City, NY: Doubleday & Company, Inc., 1961.

Stearn, Jess. *The Grapevine*. Garden City, NY: Doubleday & Company, Inc., 1964.

Stearns, Peter N. *Be a Man: Males in Modern Society*. New York: Holmes & Meier Publishers, Inc., 1979.

Steen, Mike. *Hollywood Speaks! An Oral History*. New York: G. P. Putnam's Sons, 1974.

Sternberg, Josef von. *Fun in a Chinese Laundry*: New York: Collier, 1965.

Stewart, Donald Ogden. *By a Stroke of Luck*. New York: Paddington Press, 1975.

Strachey, James, ed. *The Complete Psychological Works of Sigmund Freud*. London: The Hogarth Press, 1957. v. 11, v. 18.

Streitmatter, Rodger. *Unspeakable: The Rise of the Gay and Lesbian Press in America*. Boston: Faber and Faber, 1995.

Studlar, Gaylyn. *This Mad Masquerade: Stardom and Masculinity in the Jazz Age*. New York: Columbia University Press, 1997.

Susman, Warren I. *Culture as History: The Transformation of American Society in the Twentieth Century*. New York: Pantheon Books, 1984.

Swindell, Larry. *Screwball: The Life of Carole Lombard*. New York: William Morrow & Co., Inc. 1975.

Taylor, William R., ed. *Inventing Times Square: Commerce and Culture at the Crossroads of the World*. Baltimore: Johns Hopkins University Press, 1996.

Theoharis, Athan. *J. Edgar Hoover, Sex, and Crime: A Historical Antidote*. Chicago: Ivan R. Dee, 1995.

Thomas, Bob. *King Cohn: The Life & Times of Harry Cohn*. New York: G. P. Putnam's Sons, 1967.

Timmons, Stuart. *The Trouble with Harry Hay: Founder of the Modern Gay Movement*. Boston: Allyson Publications, 1990.

Toll, Robert C. *The Entertainment Machine*. New York: Oxford University Press, 1982.

_____. *On With the Show: The First Century of Show Biz in America*. New York: Oxford University Press, 1976.

Tornabene, Lyn. *Long Live the King: A Biography of Clark Gable*. New York: G. P. Putnam's Sons, 1976.

Townsend, Kim. *Sherwood Anderson*. Boston: Houghton Mifflin Company, 1987.

Tully, Jim. *Jarnegan*. New York: Albert & Charles Boni, 1926.

Tyler, Bruce M. *From Harlem to Hollywood: The Struggle for Racial and Cultural Democracy 1920–1943*. New York: Garland Publishing, Inc., 1992.

Unwin, Raymond. "Discussion," *Proceedings of the National Conference on City Planning* 3 (1911): 110–111.

Vale, Joan M. "Tintype Ambitions-Three Vaudevillians in Search of Hollywood Fame," M.A. thesis, University of San Diego, 1985.

Valenti, Peter. *Errol Flynn: A Bio-Bibliography*. Westport, CT: Greenwood Press, 1984.

Van Rensselaer, May King. *The Social Ladder*. New York: Henry Holt & Co., 1924.

Vickers, Hugo. *Loving Garbo: The Story of Greta Garbo, Cecil Beaton, and Mercedes de Acosta*. New York: Random House, 1994.

Vietel, Salka. *The Kindness of Strangers*. New York: Holt, Rinehart & Winston, 1969.

Ware, Caroline F. *Greenwich Village, 1920–1930*. New York: Columbia University Press, 1935.

Waugh, Evelyn. *The Loved One*. Boston: Little, Brown & Co., 1948.

Wayne, Jane Ellen. *Clark Gable: Portrait of a Misfit*. New York: St. Martin's Press, 1993.

Webster, James G., and Patricia F. Phalen. *The Mass Audience: Rediscovering the Dominant Model*. Mahwah, N.J.: Lawrence Erlbaum Associates, Publishers, 1997.

Weiss, Andrea. *Vampires and Violets: Lesbians in Film*. New York: Penguin, 1993.

Wells, Walter. *Tycoons and Locusts: A Regional Look at HollywoodFfiction of the 1930s*. Carbondale: Southern Illinois University, 1973.

West, Nathanael. *The Day of the Locust*. 1939; reprint: New York: Bantam Books, 1973.

Wexman, Virginia Wright. *Creating the Couple: Love, Marriage and Hollywood Performance*. Princeton: Princeton University Press, 1993.

White, Hayden. *Tropics of Discourse: Essays in Cultural Criticism*. Baltimore: Johns Hopkins University Press, 1985.

Wiebe, Robert. *The Search for Order, 1877–1920*. New York: Hill and Wang, 1967.

Wilder, Margaret Buell. *Hurry Up & Wait*. New York: McGraw-Hill Book Co., 1946.

Wilkerson, Tichi, and Marcia Borif, *The Hollywood Reporter: The Golden Years*. New York: Coward-McCann, Inc., 1984.

Willeford, Charles. "Jim Tully: Holistic Barbarian," *Writing and Other Blood Sports*. Tucson, AZ: Dennis McMillan Publishing, 2000.

Wilson, Elizabeth. *The Sphinx in the City: Urban Life, the Control of Disorder and Women*. Berkeley: University of California Press, 1991.

Wilson, Harry Leon. *Merton of the Movies*. New York: Cosmopolitan Book Corp., 1922.

_____. *Two Black Sheep*. New York: Cosmopolitan Book Corp., 1931.

Winters, Shelley. *Shelley: Also Known as Shirley*. New York: Ballantine Books, 1980.

Witt, Lynn, Sherry Thomas, and Eric Marcus, eds. *Out in All Directions: The Almanac of Gay and Lesbian America*. New York: Warner Books, 1995.

Wodehouse, P. G. *Laughing Gas*. New York: Doubleday, Doran, 1936.

Wolselen, Roland E. *The Magazine World: an Introduction to Magazine Journalism*. New York: Prentice-Hall, Inc., 1951.

Woods, James D. *The Corporate Closet: The Professional Lives of Gay Men in America*. New York: The Free Press, 1993.

Wright, Gwendolyn. *Building the Dream: A Social History of Housing in America*. Cambridge, MA: The MIT Press, 1981.

Wynn, Ned. *We Will Always Live in Beverly Hills: Growing Up Crazy in Hollywood*. New York: William Morrow & Co., Inc, 1990.

Zneimer, John. *The Literary Vision of Liam O'Flaherty*. Syracuse, N.Y.: Syracuse University Press, 1970.

Zolotow, Maurice. *Billy Wilder in Hollywood.* New York: G. P. Putnam's Sons, 1977.

Manuscript Collections

Academy of Motion Picture Arts and Sciences (AMPAS), Beverly Hills, CA
   Paramount Productions, Inc. Collection:
      Scripts
      Stills
      Press Books
   Annual reports submitted to the Motion Picture Producers and Distributors of America, Inc.
Biography files of various performers
Lesbian Herstory Archive, Brooklyn, New York
   Biographical files
Los Angeles City District Attorney Collection
Manuscript Division, Library of Congress, Washington, DC
   Ralph Block Papers
   Lillian Gish Papers
   Ben Hecht Papers
   Thomas H. Ince Papers
   Garson Kanin Papers
   Rowland V. Lee Papers
   Val Lewton Papers
   Alla Nazimova Papers
   May Robson Papers
   Harold A. C. Sintzenich Papers
   Miriam Cooper Walsh Papers
Motion Picture Producers and Directors Association Collection:
   Production Code Administration Files
Municipal Archives, Department of Records and Information Services, Los Angeles, CA
   City Council Collection
New York Public Library at Lincoln Center, New York, NY
   Billy Rose Theatre Collection
      Biography Clipping Files
      Cinema: Hollywood Clipping Files

Production files of various Hollywood on Hollywood films
Rosenbach Museum, Philadelphia, PA
   Mercedes de Acosta Collection
Smithsonian Institution — Library Annex, Washington, DC
   Photoplay, 1915–1933
University of Southern California Cinema and Television Library, Los Angeles, CA
   MGM Script Collection
   Warner Brothers Script Collection

Movies

Bombshell (MGM, 1933).
Ella Cinders (First National, 1926).
Go West Young Man (Paramount, 1937).
Going Hollywood (MGM, 1933).
Hollywood Boulevard (MGM, 1936).
Hollywood Hotel (Warner Brothers, 1937).
Hollywood Party (MGM, 1934).
Let's Fall In Love (Columbia, 1934).
Movie Crazy. (Columbia, 1932).
Once In a Lifetime (Universal, 1932).
Show Girl in Hollywood (First National (Warners, 1930).
Show People (MGM, 1928).
Something to Sing About (Grand National, 1937).
A Star is Born (MGM, 1937).
Stunt Pilot (Monogram, 1939).
Sullivan's Travels (Paramount, 1941).
The Talk of Hollywood (Sono Art, 1929).
What Price Hollywood? (RKO, 1932).
World Premiere (Paramount, 1941).

Newspapers and Periodicals

Los Angeles Times, 1915–1941
Los Angeles Evening Herald, 1915–1930
Los Angeles Evening Herald & Examiner, 1931–1941
The New Masses, 1930–1941
The New Republic, 1930–1941
New York Times, 1915–1941
Saturday Review of Literature, 1930–1941
Silver Screen, 1930–1938.

Index

Numbers in **_bold italics_** indicate pages with photographs.

Academy Awards 54, 64; coverage 55–56; Dietrich nomination 33; dignitaries attendance 56–57; effusive emotions 57–58; glamour 55; stars' arrivals 55–56; start 54
Academy of Motion Picture Arts and Sciences (AMPAS) 54–55
Acker, Jean 103–106, 124; *see also* Darmond, Grace; Valentino, Rudolph
Adams, John 114
Adams, John Quincy 60
Adams, Louisa Catherine 60
Adrian, Gilbert 159, 187, **_190_**
adulterers 4; appearance in semi-public party reporting 61–62; *The Big Money* (Dos Passos novel) 76–77; change with World War II 195; exposure in newspapers 60; Gable, Clark 63, 74; Hollywood bohemians thriving 153–154; scholarship on other adulterer images 6–7; *Screen Star* (Preston novel) 171; *see also* Davies, Marion; Hearst, William Randolph; Lombard, Carole
Ainsworth, Helen 133
Akins, Zoe 31–32, 84
Al Levy's Café 18
Allan, Ted 180
Allen, Jane *see* Schulman, Sylvia
Ambassador Hotel 25, 55
American Federation of Labor 119
American Film Institute 139
American Magazine 148
American Newspaper Publishers Association 56
Anna Christie (movie) 129–130
Anti-Saloon League 21
Arbuckle, Fatty 84–85, 117
Architects Ball 62
Arizona to Broadway (movie) 40
Arsenic & Old Lace (movie) 191
art department 175
art directors 122, 175
Arthur, Jean 129
Arzner, Dorothy 28–29, **_142_**, **_144_**; contemporaries' perceptions about her sexuality 129,

144; *Craig's Wife* (movie) 142; *Dance Girl Dance* (movie) 142; early life 142; *Man Woman Marriage* (movie) 145; Morgan, Marian 144–145; publicity 143–144; scholars' perceptions about her sexuality 144; *Ten Modern Commandments* (movie) 144; *The Wild Party* (movie) 142
Assembly Ball 52
Astaire, Adele 157
Astaire, Fred 157, 162, 164, 180

bachelors 12, 145–146; *see also* Cukor, George; Eltinge, Julian; *Falling Star* (Baum novel); Grant, Cary; Haines, William; Horton, Edward Everett; Montgomery, Douglass; Scott Randolph
Back Yard Café 25
back stage 160; artisan crew 173–174; depictions 161–162; *Forty-Second Street* (movie) 172; *The Gold Diggers of 1933* (movie) 172; *Sister Carrie* (Dreiser novel) 162
balls 77–78, 95–96
Bankhead, Tallulah **_31_**, 159; career after Hollywood 32; contemporaries' perceptions about her sexuality 32; *The Dancers* (play) 31; early years 30; *Footloose* (play) 31; friends in Hollywood 32–33; private parties 84; scholars' perceptions about her sexuality 33; *The Skin of Our Teeth* (play) 32; *The Squab Farm* (play) 31
Bankhead, William 29
Banks, Lionel 175
The Barn 25
Barrios, Richard 7
Barrymore, John 89
Baskette, Lina 70
The Battle Over Citizen Kane 92
Baum, Vicki 5, 147
Baumgartner, John (Los Angeles city councilman) 43–44, 54
B.B.B.'s Cellar 40, 45
Beale, Mrs. Truxton 81
"beard" 102

237

Index

Beardsley, Aubrey 178
Beaton, Cecil 125, 180
Beaux Arts Ball 62
Beery, Wallace 39
behind the scenes 162; Bankhead 32; *Bombshell* (movie) 166–168; chorus boys 171; chorus girls 171; employment 163–164; family atmosphere 162, 164; glamorous conditions 164; *Going Hollywood* (movie) 176–178; *Hollywood Hotel* (movie) 183–185, 186; *Hollywood Siren* (McGrath novel) 179–180; *I Lost My Girlish Laughter* (Allen novel) 185–187; *Jarnegan* (Tully novel) 168; *Lady's Lady* (Bell novel) 172; *Merton of the Movies* (Wilson novel; movie) 165; pre-1920 160; *Reckless Hollywood* (Lubou novel) 170–171, 178–179; *Screen Star* (Preston novel) 171; sexual behavior 164–165; *Show Girl in Hollywood* (movie) 169–170; *Show People* (movie) 165; *Something to Sing About* (movie) 181–182, 184; tourists 163; see also specific professions
Bel Air 117
Bell, Ann 172
Ben-Hur (movie) 105–107
Benchley, Robert 32–33, 164
Bennett, Constance 89
Bennett, Joan 89, 95
Benton, Travis **190**
Berle, Milton 41
Bernadotte, Prince Sigvard 63
Bernadotte, Princess Sigvard 63
Betsky, Aaron 156
Better Angel (Meeker novel) 152
Beverly Hills 24–25, 117, 140
Beverly-Wilshire Hotel 148
The Big Money (Dos Passos novel) 76–77, 110–111
The Bird of Paradise (play) 72
Biltmore Hotel 55, 95
Blackwell, Carlyle 18
Blaine, Sally 95
Block, Ralph 16
Blondie 90
The Blue Angel (movie) 33
Blue Venus (movie) 33
Blum, Ralph 34
Bodkin, Henry G. 48
La Boheme Cafe 13, 25, 26, 38–40
Bois, Curt 183, **184**
Bombshell (movie) 166–168
Boni, Albert 93
Boni, Charles 93
Borzage, Frank 95
Boys Town (movie) 58
Brand, Harry 155
Breen, Joseph 183
Brentwood 117, 140
Bret, David 108
Brian, Mary **83**

Briggs, Emily Edson 60, 79
Bringing Up Baby (movie) 28
Broadway Brevities (magazine) 40
Broadway restaurants 15
Broadway theaters 10, 15, 22–23
brothels 2
Brown Derby 4, 25, 27–28, 33, 37
Browne, Bothwell 18
Buchanan, James 53
Budd, Ruth 39; see also Norman, Karyl
Bull, Clarence 180
Bullpen 26
Burbank 116, 162–163
Burp Hollow 26
Buschlen, John Preston 5, 171; see also Preston, Jack
Butler, David 49

Cabaret 15
Cafe International 46
café society 21, 51, 82
Cafe Trocadero 4, 21
Cagney, Jimmy 181
Cain, James M. 5
Camille (1936 movie) 139
Camille (silent movie) 122
El Capitan Theater 96
The Captive (Bourdet play) 22, 128; see also *La Prisonnaire*
Carpenter, Frank 60, 79
Carter, Chloe 105
The Cat and the Fiddle (movie) 70
C.C. Hall 16
censorship 6, 135
Chaplin, Charles 117, 164; Davies and Hearst 88–89; joke in *Jarnegan* 168; Tully's employer 93
Charles Froham Company 10
Chase, Salmon P. 60
Chatterton, Ruth 187
Chauncey, George 23
Cherrill, Virginia 152; see also Grant, Cary
Chesboro, Raymond (Los Angeles city attorney) 48
Chevalier, Maurice 35
Chicago 23
Chicago Tribune 107–108, 111
Chin Chin 88; see also Davies, Marion
China Seas (movie) 113
chorus boys 171, 172
chorus girls 171
The Chosen People (play) 121
Ciro's 26
Citizen Kane (movie) 92, 129
Club Abbey 39
Club New Yorker 20, 39, 41
Coconut Grove 25–26, 55
Cohan, George M. 97
Colbert, Claudette 26, 39, 74
Colegrove 44

Columbia Pictures 95, 175–176, 192
Conkling, Roscoe 60; see also Sprague, Mrs. Kate
Cooper, Gary 140
Cooper, Georgie **184**
Cooper, Miriam 16, 117, 164
Cosmopolitan Pictures 148, 178; see also Davies, Marion; Hearst, William Randolph
The Cotton Club 25, 178; see also Sebastian, Frank
The Countess Charming (movie) 20
Cousin Lucy (play) 17
Cox, Wilma 132–134
C.R. Ashbee's Guild, 176; see also scenic art department
Cracraft, Thomas 176, 192; see also scenic art department
Craig's Wife (movie) 142
Crawford, Cheryl 33
Crawford, Joan 13, 41, 67, 96
The Crinoline Girl (play) 17
Crosby, Bing 176
cross-dressers xiv; see also female impersonation; homosexuals; lesbians; male impersonation
Cruikshank, Herbert 143
Cruze, James 142
Cukor, George 29, 32, 107; Garbo's sexuality 129; Grant's sexuality 153; images of home 147; Nazimova's sexuality 125
Culver City 25, 163
Curtis, Charles (vice president) 56–57

Dance Girl Dance (movie) 142
dance halls 2
The Dancers (play) 31
Darmond, Grace 103–105, 124; see also Acker, Jean; Valentino, Rudolph
Davies, Marion, **91**, 164, 189; in anti–Hearst newspaper 92; attends at Hollywood weddings 89; *Chin Chin* (play) 88; *Citizen Kane* (movie) 92; contemporaries' perceptions about Hearst relationship 90–91; Cosmopolitan Pictures 148; early years 88; friendship with Alma Rubens 91; *Going Hollywood* (movie) 176; Hearst's will 92–93; Ince death 86–87; at Mayfair Ball 90; public reaction 90; *Runaway, Romany* (movie) 88; Santa Monica Beach bungalow 88, 93; scholars' perceptions about her sexuality 92–93; *Show People* (movie) 165; *Stop! Look! Listen!* (revue) 88; visiting dignitaries 89–90; *The Ziegfeld Follies of 1916* (revue) 88; see also Hearst, William Randolph
Davis, Bette **83**
Davis, James E. (Los Angeles police chief) 45
The Day of the Locusts (West novel) 47–48
de Acosta, Mercedes 3, 28, 36, 129, **139**; *Camille* (1936 movie) 139; contemporaries'

perceptions about her sexuality 140–141; *Desperate* (movie) 138; early life 138; house 140; images 139–140; marriage 138; Munson, Ona 141; *Queen Christina* (movie) 138; relationships with Garbo and Dietrich 140–141; scholars' perceptions about her sexuality 141–142; *The Shining Hour* (movie) 139; see also Dietrich, Marlene; Garbo, Greta
Decatur House 135
de la Falaise, Marquis Henri 149
Delineator (magazine) 119
Delmonicos 61, 74
Del Rio, Dolores 68, 129, **176**
De Mille, Cecil B. 99; see also *The King of Kings*
De Mille, William 142
Department of Water and Power (DWP) 116
de Saulles, Blanca 172
de Saulles, John 172; see also Valentino, Rudolph
Desperate (movie) 138
Devil May Care (movie) 68
Dietrich, Marlene 26, 28–29, **34**, 65–66, 74, 125, 164; *The Blue Angel* (movie) 33; *Blue Venus* (movie) 33; contemporaries' perceptions about her sexuality 35–36, 141; early years 33; Josef Von Sternberg 35; Maurice Chevalier 35; *Morocco* (movie) 33; relationship with de Acosta 36–38; Riva (daughter) 37; Rodgers and Hart song 35–36; scholars' perceptions about her sexuality 36, 141–142; *The Song of Songs* (movie) 33
D'Orsay, Fifi 40, 177
Dos Passos, John 76, 110–111; see also *The Big Money*
Dove, Billie 27
Downey, Morton 178
Downing, Andrew Jackson 114
drag see female impersonation
The Drag (play) 22
drag balls 12
Drake, Betsy 153; see also Grant, Cary
Dreiser, Theodore 162
Dressler, Marie 58, 129–130
Du Brey, Claire 130
Dumbrille, Douglass 90
Duncan, Isadora 141; see also de Acosta, Mercedes
Durante, Jimmy 64; see also *Hollywood Party*
Durbin, Deanna 164

Earl Carroll's Theatre Restaurant 25–26
The Easiest Way (movie) 73
Eaton, Mary 89
Eddy, Nelson 148, 155, 172; contemporaries' perceptions about his sexuality 100–101; early years 98–99; marriage 101; private parties 99–100; relationship with Mother

99–100; scholars' perceptions about his sexuality 101
Edendale 44
Ehrenstein, David 6
Eicks, Mary 176
Eilers, Sally 39
Elias, Hal 70
Elks 51
Ellenberger, Allan 71–72
Elliot, Marc 154
Eltinge, Julian (William Julian Dalton) 16, *19*, 41; career end 48–49; *The Countess Charming* (movie) 20; *Cousin Lucy* (play) 17; *The Crinoline Girl* (play) 17; *The Fascinating Widow* (play) 17; house 20; *Mr. Wix of Wickham* (play) 17; movie career 18–19; publicity in vaudeville 17
Embassy Club 26
Epstein, Michael 92
The Eyes of Youth (movie) 102

Fairbanks, Douglas 91, 120, 145, 164
Fairbanks, Douglas, Jr. 125
Falling Star (Baum novel) 5, 147
Farmer, Michael 26
The Fascinating Widow (play) 17
Faulkner, William 6; see also *Sanctuary*
Fay, Frank 131
female impersonation 5, 10, 23, 44, 53; *see also* Malin, Gene; Norman, Karyl
Film Daily 185
Fish, Mrs. Stuyvesant 79
Fitzgerald, F. Scott 5, 82, 136
Fitzmaurice, Mr. and Mrs. 89
"flapper" 135, 145
Fleming, Victor 167
flower department 175
Folies Bergere Theater 15
Footloose (play) 31
Forty-Second Street (movie) 172
The Four Horsemen of the Apocalypse (movie) 103
"Four Hundred" 51
Fox Film Corporation (Twentieth Century–Fox) 44, 66; chorus boys 171; chorus girls 171; Horton publicity 154–155; script department 175; Tracy, Spencer 95; Tracy and Young 95–96
Francis, Kay 129, 187
Franklin, Ann Demitz 101
Freud, Sigmund 101, 180
Fritsch, Willy 66
A Front Page Story (movie) 154
Frye, Dwight 181
Furthman, Jules 167

Gable, Clark 32, 63, *75*, 89, 96, 165; affair with Carole Lombard 73–76; *The Bird of Paradise* (play) 72; *China Seas* (movie) 73; contemporaries' perception about his sexuality 73–76; early years 72; *The Easiest Way* (movie) 73; first wife Josephine Dillon 72; friendship with Marion Davies 91; "Hollywood Party" (song) 86; *Marie Antoinette* premiere 73; movie career 73–74; at movie premieres 73–74, 117; scholars' perceptions about his sexuality 76; second wife Ria 63, 72–74, 117; *see also* screenwriters
Gable, Ria (née Langham) 63, 72–74, 112, 113, 117; *see also* Gable, Clark; Lombard, Carole
Garbo, Greta (Greta Louisa Gustafsson) 3, 26, 66–67, 106, 135; *Anna Christie* (movie) 129–130; Bull 323; contemporaries' perceptions about her sexuality 129; dressing room décor 166; early life 126; "Hollywood Party" (song) 86; house décor 128–129; *Mata Hari* (movie) 165; movie career 127, 129; *Peter the Tramp* (movie) 126; *Queen Christina* (movie) 128; relationship with de Acosta 127, 130; scholars' perceptions about her sexuality 129–131, 141–142; Stokowski, Leopold 134; *The Torrent* (movie) 127; trousers 127–128; *Two-Faced Woman* (movie) 129; unmarried status 134–135
Garnett, Tay 84
Gaucho Theater 64
Gay Divorcee (movie) 157
Gaynor, Janet 129
gender inversion 7, 17; Eltinge image 18; female cross-dressers 27, 29; private party image 80
George M. Cohan Theater 68
George Olsen's Club 26
Gibbons, Cedric 176
Gilbert, John 219
Gish, Dorothy 117
Gish, Lillian 117
Godowsky, Dagmar 84, 105, 124
Going Hollywood (movie) 5, 176–178, 189
The Gold Diggers of 1933 (movie) 172
The Gold Rush (movie) 50; *see also* movie premieres
Golden Dawn (play) 150, 191
Gopal, Ram 141
Graham, Lee 133
Grand National (studio) 181
Grant, Cary 83, 108, *151*; *Arsenic & Old Lace* (movie) 191; contemporaries' perceptions about his sexuality 153–154; early life 150; *Golden Dawn* (play) 150, 191; *Hot Saturday* (movie) 150; marriage to Virginia Cherrill 152; movie career 150; photo shoot of house 152–153; relationship with Orry-Kelly 150, 187, 189–190; scholars' perceptions about his sexuality 154; Schulberg, B. P. 150; shared place with Randolph Scott 150–152

Index

Grant, Mrs. Julia Dent 60
Grauman's Chinese Theater 4, 63, 118
Grauman's Egyptian Theater 63
The Great Gatsby (Fitzgerald novel) 82
Greenwich Village, New York City 21, 23, 37, 150, 191
Greer, Howard 30, 185
Griffith, D.W. 56, 58

Haines, William 32, 84, 155; Cukor relationship 147; early years 148; Malin friendship 40; publicist's statement 70; publicity images 148–149; Shields, Jimmy 148; *Show People* (movie) 165
Halasz, Gyula (Brassai) 194
Hall, Radclyffe 6; see also *The Well of Loneliness*
Hamilton, Alexander 114
Hammerstein, Arthur 150
Harding, Ann 44
Harding, Laura 30; *see also* Hepburn, Katharine
Harding, Warren 54
Harlem (New York City) 18, 23
Harlow, Jean 32, 39, 112, 166–167
Harris, Warren 154
Harrison, William Henry 53
Harron, John **184**
Harry Garson Productions 103
Hart, Lorenz 35, 142
Harvey, Lilian 66–67
Harwood, Gean 154
Hawthorne, Nathaniel 118
Hay, Harry 86
Hay, John 81
Hayes, Helen 67
Haynes, Harmony 170
Hays Office 166
Head, Edith **190**
Hearst, Millicent Veronica Willson 87, 92
Hearst, William Randolph 56, **83**, **91**; anti–Hearst newspaper 92; attends at Hollywood weddings 89; *Citizen Kane* (movie) 92; contemporaries' perceptions Davies relationship 90–91; Cosmopolitan Pictures 88; courts Marion Davies 87–88; early years 87; Ince Death 86–87; at Mayfair Ball 90; political ambitions 87; private parties 84; public reaction 90; San Simeon 90, 93; visiting dignitaries 89–90; *see also* Davies, Marion
Hepburn, Katharine 29–30, 35, 95–96
Hersholt, Jean 63
Hey Diddle Diddle (Lane novel) 97–98, 100
Higham, Charles 154, 191
Highland, Chauncey 51
Hollywood Boulevard 4, 16, 25–26, 63, 117, 127
Hollywood Cemetery (O'Flaherty novel) 41–43

"Hollywood Four Hundred" 62
Hollywood Hills 94, 145
Hollywood Hotel 6
Hollywood Hotel (movie) 4, 183–185, 186
Hollywood Lesbians (Hadleigh book) 36–37
Hollywood Magazine (movie magazine) 40
Hollywood novels 5; artisans behind the scenes 178–180, 185–186; bachelor in 147; differences from other literature 6, 171; movie making technology in 160; nightclubs in 47–48; stars at private parties 93–94, 110–111; stars behind the scenes 168, 170–172; *see also* specific names
"Hollywood on Hollywood" movie 5; artisans behind the scenes 176–178, 181–185; differences from other movies 7; nightlife in 27–28; stars at premiere parties 64–65; stars at private parties 85–86; stars behind the scenes 166–170; *see also* specific names
Hollywood Party (movie) 5, 35, 64; shows premiere party 64–65; shows private party 85–86; title song 85–86
Hollywood Reporter 6
Hollywood Siren (McGrath novel) 108–109, 179
Holt, Jack 120
home: apartment buildings 114–115; architectural styles 118; character building 114, 118; depictions of women 118–119; displaying status 118; Downing, Andrew Jackson 114; early Republic Leaders attitudes 113–114; Holt images 120; *Homes of American Authors* (book) 117; *Homes of American Statesmen* (book) 117; magazine and pamphlet images 119; Pickford-Fairbanks images 120; single-family detached house 115; Swanson images 120–121; tenement housing 114; Wright, Frank Lloyd 115; *see also* Arzner, Dorothy; bachelors; Cukor, George; de Acosta, Mercedes; *Falling Star* (Baum novel); Garbo, Greta; Grant, Cary; Haines, William; Horton, Edward Everett; Kelly, Patsy; Montgomery, Douglass; Nazimova, Alla; Rowland, Beth; Scott Randolph
Homes of American Authors (book) 117
Homes of American Statesmen (book) 117
homosexuals 7, 10, 15; bachelors 145; Bankhead's jokes 32; Baumgartner's district nightclubs 49; *Better Angels* (Meeker novel) 152; *The Captive* (play) 22; contemporaries' lists 129; Cukor's circle 125; *The Drag* (West play) 22; Drake on Grant 153; *Falling Star* (Baum novel) 147; female impersonators and 50; Garbo images 128; gender inversion as clue 7, 17; *Going Hollywood* (movie) 177–178; Grant 153–154; Haines 147, 149; *Hey Diddle, Diddle* (Lane novel) 97–98; Hollywood bohemians thriving 195; *Hollywood Hotel* (movie) 183; *Hollywood Party* (movie) 64–65; *Hollywood*

Siren (McGrath novel) 179–180; Horton 156–158; *How to Sin in Hollywood* (tour book) 53, 194; image change in fiction in 1960s-1970s 196; image change with World War II 195; *Jarnegan* (Tully novel) 168; knowledge about Novarro 110; *Lady's Lady* (Bell novel) 172; Los Angeles City Council law 56; Malin image 42; Norman image 45; other city's nightlife 23; private parties 81–82; *Reckless Hollywood* (Lubou novel) 178–179; repression of 22–23; Riva Dietrich's observation 37; scholar interpretations of images 196; semi-public parties 61–62; *Show Girl in Hollywood* (movie) 169–170; *Something to Sing About* (movie) 181; statue of David 108; television in the 1970s 196; *see also* lesbians
Hoover, Herbert 56
Hopkins, George James 191
Hopper, Hedda 143
Hornblow, Arthur, Jr. 84
Horton, Edward Everett **155**, 189; contemporaries' perceptions about his sexuality 157; early life 154; *A Front Page Story* (movie) 154; *Gay Divorcee* (movie) 157; Majestic Theater 154; movie career 154–155; *Paris Honeymoon* (movie) 156; publicity 154–157; scholars' perceptions about his sexuality 158; *Top Hat* (movie) 157
Hot Saturday (movie) 150
The House of Mirth (Wharton novel) 81–82
How to Sin in Hollywood (tour book) 45–46, **46**, 194
Howe, Herbert 68, 71–72, 124
Hughes, Howard 27, 149
Hula Hut 26
Hume, Benita 40
Hunter, Catherine 3; *see also* Todd, Thelma
Huntington Library 24
Hurrell, George 180
Hutton, Barbara 189

I Lost My Girlish Laughter (Allen novel) 185–187
I Loved a Woman (movie) 138; *see also* Thompson, Alma
If I Had My Way (movie) 49
"I'm One of the Boys" (song) 35
Inaugural Balls 53–54, 92
Ince, Thomas H. 87
The Informer (movie) 41; *see also* O'Flaherty, Liam
Ingram, Rex 104
Irene **190**
Irene (play) 132
Ivano, Paul (Ivanichevitcz) 105, 108, 126, 181–182

Jackson, Andrew 53, 60
James, Henry 81

Jarnegan (Tully novel) 93–95, 168
Jefferson, Thomas 114, 118
Jimmy's Back Yard 40

Kahane, B.B. 41
Kelly, Patsy (Bridget Sarah Veronica Rose Kelly) 33, 40, 135, 155; contemporaries' perceptions about her sexuality 133; Cox, Wilma 132–134; early life 131; friendships 131–132; *Going Hollywood* (movie) 176; *Irene* (play) 132; *No, No Nanette* (play) 132; publicity images 132–133; scholars' perceptions about her sexuality 133–134; *Three Cheers* (play) 131
King Edward VII 17
The King of Kings (movie) 63; *see also* DeMille, Cecil B.
Kingsley, Grace 143
Kitty Foyle: The Natural History of a Woman (movie) 58; *see also* Rogers, Ginger
Krafft-Ebing, [Richard] 180
Kressley, Carson 159

Lachman, Harry 96
Lachman, Tai 96
Ladies' Home Journal (magazine) 119
Lady's Lady (Bell novel) 172
Lambert, Gavin 126, 144
Lanchester, Elsa 84
Lane, Lola **184**
Lane, Tamar 97, 110
LaRoque, Rod 163
The Last Mile (play) 95
The Last Tycoon (Fitzgerald novel) 5, 136
Laughter Limited (Putnam novel) 78, 97
Laughton, Charles 84
Laurents, Arthur 153
Lederer, George 88
Lee, Gypsy Rose 62
Lennon, Thomas 92, 153
Leo, Maurice 183; *see also* scriptwriters
LeRoy, Mervyn 169
lesbians 6, 7, 10, 37, 121, 180; Acker's relationships with Diamond and Nazimova 105, 107; bachelor chic image fantasy for 135; Bankhead 32–33; *The Captive* (play) 22; contemporaries' lists 129; cross-dressing women 28; Dietrich, Marlene 35–36, 66; Dressler, Marie 130; Garbo, Greta 125, 130, 166; gender inversion as clue 7, 17; Hepburn comment 30; *How to Sin in Hollywood* (tour book) 53; "I'm One of the Boys" 35–36; Kelly, Patsy 133–134; *The Last Tycoon* (Fitzgerald novel) 136; Nazimova, Alla 105, 107, 125–126; Rambova, Natacha 107; repression of 22–23; Riva Dietrich's observation 37; subculture 38; view of lesbianism 135; *see also* homosexuals
Lieder, Emily 108
Life 6, 9, 73, 116

Lincoln, Abraham 53
lobster palaces 14
Loder, John 218
Lombard, Carole 32, 63, **75**, 161; affair with Clark Gable 73–76; contemporaries' perceptions about her relationship with Gable 73–76; early years 74; *Marie Antoinette* premiere 73; movie career 74; at movie premieres 73–74; private parties 84; scholars' perceptions about her relationship with Gable 76
Loos, Anita 84, **91**, 101, 140, 164
Los Angeles: All-Year Club 116; boosterism 116–117; Cahuenga Boulevard 49; dimensions 117; Hollywood housing 117; North Vermont Avenue 44; population growth 116; water 116; West Adams 72; West 5th Street 117; West 6th Street 117; Western Avenue 54; *see also* specific government agencies; specific neighborhoods; specific street names
Los Angeles City Council 50–51
Los Angeles County Sheriff's Office 20
Los Angeles Department of Water and Power (Metropolitan Water District) 116
Los Angeles Examiner 134
Los Angeles Police Department 51, 136
Los Angeles Times 16, 33, 89
Los Feliz 117, 188
Loubou, Dorothy 170
Louis, Jean 190
Lowe, Edmund 102
Loy, Myrna 67, 70, 164, 180
Luce, Claire Booth 322

MacDonald, Jeannette 106, 99, 101
Madison, James 53
Madison, Dolley 53
Madsen, Axel 36, 134, 144
Mahin, John Lee 167; *see also* screenwriters
makeup artist 165, 175, 181–182, 184, 186
male impersonators 4, 23, 44
Malibu Beach 78, 117, 133
Malin, Gene (Jean) 37; *Arizona to Broadway* (movie) 40; death 228; early years 37–38; friendships 40, 131; movie career 40–41; publicity 39–40
Majestic Theater 154
Man Woman Marriage (movie) 145
Manley, Nelly 164; *see also* Dietrich, Marlene
Mann, Marjorie 37
Mann, William 6, 71, 134, 144, 154, 158, 191
Mannix, Eddie 36
Man's Castle (movie) 95
Marbury, Elisabeth "Bessie" 138
Marie Antoinette (movie) 73
Markey, Gene 89, 95
Martin, Paul 66
Mata Hari (movie) 165
Mathis, June 102

Matzene Feature Film Company 17
Mayer, Louis B. 54, 89, 91, 127
Mayfair Ball 62–63, 73, 76
Mayfair Club 62–63
Mayne, Judith 143–144
La Maze 29
McCann, Graham 154
McDaniel, Hattie 58
McDonald, J.A. 137
McEvoy, J. P 169
McGrath, Keane 108–109, 180
McKenzie, Twas 175; *see also* Warner Brothers wardrobe department
Meeker, Richard 152
Melrose Avenue 19
Mendl, Lady (Elsie de Wolfe) 189
Merton of the Movies (Wilson novel; movie) 165
Metro-Goldwyn-Mayer (M-G-M) 36, 89, 99, 176; Adrian, Gilbert 159; art department 176; *Bombshell* (movie) 166–168; Bull, Clarence 180; *Camille* (1936 movie) 139; de Acosta, Mercedes 138–140; Elias, Hal 70; Gable images 73–76; Garbo, Greta 127–129; *Going Hollywood* 176–178; Haines images 148–149; *Hollywood Party* 36, 64, 85; Novarro images 67–70; Selznick prevents from filming *I Lost My Girlish Laughter* 185; *The Shining Hour* (movie) 139; *Show People* (movie) 165; Thalberg, Irving 138; wardrobe department 175; work environment 25, 162, 164
Metropolitan Water District (MWD) 116; *see also* Department of Water and Power (DWP)
Miller, Patsy Ruth 105
El Mirador Hotel 34
Miss Lonelyhearts (West novel) 47; *see also* West, Nathanael
Mr. Blackwell 159
Mr. Wix of Wickham (play) 17
Montgomery, Douglass 146
Montmartre Cafe 26
Moore, Colleen 39
Morgan, Frank 84
Morgan, Marian 67, 144–145; *see also* Arzner, Dorothy; Novarro, Ramon
Morocco (movie) 33
Morrill, Justin (U.S. senator) 79
Moseley, Roy 154, 191
Motion Picture Herald (movie magazine) 28
Mountbatten, Lady Louise 89
movie premieres 50, 131; *Ben-Hur* 67–68; *The Cat and the Fiddle* 70; *China Seas* 73; *Devil May Care* 106; insider's reaction 64; *The King of Kings* 63; *Marie Antoinette* 73; *The Sign of the Cross* 65–66; *see also* Gable, Clark; Lombard, Carole; Novarro, Ramon
Moving Picture World 160
Munson, Ona 141

National Board of Review of Motion Pictures 122
National Survey 114
Nazimova, Alla (Mariam Edez Adelaida Leventon) 113, **123**, 135, 141; Arzner, Dorothy 142; Bryant, Charles 123; *Camille* (silent movie) 122; *The Chosen People* (play) 121; contemporaries' perceptions about her sexuality 103, 105–108, 125–126; early life 121; Garden of Allah 122, 125; home images 124–125, 134; Marshall, Glesca 125; movie career 121–122; private parties 84; Rambova, Natasha 122, 124; return to Hollywood 125; *Salome* (movie) 122; scholars' perceptions about her sexuality 126, 141; self-description 124–125; *Stronger Than Death* (movie) 103; *War Brides* (movie) 122; *Zaza* (movie) 125
Negri, Pola 66, 108, 138
The New Movie Magazine 93
"New Negros" 22
New Orleans 23
"New Woman" 145
New York Daily News 21
New York Herald 51
New York State Liquor Authority 16
New York Times 51, 103, 154, 182
nightclubs 13; attempts to close them 23, 43–45, 48–49; female impersonators 38–42, 48; in Hollywood novels 42, 47–48; in Los Angeles 24–27; mannishly-dressed women 27–33; in other cities 23; prohibition 21–22; Times Square 22–24; *see also* specific clubs
nightlife 13, 131; Bankhead images 31–32; cross-dressing women in *What Price Hollywood?* 27–28; *The Day of the Locusts* (novel) 47–48; Dietrich images 33–35; Eltinge images 17–20; Hepburn images 29–30; *Hollywood Cemetery* 42; Hollywood during the 1910s 16–18; Hollywood during the 1920s 24–26; *How to Sin in Hollywood* (tour book) 45–47; images of cafe society 14–15; Los Angeles City Council suppressed 43–45, 48–49; Malin images 39–40; New York 14–15, 22–24; nineteenth century 14–15; Norman images 39–40; other cities in 1920s–1930s 23; prohibition effects on 21–22; *see also* nightclubs
No, No, Nanette (play) 132
Norman, Karyl 13, **38**, 45, 51; contemporaries' perceptions about his sexuality 40, 45; early years 37; friendships 44; publicity 39, 52
Novarro, Ramon (José Ramón Gil Samaniego) **69, 71**, 108, 148; *Ben-Hur* (movie) 67–68; *The Cat and the Fiddle* (movie) 70; contemporaries' perceptions about his sexuality 70; *Devil May Care* (movie) 68; early years 67; *Mata Hari* (movie) 67, 165; movie premieres 68–70; murder 72; *The Pagan* (movie) 67; *The Prisoner of Zenda* 67; publicity about bachelor status 69–70; scholars' perceptions about his sexuality 71–72, 182

Oasis 26
Office of War Information 195
O'Flaherty, Liam 41–43; see also *The Informer* (movie)
O'Hara, Mary 67
Oil 6; *see also* Sinclair, Upton
Olivier, Laurence 32
Orry-Kelly (George "Jack") **188, 190**; *Arsenic & Old Lace* (movie) 191; contemporaries' perceptions about his sexuality 190; early years 187; friendships 188–189; home 188–189; on the studio lot 187–188; relationship with Cary Grant 187, 190; relationship with Milton Owen 189; scholars' perceptions about his sexuality 190–191
Owen, Milton 189; *see also* Orry-Kelly
Owens Valley 116

Pacific Electric (Big Red) 116
Palm Springs 34
pansy *see* homosexual
pansy craze 23, 37
Paramount Pictures Corporation 18, 116, 149; Arzner 142–144; Bankhead images 32; Dietrich images 33, 35, 65–66; Eltinge 18; Grant and Scott images 152–153; Holt publicity 120; Horton publicity 155–156; *Paris Honeymoon* (movie) 156; Ralston, Esther 144; Schulberg, B. P. 150; size 163; *Ten Modern Commandments* (movie) 144; wardrobe department 175; *The Wild Party* (movie) 142
Paris After Dark (book) 194
Paris Honeymoon (movie) 156
Parsons, Louella 33, 56, **83**, 91, 101, 183
The Party at Jack's (Wolfe story) 82
Pasadena Community Playhouse 149
Paul and Joe's 39
People 159
Peter the Tramp (movie) 126
Philadelphia Ledger 70
photographers 99, 125, 127, 154; *Hollywood Siren* (McGrath novel) 179–180; *see also* specific names
Photoplay (movie magazine) 6, 9, 122, 141; *Bombshell* (movie) 167; female screenwriters 136; Garbo articles 128–129; Haines and antiques 148; Nazimova house 124; Novarro in Italy 68–69; reader on women in masculine attire 30
Photoplayers' Club 18
Pickford, Mary 89, 120, 145, 164
Picture Play (movie magazine) 30
Pig 'n' Whistle 16

plays, homosexuals depicted 15–16
Police Commission (Los Angeles) 57
Polo, Eddie 165
Poole, Abram 138; see also De Acosta, Mercedes
Powell, William 32, 44, 74
Power, Tyronne 91
Preston, Jack 171; see also Buschlen, John Preston
The Prisoner of Zenda 67
La Prisonnaire (Bourdet play) 128; see also *The Captive*
private parties: coverage after World War I 80–81; coverage during the nineteenth century 79–80; defined 78–79; *Hollywood Party* 85–86; *Jarnegan* 93–94; literature images 81–82; Washington, D.C. 81; see also Davies, Marion; Hearst, William Randolph; Tracy, Spencer; Young, Loretta
Production Code Administration 7, 183; see also Breen, Joseph; Hays Office; Studio Relations Committee
prohibition 21, 23; see also nightlife
Providence Press 60
public parties 50–55; see also Academy Awards; inaugural balls; specific names of balls
Putnam, Nina 78, 97–98

Queen Christina (movie) 138
Queer Eye for the Straight Guy 159

Radio-Keith-Orpheum (RKO) 27–29, 40–41, 138
Raft, George 39
Ralston, Esther 144
Rambova, Natacha (Winifred Shaughnessy later Winifred Hudnut) 105–108, 122, 124, 179; see also Nazimova, Alla; Valentino, Rudolph
Rappe, Virginia 84–85
Rathbone, Basil 99
Reckless Hollywood (Lubou novel) 170–171, 178–179
Red Dust (movie) 73, 167
Reid, Wallace 117, 164
Renault, Francis 21
Republic Films 72
Rhode Island Fisherman's Ball 62
Rich, Sharon 101
Ridgeway, Kathleen 175–176; see also script department
Roach, Hal 40, 73, 131, 132
Rodgers, Richard 35, 85
Rogers, Ginger 58, 99
Rogers, Will 57
Rolph, James (California governor) 56
Roosevelt, Franklin D. 56, 89–90
Roosevelt Hotel 84
Rotarians 51

Rowland, Beth 136–137
Rowland, Richard 137
Rubayiat 39
Rubens, Alma 91
Runaway, Romany 88; see also Davies, Marion
Russo, Vito 7, 158

St. Johns, Adela Rogers 120
Salome (movie) 122, 179
Saloons 2
Samuel, Louis 67
Sanctuary 6; see also Faulkner, William
San Fernando Valley 24, 155
San Francisco Examiner 87; see also Hearst, William Randolph
Santa Monica Boulevard 25, 44, 78, 163
Savoy, Bert 21, 41
scenic art department 175, 192
Schanke, Robert A. 141
Schickel, Richard 154
Schulberg, B. P. 150
Schulman, Sylvia 185; see also Allen, Jane
Scott, Randolph *151*, 189; contemporaries' perceptions about his sexuality 153–154; early life 149; *Hot Saturday* (movie) 150; marriages 149–150; photo shoot of house 152–153; scholars' perceptions about his sexuality 154; shared place with Cary Grant 151–154
Screen Star (Preston novel) 5, 171
screenwriters 136; see also de Acosta, Mercedes; *The Last Tycoon*; Thompson, Alma
Script (magazine) 57
script department 175
Sebastian, Frank 25, 178; see also *The Cotton Club*
Selznick, David O. 27, 26, 95, 185
Selznick, Lewis, J. 122
semipublic parties 50, 58–62; coverage after World War I 60–61; Dietrich, Marlene 65–66; *Hollywood Party* 64–65; including risque characters 61–62; in Washington, D.C. 59–60; see also *The Big Money*; Gable, Clark; Lombard, Carole; Novarro, Ramon
Sennett, Mack 18
Serenade (Cain novel) 5
Sex (West play) 22
Sharaff, Irene 107, **190**
Shaw, George Bernard 89
Shearer, Norma 67
Sheehan, Winfield 95
Sherman, Vincent 129, 182
The Shining Hour (movie) 139
Show Girl in Hollywood (movie) 169–170, 178
Show People (movie) 165
Shuberts 31, 121, 150
The Sign of the Cross 66; see also movie premieres
Silver Screen (movie magazine) 9

Sinclair, Upton 6; see also *Oil*
Sintzenich, Harold 63–64
Sister Carrie (Dreiser novel) 162
sketch artists 178–179; *see also* art department
Skin of Our Teeth (play) 32; *see also* Bankhead, Tullulah
slumming 22
Smith, Al (New York governor) 87
Smith, Kate 177–178
Smith, Queenie 133
Smith, Stanley 39
Something to Sing About (movie) 181–182, 184
The Song of Songs (movie) 33; *see also* Dietrich, Marlene
Sorrell, Herbert 162
South Western Avenue 40
Sprague, Mrs. Kate (née Chase) 60; *see also* Conkling, Roscoe
Sprague, William (U.S. senator) 60
Spring Street 16, 25
The Squab Farm (play) 31; *see also* Bankhead, Tullulah
Staiger, Janet 7
Stanwyck, Barbara 36, 129
Stewart, Donald Ogden 177–178
Stewart, Jimmy 162
Stiller, Mauritz 126–127
Stokowski, Leopold 134
Stop! Look! Listen! (revue) 88; *see also* Davies, Marion
Strassner, Joseph 66
Stronger Than Death (movie) 103
Stratford, Peter 136–137
Studio Relations Committee 36
Stunt Pilot (movie) 5
Sullivan's Travels (movie) 5
Sunset Boulevard 25, 44, 46, 122, 148
Sunset Strip 22, 24, 25, 73, 122
Swanson, Gloria 26, 120–121
Sweet, Blanche 169
Swing Club 45

tabloids 5, 21, 57, 80, 137; Dietrich, Marlene 33; female impersonation 37, 40; inaugural balls 54; Nazimova, Alla 122
Talmadge, Constance 117
Talmadge, Norma 189
Taylor, Robert 182
Temple, Shirley 140
Ten Modern Commandments (movie) 144
Thalberg, Irving 138
Thompson, Alma 136–138; see also *I Loved a Woman*
Thompson, Clarence 192
Thrasher, Edward (Los Angeles city councilman) 44
Three Cheers (play) 131
Three Radio Rogues 177–178

Time 6, 9, 143, 159
Times Square 22–24, 39
Toad in the Hole 26
Todd, Thelma 3, 26, 141, 131–132
Too Young to Marry (movie) 95
Top Hat (movie) 157
The Torrent (movie) 127
Tracy, Lee 166
Tracy, Spencer 30, 58; *Boys Town* (movie) 58; contemporaries' reactions to Young relationship 96; early career 158–159; Hepburn relationship 28, 95; *The Last Mile* 95; *Man's Castle* (movie) 95; relationship with Loretta Young 95–96; scholars' reactions to Young relationship 96
traffic dispatcher 176
Trocadero 5, 26, 74
Trusty, Joe 175; *see also* flower department
Tully, Jim 93, 98, 168; see also *Jarnegan*
Turner Classic Movies 153; *see also* Drake, Betsy
Twain, Mark 59
Twelvetrees, Helen 96
Twentieth Century–Fox *see* Fox Film Corporation
"twilight tandem" 102, 185
Two-Faced Woman (movie) 129

United Artists 163,
Universal 57, 165
University of Southern California 24
Universum Film AG (UFA) 33

Valdi, Nita 108
Valentino, Rudolph (Rodolfo Alfonso Piero Filiberto Guglielmi) 50, 67, **106**; *The Big Money* 111; *Camille* (movie) 122; *Chicago Tribune* editorial 107–108, 111; contemporaries' perceptions about his sexuality 105, 107–108; de Saulles affair 102; early years 102–103; *The Eyes of Youth* (movie) 102; *The Four Horsemen of the Apocalypse* (movie) 103; friendship with Marion Davies 91; marriage to Jean Acker 103–104; marriage to Natcha Rambova 105–107; scholars' perceptions about his sexuality 108
Van Buren, Martin 53
Vanity Fair 93
Variety 160, 178
Vaudeville 10, 41, 44; Acker, Jean 103–105; Davies, Marion 88; Eltinge publicity 17–18; Grant, Cary 150; Horton, Edward Everett 154; Kelly, Patsy 131; Norman, Karyl 37, 39; Novarro, Ramon 67; Orry-Kelly 187; Three Radio Rogues 177
Veiled Prophets Ball 52
Vendomes 29
Venice Beach 16
Venice Pier Amusement Park 74, 84

Vernon 25
Victor Hugo Café 63
Viertel, Berthold 130
Viertel, Salka 130
Vine Street 25 27
volume restaurants 5, 24
Von Sternberg, Josef 33

Wald, Jerry 183; *see also* scriptwriters
Wales Padlock Law 10
Walker, James J. (New York City mayor) 90
Walsh, Miriam Cooper *see* Cooper, Miriam
Walsh, Raoul 16
War Brides (movie) 122
Warner, Jack 183, 187, 189
Warner Brothers 4; flower department 175; *Hollywood Hotel* (movie) 183; *I Loved a Woman* (movie) 138; Orry-Kelly 175, 187–190; size 162, 164; wardrobe department 175
Washington, George 118
Washington Evening Star 80
Webb, Millard 89
The Well of Loneliness 6; *see also* Hall, Radclyffe
Wells, Orson 92, 185
West, Mae 10, 32, 150; see also *The Drag* (play); *Sex* (play)
West, Nathanael 47–48; see also *The Day of the Locusts* (novel); *Miss Lonelyhearts* (novel)
West Hollywood 25
Westmore, Ernst 84
Westmore, Monte 108
Westmore, Perc 189
Wharton, Edith 81
What Price Hollywood? (movie) 27–29, 31
What's Wrong with the Movies? (Lane non-fiction book) 97
Whitaker, Alma 140
White, Alice 169

The White Horse 49
The Wild Party (movie) 142
Willinger, Lazlo 180
Wilshire-Pico 44
Wilson, Henry Leon 165
Winchell, Walter 26
Winters, Shelley 190
Wolfe, Thomas 82
Women's Christian Temperance Union 14
Woolf, Edgar Allan 84
World War I 15, 21; Arzner's ambulance corps service 142; breakdown of genteel culture 8; Hearst and Bonus Army 90; Hollywood homes after 119; Hollywood nightlife after 24; Ivano to Hollywood after 105; private party coverage after 80–81; Scott's Army service 149; semi-public party coverage after 60
World War II 66, 93, 129, 149, 195
Wright, Frank Lloyd 115

You Can't Take It with You (Wolfe novel) 82; see also *The Party at Jack's*
Young, Clara Kimball 102–103; *see also* Valentino, Rudolph
Young, Loretta 76; contemporaries' reactions to Tracy relationship 96; early career 95; family 95; *Man's Castle* (movie) 95; relationship with Clark Gable 96; relationship with Spencer Tracy 95–96; scholars' reactions to Tracy relationship 96–97; *Second Floor Mystery* (movie) 95; *Too Young to Marry* (movie) 95
Young, Polly Ann 95
Young, Robert 64–65

Zerbe, Jerry 32, 154
The Ziegfeld Follies of 1916 (revue) 88; *see also* Davies, Marion

www.ingramcontent.com/pod-product-compliance
Lightning Source LLC
Chambersburg PA
CBHW051217300426
44116CB00006B/611